# A COMPLETE PRACTICAL GUIDE

## HOW TO

# GET THE BIBLE
# INTO MY LIFE

## STEPHEN M. MILLER

THOMAS NELSON PUBLISHERS
*Nashville*

Published in Nashville, Tennessee, by Thomas Nelson, Inc.

Unless otherwise indicated, all Scripture quotations are from the Contemporary English Version (CEV), copyright © 1995 by the American Bible Society. Used by permission.

Verses marked "NKJV" are taken from the New King James Version, copyright © 1979. 1980, 1982 by Thomas Nelson, Inc.

The Scripture quotations contained herein from the New Revised Standard Version (NRSV) of the Bible are copyright © 1989 by the Division of Christian Education of the National Council of the Churches of Christ in the U.S.A., and are used by permission. All rights reserved.

Verses marked "RSV" are taken from the Holy Bible: Revised Standard Version, second edition, copyright © 1946, 1951, 1972 by the Division of Christian Education of the NCCCUSA.

Verses marked "NIV" are taken from the Holy Bible: New International Version, copyright © 1973, 1978, 1984 by the International Bible Society. Used by permission of Zondervan Publishing House. All rights reserved.

Scripture quotations marked "NLT" are taken from the Holy Bible, New Living Translation, copyright © 1996. Used by permission of Tyndale House Publishers, Inc., Wheaton, Illinois 60189. All rights reserved.

Miller, Stephen M., 1952–
    How to get the Bible into my life
    ISBN 0-7852-4549-9

Printed in the United States of America

2 3 4 5 6 7 — 06 05 04 03

# CONTENTS

# AUTHOR'S PREFACE

Welcome to a sequel. And thanks to those of you who bought the first volume, *How to Get Into the Bible*. You made it a best-selling Christian reference book, and prodded the editor to ask for an encore.

The first volume introduces readers to the world of the Bible, spotlighting big scenes, famous people, and modern discoveries that help us better understand what life was like in Bible times and how it influenced what the writers said.

This second volume, *How to Get the Bible Into My Life*, shifts the focus to today. We look at the big scenes in the Bible, but zero in on what those scenes teach us about how to live the Christian life today. We look again at the starring characters in the Bible, but this time it's to see what we can learn from their lives. In addition, we explore differing opinions among Christians about how to understand controversial issues, such as abortion, the death penalty, alcohol, tithing, the "unforgivable sin," women leaders in the church, and how to discipline church members. That's just a sampling.

This book isn't going to tell you how to live your life. That's God's job. But we've done our best to put you front row, center, so you can watch some of the Bible's greatest and most timeless scenes—those with important messages for people in any century or culture.

Why bother?

It's not enough to know the Bible and believe it. God wants us to behave it. When we do, we make this world a better place.

## A FEW FRIENDS

I'd like to thank the following people who helped bring this book to life:

- Linda, my wife, proofreader, and encourager. Thanks for holding down a real job, as a nurse, while I study and write my days away.
- Rebecca and Bradley, my children, who agree to let me be a writer during the day if I'm a dad in the evening, and promise never again to wash red and white clothes in the same load.
- Paul Gross, whose drawings bring the Bible scenes to life. I appreciate your gift of art and your commitment to getting the picture research right.
- Lee Hollaway, the skilled reference editor who pulled this entire project together. Thanks for your great work on both books.
- Giles Anderson, a delightful agent, which makes him an oxymoron. Your sense of humor and approachable personality make it a joy to work with you.

God bless them, every one.
And God bless you.

Steve Miller

# HOW TO USE THIS BOOK

As you turn the pages of this book, here's what you'll find.

- **The Bible's Top Guidelines for Today.** Want a spiritual to-do list for energizing your life? And want it to be the most important in the Bible? There are three short passages you should read. We put them right at the beginning of the book instead of slipping them in later, where they would go chronologically. They deserve special treatment.
  - ○ **Ten Commandments.** These are the most basic laws we need to know if we want to get along with God and our fellow human beings. Every one of the hundreds of Old Testament laws flows out of these ten.
  - ○ **The Greatest Commandment.** Asked to identify the greatest commandment in the Bible, Jesus said: Love God and love each other.
  - ○ **Sermon on the Mount.** This most famous sermon of Jesus is the keynote address of his life. Here he tells his followers exactly what he expects of them.

- **Genesis through Revelation.** From the first book to the last, you'll get a captivating introduction to the Bible and how it applies to you.
  - ○ **A Quote for You.** From each Bible book, one of the most pertinent quotations for life today.
  - ○ **Background Notes.** A concise summary of each book, with snippets about the writer and setting.
  - ○ **Influential People.** Main characters and the examples—good or bad—that they set for us.
  - ○ **Key Ideas You Need to Know.** Quick summary of important themes to help you understand the book and apply it to your life.
  - ○ **To-Do List.** Quotes from the book that tell us what God expects of his people.
  - ○ **Fascinating Facts.** Surprising nuggets of insight about each book.
  - ○ **Q & A.** Questions people ask about key teachings in the book, and answers that Bible experts give—though the experts sometimes disagree.
  - ○ **Red Flag Issues.** Hot topics in the book that spark debate among Christians.
  - ○ **For the Record.** Examples from history about how people abused the book, or used it to improve the world. A classic example of abuse is when slave owners quoted select verses out of context to justify slavery.
  - ○ **Bible Scenarios You Can Use.** This is the heart of the book. What you get here is a brief review of selected scenes from each Bible book—scenes that we show are especially relevant for us today.

## GETTING STARTED

This isn't the kind of book you need to read from cover to cover, starting at the beginning. But you can if you like. Actually, it's more of a light-reading reference book—something you can refer to when you're studying a particular book in the Bible.

Here's one way you might use the book. Start by reading "The Bible's Top Guidelines for Today." This will give you Christianity's big picture, since nearly every life lesson you'll learn from the Bible starts with one of these principles.

Next, as you read your Bible during your personal devotions, Bible study, or in preparation for small-group meetings, read the accompanying section in *How to Get the Bible Into My Life.* If, for example, you're beginning a Bible study in the Gospel of Matthew, read the Matthew section in *How to Get the Bible Into My Life.* It won't take long, and it'll give you an excellent overview of the book.

As you study the Bible, there are dozens of Bible translations from which you can choose. Some are easier to read than others. Some are more literal in their translation, which sometimes makes them harder to read but often the preferred choice among Bible scholars. We especially like the Contemporary English Version because of its readability. In fact, unless we indicate otherwise, it's the version we use throughout *How to Get the Bible Into My Life.*

One final tip. It's about looking up Bible references. If you see "John 3:16," for example, John is the name of the book, and 3:16 means chapter 3, verse 16.

I hope you enjoy this Bible companion. And I hope it helps you discover new ways to apply the ancient stories and teachings of the Bible to your life. The writing has certainly done that for me. I pray that the reading will do it for you.

# THE BIBLE'S TOP GUIDELINES FOR TODAY

# Ten Commandments

It wasn't Moses who first delivered the Ten Commandments, the foundational Jewish laws on which all other laws are built. It was God. He spoke the laws for all Israel to hear before Moses ever climbed Mt. Sinai to get the written version, etched onto stone tablets.

After the Israelites fled Egypt, they camped at the foot of Mt. Sinai. There, God offered to make a contract, or covenant, with the people. He would bless and protect them if they obeyed him. Astonished at the miraculous power he had shown in freeing them, they eagerly agreed. During the many months they camped at Mt. Sinai, God delivered the hundreds of laws that would govern the people. But he started first with the heart of these laws—the Ten Commandments. And he delivered them in person, so the people would know they came from God, not Moses.

After three days of getting ready for God to come, the Israelites gathered at dawn by the foot of Mt. Sinai. Thunder and lightning filled the sky as God descended on the mountain peak in a fire. The ground shook and mysterious trumpets blasted. The people were terrified.

"I am the Lord your God, the one who brought you out of Egypt where you were slaves," God said in a voice that filled the plain (Exodus 20:2).

Then he began to deliver what became known as the Ten Commandments— timeless laws intended to teach us what God is like and what we should be like. The first three laws deal with humanity's relationship to God: worship God, don't worship anything else, and don't abuse God's name. The last seven deal with relationships between humans: rest one day a week, respect your parents, and don't murder, commit adultery, steal, lie, or crave what belongs to another.

Many laws of the Old Testament became obsolete after Jesus (Hebrews 8:13). That's because Jesus established the new covenant God said he would make (Jeremiah 31:31). No longer do we have to follow the hundreds of civil and ritual laws in the Old Testament, such as laws about sacrifices and kosher food. Instead, God has put his laws in our heart—laws of morality.

When we read the Ten Commandments, we get a taste of what God meant by laws put in our heart. We recognize in our heart that these are laws for everyone. And we know from experience that we're all better off when we obey them, and worse off when we don't.

## 1. Worship only God (20:3)

"Do not worship any god except me."

That's the first and most important of the Ten Commandments. It's also perhaps the hardest to obey—for the Israelites as well as us.

It's hard for the Israelites because they live in a culture where people worship lots of gods. Popular wisdom says that the more gods you worship, the better off you'll be. In Egypt, Hapi is the river god thought to provide the water that nourishes the nation. In Canaan, Baal is said to offer fertility in the fields, flock, and family. For security—insurance, we could say—some Israelites worship a gallery of gods, the Lord included.

Even today it's hard to worship only God. We live in a culture where people revere themselves and their achievements. Our popular wisdom says if we want something bad enough, we can get it: wealth, power, fame. The priority we give these desires can displace God as first place in our hearts. We can end up abandoning God in our quest for achievement and personal security.

But Law Number One says this: if we have God, we have all we need.

## 2. Don't make idols (20:4–6)

"Do not make idols that look like anything in the sky or on earth or in the ocean under the earth."

This is a partner to the first commandment—the next logical step for a culture that makes statues and shrines as worship aids to represent the gods. But instead of just representing the gods, these idols become the gods. People worship them and pray to them.

We may not worship idols, but we sometimes elevate worship objects to god-like status. The Israelites did this to the bronze serpent Moses made to ward off poisonous snakes. Centuries later, King Hezekiah smashed the serpent to pieces because people were praying to it (2 Kings 18:4).

We misplace our worship when we allow religious objects to become more than symbols. We might pray to a crucifix or to a private shrine that has pictures of Jesus or saints. Or we might treat holy water, anointing oil, or the Bible as though they have magical power.

In a way, we make idols whenever we allow anything to take the place of God as the object of our deepest devotion—whether it's a religious relic or something else: our job, our family, our treasured possessions. Our greatest treasure is something we can't paint, sculpt, touch, or wrap. That's because it's not physical. It's spiritual. It's God.

## 3. Don't abuse God's name (20:7)

"Do not misuse my name."

Other Bible passages explain what this means. It can mean using God's name to swear that the lie you're telling is true (Leviticus 19:12). It also can mean using God's name or heaven to swear that you'll keep your promise (Matthew 5:34). People also used God's name in magic and sorcery. In time, devout Jews avoided using God's name at all. When they came across it while reading Scripture, they said "Lord" instead.

Today, people use God's name frivolously and disrespectfully so often that we don't give it a second thought. We use it as a one-word exclamation of disgust, as part of a heated curse, or in flippant, crude jokes.

The way we use God's name shows how we feel about him. It also gradually reshapes our attitude toward him. If we keep using his name in curses, we begin to associate God with evil—exactly the opposite of what he is.

## 4. Rest and worship every seventh day (20:8–11)

"Remember that the Sabbath Day belongs to me. You have six days when you can do your work, but the seventh day of each week belongs to me, your God. No one is to work on that day."

Whether we're shepherds in ancient Israel or movers and shakers in a modern metropolis, we need a regular time of spiritual and physical renewal. God has set aside one day a week for his people to relax and enjoy time with him and others. Jews celebrate the Sabbath from sundown on Friday through sundown on Saturday. Christians, in tribute to Christ's resurrection, make Sunday their day of rest.

Today, many people work on Saturday and Sunday. Their day of rest can come mid-week. There's no hard-and-fast rule about when and what a Sabbath Day should be like. To religious leaders who thought otherwise and wanted to dictate how people should observe the Sabbath, Jesus said, "People were not made for the good of the Sabbath. The Sabbath was made for the good of people" (Mark 2:27).

## 5. Respect your parents (20:12)

"Respect your father and your mother."

Elsewhere in the Bible God gives examples about how to respect our parents. To begin with, children shouldn't hit their parents or curse them (Exodus 21:15, 17). But respect is far more. It's speaking kindly about them. It's treating them with courtesy. And it's obeying them, when their requests don't contradict God.

Some parents are hard to get along with. Some are even cruel and abusive. Perhaps they fit in a category that the apostle Paul later talked about: "If it is possible, as far as it depends on you, live at peace with everyone" (Romans 12:18, New International Version).

In this world where it seems so many people stand against us, we can certainly use the love and support of our family. But before that can happen, there needs to be mutual respect within our family—parents who honor their children and children who honor their parents. If this hasn't happened yet in your family, perhaps you could take the first step toward starting something good and lasting.

## 6. Don't murder (20:13)

"Do not murder."

Except in war, executions, and for self-defense, the Israelites are forbidden to kill people. The punishment for murder, in this biblical era without prison facilities, is usually execution—often by one of the victim's relatives, called the "blood avenger" (Numbers 35:19). Exceptions include humanity's first murder: Cain's slaughter of his brother, Abel. God banishes Cain from the land. King David also escapes execution after ordering the murder of Bathsheba's husband.

Jesus broadens the command, saying anger is no less an offense in God's eyes (Matthew 5:22). Anger and murder are both exactly the opposite of how God wants us to treat each other: "Stop being angry and don't try to take revenge. I am the Lord, and I command you to love others as much as you love yourself" (Leviticus 19:18).

God says this with such authority that it's as though he has given us the power to will anger and murder out of our life. When the hostile thoughts come, we can make them go. In the event of mental disorders, the process may involve medicine. But for most of us, it may mean simply refusing to dwell on the source of the anger.

## 7. Don't commit adultery (20:14)

"Be faithful in marriage."

Adultery is portrayed in the Bible as treachery of the worst sort—betrayal of the one person who needs us most. Perhaps because adultery devastated a family, which was the main resource for survival in the ancient world, it drew the death penalty. By New Testament times, executions were replaced with divorce.

Today, adultery is so common that we expect it of people who achieve even a moderate measure of wealth, fame, or influence—and we are actually surprised if they remain faithful. But the sad fact that adultery is common doesn't make it right. As in ages past, it breaks hearts forever and decimates families for generations.

## 8. Don't steal (20:15)

"Do not steal."

"You have sinned if you rob or cheat someone," God adds in a later law, "When this happens, you must return what doesn't belong to you and pay the owner a fine of twenty percent" (Leviticus 6:2, 4).

Stealing is a sin against the person whose property we take—and against God for not trusting that he'll provide for our needs.

In our greedy society, people seem forever on the take. We overcharge. We do sloppy work for our wages. We create unfair laws that make the rich richer and the poor poorer. This selfishness breeds mistrust, anger, violence and—eventually—revolution. The only way to stop it is one person at a time. You are that person.

## 9. Don't lie (20:16)

"Don't tell lies about others."

The original language of this verse pictures a court scene. A more literal translation is, "You shall not give false testimony against your neighbor" (New International Version). But the Bible broadens this elsewhere by condemning lies in any setting. Jesus warned, "I promise you that on the day of judgment, everyone will have to account for every careless word they have spoken" (Matthew 12:36).

That includes unsubstantiated rumors, self-serving exaggerations, and strategically planted disinformation—all of which are common tactics for getting ahead in this world. But in the long haul, these tactics spawn trouble in this life and condemnation in the next.

A wiser approach is one chosen by a poet who understood God and the value of God's laws for humanity, "I have chosen the way of truth; I have set my heart on your laws" (Psalm 119:30, New International Version).

## 10. Don't crave what belongs to another (20:17)

"Do not want anything that belongs to someone else."

God gives a few examples: "Don't want anyone's house, wife or husband, slaves, oxen, donkeys or anything else."

Our crave list might be much the same. But instead of slaves and livestock, we could pencil in a sailboat, sports car, and a thriving stock portfolio.

The craving God is talking about isn't the innocent, "I'd like to have one of those," so you go to the store and buy one. It's the unhealthy, "I don't see why I can't have that. It's not fair." It's the kind of thing you might say on your way out of a mansion, or that a citizen of the developing world might say on the way out of your home.

God wants us to cherish the gifts he has given us, not pout for more.

One sage writer put it this way: "Be satisfied with what you have. For God has said, 'I will never fail you. I will never forsake you'" (Hebrews 13:5). If there's any envying to be going on, it should be people envying the joy we have in the Lord.

## THE GREATEST COMMANDMENT

### Love God and people
(Matthew 22:36–40)

If we tally up the Ten Commandments and all the Old Testament laws that flow out of them—as Bible scholars do in Jesus' day—we'll be looking at more than 600 laws. No wonder one of the scholars asks Jesus to boil them down.

"Teacher," the scholar says, "what is the most important commandment?"

Jesus instantly replies with two commandments he says share the top spot.

- "Love the Lord your God with all your heart, soul, and mind."
- "Love others as much as you love yourself."

"All the Law of Moses and the Books of the Prophets are based on these two commandments," Jesus says.

For those of us who need help on how to put those two commandments into practice, we have the rest of the Bible. But the short course is this: obey God and help others.

# Sermon on the Mount

If you're in a hurry to find out what Jesus taught—to discover the heart of his message—you can turn to his most famous sermon, recorded in Matthew 5—7. Bible experts say the Sermon on the Mount reads like the keynote message of his life, a summary of most of the spiritual ideas you'll find in his parables, miracles, and teachings.

Be warned. This sermon contains lightening bolts that will shock you out of your comfort zone—challenging you to embrace new and godlier patterns of thought and action. For instance, to those who think they've obeyed the law that forbids adultery, Jesus says lust is no less sinful.

As the sermon begins, Jesus is sitting on a hillside, perhaps near the Sea of Galilee where some of his disciples had worked as fishermen and where Jesus conducted much of his ministry. Surrounded by masses of people who had come from throughout the region to hear him, Jesus starts with what will become the most famous section of his celebrated sermon—the best of the best: the Beatitudes.

## 1. The Beatitudes (5:3–12)

In what sounds like a prescription for spiritual happiness, Jesus delivers a collection of short sayings. Each one describes the kind of people God blesses. It's a startling list, because some of the sayings are exactly the opposite of what many in his audience would expect. Generally, the Jews thought people who were high and mighty and free of suffering were that way because of God's blessing—a reward for being good.

Not so, says Jesus. God blesses the humble, the grieving, and the persecuted.

The Beatitudes, from a Latin word meaning "blessed," is a succinct list of attitudes God wants to see in us: devotion to him no matter what, obedience, mercy, purity in heart, and lovers of peace.

"Be happy and excited!" Jesus says of people like this. "You will have a great reward in heaven."

## 2. Be light in a dark world (5:14–16)

"You are like light for the whole world," Jesus says. "Make your light shine, so that others will see the good that you do and will praise your Father in heaven."

Jesus compares godly people to a lighted city on a hilltop at night, with its light shining for miles around. People passing by can't miss it.

Nor should people passing our way fail to notice the spiritual light in us. The light Jesus is talking about includes all the good attributes we see in him: compassion, generosity, mercy, forgiveness, and patience. When people see these in us and discover we're Christians, they're drawn to the faith—like lost travelers to the nighttime lights of a city.

## 3. Obey God's laws (5:17–20)

Jesus tells the people if they want to belong to God's kingdom, they'd better obey God's laws more faithfully than the Jewish leaders do—which may seem impossible.

Jesus' implication is that the leaders obey the letter of the law but ignore the spirit of it. Instead of letting the laws of God do their job of elevating a person's character, the leaders create loopholes. For example, instead of financially helping their parents, they can say their money is devoted to God (Mark 7:11). A loophole. The leaders obey the Ten Commandments outwardly—so they look religious—but they won't let it change them inwardly, making them more sensitive to God and others.

"You must obey God's commands better than the Pharisees," Jesus says. That means obeying them because we love God, not because we love the praise of others.

## 4. Don't let anger control you (5:21–26)

One of God's most basic laws prohibits murder. But in a startling announcement, Jesus adds that anger is no less a sin. It violates God's basic law to love others as much as we love ourselves.

We can't always control bursts of outrage when someone hurts us or someone we love. But we don't have to cling to the anger like it's a medal of honor. Anger, like untreated cancer, can grow and consume us. It can steal our spiritual life as surely as disease can kill us.

God certainly wants us to control our physical actions, such as refraining from hitting others. But he wants us to control our thoughts as well, for if we don't control our anger it will control us.

## 5. Stay faithful in marriage (5:27–30)

"You know the commandment which says, 'Be faithful in marriage,'" Jesus tells the people gathered on the grassy slopes. "But I tell you that if you look at another woman and want her, you are already unfaithful in your thoughts."

So the old adage, "You can look but don't touch" is dangerous. Looks can linger in our mind, becoming mental adultery that has the power to erode our marriage with unrealistic expectations and lure us into physical adultery. Job had a better idea, very much in sync with Jesus' teaching: "I promised myself never to stare with desire at a young woman" (Job 31:1).

## 6. Don't divorce over problems you can mend (5:31–32)

Women in the time of Jesus have pitifully few legal rights. Their husbands can divorce them for just about any reason—like today—but the women don't get a share of the property. To survive, they are generally forced to return to their parents, remarry, or take up prostitution.

Jesus says it isn't right. Divorce, with all its tragedy, shouldn't be considered an option for anything less than adultery. And even then marriage can survive, if repentance and forgiveness prevail. The apostle Paul later adds that abandonment is another grounds for divorce (1 Corinthians 7:15).

God intended marriage to last a lifetime. When it doesn't, the pain that follows generally does. So divorce should be nothing less than a last resort.

## 7. Keep your promises (5:33–37)

In Jesus' day, people are making promises they have no intention of keeping. Yet they insist their word is good, and do so by invoking a vow in the name of God or something else sacred.

Jesus tells the people, "Just say a simple, 'Yes, I will,' or 'No, I won't.' Your word is enough. To strengthen your promise with a vow shows that something is wrong" (New Living Translation).

In our day of written contracts, some verbal promises aren't worth the paper they're not written on. They're nothing but a puff of hot air.

That's not how it should be, Jesus says. God doesn't lie, nor should we. If we make a promise, we should keep it. And if we break it, we should seek forgiveness and make restitution for any harm our dishonesty caused.

## 8. Don't seek revenge (5:38–42)

Forget "an eye for an eye and a tooth for a tooth," Jesus tells the crowd. Though that ancient law was intended to limit punishment—so it fit the crime instead of exceeding it—Jesus limits the law even more. Don't retaliate, he says to Jews in an occupied nation, where they're often abused by Roman soldiers.

If you're backhanded, which is how a right-handed person would hit your "right cheek," Jesus says turn the other cheek. That means take the insult without returning violence. Retaliation breeds more retaliation, which escalates the hatred and violence. It works that way one on one and nation on nation. We read about it in the news every day. Someone needs to stop the cycle of violence. We are that someone. We follow Jesus, who died without striking back.

## 9. Love your enemies (5:43–48)

"You have heard people say, 'Love your neighbors and hate your enemies,'" Jesus tells the crowd. "But I tell you to love your enemies and pray for anyone who mistreats you."

There's nothing special about loving a friend, Jesus adds. But the capacity to love and pray for someone who hurts us comes from God. Stephen did it when he asked God to forgive the mob executing him (Acts 7:60). And so did Jesus, of the soldiers crucifying him (Luke 23:34).

Our challenge is to look beyond the pain we feel, and see the soul of one who needs God. If we can see that in them, perhaps they will see God in us.

## 10. Help the needy (6:1–4)

The Old Testament is filled with reminders for God's people to help the needy, especially widows, orphans, and strangers in the land who have no one else to turn to. For this reason, helping the needy becomes a badge of holiness that some charity donors wear proudly.

Jesus says don't wear the badge. "When you give to the poor, don't let anyone know about it. Then your gift will be given in secret. Your Father knows what is done in secret, and he will reward you."

Though we can't always give secretly, we can usually keep a low profile. Jesus' point is that the kind of giving God loves to see is unselfish giving, intended to help others instead of drawing attention to ourselves.

## 11. Pray sincerely instead of for show (6:5–15)

"When you pray," Jesus tells the people, "don't be like those show-offs who love to stand up and pray in the meeting places and on the street corners. They do this just to look good."

Some religious leaders in Jesus' day pray long-winded, holy-sounding prayers in public, to impress the spectators. Jesus says the spectators might be impressed, but God isn't. To show the people how to pray, Jesus offers a short series of praises and requests to God now known as the Lord's Prayer—a model of simplicity and sincerity.

There's no magic formula for talking with God. We can tell God about our hopes, disappointments, and gratitude in plainspoken words, as we would if we could see him sitting with us. Long speeches and religious jargon only get in the way.

## 12. Don't fast to show off (6:16–18)

In Jesus' day, Jews had to go without food for only one day a year, on *Yom Kippur*, a national day of repentance. But many religious leaders also fasted twice a week. Some made it obvious they were fasting—on fast days they wore ragged clothes, covered themselves with dust, and tried to look hungry. They thought this would make them appear holy, and would generate respect from others.

Not from God, Jesus says.

Fasting is a spiritual discipline we can use to reinforce our prayer time and to help us concentrate on a special concern. It can also help us to practice self-discipline, which most of us need more of in various areas of our life. But fasting isn't something we should do for show, to convince others how religious we are.

## 13. Money shouldn't be our top priority (6:19–24)

"Your heart will always be where your treasure is," Jesus says. "You cannot serve both God and money." Anyone who tries will fail. "You will like one more than the other or be more loyal to one than the other."

We live in a material-minded society, where people are obsessed with making, storing, and enjoying money. For many, income potential determines their career—money dictates how they'll spend the bulk of their life's energy.

Money sometimes displaces God as our top priority perhaps because we trust ourselves to take better care of us than God can. That's a bit like our toddlers telling us they know what's best for them. Too often they learn their lesson the hard way. And too often, so do we. (See what Paul says about the love of money: 1 Timothy 6.)

## 14.  Don't let worry control you (6:25–34)

I tell you not to worry about your life," Jesus says to the people, many of whom are poor and working class folks. "Don't worry about having something to eat, drink, or wear. Isn't life more than food and clothing?"

Jesus isn't saying we shouldn't plan for the future or try to put food on the table and a roof over our head. He's saying not to let concerns about such things dominate us. That's what worry is. It takes us over, making it nearly impossible to think about anything else.

Life is more than the physical. Life is spiritual, too. Long after our physical life is gone—with all its concerns and needs—our spirit will be thriving. But if we spend much time worrying about the temporary things of life, we'll miss out on some eternal matters.

## 15.  Don't harshly judge others (7:1–6)

"Stop judging others," Jesus says. "For others will treat you as you treat them. Whatever measure you use in judging others, it will be used to measure how you are judged" (New Living Translation).

Sometimes we have to confront and condemn people about how they're hurting themselves and others. But that's not what Jesus is talking about. He's talking about the hypocritical, self-righteous tearing down of other people. On the other hand, if our criticism is motivated by a desire to help the offending person, our gentle words of advice might actually build them up instead of tear them down.

The judging Jesus talks about is different. It feeds on hatred. There's no place in Christianity for this kind of judgment—of anyone.

## 16.  Ask God for whatever you need (7:7–11)

"Ask, and you will receive," Jesus says about requests people have for God. "Search, and you will find. Knock, and the door will be opened for you."

Jesus doesn't mean we'll always get what we ask for. God knows what we need better than we know ourselves. But Jesus promises that God won't ignore us or give us something less than a child might expect from a loving parent. "As bad as you are," Jesus says, "you still know how to give good gifts to your children. But your heavenly Father is even more ready to give good things to people who ask."

So go ahead. Ask God for whatever you need, asking in the spirit you'd want your child to ask you for something you could give. See what happens.

## 17. **The Golden Rule** (7:12)

"Treat others as you want them to treat you," Jesus says. "This is what the Law and the Prophets are all about."

Known as the Golden Rule, this advice is very close to what Jesus elsewhere describes as one of the most important commandments in the Bible: love others as much as you love yourself (Matthew 22:39). One way to show our love for people is to treat them with the respect we like to get.

When an accountant messes up our bank statement, we exercise the restraint we'd want a customer to show us if we were the accountant who made the mistake. And when someone cuts us off in traffic, we remember when we were that distracted, rushed, or grumpy. So we wave instead of honk.

## 18. **The only highway to heaven** (7:13–14)

"The gate to destruction is wide," Jesus says, "and the road that leads there is easy to follow. . . . But the gate to life is very narrow. The road that leads there is so hard to follow that only a few people find it."

What is that narrow road to eternal life? "I am the way, the truth, and the life!" Jesus explains on another occasion. "Without me, no one can go to the Father" (John 14:6).

Faith in Christ is the narrow road that leads to life. It's hard to follow that road, though, since we'd rather trust in ourselves. Perhaps that's because we know ourselves better than we know Jesus. If so, we can get to know Jesus better and discover for ourselves that he's worthy of our trust.

## 19. **Building our life on Christ's teachings** (7:15–29)

"Watch out for false prophets!" Jesus warns. These are people who say they're godly, but whose actions betray them.

Instead, we're to follow the teachings of Jesus, such as those in this Sermon on the Mount. "Anyone who hears and obeys these teachings of mine is like a wise person who built a house on solid rock."

Jesus promises that if we build our faith on his teachings, we'll weather the storms of life. He should know. He lived, died, and rose again by those teachings.

# MESSAGES FROM THE BIBLE'S BOOKS

# GENESIS

## The Best Part of Creation

Beginning. That's what the ancient Greek word *genesis* means. It's the kind of title God might read and say, "It is good."

After all, Genesis is the beginning of the Bible. And Genesis talks about other beginnings: of the universe, human beings, sin, and God's plan to get rid of sin—a plan that starts with the beginning of the Jewish nation "that will be a blessing to all other nations on earth" (Genesis 18:18). Jesus later comes from this nation.

Yet, Genesis isn't just about beginnings. It's about now. About you.

In this book, you'll read of a primordial earth shrouded in darkness, of a 100-year-old man with no children but whom God promises a big family, and of human civilization wiped out by a flood. But you'll also read of God filling the earth with light and life, of old Abraham having a son whose descendants become the Jewish nation, and of Noah launching a new beginning for the human race.

The message for you?

With God there's always hope. No matter how dark the situation, how ridiculous the odds against you, or how sinful your surroundings, there's hope.

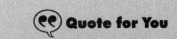 **Quote for You**

"God created people in his own image; God patterned them after himself" (1:27, New Living Translation) *You have many of God's attributes: an eternal spirit, along with the ability to reason, make choices, create, love, and forgive.*

Why should you believe that? The answer lies in the creation story, which explains who we human beings are. When God created us, he breathed part of his life into us. He created us to be like himself and to rule over his creation. After days one through five of creation, God reviewed his work—and each day said it was good. But on the sixth and last day, after he created human beings, he looked at what he had done and said it was extraordinary.

As far as God is concerned, you're the best part of creation. God loves you, and that's why there's hope.

## When It Happened

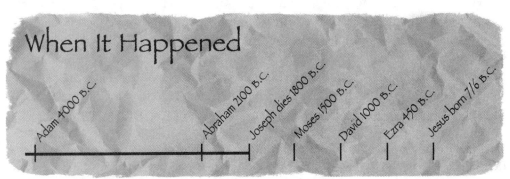

Adam 4000 B.C.    Abraham 2100 B.C.    Joseph dies 1800 B.C.    Moses 1500 B.C.    David 1000 B.C.    Ezra 450 B.C.    Jesus born 7/6 B.C.

# Info You Can Use

 **Background Notes**

**Writer:** Genesis never identifies the writer. Jewish tradition says Moses wrote it and the four books that follow. Moses lived about 400 years after the last events described in Genesis. So if he wrote the book, he relied on earlier records passed along in writing or by word of mouth. He may also have received information directly from God, as he did with the Ten Commandments (Exodus 34:28–32) and other laws. Many Bible scholars, however, say Genesis reads like a book masterfully edited together from several ancient sources. One clue is that there seem to be two accounts of creation—the first in chapter 1 and the second beginning in 2:4, with each using a different Hebrew name for God. The first story uses *Elohim*, meaning God. The second uses *Yahweh Elohim*, meaning Lord God.

**Time:** The stories in Genesis stretch from the time of creation until Joseph died in Egypt, in about 1800 B.C.

**Place:** The stories take place throughout the Middle East, along a thousand-mile stretch in what is now

- Iraq in the east (where Abraham was raised),

- Israel (in ancient times called Canaan, the land God promised to Abraham),

- Egypt in the west (where the Hebrews moved temporarily during a drought, and ended up living as slaves).

**Bottom-Line Summary:** God makes a beautiful world, and humans to take care of it. The first humans—Adam and Eve—disobey God by eating fruit from a forbidden tree. This severs the close relationship between God and humanity: Adam and Eve are banished from the Garden of Eden, where they had walked with God. This disobedience also unleashes sin into creation. In ways we can't fully understand, sin becomes a force that changes people and much of God's good creation. Wickedness, suffering, hard labor, and death all make their debut after humanity's first sin.

Human beings grow so evil that God uses a flood to wipe out everyone except the family of earth's only righteous man: Noah. Afterward, God launches a long-term plan to break sin's grip on humanity and to restore the goodness of his creation. In Genesis, this plan begins with the birth of the Jewish nation, a people set apart to serve God and to become a model of godliness for the rest of the world. Later, Israel's prophets, Jesus, and the Holy Spirit will all play critical roles in the plan, leading people away from sin. Standing at the completion of God's plan, sometime in our future, one of God's prophets describes the scene: "I saw a new heaven and a new earth . . . God's home is now with his people" (Revelation 21:1, 3). Paradise lost becomes paradise restored.

# Influential People

**Adam and Eve,** the world's first human couple. At first, they enjoy blissful fellowship with God. Then they disobey God and are expelled from the idyllic Garden of Eden, which graphically shows how sin rips us away from God and wrecks our life.

**Cain,** oldest son of Adam and Eve. He murders his brother, Abel, and becomes a tragic example of what jealousy can drive us to do.

**Noah,** a godly man who, with his family, builds an ark and survives the Flood. He's an example of God protecting those who love him.

**Abraham,** father of the Jewish people. His riches, long life, and revered reputation all grow out of his extraordinary faith in God. He consistently obeys God, and is rewarded for it.

**Jacob,** son of Isaac and grandson of Abraham. Though he tricks his brother and his elderly father to get a part of the family inheritance that doesn't belong to him, an encounter with God helps change him into a righteous man. His sons become founding ancestors of Israel's 12 tribes.

**Joseph,** Jacob's favorite son. His brothers sell him to slave traders and he ends up as the Egyptian king's second in command. A model of compassion, Joseph forgives his brothers and takes care of them and their families during a seven-year drought.

## Key Ideas You Need to Know

**Sin pushes you away from God.** You see this in stories throughout Genesis and the entire Bible, but most graphically in the story of Adam and Eve. Before their sin, God walks and talks with them in the beautiful Garden of Eden. After their sin, God orders them out of his presence and his garden. If you reject God's way of living—a way of living that puts your best interests first—you're saying no to God. That drives you away from him. It works the same way with people in your life. Each time you reject them, you push yourself further and further away from them.

**God punishes people for sinning.** God hates punishing people, just as parents hate punishing their children. Yet Genesis brims with punishment, including some of the most cataclysmic in all the Bible: the fiery destruction of the cities of

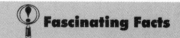

### Fascinating Facts

Though God created Eve as Adam's "helper," (2:18, King James Version) that doesn't mean women are inferior to men. The Hebrew word for "helper" is more accurately translated "partner" or "companion." In fact, it's the same word the Psalm writer uses to describe God: "He is our *help* and our shield" (Psalm 33:20, King James Version).

Adam's name, which can be translated "human being," is a play on the Hebrew word *adamah*, meaning "soil" or "ground."

Sodom and Gomorrah, and the Flood that nearly wipes out humanity. But even in these events, the goal of the punishment is to teach. So what do the citizens of Sodom and Gomorrah and the neighbors of Noah learn, besides how to die? Perhaps nothing, but in these extreme cases the lesson isn't for them. The lesson is for the rest of us. If you follow the Creator's plan for living, you'll be blessed and fulfilled. If you reject the Creator's plan, you become a creature out of sync with creation. And you'll suffer the consequences.

**Showing favoritism in your family is a shortcut to trouble.** Genesis illustrates this with three stories.

1. Isaac loves his oldest son, Esau the hunter, best. But Rebekah favors the younger boy, Jacob. The result is a feud in which Esau vows to kill Jacob, forcing Jacob to flee the country. He never again sees his mother.

2. Jacob marries two women, and loves Rachel more than Leah. The women and their children become bitter rivals, competing for Jacob's attention.

3. Jacob loves Rachel's first son, Joseph, more than any of this other sons. Joseph gets light work duty, a fancy robe, and other favors. Then he flaunts it all. His ten older brothers get fed up and sell him to slave traders headed for Egypt.

There are lots of take-home messages in these stories, but one of the most obvious is this: don't show favoritism in your family. Try to make everyone feel equally loved and respected.

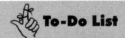 **Q&A**

**What's wrong with polygamy?** Many of Israel's respected leaders had more than one wife. That includes the most respected Israelite of all: Abraham, the father of Israel.

But Adam didn't. God gave Adam just one wife. That was God's plan for human companionship: one man, one woman. "A man leaves his father and mother and is joined to his wife, and the two are united into one" (Genesis 2:24, New Living Translation).

**To-Do List**

- "Be masters over all life—the fish in the sea, the birds in the sky, and all the livestock, wild animals, and small animals" (1:26, New Living Translation). *It's God's creation, but he has put you in charge. Take good care of it.*

- "Am I my brother's keeper?" (4:9, King James Version). *Yes. So be supportive of your brother—and the other loved ones in your circle of influence.*

- "[Noah] constantly followed God's will and enjoyed a close relationship with him" (6:9, New Living Translation). *You may not always know what God wants you to do. But when you know it, do it. Your life will be better for it.*

Yet it became common in ancient times for men to marry more than one wife, so they would have lots of children. The bigger the family, the more workers for the herds and fields. And as the children grew up and the extended family blossomed, the parents could rest in greater assurance that they'd be well cared for in their old age. A big family was about all the Social Security the ancients had.

Yet, when you read the Bible stories of men with multiple wives—men like Jacob, David, and Solomon—you're going to be served a full plate of scheming, bickering, and yelling, along with an occasional murder. These were not happy families.

**Is it okay to ask God for a sign to show you what to do?** Abraham asked his most trusted servant to find a wife for Isaac, Abraham's 40-year-old son. The bride had to come from Abraham's former country, hundreds of miles away. When the servant arrived there, he stopped by a village well and asked God for a sign. The servant told God that as the village women came to get water, he should ask for a drink. The sign: Isaac's future bride would offer to water the camels as well. Rebekah did just that (Genesis 24:46).

Others throughout the Bible asked God for signs, and got them. Should you do the same today? You can, but you probably won't need to. You have God's direction in the Bible, which people in Abraham's day didn't have. You have God's Holy Spirit within you, a source of divine guidance available to only a select few before the Day of Pentecost (Acts 2). And you have the experienced advice of godly people older than yourself.

Besides, searching to discover what God wants you to do—by seeking answers in prayer and the Bible—can make you spiritually stronger.

# Red Flag Issues

**Evolution.** The Bible says God created the world, but it doesn't say how.

Some Christians read the creation story literally, and say God made the universe in six 24-hour days, and humans from the dust of the ground on the sixth day. Other Christians say the "days" probably refer to long periods of time, and that the earth may have developed through a process of evolution over billions of years. In fact, 24-hour days as we know them couldn't have taken place until the fourth day of creation, when God made the sun and moon—"to mark off the seasons, the days, and the years" (Genesis 1:14, New Living Translation).

If humans evolved, there was a point at which God breathed into humanity the breath of life—granting them an eternal soul.

The theory that the earth is young emerged in the 1600s, when Archbishop James Ussher tried to calculate the date of creation by counting the generations backward to Adam. He came up with a creation date of 4004 B.C. Bible scholars later determined that the Bible's genealogy lists don't include everyone, but only the most notable people in Bible families. In these lists, the word once translated "son" means "descendant." So the genealogy lists sometimes skip many generations.

Though Genesis doesn't answer our questions about the how and when of creation, it's clear about the who—which is the point of the creation story. In ancient times, there were a lot of creation legends making the rounds—some of which have been discovered by archaeologists. Genesis wants to set the record straight that the Creator is God.

**Capital punishment.** Some Christians are for it. Others are against it. That's partly because the Bible seems for it at times, and against it at others. God tells Noah, "You must execute anyone who murders another person" (Genesis 9:6, New Living Translation). Moses later gets a similar message (Numbers 35:16). But God didn't execute Cain, the first murderer. And when a group of Jews asked Jesus if they should stone to death a woman caught in adultery—a capital offense according to the laws of Moses—Jesus said, "All right, stone her. But let those who have never sinned throw the first stones!" (John 8:7, New Living Translation). The woman walked.

Perhaps God didn't execute Cain because the emerging human race couldn't afford to lose another male. Yet that would seem to apply to Noah's situation, too, since the execution law came after humanity's near annihilation in the Flood.

God's stated reason for the execution law was this: to show that human life is more important than anything else in creation. That includes the life of the accused. Partly because it's not always possible to determine a person's guilt with absolute certainty, many Christians argue that even the guilty deserve mercy with a sentence of life in prison (an option not available in ancient times). Others believe that even murderers forgiven by God should pay with their life.

**Homosexuality.** When a gang of men in Sodom tries to rape male messengers sent by God, Lot pleads with his neighbors, "Friends, please don't do such a terrible thing!" (Genesis 19:7). God destroys Sodom in a fireball. Later, God tells the Israelites, "Do not practice homosexuality; it is a detestable sin" (Leviticus 18:22, New Living Translation). And shortly after the time of Christ, Paul told the church at Rome that homosexual behavior is "shameful" (Romans 1:27).

Many people say homosexuality is programmed into people—by genetics or childhood episodes that are beyond the person's control. Whether or not that's correct, the Bible gives the homosexual the same warning it gives to unmarried heterosexuals and to married people attracted to someone not their spouse: "No one who is immoral . . . unfaithful in marriage . . . or behaves like a homosexual will share in God's kingdom" (1 Corinthians 6:9–10).

Christians don't agree on how to deal with homosexuals today. Some refuse to have anything to do with homosexuals. Others welcome them into the church and approve of same-sex marriages. Still others search for a middle ground, taking their cue from Jesus, who scatters the attackers of a woman caught in adultery. Jesus refuses to pass judgment on her, and sends her home with these words kindly spoken, "You may go now, but don't sin anymore" (John 8:11).

## For the Record: Genesis Abused

**Slavery.** To justify enslaving black people, some early American slave owners quoted Bible passages, such as God's curse on Noah's son, Ham, whose descendants included some African people. The curse was for Ham seeing his father drunk and naked, and then telling his brothers instead of respectfully covering his father. The curse was actually on Ham's son, Canaan, whose descendants lived in what is now Israel: "A curse on the Canaanites! May they be the lowest of servants to the descendants of Shem and Japheth [brothers of Ham]" (Genesis 9:25, New Living Translation).

This punishment was fulfilled later, when the Jewish people conquered the Canaanites. This passage doesn't condone slavery today, nor does any other passage. The Bible reports that slavery was common in ancient times, but early Christianity began the long process of changing this by teaching we are all equal in God's eyes: "There is no longer Jew or Gentile, slave or free, male or female" (Galatians 3:28, New Living Translation).

Some have taught that the mark God put on Cain, after Cain murdered his brother Abel, was black skin—and that all dark-skinned people are Cain's descendants and should be treated as a race cursed by God.

The Bible doesn't say what the mark was. What's clear is that the mark was not a curse. Cain's curse was banishment, which forced him to wander as a fugitive. The mark was the opposite of a curse—it was a sign of God's mercy. After Cain said the curse was more than he could take and that all who saw him would try to kill him, God put a mark on Cain "to warn anyone not to kill him" (Genesis 4:15).

# Bible Scenarios You Can Use

## 1. God creates the universe (1:1–2:1)

In the beginning, there was no physical world. But over a period of six days, which may refer to long stretches of time, God miraculously makes everything that exists.

He makes light on the first day, sky on the second, and seas and land on the third. Then on the fourth day he creates the sun, moon, and stars. On the fifth day he creates all the fish and birds. On the sixth and final day of creation, he makes all the other animals. As a final act of creation, he makes human beings in his own image, "to be like himself."

For every good thing we have in this world, we can thank God. The air we breathe, the food we eat, the shelter we enjoy beneath starry skies—it all comes from God.

## 2. Humans are in charge (1:26–30)

After God creates man and woman, he blesses them and says, "Fill the earth with people and bring it under your control. Rule over the fish in the ocean, the birds in the sky, and every animal on the earth." The plants, too, are under our authority—given to us as a provision to keep us alive.

What we do with the planet is up to us. God has entrusted us with the job of taking care of it.

To keep our profit margins high, we can drain toxic chemicals into our water supply. And we can load the air with unfiltered pollutants that damage our lungs. But God made this planet with care. He expects us to handle it with care.

## 3. Eve eats forbidden fruit (3:1–24)

Adam and Eve enjoy a life of intimacy with God. There's only one rule: don't eat fruit from one tree because it's deadly. Yet, Eve eats and persuades Adam to do the same.

As punishment, Eve will endure the pains of childbirth. Adam will "struggle to grow enough food." Worse, humans will die: "You were made out of soil, and you will once again turn into soil." Still, God shows concern for Adam and Eve by sacrificing animals to make clothing for them.

This story begins a cycle repeated throughout the Old Testament. People disregard God's rules and suffer the consequences. But God never stops loving them. When we sin, we suffer the inescapable consequences. Yet God keeps loving us.

## 4. Cain kills his brother (4:1–16)

**A**dam and Eve have two sons. Cain, the oldest, becomes a farmer. Abel becomes a shepherd. At harvest, Cain gives God some crops, perhaps in an offering burnt on an altar. Abel kills a choice lamb and gives God the best parts.

God rejects Cain's offering, though the Bible doesn't say why. Perhaps Cain didn't give the best of his crops. God later warns Cain: "You did the wrong thing, and now sin is waiting to attack you like a lion. Sin wants to destroy you, but don't let it!"

Cain lets it. He murders Abel. Cain's relatively minor sin explodes into a massive sin with tragic results. He is banished from his homeland.

Sin can mushroom. But it's not inevitable. As God told Cain, if we do the right thing, we'll be smiling.

## 5. The Flood nearly wipes out humanity (6—9)

**B**y ten generations after Adam, the human race is so hopelessly sinful that God decides to wipe them out and start over. "Cruelty and violence have spread everywhere," God tells Noah, the only righteous person left. "I'm going to destroy the whole world and all its people." God sends a colossal flood that covers even the mountaintops. Noah and his family, along with pairs of all varieties of animals, survive in a covered barge.

The Bible's portrait of sin is more horrifying than a lethal plague. God takes extraordinary steps to stop it. He decimates the planet, to cleanse it. In New Testament times he takes another extraordinary step by sending his Son, Jesus, to empower humans to win the battle against sin.

## 6. People start the Tower of Babel, a monument to themselves (11:1–9)

**N**oah's descendants migrate east, to a plain in the land of Babylon, in what is now Iraq. "Let's build a great city," they say, "with a tower that reaches to the skies—a monument to our greatness!"

God topples their ego by making the people speak a lot of different languages. Unable to communicate, they abandon their work and eventually scatter, apparently by language groups.

We can probably name rich and famous people today who have actually built towering monuments to their own glory—a skyscraper named after the owner, a college building named after a donor. We're all tempted to call attention to our achievements. But as far as God is concerned our identity and worth come not from what we accomplish, but from who we are: people created in his image.

## 7. God promises Abraham a nation (12:1–4)

**A**braham is 75 years old and childless when God makes him an astonishing offer: "Leave your country, your family, and your relatives and go to the land that I will show you. I will bless you and make your descendants into a great nation."

This is another pivotal moment in God's plan of defeating sin. God starts with one righteous man, through whom he plans to establish a nation of people committed to a relationship with him. Through this nation, God intends to bless the entire world. In fact, Jesus—a descendant of Abraham—later becomes one such blessing.

The Bible never says why God singled out Abraham, but the stories that follow show this father of the Jewish people to be firmly devoted to God. Abraham's faith provided a way for God to do great things for people. Our faith can do the same.

## 8. Sodom and Gomorrah burn (18:20—19:29)

**E**vil is running out of control in the twin cities of Sodom and Gomorrah, in a plain somewhere in Canaan. God sends divine messengers to investigate, and they discover incredible depravity. In fact, men of Sodom try to gang rape them. God destroys the cities in a firestorm, but only after his messengers escort the family of Abraham's nephew, Lot, out of town.

The Old Testament shows God is patient in dealing with sin, especially when it involves entire cities and nations. God often waits years and sometimes centuries, to give the people time to repent. When it becomes clear they won't—and evil does nothing but grow—God steps in. His action isn't always this drastic, but if we don't deal with blatant, destructive sin, God will.

## 9. Abraham and Sarah have a son (21:1–7)

**A**braham is 75 years old and childless when God promises to give him many descendants if Abraham will move to Canaan in what is now Israel. Abraham obeys God and moves. But God doesn't begin to make good on this promise until 25 years later. When Abraham is 100 and Sarah is 91, they miraculously have a son: Isaac. Maybe God waited this long to show that with him the impossible is possible.

God keeps his promises. As you read the Bible, you'll see this message played out time and again. So when you read Bible promises directed to all of us, believe them. Promises such as this one from Jesus: "God blesses people whose hearts are pure. They will see him!" (Matthew 5:8).

## 10. Abraham prepares to sacrifice his son (22:1–19)

**G**od's command to Abraham seems cruel and irrational. "Go get Isaac, your only son, the one you dearly love!" God says. "You must sacrifice him to me on the fires of an altar."

This is the son through whom God promised to create the Jewish nation.

Yet, Abraham obeys. As Abraham raises his knife to kill the boy, an angel stops him, saying, "Now I know that you truly obey God, because you were willing to offer him your only son."

This was a test to strengthen Abraham's trust in God. We endure tests as well, though usually not as difficult as this. Abraham's test, as horrifying as it seems, was also a foreshadowing of Jesus. What Abraham was willing to do, God actually did, offering his only son as a sacrifice for our sins.

## 11. Jacob and his mom cheat Esau (27:1–45)

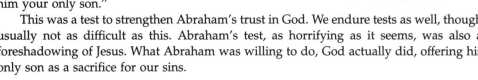

**I**saac and his wife, Rebekah, have twin sons: Esau, the firstborn, and Jacob. Isaac favors Esau, the hunter. Rebekah favors Jacob, who stays in camp. When Isaac becomes old and almost blind, and fears he might die, he asks Esau a favor. Isaac wants fresh meat, and then he will give Esau the blessing traditionally given to the oldest son.

The blessing is an irrevocable promise intended for the next family leader. Once spoken, the words are believed to become fact. Rebekah convinces Jacob to trick Isaac. Jacob serves Isaac his favorite meal and gets the blessing. When Esau learns of this, he vows to kill Jacob. Rebekah sends Jacob hundreds of miles north.

Showing favoritism in the family can wreck lives. Jacob and Esau later reconcile, but Rebekah never sees Jacob again.

## 12. Jacob is tricked into marrying the wrong woman (29:14–30)

**J**acob moves in with his uncle Laban, Rebekah's brother, who lives in what is now southern Turkey. Jacob falls in love with one of Laban's daughters, Rachel, and agrees to work seven years for the right to marry her.

But Jacob, who had cheated his brother, now gets cheated himself. Laban switches brides. Behind the veil is Leah, Rachel's older sister. Jacob doesn't discover the deception until the next morning. Jacob gets Rachel as a second wife, but has to work another seven years.

You reap what you sow, as the apostle Paul once wrote (Galatians 6:7). The way you treat others is the way you can expect to be treated yourself. That's at least partly because word spreads about the kind of person you are.

## 13. Joseph's brothers sell him to slave traders (37:12–28)

Jacob's favorite son is Joseph—the first son of his favorite wife, Rachel. There's already a lot of tension in this family because Jacob has two primary wives and two secondary wives, and he has fathered children by all four. So everyone is competing for Jacob's love and attention.

Joseph, age 17, knows he's the favorite son, and he flaunts it by bragging and tattling. His older brothers get so fed up that they sell him to slave traders on their way to Egypt. The men tell their elderly father a wild animal killed Joseph.

Jacob is heartbroken. But he's partly to blame. He pumped up the tension by giving Joseph special treatment, such as a fancy robe. Favoring one of our children over another is a sure way to drive our kids apart.

## 14. Joseph runs from his master's wife (39:1–20)

Joseph winds up running the household of an Egyptian official, Potiphar. Joseph is handsome, and Potiphar's wife asks him to have sex with her. Joseph refuses and tries to avoid her, but she keeps harassing him. One day she grabs him and demands, "Make love to me!" Joseph runs, leaving her holding his cloak.

She tells her husband Joseph tried to rape her, and shows the cloak as proof. Potiphar seems doubtful, because he imprisons Joseph instead of executing him.

Joseph's response to sin is worth imitating. First, when it invites you, say no—as many times as necessary. Second, if you know where it lingers, stay away. Third, when it reaches out to grab you, run.

## 15. Joseph forgives his brothers (45:1–15)

Famine in the Middle East sends Joseph's brothers on a mission to buy grain in Egypt. Joseph, now 30, has been put in charge of grain distribution. The men meet him, but don't recognize him.

"I am your brother Joseph, the one you sold into Egypt," he tells them. "Don't worry or blame yourselves for what you did. God is the one who sent me ahead of you to save lives." In fact, Joseph arranges for his entire extended family—the people who would become the Israelites of the Exodus—to come to Egypt and wait out the famine.

God can take a bad situation and use it to do good. When others try to hurt you, remember that God can use even their evil to accomplish wonderful things in your life.

# EXODUS

## Feeling Trapped?

Who could have been more trapped than the Hebrews of Moses' day? Enslaved by Egypt, they had no control over their lives. Someone else decided when they woke, what they did with their day, and whether they or their children lived to see sundown.

It was a slow-motion Holocaust Limited. The Egyptians tried working the Hebrews to death and slaughtering newborn boys—not to wipe out the race, but to thin the staggering number of Hebrews taking up space.

After some 400 years in Egypt—no one knows how long as slaves—the Hebrews somehow rediscovered their spiritual roots and cried out for help from the God of their ancestors Abraham, Isaac, and Jacob. God answered their cry. He sent a deliverer. And he came in person—a spirit who invaded human history with miraculous results that seem to defy physics.

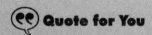 **Quote for You**

"I have seen how my people are suffering . . . and I have heard them beg for my help. . . . I have come down to rescue them" (3:7–8).

What God did for the trapped Israelites, he can do for us today. You might not have a kilt-wearing Egyptian slave driver forcing you to make mud bricks. But you might be trapped in a horrible job. With the slave driver boss you do have and the demands dumped on you, brickwork in Egypt could seem a step up.

Maybe it's debt that has you trapped, or an abusive relationship, or destructive habits. When you call on God for help, he hears, he cares, and he delivers. The deliverance may not come easy. It certainly didn't for the Israelites. And the deliverance may require the help of others. But deliverance does come.

As Jesus once said, at another time when God invaded human history, "Ask, and you will receive. Search, and you will find. Knock, and the door will be opened for you" (Matthew 7:7).

When It Happened

(Dates are approximate)

Adam 4000+ B.C.  Abraham 2100 B.C.  Moses 1500 B.C.  Exodus 1440 B.C.  David 1000 B.C.  Ezra 450 B.C.  Jesus born 7/6 B.C.

# Info You Can Use

## ◈ Background Notes

**Writer:** Probably Moses, though the book never says. However, Exodus 17:14 says Moses wrote at least the Exodus story of how the Israelites defeated the Amalekites—the battle in which Moses had to hold his arms up throughout the battle. And the Gospel of Mark refers to the story of the burning bush, which appears in Exodus, as being in the book of Moses (Mark 12:26).

**Time:** It's unclear when Moses lived and the Exodus took place. Some scholars say the Exodus happened during the 1400s B.C. They base this on 1 Kings 6:1, which says Solomon dedicated his temple 480 years after the Exodus. Since the temple was dedicated in about 960 B.C., that means the Exodus began about 1440 B.C.

Other scholars say Moses lived during the 1200s B.C. They base this on Exodus 1:11, which says the Hebrews built cities such as Rameses. Archaeological evidence suggests the pharaoh Rameses I ruled from about 1293–1291 B.C. His grandson, Rameses II (1279–1212 B.C.), was especially famous for his massive building projects, and may have been the stubborn ruler Moses dealt with.

Archaeologists haven't found any Egyptian reference to the Exodus. But the Egyptians generally reported only success stories, since the pharaohs at that time ruled as gods. A later pharaoh, Merneptah (1212–1202), tells of invading and defeating the Israelites—perhaps during the time of the judges, if the 1440 B.C. date of the Exodus is correct. His report, preserved as an inscription: "Israel is laid waste, his seed is not."

**Place:** The story begins in the Nile Delta of northern Egypt, where the Hebrews worked as slaves on massive construction projects for the government, building entire cities. Freed, they fled east into the barren Sinai Peninsula. There, they camped at the foot of Mt. Sinai for nearly a year, receiving God's laws. Then they moved north, toward their homeland in Canaan (Israel). For disobedience, God ordered them to stay in the wilderness 40 years. They apparently spent much of that time at the oasis of Kadesh Barnea near Canaan's southern border.

**Bottom-Line Summary:** Four hundred years before Moses, Jacob moves his extended family from Canaan to Egypt to escape a seven-year drought. Jacob's descendants stay, where they've grown accustomed to grazing their herds in prime pastures of Goshen, near the Nile Delta. In time, the Hebrews grow so large in number that Egypt feels threatened and enslaves them.

God sends Moses to free the people and lead them back to Canaan. It takes a lot of miracles for God to secure their release and lead them safely through the desert—more miracles than in any other book of the Old Testament. At Mt. Sinai, God gives the people a code of laws that begins establishing them as a nation.

Once they arrive on the southern border of Canaan, they refuse to go any further—terrified by their scouts who report that giants live there, and that the cities are defended by walls and armies. For failing to trust God—even after all the miracles they've seen—the Hebrews are condemned to stay in the desert 40 years. Returning home will have to wait for a new and more faithful generation.

## Influential People

**Moses,** he leads the enslaved Hebrews out of Egypt. Though he's a reluctant leader who tries to talk God out of using him, he becomes a model of courage, obedience to God, and compassion for his people.

**Pharaoh,** unidentified king of Egypt. He's an example of how one person's pride can hurt a lot of people. His stubborn refusal to free the Hebrews caused his entire nation to suffer ten horrifying plagues.

**Aaron,** older brother of Moses and leader responsible for building the golden calf idol. Though Aaron fails God on several important occasions, he receives forgiveness and becomes the nation's chief priest—a tribute to God's mercy.

**Miriam,** older sister of Moses. After God parts the waters of the Red Sea so the Hebrews can escape the pursuing Egyptian army, Miriam shows her people how to praise God. She grabs a tambourine and starts singing and dancing.

## Key Ideas You Need to Know

**God gets involved in your life.** God is all over the landscape of ancient Egypt. He's talking to Moses from a burning bush. He's releasing swarms of locusts, flies, gnats and other plagues to convince the Egyptians to free the Hebrews. With their freedom secured, he's leading them as a pillar of fire and smoke. When Egyptian charioteers give chase, he's parting the sea to make an escape route for his people. At Mt. Sinai, he's delivering a code of laws that defines the emerging nation. In the desert, he's producing water from solid rock and manna bread from who knows where. In camp, he's present among his people in a tent worship center.

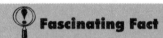

### Fascinating Fact

**God versus gods.** Scholars say the ten plagues probably target Egyptian gods, to show that the Hebrews serve the only true God. With the first eight plagues, God demonstrates his power over gods of the Nile, livestock, earth, sky, health, and the protector from locusts and other pests. Plague 9—turning the land dark—overpowers Egypt's chief god, Ra, the sun god. Plague 10, which kills all the oldest sons of the Egyptians—Pharaoh's included—shows his power over Pharaoh, who is worshiped as a god.

Granted, this was an unusual time in human history. To establish a nation devoted to him, God became more visible and obvious than usual. But the story of Israel's great escape shows that God isn't limited to a separate spiritual dimension. The spiritual can get physical in a big way. When you pray to God, you're not blowing in the wind.

# ❓ Q&A

**Why did God make Pharaoh stubborn?** Before God unleashed the eighth plague—swarming locusts to eat the crops—he told Moses, "Go back to the king, I have made him and his officials stubborn, so that I could work these miracles" (10:1).

Did God actually force Pharaoh to disobey him—to refuse God's order to free the Hebrews?

Pharaoh had already refused God through seven plagues. His pattern of disobedience was well established. What God did was to use this pattern of disobedience for the good of his chosen people. The pattern—and the miracles—would continue a little longer. The stories that came out of these confrontations graphically show God's power to help us.

What exactly God did to enhance the king's stubborn streak is a mystery. But why he did it is clear: "I did this because I want you to tell your children and your grandchildren about my miracles," God told Moses. "Then all of you will know that I am the Lord" (10:2).

## ☝️ To-Do List

- "Do not worship any god except me" (20:3). *The first— and considered the most important—of the Ten Commandments. For more about these basic laws, see pages 3–8.*

- "Make sure that the poor are given equal justice in court" (23:6). *Unlike law codes in other ancient cultures, the laws God gave the Israelites demand equal justice for all, and oppose special treatment for the rich.*

**Does God change his mind?** While Moses was on Mt. Sinai, talking with God, the Israelites were worshiping a golden calf. God told Moses he was so angry at the people that he would kill them all and start over, making the family of Moses into a great nation. Moses pleaded with God not to kill the Israelites. The result? "Even though the Lord had threatened to destroy the people, he changed his mind and let them live" (32:14).

There are other Bible stories about God changing his mind, too. One of the most famous is when he sent Jonah to Nineveh with the message that the city would be overrun in 40 days. The people repented, and God changed his mind.

How can you change the mind of someone who knows everything?

Perhaps it isn't God who's changing, but us. God has a course of action set in place, but it's one that can be affected by our behavior. His plans change when we change. The people of Nineveh repent, and God forgives them instead of punishing them. Moses pleads for the Israelites, and something happens—maybe he becomes better equipped to deal patiently with this generation of serial complainers.

# ⬧ Red Flag Issues

**Abortion.** The Bible doesn't talk directly about abortion. In Bible times, there weren't doctors who could easily stop an unwanted pregnancy. Even so, Christians on both sides of the controversy search the Bible for guidance.

Exodus has a passage implying that the value of an unborn child isn't equal to the value of the mother. "Suppose a pregnant woman suffers a miscarriage as the result of an injury caused by someone who is fighting," God tells Moses. "If she isn't badly hurt, the one who injured her must pay whatever fine her husband demands and the judges approve. But if she is seriously injured, the payment will be life for life, eye for eye, tooth for tooth" (21:22–24). If the mother dies, the attacker dies. But if the child dies, the attacker merely pays a fine.

Christians who oppose abortion sometimes quote a song lyric from the Bible: "You are the one who put me together inside my mother's body" (Psalm 139:13). These Christians also remind us that life is from God, and we shouldn't discard that life simply because it's the most convenient thing to do—especially with so many couples wanting desperately to adopt.

The issue is complicated. It involves more than surprise, inconvenient pregnancies. It involves kids having kids, rape, and incest. With an issue this complex, perhaps the most effective Christian response is one that's equally wide-ranging: love. Or to quote Jesus, "Treat others as you want them to treat you" (Matthew 7:12).

## For the Record: Exodus Abused

**Slavery.** Not only does the Bible stop short of condemning slavery, in places it provides rules to govern slavery. Exodus is one such place. God himself gives Moses laws about the purchase and sale of slaves. "If you buy a Hebrew slave," God says, "he must remain your slave for six years. But in the seventh year you must set him free" (21:2).

Passages like this were used by many Christians in the 1600s–1800s to condone slavery. Rev. William Graham, an instructor in the late 1700s in what is now Washington and Lee University in Lexington, Virginia, taught his students that the Bible isn't a tool to change public policy, but to bring the message of salvation.

This passage, however, deals with Hebrews who voluntarily sold their services to another Hebrew for an extended time. Slavery supporters skimmed past verse 16 in the same chapter—a verse that seems specially suited to slave traders who harvested their cash crop by raiding African villages and selling the captives abroad: "Death is the punishment for kidnapping. If you sell the person you kidnapped . . . the penalty is death" (21:16).

Other passages in the Bible present slavery as a fact of life throughout the world—an issue that was still considered morally neutral. The New Testament emphasis on equality and spiritual freedom, however, planted the seeds that helped convince many nations in the 1800s to abolish slavery.

# Bible Scenarios You Can Use

### 1. Enslaved Israelites grow despite persecution (1:8–14)

The Israelites move to Egypt to escape a famine in Canaan. A few generations later, the Israelites are still there and have produced so many children that the country's new ruler considers them a threat to national security. The Egyptians enslave the Israelites and try to wear them down with hard work, such as making bricks to build cities. But God continues to bless these descendants of Abraham—and their families keep growing.

Difficult circumstances can break your spirit and body. That's what the Egyptians were counting on for the Israelites. On the other hand, difficult circumstances can have the opposite effect. They can give your spirit and body a workout that makes you stronger. When you face tough times, ask God to use the experience to strengthen you.

### 2. God chooses Moses to free the Israelites (3:1—4:17)

Moses is raised by a daughter of Pharaoh, but later flees Egypt after killing an Egyptian for beating a Hebrew slave. Moses becomes a shepherd. One day, while leading a flock in the Sinai, he sees a bush on fire that doesn't burn up. There, God instructs him to go back to Egypt and free the Israelites.

Moses doesn't want to do it. He says he's a nobody. But God says, "I will be with you." Moses says the Egyptians won't listen. But God promises miracles that will make the Egyptians listen. Moses says he's not a good speaker. But God says Aaron—Moses' older brother—is already on his way and he will help with the speaking.

God's ability is greater than our inability.

### 3. God sends ten plagues (7:14—12:30)

As Moses suspected, the Egyptian pharaoh is too proud to take orders from any Hebrew—even one who claims to speak for God. Pharaoh, after all, considers himself a god—the son of Ra, mighty god of the sun.

Moses delivers one plague after another to convince Pharaoh that the only true God is demanding release of the Hebrews. Each plague graphically proves God's power over supposed Egyptian gods. The first plague—turning the Nile River red—shows the impotence of the Egyptian Nile god, Hapi. The tenth plague—killing the oldest son in each Egyptian family, including the royal family—shows God's power over Pharaoh himself, and breaks the ruler's stubborn spirit.

As you face obstacles in your life, remember that no power is greater than the God you serve.

## 4. The first Passover meal (12:1–27)

**T**he night of the tenth and final plague, God institutes the first of Israel's annual festivals: Passover. God says he will pass through Egypt, killing the oldest son in each family. But he will pass over Israelite families, leaving them unharmed.

God tells each Israelite family to eat what becomes known as a Passover meal: roast lamb or goat, herbs and thin bread. "Do this each year," God says, "as a way of remembering the day that I brought your families and tribes out of Egypt."

God wants us to remember where we came from, and who got us where we are now. Remembering helps us face hardship. As followers of Jesus, we have been delivered from our slavery to sin. To commemorate this, Jesus asked us to eat a meal of bread and juice: communion.

## 5. God parts the Red Sea (14:1–31)

**"G**et your people out of my country," Pharaoh tells Moses, after the tenth plague claims his oldest son. The Israelites leave that same morning, marching east toward the Sinai Peninsula and the Red Sea. Pharaoh's grief soon mutates into rage, and he dispatches his chariot corps, which traps the Israelites by the sea. In one of the Bible's most famous scenes, God blocks the Egyptians with a column of smoke and fire, and sends a strong east wind from the desert to blow a path across the body of water—opening an escape route along the sea floor. When the Egyptians try to follow, the sea walls crash in on them, ending the Egyptian threat.

At times, we all find ourselves trapped with no way out. But God can open doors we didn't know existed.

## 6. Israelites complain of hunger and thirst (15:22—16:15)

**A** month after leaving Egypt, many Israelites wish they had never left. "There, we could at least sit down and eat all the bread and meat we wanted," they tell Moses. "You have brought us out here into this desert, where we are going to starve."

God responds by supplying food. For meat, God provides what scholars guess are migrating quail, resting and too exhausted to escape. For bread, God supplies what the Hebrews call *manna*, meaning "What is it?" This mysterious substance looks like thin, white flakes and tastes sweet.

You may not run out of food, but you'll face other shortages that punch up your stress levels. Money runs low. Time runs short. But when you call on God, he provides what you need.

## 7. God delivers the Ten Commandments (20:1–17)

**B**efore Moses delivers the Ten Commandments on stone tablets, God delivers them himself in a dramatic spectacle. At dawn the Israelites assemble at the base of Mt. Sinai. Thunder and lightning fill the sky as a thick cloud settles on the mountain. With a voice that fills the landscape, God speaks the Ten Commandments.

These ten basic rules for living become the building blocks on which all other Jewish laws rest. These laws teach us how to treat God (respect him above all else), ourselves (take a day off work every week), and others (don't murder, steal, lie, commit adultery, or crave what belongs to someone else).

Life is miserable when we disobey these rules. God gave us these rules to bring peace to our life. (For more about the Ten Commandments, see page 3.)

## 8. Israelites build a tent worship center (25:1–9; 26:1–37)

**P**eople worship their gods in temples. But the new and mobile nation of Israel has no place to worship God. It's not practical to build a temple, since the Israelites are on what will become a 40-year journey. So God instructs them to build a tent worship center they can set up in the center of camp. God describes the tabernacle, as it becomes known, as "a special place where I can live among my people."

God doesn't need a place to live, but the Israelites need a visible reminder that he is with them. And they need a place to gather for worship. We need a place to worship God, too. It may be a church, a rented school building, or someone's living room. Wherever it may be, it's a special place where God is present.

## 9. Israelites worship a golden calf (31:18—32:35)

**A**fter God's dramatic speech, in which he presents the Ten Commandments, the people are so frightened they ask Moses to serve as God's intermediary. Moses climbs Mt. Sinai, where God gives him "two flat stones on which he had written all of his laws with his own hand." Moses is gone 40 days, long enough for the people to conclude he died. They talk his brother, Aaron, into building a golden calf, "an image of a god who will lead and protect us." Bull idols are worshiped in Egypt. When Moses returns and sees this, he breaks the stones—just as the Israelites had broken the first commandment to worship God alone.

Old habits can lure us back, especially when we're feeling vulnerable. But God can help us break the habits, before they break us.

# LEVITICUS

## A Holiness How-to Manual

We're made in God's image—which means we're like him in many ways. Because of this, it's natural that we want to spend time with him.

But there's something that gets in our way: sin. That's one big difference between God and us. God is the definition of goodness. He has never sinned, and never will. But we have sinned in days past, and may well sin again.

So how can sinful people and a holy God develop a relationship? Sin and holiness are opposites that don't attract. They're more like matter and antimatter, which can't exist together. Leviticus is a manual to teach the Israelites how to live in the presence of a holy God.

Leviticus condensed is this: sinful people develop a relationship with a holy God by becoming holy themselves. We do this by seeking God's forgiveness when we sin and by devoting ourselves to him.

We tend to think of priests as holy men, or men of God, because they devote their lives to God. Israel, however, was to be a nation of priests. God told them, "You will be my holy nation and serve me as priests" (Exodus 19:6), representing God before the world. Leviticus showed the Israelites how to find cleansing for sin and how to develop a lifestyle pleasing to God.

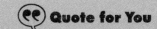 **Quote for You**

"You must become holy, because I am holy" (11:44). God isn't talking about living perfect lives. He means being devoted to goodness. When we slip up, forgiveness is available.

Some of the guidelines in Leviticus are obsolete now, because they deal with sacrifices and rituals in the ancient worship center, which doesn't exist anymore. Yet this law code is one of the important steps God took in his plan to save humanity from sin. So Leviticus precedes the new manual coming from Jesus, "the author and finisher of our faith" (Hebrews 12:2, King James Version).

When It Happened

(Dates are approximate)

Adam 4000+ B.C.    Abraham 2100 B.C.    Moses 1500 B.C.    Exodus 1440 B.C.    Wandering Ends 1400 B.C.    David 1000 B.C.    Ezra 450 B.C.    Jesus born 7/6 B.C.

# Info You Can Use

## Background Notes

**Writer:** The unnamed writer is probably Moses, who according to ancient Jewish tradition wrote each of the first five books of the Bible. Most of the book is a collection of quotes from God to Moses, in which God gives detailed instructions about how the people are to conduct themselves in everyday life and worship.

**Time:** God delivers the laws that make up most of Leviticus during the nearly one year that the Israelites are camped at the foot of Mt. Sinai. This first year after their miraculous escape from Egypt becomes a time to rest, recover, and begin organizing themselves into a nation. The date is roughly 1440 B.C. according to some scholars, or in the 1200s B.C. according to others. (For more about the date, see "Background Notes, Time" for Exodus, page 32.)

**Place:** The setting for this book is at the foot of Mt. Sinai. It's unclear exactly where this is. The Israelites fled east out of Egypt, and into the rugged and barren Sinai Peninsula—a region that looks a bit like a cross between a desert and rocky badlands.

Near the southern tip of the peninsula is a 7,500-foot-high rock mountain that has been identified as Mt. Sinai since ancient times. It's called Jebel Musa, an Arabic name that means "mountain of Moses." In the fourth century A.D., Christians built a monastery there to commemorate the place where God met Moses at the burning bush, and later gave him the Ten Commandments. A nearby oasis may have provided the Israelites with water and a comfortable resting place.

**Bottom-Line Summary:** After fleeing Egypt and escaping the chariot corps that Pharaoh sent to bring them back, the Israelites camp at the foot of Mt. Sinai, the same mountain where Moses first met God at the burning bush.

They stay there for nearly a year, while God gives Moses the Ten Commandments and more than 600 other laws—many of which are preserved in Leviticus. A lot of these laws are religious and deal with how to worship God in the newly built tent worship center, called the tabernacle. Other laws deal with civil issues, such as how to help the poor and how to punish people for crimes.

With this wide array of laws, God is teaching us that he is our Lord not just when we worship, but in every moment of our life.

## Influential People

**Moses** receives and puts into place the detailed laws God gives him to establish Israel as a nation devoted to the Lord. In so doing, he shows his devotion to God, leading by his actions as well as his words.

**Aaron,** older brother of Moses, is appointed by God as the chief priest, responsible for overseeing the sacrifices and other sacred rituals that God set up. As such, he is Israel's worship leader—this man who earlier led the Israelites in worshiping a golden calf. Aaron is a model of God's mercy and willingness to give people a second chance.

# 🔑 Key Ideas You Need to Know

**Holiness.** Leviticus mentions holiness 152 times—more than any other book in the Bible. The word has several meanings. Many people think it means living a perfect life, but it doesn't. It means being devoted to God. Bowls or lamp stands were considered holy when they were used in rituals at the worship center. The Israelites were holy because they were devoted to God (even though they made plenty of mistakes). We are holy, too, when we devote ourselves to God.

When Leviticus talks about the holiness of God, that's another matter. In this case, holiness is God's defining quality—goodness off the scale and rocketing to infinity. Holiness includes God's purity, righteousness, love, mercy, and justice. It's impossible to describe the spiritual essence of God in human terms. But the word "holiness" takes it as far as we're able to follow, then leaves us wondering how we can ever hope to understand how good God is.

**Worship.** God expresses his love to the Israelites in many ways, as in protecting them along their journey in the desert. To let them reciprocate, he sets up a wide-ranging worship system.

One day a week, they rest and gather for worship. Seven times a year they mark religious holidays, often to celebrate the harvest and other blessings from God. Throughout the year they can bring many kinds of offerings to the worship center, such as a burnt offering to express sorrow for a sin, a grain offering as thanks for God's provision, and a fellowship offering that calls together family and friends to share a meal of thanksgiving.

> ## 💡 Fascinating Facts
>
> Leviticus gives us the word "scapegoat," which describes a person who takes the blame for someone else. On Israel's annual day of repentance, known in Hebrew as *Yom Kippur,* the high priest lays his hands on a goat to symbolize the nation's sins being transferred to the sacrificial animal. The animal is then driven into the desert to die. Its departure represents the nation's sins leaving as well.
>
> Leviticus was once called the Priest's Manual because the book is full of detailed instructions about worship, which is led by priests. The name *Leviticus* came later, and means "about the Levites," the family descended from Jacob's son Levi, who produced Israel's priests.

Some of these worship experiences take place at home, surrounded by family. Others take place at the worship center, surrounded by friends and strangers. In either setting, the people recall what God has done for them in years past, what he is doing now, and what they are asking of him in the days ahead. Some of the worship is boisterous, with singing, dancing, and plenty of food. Other worship, as in the annual day of repentance—*Yom Kippur*—is a time of fasting, quiet reflection, and rededication.

Worship today is more than a sermon, a few songs, and passing the collection plate. It's time you spend with God on your mind, whenever and wherever that is: over a mealtime prayer, enjoying the Heavenly Artist painting a sunset, or reading to your child a Bible story.

## Q&A

**Why sacrifice an animal for sins?** Since the days of Adam and Eve, animals have been dying for the sins of humanity. After the first couple ate the forbidden fruit and became embarrassed by their nakedness, "God made clothes out of animal skins for the man and his wife" (3:21). The death of these animals—the first death of any kind recorded in the Bible—illustrates that sin is deadly serious.

"Life is in the blood," God explained. "I have given you the blood of animals to sacrifice in place of your own" (17:11). Blood offerings is the method God chose for people in Old Testament times to find forgiveness. God never explained why he chose this method, but it certainly became a graphic way of helping people associate sin with death.

The sacrificial system became obsolete when Jesus died for humanity's sin: "Christ obeyed God and offered himself once for all . . . a sacrifice that is good forever" (Hebrews 10:10–11). Jews stopped offering sacrifices when Rome destroyed the temple in A.D. 70. The temple has never been rebuilt. On the Jerusalem hilltop where it once sat is a 1,400-year-old Muslim worship center called the Dome of the Rock.

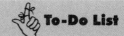 **To-Do List**

- "Love others as much as you love yourself" (19:18). *Jesus later calls this the second most important commandment, after loving God with all your heart (Matthew 22:39).*

- "Show respect for older people" (20:32).

- "If any of your people become poor and unable to support themselves, you must help them" (25:35).

**Why circumcise Jewish males?** On the eighth day of a Jewish boy's life, he was circumcised—the foreskin of his penis was cut off (Leviticus 12:3). Circumcision was common in the ancient Middle East, though it was usually a rite of passage, performed on boys approaching puberty or marriage.

God gave this ritual a different meaning among the Israelites. The ritual started hundreds of years before Moses, in the time of Abraham. "You and all future members of your family must promise to obey me," God told Abraham. "As the sign that you are keeping this promise, you must circumcise every man and boy in your family" (Genesis 17:9–11). This ritual became a perpetual reminder of the agreement between God and Israel. The people would obey God, and God would make Israel into a great nation.

Why God chose this ritual is unclear, but it may have been a practical, healthy choice. Circumcision can make it easier to keep the skin clean and prevent transmitting infections during sex—which could be a problem of special concern for people living in desert regions where bathing is a luxury.

Early Christians decided that non-Jews didn't have to submit to this ritual.

Requiring it would have meant that a person had to convert to the Jewish faith before becoming a Christian. "Being circumcised or uncircumcised isn't really what matters," Paul wrote the church in Corinth. "The important thing is to obey God's commands" (1 Corinthians 8:18–19). Paul wasn't referring to God's detailed instructions for Jews in Old Testament times, but to the basics of God's law, which were expressed in the Ten Commandments and are relevant to everyone, not just the Jews.

 ## Red Flag Issues

**No work on Sundays.** "You have six days when you can do your work, but the seventh day of each week is holy because it belongs to me. No matter where you live, you must rest on the Sabbath and come together for worship. This law will never change" (23:3).

For Jews, the Sabbath is from sundown on Friday through sundown on Saturday. Christians set aside Sunday as a day of rest and worship, in celebration of Christ's resurrection on Easter Sunday.

In Israel today—and in some Jewish communities abroad—many businesses are closed on Saturday. In the United States, some businesses are closed on Sunday, though this isn't as common as it was a generation or two ago.

Jews and Christians have long debated among themselves what should and shouldn't be allowed on the Sabbath. In response to a strict list of do's and don'ts, Jesus had a simple reply. "The Sabbath was made for the good of people," he said. "People were not made for the good of the Sabbath" (Mark 2:27).

In our busy world, God wants us to take a day off each week. It's his gift to us, to refresh our body and spirit.

**Stay away from psychics.** "If any among the people are unfaithful by consulting and following mediums or psychics, I will turn against them" (20:6, New Living Translation).

A medium, or psychic, tells the future by contacting spirits of the dead. God didn't want his people to have anything to do with psychics, and he ordered that any psychics consulting the dead should join the ranks of the dead—it drew the death penalty (20:27).

The Bible never explains why God considers this such a serious offense. It's clear he wants to protect us, but from what? Perhaps from being taken advantage of by frauds. And for psychics who may have real contact with the spirit world, perhaps God wants to protect us from evil spirits who have no desire to do anything but hurt us.

For any godly person who wants to know the future, or who wants answers to other questions that might be hidden in the spirit world, God wants us to turn to him—the Spirit who has demonstrated his love for us. And if the answers don't come, he wants us to trust him to hold those answers for us until the time is right for us to receive them.

# For the Record: Leviticus Abused

**Witch hunts.** During the 1500s and 1600s, an estimated 300,000 accused witches—mostly women—were imprisoned, tortured, or executed throughout Europe and America. Hysteria drove the hunt, which started after publication of *The Witch's Hammer,* an anti-women's book written by two priests vividly describing the satanic and sexual activities of witches. In America, witch mania was also fed by preaching that the devil would become more active as the Second Coming of Jesus drew near.

One of the last outbreaks took place in 1692 in Salem, Massachusetts, after several young girls caught practicing magic said they were bewitched—and started naming witches. One hundred and fifty people were arrested, and 20 were hanged. No one listened to Martha Corey, a victim who said her accusers were "poor, distracted children."

Tituba, a slave from the West Indies, told fortunes of Salem girls. She admitted this, as well as making a pact with the devil. But she never came to trial because only those who insisted they were innocent were hanged.

Seeking biblical approval for the executions, people turned to Leviticus and other passages, such as Exodus 22:18, which says the guilty should die. But in the witch hunts, it was usually the innocent who died.

# Bible Scenarios You Can Use

### 1. A lamb dies for a person's sin (4:27–35)

**G**od creates an intricate system of sacrifices to help people express their feelings to him. Some offerings are of crops or fragrant incense, to thank God. Other offerings are of animals, such as a lamb, to express sorrow for sin.

The animal's death is a powerful visual aid reminding people that sin causes spiritual death. Before killing the animal, the worshiper lays a hand on it, perhaps to symbolize that the animal is about to lose its life because of the person's sin.

The sacrificial system becomes obsolete after Jesus dies as "the Lamb of God who takes away the sin of the world" (John 1:29). About 40 years later, Romans destroy the Jerusalem temple—ending the sacrificial system among Jews. Still, sin remains a deadly serious matter that leads to spiritual death. But it doesn't have to. There's no need to offer a sacrifice, since Jesus is your sacrifice. Just tell God you're sorry for your sin—whenever you sin—and stay devoted to him.

### 2. Eating only kosher food (11:1–47)

**G**od takes some meat off the menu. The Israelites can eat cattle and sheep, fish that have scales, and even some insects, such as locusts and grasshoppers. But they can't eat pigs, rabbits, shellfish, and certain birds, such as eagles and storks. If Israelites even touch non-kosher food, they have to go through cleansing rituals before worshiping God.

The Bible doesn't explain why God makes these rules. Some scholars guess God was trying to protect the people from health problems or idolatry (pigs were popular sacrifices to idols, but so was cattle). Perhaps God was providing another way to show everyone that Israel was a unique nation—devoted to God. You could tell Israelites from other people by their behavior. Among other things, they rested on the Sabbath and they refused to eat certain foods. This called attention to Israelites. And when others saw how God was taking care of them, it called attention to him as well.

The New Testament says we don't have to follow kosher food laws anymore (Matthew 15:11). But God wants our behavior to identify us as people devoted to him. This happens when we gather to worship, lend a helping hand, or speak kindly of others.

## 3. Gathering for worship festivals (23:1–44)

**B**esides giving the Israelites one day a week for rest and worship, God instructs the Israelites to set aside another 19 days for seven national religious holidays. The annual celebrations, in the order they fall, are as follows:

**Passover** (1 day) comes in early spring, usually between mid-March to mid-April. The Israelites eat a meal like they ate on the night before their release from Egyptian slavery.

**Festival of Unleavened Bread** (7 days) follows Passover, and reminds the people of the Exodus. They rest from work on the first and last day of the festival. And they don't eat bread made from yeast. Since yeast takes time to rise, the Israelites couldn't use it as they fled from Egypt. So eating the thin bread reminds them of their deliverance.

**Festival of Early Harvest** (1 day) also comes in early spring. It's a time to thank God for barley, flax, and other crops harvested early. People bring grain offerings to the worship center.

**Festival of Harvest** (1 day) is later known as Pentecost, from a Greek word for "fifty." That's because it comes 50 days after Passover and the Festival of Unleavened Bread. It celebrates the wheat harvest, with people bringing more grain offerings to the worship center.

**Festival of Trumpets** (1 day) usually comes in September or October. Israelites blow horns in what later becomes the Jewish New Year, *Rosh Hashanah* in Hebrew.

**Day of Forgiveness** (1 day) comes ten days later. Called *Yom Kippur* in Hebrew, this is a national day of repentance—the most solemn day of the Jewish year.

**Festival of Shelter** (7 days) comes five days later and is a celebration of God's protection during the Exodus. Later generations would camp out in huts or shelters made of branches, to commemorate Israel's years in the desert after the Exodus.

Christians today celebrate few if any of these ancient festivals, though some celebrate Passover. But we have Sunday, Christmas, Easter, and other important days on the Christian calendar—such as Pentecost Sunday (marking the arrival of the Holy Spirit) and Ascension Sunday (when Jesus rose into the heavens). These special times with family, friends, and fellow Christians give us a chance to reflect on what God has done for us, to thank him, and to renew our commitment to him.

# NUMBERS

## When God Has It Up to Here

This is a Bible book for complainers—chronic or casual. The message is this: there's a point when complaining becomes sin, when your incessant grumbling offers proof positive that you've lost all trust in God.

For a nation of newly freed slaves headed to the land of milk and honey, the Israelites complained a lot. First it was the food. They missed their fish from the Nile and fresh veggies. Then they complained about Moses, figuring they needed a leader other than God's man. The complaint that broke the camel's back was when they refused to go into Canaan after some of their scouts reported there were giants in the land.

God suggested cleaning the gene pool. "I have done great things for these people, and they still reject me by refusing to believe in my power," God told Moses. "I will destroy them, but I will make you the ancestor of a nation even stronger" (14:11–12).

Moses asked God to spare the Israelites—as Moses had done before. And God honored the request—again. But God insisted that this complaining generation should get their wish and never set foot on the promised land. By rejecting God, the Israelites rejected the milk and honey that was waiting for them. They paid the price. So did their children, who had to grow up in the desert.

> ### 💬 Quote for You
>
> "You [God] will punish everyone guilty of doing wrong—not only them but their children and grandchildren as well" (14:18). *Sin can have long-lasting consequences, sometimes scaring a family for generations. For instance, one of Israel's sins kept them in the desert for 40 years.*

## When It Happened

(Dates are approximate)

Adam 4000+ B.C.

Abraham 2100 B.C.

Moses 1500 B.C.

Exodus 1440 B.C.
Wandering Ends 1400 B.C.

David 1000 B.C.

Ezra 450 B.C.

Jesus born 7/6 B.C.

# Info You Can Use

## Background Notes

**Writer:** Though the writer isn't identified, ancient Jewish tradition says Moses wrote Numbers, along with each of the first five books of the Bible. Numbers 33:2 says he kept a log of the places the Israelites camped. So he wrote at least that section. Others may have contributed to the book by writing down stories that had been passed along by word of mouth for generations. It seems unlikely, for example, that Moses wrote this: "Moses was the most humble person in all the world" (Numbers 12:1).

**Time:** These stories take place during the 40 years the Israelites stayed in the desert, after fleeing slavery in Egypt. Many scholars place that from roughly 1440 B.C. to 1400 B.C.

**Place:** Numbers is set in the barren stretch of rocky desert between Egypt in the southwest and Israel in the northeast. The Israelites break camp at the foot of Mt. Sinai, possibly somewhere in the southern Sinai Peninsula, and then migrate north toward Canaan. They likely spend most of their 40 years in the desert at the oasis of Kadesh Barnea, near Canaan's southern border.

**Bottom-Line Summary:** After nearly a year camped at the foot of Mt. Sinai, where God gives Moses the hundreds of laws that will establish and govern the nation, God orders Moses to take a census of the people and then lead them to the promised land of Canaan, now Israel. (The book gets its name from two census reports: one before the people leave Mt. Sinai, and another one about 40 years later, as they prepare to enter Canaan.)

Traveling through the desert from mid-spring to late summer, they run low on water and food. Rather than ask help from God who freed them from Egypt and performed many miracles to protect them, they bitterly complain to Moses and say they wish they were back in Egypt. Their complaints reach an all-time high when they arrive on Canaan's southern border. Scouts sent into Canaan return with a horrifying report that giants live in the land and the cities are massively fortified with high walls.

God or no God, the Israelites refuse to go any further. "We'd be better off in Egypt," they say. "Let's choose our own leader and go back" (14:3–4). Because of their lack of confidence in God's power—in spite of all the miracles they've witnessed in the last couple of years—God banishes this faithless and complaining generation to the desert. A new and braver generation will reclaim the promised land.

After Israel is finished serving its sentence, a new generation sets out for Canaan and arrives at the region that becomes the staging area for their invasion: pastures east of the Jordan River, in what is now Jordan.

**Influential People**

**Moses** leads the Israelites out of slavery in Egypt and to the very edge of the promised land. But an act of disobedience keeps him from crossing into Canaan— a reminder that even spiritual leaders can make tragic blunders.

**Aaron,** high priest of Israel and brother of Moses, seeks equal power with Moses, and becomes a reminder that even those who are envied can get jealous.

**Miriam,** sister of Moses, unfairly criticizes him and seeks equal power with him. God strikes her with leprosy, and she becomes an object lesson about what God thinks of envy and a critical spirit.

**Joshua,** a scout, shows his confidence in God by urging the Israelites to enter Canaan even though the land is heavily defended. When Moses dies, he will become the new leader and a symbol of how God rewards faithfulness.

**Balaam,** a seer hired by the king of Moab to put a curse on Israel, is convinced by an angel to bless Israel instead. His blessing shows that God can use even the ungodly to help his people.

 **Key Ideas You Need to Know**

**God won't ignore sin.** Ignoring sin doesn't make it go away. Ask any parent who has dealt with a rebellious child, or a supervisor with a disruptive worker. God will show concern, patience, and loving forgiveness. But he won't put up with sin. If the sin lingers, punishment follows. Sometimes the consequences of the sin last a lifetime, as it did for the Israelites who spent the rest of their lives in the desert. But even in the desert, God didn't desert them. He was with them every step of the way.

**Red Flag Issues**

**Interracial marriage.** "Moses had no right to marry that woman from Ethiopia!" (12:1). That's a complaint from his brother and sister. Moses was of the Hebrew race. His wife was probably from either Africa or Arabia. Scholars debate how to translate the name of her country; some say it was Ethiopia in northern Africa and others say it was Cush in northern Arabia.

---

**Fascinating Facts**

"Slow as Moses" is a phrase that comes from the fact that it took the Israelites 40 years to cover the 400 miles between Egypt and Canaan—an average speed of less than a mile a month. Take 60 steps and call it a day. Actually, the Israelites were camped just about all of those 40 years because God ordered them to stay in the desert.

Israel's national symbol, the Star of David, comes from Balaam's prophecy about a king of Israel who "will appear like a star" (24:17) and conquer the desert nations.

Balaam's name has turned up on a seventh century B.C. plaster inscription found in non-Israelite ruins in Jordan—the region where a desert king asked him to come and curse the invading Israelites. The inscription calls Balaam a "seer of the gods" who received a divine message about a coming disaster.

In either case, she wasn't a Hebrew. God defends Moses, saying, "You have no right to criticize my servant." Apparently for her role in leading the criticism, Miriam is temporarily stricken with leprosy.

## For the Record: Numbers Abused

**You're sick because you sinned.** Some religious leaders have said AIDS is a curse from God—a divine judgment on homosexuals, prostitutes, and drug users. For support, they turn to Numbers and other Bible books that talk about plagues and disasters caused by sin. Miriam got leprosy for criticizing her brother (12:9). The ten scouts who advised Israel to ignore God's instructions and stay out of Canaan died of a "deadly disease" (14:37). And after an uprising against Moses, 14,700 Israelites died of a fast-spreading disease (16:49). In each case, God said he was the one dispensing judgment.

If God is responsible for AIDS, he's not admitting it. And God has a long history of giving warnings before and mercy after any judgment. Even if AIDS is from God, our response should be no less than the response Moses gave to his people. He prayed for Miriam's healing. He likely mourned the death of the scouts. And he found a way to stop the plague that killed thousands.

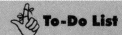 **To-Do List**

- "Obey his [God's] commands instead of following your own desires and going your own ways, as you are prone to do" (15:39, New Living Translation).

# Bible Scenarios You Can Use

## 1. A pillar of cloud leads the Exodus (10:11–36)

In mid-spring, 11 months after the Israelites made camp at the foot of Mt. Sinai, God lets them know it's time to move on. The pillar of cloud and fire hovering above the worship center—the same pillar that had led the Israelites out of Egypt—begins to move away from camp. From here, the journey to Canaan is perhaps 300 miles and would take a large group of refugees about three to four months. When the divine cloud moves, the Israelites follow. When the cloud stops, the people make camp.

This is an extraordinary time in Israel's history. They are emerging as a nation destined to bless the world through their example of godliness and the gift of the Messiah. They need dramatic evidence that God is with them.

We need to know God is with us, too. We probably won't see him in any beams of light or luminous clouds above our church. But we don't need to. We have his Spirit within us. And we have the Bible to remind us of what Jesus told his disciples, "I will be with you always, even until the end of the world" (Matthew 28:20).

## 2. Refusing to enter the promised land (13:1—14:44)

During harvesttime in late summer, the Israelites arrive at an oasis near Canaan's southern border. Moses sends 12 scouts to find out if the land is good, how many people live there, and if the cities are heavily defended. The scouts spend 40 days in Canaan and return with mixed reviews. Ten scouts say the land is poor, the cities have walls, and the people are huge: "They were so big that we felt as small as grasshoppers." Two other scouts—Joshua and Caleb—show off grapes, pomegranates, and figs they brought back, and argue for taking the land: "The Lord is on our side, and they won't stand a chance against us."

The Israelites are terrified by what the ten scouts say and refuse to go any further. For this lack of trust, God condemns the nation to stay in the desert 40 years—one year for each day the scouts were in Canaan.

When you have decisions to make, don't let the negatives keep you from seeing the positives—and don't underestimate God's power.

## 3. Leaders rebel against Moses (16:1–35)

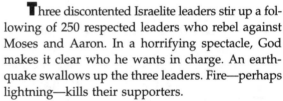

**T**hree discontented Israelite leaders stir up a following of 250 respected leaders who rebel against Moses and Aaron. In a horrifying spectacle, God makes it clear who he wants in charge. An earthquake swallows up the three leaders. Fire—perhaps lightning—kills their supporters.

It's natural to have ambition, but not ambition on steroids, puffing up our ego and convincing us we deserve what belongs to someone else. Ambition like that is greed. It can hurt you and the people you love. Instead of wishing you were like someone else, concentrate on who you are and the talents God has given you.

## 4. A new generation prepares to enter Canaan (20:14—21:35)

**A**fter the Israelites spend 40 years in the desert, God tells Moses it's time for them to go to Canaan, where their ancestor Abraham lived. Nearly all the adults from the previous generation have died. Moses will die, too, after he sees Canaan from a mountaintop. Only Joshua and Caleb of the Exodus generation will get to step foot on the land.

Despite Israel's chronic and bitter complaining, along with their remarkable lack of trust in God after all the miracles they saw him do, God doesn't give up on the nation. These are his people, spiritually immature though they are. We are his people, too. Though we'll make our share of mistakes as we grow in the faith, God will keep leading us as long as we keep following.

## 5. A seer refuses to curse Israel (22:1—24:25)

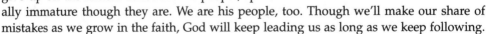

**A**s the Israelites turn north along the eastern border of Canaan, they approach the nation of Moab in what is now Jordan. Moab's king panics. He sends for Balaam, a famous seer. The king says a huge group of people is coming, and his army can't stop them. Moab's only hope is if the seer puts a curse on the invaders.

Balaam agrees to come, but along the way meets an angel who warns him to say only what God commands. The king takes Balaam to a mountaintop overlooking the Israelite camp. Instead of cursing the people, Balaam blesses them: "You will defeat your enemies."

God has plans for your life, just as he had plans for Israel. People who don't care about you or God may stand in your way. But they won't be able to stop what God is going to do through you. God may even use their evil intentions to help you.

# DEUTERONOMY

## Listening to People Who've Been There

We don't take advice well. Yet, people who love us keep giving it.

They've learned from their experiences—the successes and failures. And they want us to learn, too, without having to go through the anguish they suffered. Trouble is, we don't want someone else telling us what to do. Besides, the advice of others often sounds like someone else's history—not relevant to us.

Moses loved the Israelites. And as he prepared to die, he did the loving thing. He gave them advice. They needed it. This was a new generation of Israelites. They weren't around to experience the escape from Egypt, the parting of the Red Sea, or the miracles in the desert. They didn't stand at the foot of Mt. Sinai and make the agreement with God to obey him in return for protection and blessing. And they didn't witness the disasters that took place when their parents disobeyed God.

So Moses told them the story. Then came the advice, based on solid and timeless experience: obey God's laws "and he will bless you in many ways" (28:2), disobey and "you won't last long, and you may even meet with disaster" (28:20).

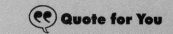 **Quote for You**

"Love the Lord your God will all your heart, soul, and strength" (6:5). *Jesus quoted this verse when asked to identify the most important commandment in the Bible.*

At first, Israel chose option one, and a strong nation was born. Later generations chose option two, and the nation crumbled.

God's most basic laws, summed up in the Ten Commandments, aren't someone else's history. They're our future. And we have a choice to make.

When It Happened

(Dates are approximate)

Adam 4000+ B.C.

Abraham 2100 B.C.

Moses 1500 B.C.
Exodus 1440 B.C.
Wandering Ends 1400 B.C.
Conquest Begins 1400 B.C.
David 1000 B.C.

Ezra 450 B.C.

Jesus born 7/6 B.C.

# Info You Can Use

## Background Notes

**Writer:** As the first verse says, "This book contains the speeches that Moses made while Israel was in the land of Moab." The final chapter, about his death, may have been added by Joshua or a priest who witnessed the death and helped bury him.

**Time:** Moses delivered these last words to his people shortly before his death and Israel's invasion of the promised land. The date may have been about 1400 B.C., though many scholars say it took place in the 1200s B.C. For more on the date of the Exodus, see "Background Notes, Time" on page 32.

**Place:** The Israelites are camped near the eastern banks of the Jordan River, on the plains of Moab in what is now Jordan.

**Bottom-Line Summary:** Just before the Israelites cross the Jordan River into Canaan, Moses calls them together. He won't be going with them, because he's about to die. But he wants to give his people some important advice. Nearly all the Israelite adults who had witnessed the miraculous escape from Egypt are dead. So the people before Moses are a new generation who didn't stand at the foot of Mt. Sinai and make an agreement with God to follow his laws in return for his blessing. So Moses gives them all a sacred history lesson, and then urges them to honor their nation's agreement with God. That's why the book is called Deuteronomy, which is from a Greek phrase that means "repeated law."

"Today I am giving you a choice," Moses says. "You can choose life and success or death and disaster. . . . Choose life! Be completely faithful to the Lord your God, love him, and do whatever he tells you . . . and he will let you live a long time in the land that he promised to your ancestors Abraham, Isaac, and Jacob" (30:15, 19–20).

Moses commissions Joshua to lead the nation into Canaan. Then, in his final act, he climbs a mountain and looks across the fertile Jordan River valley into the promised land. There, on the mountain, Moses dies.

## Influential People

**Moses,** a Hebrew who leads his emerging nation out of Egypt and through the desert. Now, he leads them once more in a service of remembering the past and trusting God for the future. His tremendous faith in God inspires the closing words of Deuteronomy: "No one else has ever had the power to do such great things as Moses did for everyone to see."

**Joshua,** a scout and warrior who showed his confidence in God by trying to convince the Israelites to enter Canaan 40 years earlier. For his faith, God selects him to lead Israel into the promised land.

# Key Ideas You Need to Know

**Remember your history with God.** God's story runs through the Bible and into your life. You can ignore it. Many do. But when you read about the great acts of God throughout history, and when you reflect on how he has worked in your life, it changes you. It makes you bolder and more devoted to him. Moses reminded the second generation Israelites about what God did 40 years earlier to free their parents from slavery. And the new generation had already witnessed recent military victories on their trek to Canaan. They had a history with God. So do we. The Israelites, with confidence based on their history, marched into Canaan—in spite of the giants and heavily fortified cities ahead. Remembering our history helps us overcome our obstacles, too.

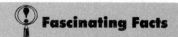

> **Fascinating Facts**
>
> An Israelite man wasn't to leave home for war or extended trips during his first year of marriage. He was to stay home and "be happy with his wife" (24:5).
>
> Because Deuteronomy is such a complete summary of the agreement between Israel and God—a contract calling for Israel to obey God's law—rabbis in ancient Israel called the book "five-fifths of the law."

# Q&A

**Why did God order the Israelites to kill all the Canaanites—men, women, and children?** "If you allow them to live," Moses explained to the Israelites, "they will persuade you to worship their disgusting gods, and you will be unfaithful to the Lord" (20:18). Children spared would grow up and search for their birth family's roots, a quest that would lead to temple prostitution, human sacrifice, and other features common to Canaanite religion.

In fact, the Israelites didn't kill all the Canaanites. And what Moses said would happen, did happen. In the years that followed, the Israelites started worshiping Canaanite gods.

**Why did God choose Israel for special attention over other nations?** As Moses told the Israelites, "The Lord did not choose you and lavish his love on you because you were larger or greater than other nations, for you were the smallest of all nations! It was simply because the Lord loves you, and because he was keeping the oath he had sworn to your ancestors" (7:7–8, New Living Translation). Actually, it was Abraham that God chose. For Abraham's faithfulness, God promised to make his descendants into a large and enduring nation. God rewards faithfulness. And he keeps his word.

# Red Flag Issues

**Cross-dressing.** "A woman must not wear men's clothing, and a man must not wear women's clothing. The Lord your God detests people who do this" (22:5, New Living Translation). Some Christian leaders a few decades ago used this verse to argue that women should wear dresses and skirts, not slacks. Fashions change, however. At the moment, it's not unusual to see men and women wearing identical types of clothing: jeans, sweat suits, fur coats.

God wasn't making a fashion statement. Some scholars think God was referring to transvestite activities in pagan worship. Canaanites would sometimes worship their chief god, Baal, by having sex with temple priests—who were male or female. This was intended to sexually arouse Baal, god of rain. The rain was considered Baal's semen.

Other scholars say God was forbidding reversal of sex roles and God's natural order. Today, as in ancient times, there are men who want to be women, and women who want to be men. Surgery and hormone therapy attempt to cure the problem by expanding the physical transformation that cross-dressing begins. But some Christian therapists aren't convinced that transsexual surgery heals the underlying emotional problem that may have caused the confused sexual identity in the first place. And they fear the surgery only further blurs the natural sex roles. Other Christians argue for tolerance and for leaving the judgment to God.

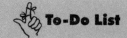 **To-Do List**

- "Memorize his [God's] laws and tell them to your children over and over again. Talk about them all the time, whether you're at home or walking along the road or going to bed at night, or getting up in the morning" (6:6–7).

- "You know God's laws . . . You can't say, 'How can we obey the Lord's commands? They are in heaven, and no one can go up to get them?' . . . No, these commands are nearby and you know them by heart. All you have to do is obey!" (30:11–14).

 ## For the Record: Deuteronomy Well Used

**Runaway slaves.** The United States Congress in 1850 passed the Fugitive Slave Law, making it illegal to help runaway slaves. Punishment: up to six months in prison, and a fine of $1,000—far more than most people made in a year. Many Christians defied the law by working on the Underground Railroad—a secret network of safe houses—to shuttle runaway slaves to Canada. Christians cited an authority higher than Congress: God. "If slaves should escape from their masters and take refuge with you, do not force them to return. Let them live among you in whatever town they choose, and do not oppress them" (23:15–16). Thirteen years later, in the Emancipation Proclamation, President Abraham Lincoln declared all slaves in the country "forever free."

# Bible Scenarios You Can Use

### 1. Parents teach their children about God (6:1–9)

In one of the last speeches before his death, Moses reminds the Israelites of all God has done for them in freeing them from Egyptian slavery and bringing them within sight of their homeland. He reminds them, too, that they have a contract with God. Their nation agreed to obey God's laws in return for continued protection and blessing.

"Memorize his laws," Moses says, "and tell them to your children over and over."

Like the Israelites, we too have a rich spiritual heritage that deserves to be passed on to our children. The growing generation needs to know about the stories and teachings in the Bible—about the miracles of God, the successes and failures of Israel, and the life and ministry of Jesus. They also need to hear about what God has done in our own lives—such as a prayer of thanks for the joy that his gift of children has brought to our lives. As parents who love God and our children, no one is better able to do this than we are.

### 2. Israelites bring offerings to the worship center (14:22–29)

Once the Israelites settle in Canaan and start raising crops and herds, each year they are to bring to the worship center a tenth of their crops and the firstborn males of their flocks and herds—the most prized animals. If they can't transport it all, they're to sell it and bring the money. When they arrive at the worship center, they're to use some of the harvest or money for a festive meal. Some of the proceeds go to the Levites, the nation's worship leaders, who don't own land. The remaining food and money go to local people in need: orphans, widows, and immigrants.

Tithing—devoting a tenth of our income to God—is an old idea that comes from God himself. Tithing gives us a tangible way to thank God for taking such good care of us, and to celebrate his provision. It gives us a way to maintain our worship facilities and support our worship leaders. It also gives us a disciplined and organized way to help the poor in our communities. In Israel, God sets up nationwide laws to help the poor—such as letting them pick crops from the borders of the field. But he also expects help on a local and more personal level: people giving a financial boost to needy family members, neighbors, and strangers in town.

### 3. Setting up safe towns for fugitives (19:1–13)

**W**hen the Israelites settle in Canaan, they are to designate six cities as "safe towns" where people accused of manslaughter can find sanctuary from revenge-seeking family members of the victim, and can get a fair trial.

At this time in ancient history, it is custom for the closest male blood relative of a victim to avenge the death—whether or not the death is accidental. God provides a way for the Israelites to pursue justice instead of revenge. The six safe towns are scattered throughout the region, so an Israelite living in the promised land will always be within about a day's travel of protection. The trial is conducted by city elders. If the person is found guilty of murder, the person is executed. But no one can be executed on the testimony of just one witness (17:6). If the person is innocent, that person may stay in the city for protection.

When someone is killed, we want the guilty person punished. But sometimes in our grief and rage we punish—and sometimes execute—innocent people for crimes they didn't commit. That wasn't justice in ancient Israel, and it isn't justice today. Before we sentence someone to death, we should be absolutely certain of the person's guilt—not just convinced "beyond a reasonable doubt."

### 4. Renewing the agreement with God (28:1—29:29)

**F**orty years after the Israelites stood at the foot of Mt. Sinai and pledged their allegiance to God, Moses calls the nation together again and urges the new generation to do the same. The agreement, or covenant, calls for the people to obey God's laws. In return, God will bless them above all nations, giving them large families, productive fields, and fertile herds. If they break their agreement, the opposite will happen and they will be "scattered to every nation on earth."

Israel would eventually break its agreement. For centuries, God would work patiently with them, sending lesser punishments than deserved along with stern warnings from prophets. But in 586 B.C., he would let Babylon conquer and scatter them.

God punishes disobedience. But he forgives, too. (Scattered Israel repented and eventually returned home.) And when we honor his most fundamental laws, summed up in the Ten Commandments, he rewards us. These laws track with the design and flow of creation. We can swim upstream if we want, but we'll have a better journey if we go with the flow.

# JOSHUA

## The Key to Success

There are lots of Bible stories about giving. This one's about taking.

The Israelites take the territory of Canaan—the general area of modern-day Israel—from the people who have lived there for centuries. But 700 years before the Israelite invasion, God called Abraham to the center of this land and told him to look around. "I will give you and your family all the land you can see," God said. "It will be theirs forever!" (Genesis 13:15). So the Israelite invasion was actually a reclamation of their ancestral homeland—the place where Abraham, Isaac, and Jacob had raised their families.

If a war must be fought, who better to lead the people than a proven warrior? Joshua was that man. He was the successor to Moses and had been fighting Israelite enemies since early in the Exodus, 40 years before. His name first appears when Moses chooses him to lead the fight against attacking desert nomads.

> ### 🗨 Quote for You
>
> "Don't ever be afraid or discouraged! I am the Lord your God, and I will be there to help you wherever you go" (1:9).

Joshua's military expertise seems to be the key to Israel's success at conquering Canaan. It's not. Joshua is the right man for the job, but not because of his military skill or bravery. He's the right man because he trusts God and obeys him.

"Obey all the laws Moses gave you," God says. "Only then will you succeed" (1:7–8, New Living Translation).

Joshua obeys. And before the war starts, as well as before several key campaigns, God assures Joshua that victory is certain. God brings the walls of Jericho down. And God's hailstorm kills more Canaanites at the battle of Gibeon than Joshua's men do.

The key to success is to obey God. His track record—with the faithful in ancient times as well as today—shows he has earned that trust.

## When It Happened

(Dates are approximate)

Adam 4000+ B.C.    Abraham 2100 B.C.    Moses 1500 B.C.    Exodus 1440 B.C.    Conquest Begins 1400 B.C.    David 1000 B.C.    Ezra 450 B.C.    Jesus born 7/6 B.C.

# Info You Can Use

## Background Notes

**Writer:** The writer is never mentioned. But since ancient times, many Bible students assumed Joshua wrote it, or at least supplied the information—some of which are private conversations between God and Joshua. Information about Joshua's death, reported at the end of the book, may have been supplied by Aaron's son or grandson, priests Eleazar or Phinehas.

**Time:** Israel invaded Canaan in about 1400 B.C. or perhaps a couple centuries later. Scholars disagree on exactly when the Exodus and conquest occurred. For more about this, see "Background Notes, Time" on page 32.

**Place:** The story begins along the east banks of the Jordan River, in what is now the country of Jordan. The Israelites cross into Canaan (now Israel) and begin conquering the cities. By book's end, they are settling throughout Canaan and the surrounding region in what are now parts of Jordan, Syria, and Lebanon.

**Bottom-Line Summary:** After 430 years in Egypt, followed by 40 years in the desert, the Israelites go home. Their ancestors—Abraham, Isaac, and Jacob—had all lived in Canaan, a land that God promised Abraham would belong to his descendants forever (Exodus 32:13).

With Moses dead, Joshua leads the Israelites on a mission to recapture the land, clear it of the idol-worshiping people who live there, and establish a nation of people devoted to God. The first to fall is the border town of Jericho, just west of the Jordan River. Afterward, the Israelites sweep south through the rugged highlands, conquering one city after another. Then they turn north and overrun cities in the hills by the Sea of Galilee and beyond. With much of the resistance gone, Joshua divides the land among the 12 tribes of Israel and orders them to clear their assigned land of any remaining Canaanites.

## Influential People

**Joshua,** military commander of the Israelites. His army consists of lightly armed civilians. His enemy includes seasoned warriors—some of them giants—heavily armed and often protected behind city walls. But Joshua's confidence in God is as absolute as a child's trust in a faithful, loving parent. Joshua's life is a model of trust in God, and of the rewards that come with that trust.

**Rahab,** a Jericho prostitute who hides the Israelite scouts and asks for protection when Jericho is inevitably captured. The New Testament Book of Hebrews later commends her faith in God. Matthew lists Rahab—probably the same woman—among the ancestors of Jesus, suggesting she changed her way of life, married an Israelite, and devoted herself to God.

**Achan,** an Israelite who, against God's orders, takes possessions from dead enemies. For this infraction, the Israelites lose their next battle. Achan becomes a reminder that one person's sin can affect the entire community.

 ## Key Ideas You Need to Know

**Your battles are won before they start.** Over and over, God tells Joshua that the battle ahead is already won.

Before the war for Canaan starts: "Everywhere you go, you will be on the land I have given you" (1:3, New Living Translation).

Before Jericho falls: "I have given you Jericho" (6:2, New Living Translation).

Before fighting combined armies of the north: "By this time tomorrow they will be dead" (11:6).

Joshua still has to fight, but he knows the outcome. That makes a difference. It energizes him with confidence and strength.

If we obey God, we can know the outcome, too. Our promised land is heaven. It will be ours forever. In the meantime, we fight life's battles knowing we're already the winners.

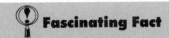

> **Fascinating Fact**
>
> The Jordan River stops flowing as the Israelites cross it going into Canaan. It dams up near the city of Adam, to the north. An earthquake in 1927 produced the same effect. Dirt from the riverbank cliffs near Adam fell and blocked the river for 21 hours.

**The "if" clause.** Canaan isn't an automatic given, and the battles aren't foregone conclusions. There's an "if" clause in God's promises: "If you obey," God tells Joshua, "you and Israel will be able to take this land" (1:8).

In fact, they lose one easy battle because someone disobeys God. A man named Achan confesses he couldn't resist taking from the ruins of Jericho about five pounds of silver, a pound of gold, and a cape imported from Babylon. God had told the Israelites to take nothing from Jericho.

As a result, the 3,000 Israelites Joshua sends to capture the tiny village of Ai are routed. They capture Ai only after executing Achan and his entire family—a horrifying example of how important obedience is at this critical stage in Israel's history.

Today, we independent-minded people often argue that our sin is our own business. But one person's sin affects others in ways we don't often realize at first. It's easy to see the effects when adultery leads to a family breakup, or when coveting leads to consuming debt. It's not so easy to see with less conspicuous sins. But the dominoes will tumble against each other to inevitable collapse.

## Q&A

**Does archaeology prove Israel captured Canaan?** No. This is a hot topic among archaeologists. Some say the evidence suggests no single exodus and conquest, and that the Israelites migrated to Canaan over a long period of time, and without much fighting. Others say the Israelites did invade, but captured primarily the hilly regions where few Canaanites lived.

So far, the archaeological evidence hasn't shed much light on exactly what happened.

Excavations at Hazor, a city north of the Sea of Galilee, seem to support the Bible's account that it was defeated twice: in the time of Joshua (11:10), and later in the time of the Judges (Judges 4:2, 23). The dates of these two destructions: about 1400 B.C. and in the mid-1200s B.C. Soot on the ruins confirms the city was burned, as reported in Joshua.

Jericho is another story. Archaeologist Kathleen Kenyon, excavating Jericho in the 1950s, said the city was gone at least 150 years before Joshua got there—that it was leveled in about 1550 B.C. Scholars who recently reviewed Kenyon's work said she misdated Jericho's pottery pieces. (Pottery designs for various eras are well known and help establish the date of ancient cities). These scholars argue that Jericho fell in about 1400 B.C.

Archaeologists still debate when and how Israel took control of the land.

> ### ☝ To-Do List
>
> - "Love the Lord your God, walk in all his ways, obey his commands, be faithful to him, and serve him with all your heart and all your soul" (22:5, New Living Translation).
>
> - "Choose today whom you will serve" (24:15, New Living Translation). *Joshua's challenge to the Israelites to renew their commitment to God.*

## ◈ Red Flag Issues

**War.** Some Christians refuse to fight in wars. Entire denominations stand opposed to any kind of violence—especially killing. They argue that committing murder is against one of God's most basic laws and that Jesus taught his followers to turn the other cheek when struck. Though pacifism is a minority opinion today, in the early centuries of Christianity the church taught it was wrong to fight and to shed another person's blood.

Most Christians today, however, seem to believe we have a responsibility to help the weak—and that sometimes we must go to war to protect people from oppressive leaders and rogue governments.

The Bible doesn't settle the matter for us. In the Book of Joshua, God tells the Israelites to fight. He even leads them in battle, contributing to the slaughter. Yet for many pacifists, a war declared by God is much different than a war declared by human leaders. God, as creator, has the right to say who lives and dies. So Joshua and his armies were instruments God used to cleanse sin from Canaan, just as God had used a flood to cleanse the earth in Noah's day, and a fire to cleanse the plains of Sodom and Gomorrah in Abraham's day.

Christians at the other end of the argument say it's not only appropriate to defend justice, it's a sin not to defend it. They say it's proper, for example, to criticize the United States for waiting so long to get involved in the fight to stop Hitler. And they say that powerful nations like ours should take a stand for innocent world citizens being terrorized by despots—that we should be the world's police force, or at least a leader in establishing justice and peace in the world.

These two positions seem at odds. But if they flow from the hearts of compassionate Christians, God can use them both. This is, after all, the God who can take evil intent and use it for good—as he did with Joseph's brothers who sold him to slave traders. Joseph ended up the number two man in Egypt, in a position that preserved his family and many others from a seven-year famine.

# Bible Scenarios You Can Use

## 1. God promises Joshua victory (1:1–9)

**M**oses is dead. It's up to Joshua to lead the people across the Jordan River and into a long series of battles for Canaan. Joshua has expressed unwavering confidence in God in the past. Still, on the eve of the invasion, Joshua must feel tremendous pressure and some doubt. God comes to assure him. "Wherever you go, I'll give you that land," God says. "I'll always be with you and help you."

That first phrase is for Joshua and his people, in their particular day. But those final words are for all God's people, on any day. Whatever battles we face, God is with us. The immediate outcome may not always look like a victory from our earthly prospective, but if God is with us, we have no reason to be afraid or discouraged.

## 2. Israel crosses the Jordan River (3:6—4:7)

**P**riests carrying the sacred chest with the Ten Commandments lead the way toward the Jordan River, which marks the eastern border of Canaan. When they step into the river, the water upstream stops flowing—as if someone had built a dam. The people cross into the promised land much as they left Egypt, by way of a miraculous path through the water. God instructs them to pick up stones from the riverbed and build a simple monument, as a reminder for their children of what happened here.

God does marvelous work in our lives, too, and we should tell others about it. When we do, we keep the memories of God's faithfulness alive—for us as well as for those we tell. We need those reminders when tough times arise.

## 3. Jericho's walls collapse (6:1–27)

**T**he border town of Jericho stands about five miles from the Jordan River, making it the first Canaanite target for the Israelites. Before the battle, the Lord tells Joshua, "I have given you Jericho" (6:2, New Living Translation). The battle is over before it starts. The outcome is certain. As instructed by God, the people march around the city once a day. On the seventh day they march around it seven times, then scream and blow ram's horns. The city walls collapse, and the Israelites charge in from all sides.

Joshua fought a defeated enemy. So do we. Every day we fight Satan and evil forces aligned with him. But they have already lost (Revelation 20:10). So fight with confidence.

## 4. The sun and moon stop (10:1–28)

**C**oalition armies from five cities gather in the hills 15 miles west of Israel's camp. Joshua stages an all-night march and catches the combined armies by surprise. The Canaanites run—with the Israelites giving chase. About noon, Joshua prays for God to stop the sun and moon in the sky, to give his men time to finish the job so the Canaanites won't survive to fight another day. The sun stands still "for about a whole day."

Whether God set aside the laws of physics or changed the perception of time, he got involved in human events. He still does. He's not sitting around in some spiritual, parallel dimension watching us like we watch TV. He steps right into our lives and helps—sometimes in ways that defy explanation.

## 5. Israel settles in the promised land (chapters 13–22)

**A**fter seven years, the Israelites have overrun cities throughout Canaan—from the desert in the south to Mount Herman in the north. Joshua divides the land among the 12 tribes—extended families descended from Jacob's sons—and then tells each tribe to finish securing their assigned territory.

These seven years of war must have seemed a long and difficult time for the Israelites. They probably wondered if it would ever end. We sometimes face long periods of hardship, too; illness, grief, job turmoil, or clawing our way out of debt. Through it all, God is there, comforting, strengthening, and inspiring us. He is our source of peace even as the battle rages.

## 6. Israel renews its pledge to God (24:1–25)

**E**lderly Joshua calls the people together—as Moses did before he died—to give each person a chance to renew their pledge of loyalty to God. "If you don't want to worship the Lord, then choose right now!" Joshua says. "My family and I are going to worship and obey the Lord!" The people agree to do the same. Not completely satisfied with their quick response, Joshua warns them to serve God with absolute loyalty or face the consequences of losing the land.

There are times in life when other believers and we need to retreat from our normal routine and renew our pledge of devotion to God in a serious and deliberate act of worship. As Joshua fully understood, pledging our allegiance to God in the company of others strengthens our commitment to the one who is most committed to us.

# JUDGES

## You Can Always Come Home to God

Remember the story of the Prodigal Son who left his father's home to live a wild life using his inheritance, but ran out of money? This book is the story of the Prodigal Nation—Israel—who leaves the God of their fathers to do exactly as they please now that they have their inheritance: the promised land.

Like the Prodigal Son, the Israelites follow their own bad judgment and wind up in big trouble: oppressed, destitute, and nowhere to turn but to the God they left behind.

When the Israelites cut themselves off from God, by abandoning their agreement to follow his laws, they cut themselves off from his protection and blessing as well—but not from his love. Like the father of the Prodigal Son, God waits for Israel to come back to him.

The trouble with Israel is that after coming home to God, they leave again by worshiping idols. Then they get into trouble, usually by a neighboring nation attacking them. They come home, by repenting of their sins and asking God for help. God forgives them and sends a warrior hero to save them from their enemies. Then Israel leaves God yet again. They repeat this distressing cycle at least a half-dozen times.

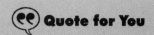 **Quote for You**

"The people did whatever seemed right in their own eyes" (21:25, New Living Translation). *The book's closing line reflects a sad state of affairs: Israelites do as they please, not caring what God wants.*

I wonder if after all this the father of the Prodigal Son would have welcomed his boy home with open arms. Actually, there's no need to wonder. The father in Jesus' parable is God—the father of the Prodigal Nation. When his child is away, God always leaves the light on.

No matter what you've done or how many times you've done it, you can always go home to God.

When It Happened

(Dates are approximate)

Abraham 2100 B.C.

Moses 1500 B.C.

Exodus 1440 B.C.

Death of Joshua 1375 B.C.

Coronation of Saul 1050 B.C.

David 1000 B.C.

Ezra 450 B.C.

Jesus born 7/6 B.C.

# Info You Can Use

## Background Notes

**Writer:** The writer isn't identified. Ancient Jewish tradition says the writer was Samuel, Israel's prophet and religious leader a few decades after the judges. Samuel, in his later years, anointed Saul as Israel's first king. It's clear the stories were written after Israel had a king, because the writer repeatedly says the stories took place "before kings ruled Israel" (17:6).

Many scholars today say the stories were probably passed along orally from generation to generation, then written down many centuries after Samuel—perhaps after the Jews were taken to exile in Babylon in 586 B.C. If so, these stories would have helped Jews in exile understand why they were there: God has a long history of punishing Israel when the people worship idols.

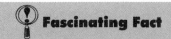

### Fascinating Fact

The country of Israel gets its name from the man whose sons produced the nation's 12 tribes. "Your name will no longer be Jacob. You have wrestled with God and with men, and you have won. That's why your name will be Israel" (Genesis 32:28).

**Time:** The book covers about 300 years, starting when Joshua dies in about 1375 B.C. and ending just before Saul is crowned king in about 1050 B.C.

**Place:** The setting is Canaan, roughly the same area as modern-day Israel and parts of the neighboring nations of Jordan, Syria, and Lebanon.

**Bottom-Line Summary:** Israel's invasion of Canaan is over. Joshua dies of old age, and the Israelites settle into Canaan's highlands. Their remaining chore is to finish clearing the region of Canaanites and their idols. Instead, the Israelites learn to live alongside the surviving Canaanites, and begin adopting their religion and sinful way of life.

God punishes the Israelites by allowing neighboring nations to overrun and dominate them. When the suffering becomes intolerable, the Israelites call on God—asking for forgiveness and help. He sends a leader—a judge—who saves the people. This cycle of sin and deliverance is repeated at least a half-dozen times, ending where it started—with the people in sin. It seems that nearly each Israelite generation is determined to learn their spiritual lessons the hard way.

## Influential People

**Samson,** Israel's strongman and last of the 12 judges. Surprisingly unrighteous and earthy for a hero chosen by God, Samson's story is prime evidence that God can do marvelous things through less-than-marvelous people.

**Delilah,** Samson's fatal attraction, and a testimony to the proverb: "The words of an immoral woman may be as sweet as honey. . . . But all that you really get from being with her is bitter poison and pain" (Proverbs 5:3–4).

**Gideon,** a farmer turned commander who routed invaders and then led Israel in an era of peace. He's another reminder that God can use ordinary people in extraordinary ways.

**Deborah,** Israel's only female judge and a model of bravery for her willingness to accompany the Israelites in battle.

**Barak,** Deborah's military commander, and a skeptic who refuses to go into battle without her.

##  Key Ideas You Need to Know

**Compromise.** Usually, compromise is a good thing—a middle ground between two harsh extremes. But there is no middle ground with sin—no acceptable compromise. Israel's mistake is not realizing this. God has ordered them to get rid of all the idol-worshiping Canaanites—to cleanse the land of sinfulness like God had done with the Flood and later at Sodom and Gomorrah. Instead, the Israelites get used to having the Canaanites around. Before long, it's hard to tell an Israelite from a Canaanite. Both worshiped idols.

The Book of Judges isn't a call to arms to clear our community of people who don't share our faith. That message was unique to ancient Israel, at a time when God was establishing a holy nation devoted to him, and through whom he would later send his son as savior of the world.

For us, Judges is a reminder not to compromise our essential beliefs, such as our commitment to God and to all things good: honesty, justice, and compassion. It's a reminder that you should be able to tell a Christian from a non-Christian.

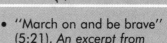

**To-Do List**

- "March on and be brave" (5:21). An excerpt from Deborah's song of praise to God, telling how her volunteer militia defeated an invasion force.

- "You will be strong because I am giving you the power" (6:14). God's message to Gideon, a farmer reluctant to lead Israel in a fight against raiders.

## Q&A

**After all God had done for Israel, why were they attracted to idols?** For one thing, each new generation didn't know all God had done for their nation. There were no history books to check out from the library. And the parents didn't do a good job teaching their children about God (2:10).

Also, idols were popular throughout the ancient Middle East. Worshiping an invisible God was not. The Canaanites, who lived as Israel's neighbors, worshiped many gods—including Baal, the god of fertility in family, flock, and fields. Perhaps the Israelites—rookie farmers—saw how well the Canaanite crops grew. So to raise better crops themselves, they started praying to Baal, rationalizing that the Lord was just one of many gods, and that he was primarily a god of war.

**Can we put out a fleece for God?** Gideon wanted proof of God's intent to help him defeat the desert raiders, so he asked for a miracle. One morning he put a piece of wool on a stone floor outside. "If you really will help me rescue Israel," Gideon said, "then tomorrow morning let there be dew on the wool, but let the stone floor be dry" (6:37). God did that. The next day Gideon asked for the opposite, a dry fleece and a wet floor. God did that, too, convincing Gideon.

Should we be fleecing God, looking for supernatural evidence to discover his will? In some circumstances, it could be perfectly acceptable. But, frankly, we know God better than Gideon did. We have the Bible, the life of Jesus, and the Holy Spirit—all of which teach us what God is like and point us to his will.

God wants us to trust him. Jesus put it this way to doubting Thomas, who told the other disciples he wouldn't believe Jesus was raised from the dead until he saw it for himself: "Thomas, do you have faith because you have seen me? The people who have faith in me without seeing me are the ones who are really blessed!" (John 20:29).

Some people with a low supply of faith or limited knowledge of God apparently need to see a miracle or some kind of sign before they trust him. But God wants us to learn from his involvement in the history of the world—and in our own lives—that we can count on him. [For more on this, see the Genesis Q&A, "Is it okay to ask God for a sign to show you what to do?" on page 23.]

# Bible Scenarios You Can Use

## 1. Generation Next starts worshiping idols (2:6–23)

Joshua's generation stays faithful to God. The kids don't. "The next generation did not know the Lord or any of the things he had done for Israel." They start worshiping Canaanite gods. God responds by allowing neighboring nations to dominate Israel. From time to time, the oppression becomes so unbearable that Israel turns to God for forgiveness and help—both of which he delivers. But the spiritual renewals don't seem to last more than a generation or so.

If we have any hope of passing our beliefs on to the next generation, we need to take the advice God gave the Israelites: "Tell them to your children over and over again" (Deuteronomy 6:7). Our kids need God as much as we do.

## 2. In trouble, Israel calls on God (3:9–11)

During the first generation after Joshua, the Israelites are attacked and apparently enslaved by a ruler from what is now northern Syria or perhaps Iran. With nowhere else to turn, "the Israelites begged the Lord for help." He sent a leader named Othniel to rally the Israelites. He defeated the invaders and maintained peace for about 40 years. But the cycle of sin, followed by attacks, the Israelites calling on God, and God sending a deliverer is repeated at least a half-dozen times.

Sin produces sad, sometimes tragic, consequences. Thousands of Israelites were likely slaughtered, injured, or enslaved during the era of the judges. But each time the people called on God, he was always there for them. No matter what we've done, or how many times we've done it, God always accepts our sincere repentance. Love is like that.

## 3. Gideon's small army stops an invasion (6:1—7:25)

A new generation repeats the sins of the past. As a result, during each harvest time Israel is swarmed by thousands of desert raiders. When the Israelites ask God for help, he calls on Gideon who replies, "How can I rescue Israel? My clan is the weakest one in Manasseh, and everyone else in my family is more important than I am." God convinces the reluctant leader to raise a tiny army of 300. With this, Gideon launches a nighttime attack on the massive raider camp—sending the invaders running for their lives. The Israelites live in peace for the rest of Gideon's life.

There's a Christian chorus with the line, "little is much when God is in it." Gideon's story is evidence of that. It doesn't matter how insignificant we feel or how limited our resources. We bring what little we have, God brings the rest, and great things happen.

### 4. Samson fights the Philistines (15:1—16:31)

**S**amson isn't like any other judge. He's a one-man army with incredible strength. Philistines kill his bride, so he slaughters a thousand of their soldiers with the jawbone of a donkey.

Samson is driven by his appetites, especially for immoral women. He escapes one Philistine trap at a prostitute's house. But they later capture him with the help of Delilah, who learns that his strength is tied to his vow never to cut his hair.

Soldiers gouge out Samson's eyes and later parade him in their temple as a war trophy. There, Samson prays for strength to take revenge. He breaks pillars that collapse the roof, killing himself and at least 3,000 Philistines. Though Samson is flawed, God uses him to drive a wedge between Philistines and Israelites—an important job, since both nations are getting along well and Israel is in danger of being assimilated into the stronger Philistine nation.

God's resources for helping us are unlimited. He's able to work through saints (like Deborah) and sinners (like Samson) to give us whatever help we need.

### 5. Civil war in Israel (19:1—21:25)

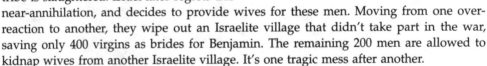

**A**n Israelite religious leader traveling with his wife spends the night in a town assigned to the tribe of Benjamin. A mob takes the man's wife and rapes her to death. The husband cuts her to pieces and sends the body parts to Israel's 12 tribes, with a plea for justice.

The tribe of Benjamin refuses to punish the rapists. So the other tribes unite in a war that nearly wipes out the tribe of Benjamin— only 600 men survive. Everyone else in the tribe is slaughtered. Israel later regrets this near-annihilation, and decides to provide wives for these men. Moving from one over-reaction to another, they wipe out an Israelite village that didn't take part in the war, saving only 400 virgins as brides for Benjamin. The remaining 200 men are allowed to kidnap wives from another Israelite village. It's one tragic mess after another.

Sadly, the book ends with Israel in a state of anarchy: "The people did whatever seemed right in their own eyes" (21:25, New Living Translation). It takes more than common sense and conventional wisdom to solve some of the complex problems we face—especially problems of life and death. It takes God's help.

# RUTH

## Wanted: Outsiders Struggling to Fit In

Ruth is one of those people we've all been from time to time: a disenfranchised outsider. No influence. No respect. No control over her situation.

Why?

- She's a woman, in a day when men rule. Under ancient law, she can't even own land.

- She's childless. From the ancient's point of view, a woman's main job is to have children. Those who don't are thought cursed of God for some terrible sin.

- She's a widow. With no husband or son to take care of her, she's destitute and dependent on the mercy of others for her survival.

- She's a foreigner, a Moabite who suddenly shows up in Bethlehem. She arrives with her mother-in-law, Naomi, who's also a destitute widow. But at least Naomi is an Israelite with distant relatives who might help her. Moabites are people in what is now Jordan who tried to stop Moses and the Israelites from entering the promised land. That was the beginning of a long and hostile relationship between the two nations.

As far as the ancient Israelites are concerned, Ruth is cursed of God.

But the story is just starting, and incredible blessings are on their way. Ruth becomes a wife again, a mother, and an Israelite. And, as an ancestor of Jesus and David, she becomes the mother of kings from heaven and earth. Jews still honor her by reading her story at harvest festivals each spring.

God gives her influence, respect, and a starring role in history. Insider or outsider—it doesn't matter to God. He loves them both.

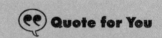 **Quote for You**

"The Lord bless you" (2:4). The respectful greeting exchanged between a farmer, Boaz, and his harvest workers.

## When It Happened

(Dates are approximate)

Abraham 2100 B.C.

Moses 1500 B.C.

Exodus 1440 B.C.

Death of Joshua 1375 B.C.

Saul 1050 B.C.

David 1000 B.C.

Ezra 450 B.C.

Jesus born 7/6 B.C.

# Info You Can Use

 **Background Notes**

**Writer:** This is one of the most captivating stories in all of Hebrew literature, yet the writer remains unknown. Jewish tradition says Samuel wrote it, but that's unlikely. The reason is that the book's climax reveals Ruth is King David's great-grandmother. Samuel died before David was crowned king.

Like many stories of the Old Testament, the Book of Ruth was probably passed along by word of mouth from generation to generation before someone wrote it down. The reason for preserving the story is uncertain. It may have been to trace the family tree of David, Israel's most popular king. Another theory is that it was written after the Jews returned from exile in Babylon during the 500s B.C., and as a counterpoint to the priest Ezra's command for Jewish men to divorce their non-Jewish wives (Ezra 10:11). Ruth wasn't a Jew, yet she married a Jew and became the mother of Israel's beloved family of kings: David and his son Solomon.

**Time:** The story takes place during the rough and tumble times of the judges, "before Israel was ruled by kings" (1:1). The Israelites were settled in the land, but there were occasional outbreaks of oppression by neighboring nations: raids, and even hostile occupation and enslavement. It's uncertain whether Ruth's story unfolds in peacetime or during hostility. But the fact that Boaz sleeps in his field at harvest time suggests he's afraid someone will steal his grain.

**Place:** Bethlehem is where the story begins and ends. In between, the story shifts briefly to Moab, Israel's neighbor east of the Dead Sea in what is now Jordan. Naomi, along with her husband and their two sons, are from Bethlehem. Ruth is from Moab.

**Bottom-Line Summary:** Drought devastates Israel, killing crops and pastures. A Jewish man in Bethlehem moves with his wife and two sons to a neighboring country in the east. There, the sons marry local women. Tragically, all three men die, leaving their widows destitute. The mother, Naomi, decides to go back to Bethlehem in the hopes that her extended family will take care of her. She urges her daughters-in-law to return to their families as well. One does. But Ruth refuses to abandon the elderly woman.

The two widows arrive in Bethlehem in early spring, during the barley harvest. A farmer related to Naomi lets Ruth pick some barley for her and Naomi. Ruth marries the farmer and they have a son: Obed, the grandfather of King David.

## Influential People

**Ruth,** a widow from Moab and great-grandmother of David. She is an example of love and loyalty to her widowed mother-in-law, Naomi.

**Naomi,** Ruth's mother-in-law from Bethlehem. She becomes destitute when her husband and sons die, but her character elicits love and admiration from both of her daughters-in-law.

**Boaz,** Ruth's second husband. He's a man of honesty, moral integrity, and devotion to his family responsibilities.

 # Key Ideas You Need to Know

**Loyalty.** The old and widowed Naomi shows her selfless devotion to her widowed daughters-in-law. Instead of asking them to come with her back to her hometown of Bethlehem, 50 or more miles away in the Judean hills, she puts their interests first. She urges them to go back to their hometowns in Moab, where they would be more likely to find another husband.

Ruth shows her incredible loyalty to Naomi by refusing to abandon her and by pledging, "your people will be my people, your God will be my God. I will die where you die and be buried beside you" (1:16–17).

God rewards both women for their devotion to each other. God honors the unselfish.

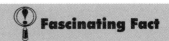
> **Fascinating Fact**
>
> According to Jewish law, if a childless woman outlived her husband she couldn't remarry outside the family. Her husband's brother or another family member was obligated to marry her and take care of her (Deuteronomy 25:5–6).

**May the Lord bless you.** Throughout this story, you'll often find people saying this to each other. It's not just a greeting. It's a prayer, asking God to reward someone for the kindness they've expressed. Boaz greets his workers this way, and they return the greeting. Naomi blesses Boaz for giving extra grain to Ruth. And Boaz blesses Ruth for her devotion to Naomi.

The Israelites believed they had the right to offer blessings in God's name—and that God would answer those prayers. We have the same right. A blessing is nothing to sneeze at.

# Q&A

**Why did Ruth slip under the covers of sleeping Boaz?** Naomi told her to, apparently so Ruth could propose marriage. Naomi said, "Take a bath and put on some perfume, then dress in your best clothes" (3:3). After Boaz fell asleep outside by the pile of barley harvested that day, Ruth sneaked under the covers at his feet. He awoke in the middle of the night and saw her.

The first words they exchanged suggest she was following an accepted custom. As a childless widow, she had the right to ask a relative of her husband to marry her and produce a son who could inherit his dead father's property.

"You are the relative who is supposed to take care of me. So spread the edge of your cover over me" (3:9). Even today, marriage ceremonies in the Middle East often feature the groom extending his cloaked arm to embrace and cover his bride, as a symbol of his promise to protect her.

"This shows how truly loyal you are to your family," Boaz replies. "I'll do what you have asked" (3:10–11).

## Red Flag Issues

**Interracial marriage.** Ruth's dramatic story is a call for tolerance toward interracial marriage. Jews in Bible times preferred to marry Jews. That's because they feared that foreign mates would lure them away from worshiping God and convince them to worship foreign gods instead.

That's exactly what happened to Solomon. "As Solomon got older, some of his wives led him to worship their gods. . . . Solomon worshiped Astarte the goddess of Sidon, and Milcom the disgusting god of Ammon" (1 Kings 11:4–5).

> ### To-Do List
>
> • "You were kind to my husband and sons, and you have always been kind to me" (1:8). *Naomi, speaking to her two daughers-in-law.*

After the Jews returned from exile in Babylon—an exile orchestrated by God as punishment for Israel's idolatry—a priest named Ezra stood before a Jerusalem crowd and said, "We must promise God that we will divorce our foreign wives and send them away, together with their children" (Ezra 10:3). Ezra didn't want the nation to fall back into idolatry and suffer another exile. The Jews complied.

Ruth's story, however, offers the compelling argument that foreigners are capable of embracing Israel's faith in God. And God is clearly willing to embrace them, as evidenced by the blessings he pours out on Ruth. Though God starts by teaching righteousness to one nation—Israel—he never intended to stop there.

In the 1800s, mixed-race marriages were illegal in most American states, though not for religious reasons. Even as late as 1959, a Virginia judge ruled against the marriage of a white man and a woman of African and Native American descent. He said, "Almighty God created the races white, black, yellow, Malay, and red, and he placed them on separate continents. The fact that he separated the races shows that he did not intend for the races to mix." In 1967, the Supreme Court ruled on this same case, *Loving v. The State of Virginia.* All nine justices agreed that laws prohibiting mixed-race marriages were unconstitutional.

# Bible Scenarios You Can Use

---

### 1. Ruth stays with her mother-in-law (1:1–22)

**A** drought in Israel drives a Bethlehem family to Moab, a neighboring country to the east, in what is now Jordan. The man and his wife, Naomi, take their two sons with them. The sons marry women from Moab. Tragically, within 10 years all three men die. In ancient culture, women are treated much like minors are today. They have very few rights and aren't permitted to own property and make business transactions. That means Naomi and her daughters-in-law are destitute. Naomi hears the drought in Israel is finally over, so she plans to return home—hoping one of her relatives will take her into their home. She urges her daughters-in-law to return to their families, with the prayer that God will give them each another husband.

One daughter-in-law reluctantly agrees. But Ruth adamantly refuses: "I will go where you go, I will live where you live; your people will be my people, your God will be my God."

Common sense would say Ruth should have stayed behind—that she'd be more likely to find a husband among her own people than among foreigners. But she put the needs of another above her own. God would bless Ruth for that, just as he blesses us when we do the same.

### 2. Boaz marries Ruth, saving her from poverty (3:1—4:13)

**R**uth and Naomi arrive in Bethlehem in time for the spring barley harvest. By law, Israelite farmers are supposed to let the poor pick leftover crops, following behind the harvesters. Naomi goes to the field of Boaz and gets permission to do this. Boaz tells the harvesters to leave extra for her.

When Naomi finds out about this, she's delighted. Boaz is related to her late husband. By law, the closest male relative of the dead husband is supposed to marry the widow if she has no children to take care of her. Ruth has no children. So at Naomi's instruction, she proposes to Boaz. He has already taken a liking to her, and admires her loyalty to Naomi and the Israelite traditions. He accepts, and they marry.

The Israelite term describing Boaz is "family redeemer." He saves Ruth and Naomi from poverty, and becomes the legal head of their household. Like Ruth, we also have a Redeemer—one who is willing to lead our family out of spiritual poverty. It seems fitting that Boaz of Bethlehem is an ancestor of our Redeemer: Jesus.

### 3. Ruth and Boaz have a son (4:13–22)

**W**hen Ruth becomes pregnant, the Bethlehem women gather around Naomi and celebrate. "Praise the Lord who has given you a family redeemer today!" they say. "May he be famous in Israel. May this child restore your youth and care for you in your old age" (4:14, New Living Translation).

Naomi, living with Ruth and Boaz, takes care of her grandson as if he's her own child. In fact, the Bethlehem women call him "Naomi's Boy." Actually, his name is Obed. He grows up to become the father of Jesse, grandfather of King David, and great-grandfather of King Solomon.

The fact that a woman from Moab became the mother of Israel's most revered family of kings sends an important message. Israelites aren't the only people of God. The Lord welcomes and accepts everyone who comes to him, no matter what his or her background. The Israelites were a chosen people, but they were chosen to be the first in a world of people devoted to God. Israel was a beacon to draw others to the Lord—"a blessing to every nation on earth" (Genesis 26:4).

New Testament writers realized this, which is why they included Ruth in Jesus' family tree (Matthew 1: 5). Jesus descended from the marriage of a Jew and a non-Jew. And the salvation he provides is for everyone on earth—a blessing indeed.

# 1 SAMUEL

## When God's Not in Charge

God can do as he pleases. That's one perk of being God. But he pleases not to push himself on us. We can accept him, or reject him. First Samuel is a story about both kinds of people—and what happens to them as a result of their decisions. That's good news for us, because we get to learn from someone else's mistakes and—on occasion—their smart choices.

The book opens with a heartbreaking scene about an infertile wife who's being ridiculed because she can't have a baby. Her husband loves her and tries to console her. But she knows that in her culture a woman's most important responsibility is to provide her husband with children. She sees herself as a failure. She doesn't take her problem to the Canaanite god of fertility, as many other Israelites are doing. She keeps God in charge and prays to him. Samuel is born a year later.

The tribal leaders of Israel do not choose so wisely. Their contract with God makes Israel different than any other nation. God leads them. He is their king. But what do the elders want? "We want a king to be our leader, just like all the other nations" (8:5).

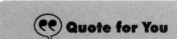

**Quote for You**

"They don't want me to be their king any longer," (8:7, New Living Translation). *God, speaking to Samuel after the Israelites ask for a king.*

God gives them fair warning to be careful what they wish for. A king comes with baggage. A king does as he pleases. That's one perk of being king. And he won't hesitate to push himself on others. The tribal leaders insist they know what they're doing, so they trade down—a King for a king. Sad stories follow.

Fortunately, a sad story doesn't have to be the history we're writing with our own lives. There may be some sad moments, but we can count on a happy ending if we keep God in charge of our life.

When It Happened

(Dates are approximate)

Abraham 2100 B.C. | Moses 1500 B.C. | Exodus 1440 B.C. | Death of Joshua 1375 B.C. | Birth of Samuel 1150 B.C. | Death of Saul 1010 B.C. | Ezra 450 B.C. | Jesus born 7/6 B.C.

# Info You Can Use

## Background Notes

**Writer:** First and Second Samuel were written by an unknown writer—perhaps many writers over several generations or centuries. Because the two books give personal information about the prophet Samuel and kings Saul and David, the writer probably had access to government records. Such records did exist: "Everything David did while he was king is included in the history written by the prophets Samuel, Nathan, and Gad" (1 Chronicles 29:29). Samuel probably wrote about his life as well as Saul's reign.

It's unclear when the stories of 1 and 2 Samuel were pulled together into a single book. Many scholars say Israel's early history as an emerging nation—from the books of Joshua through 1 and 2 Kings—probably weren't completed until after Babylon defeated Israel and took the people into slavery. Without a temple in which to worship God, literature about the story of God's dealings with Israel became more important.

**Time:** The stories in 1 Samuel begin with the birth of Samuel in about 1150 B.C. and end with the battlefield death of King Saul in about 1010 B.C.

**Place:** Israel is the setting for the stories. Shiloh, a town about 20 miles north of Jerusalem, is the religious center of the nation before Israel appoints a king. This is where the tent worship center is set up, and where Eli and Samuel live. After Saul becomes king, he establishes his capital in his hometown of Gibeah, a few miles north of Jerusalem. At this time Jerusalem is a mountain stronghold still controlled by Canaanites.

**Bottom-Line Summary:** Israel isn't a nation as we think of one—with a central government and army. They are a loosely united group of extended families (tribes) led by God. They come together for annual religious festivals at the village of Shiloh, where the worship center is located. As the book opens, a priest named Eli is the nation's spiritual leader. His sons die in battle. So Samuel, whom Eli has raised as a child uniquely devoted to fulltime service for God, grows up to become Israel's next spiritual leader. He serves as a prophet who delivers God's messages to the people, and as a traveling judge who settles disputes. When he grows old, he appoints his two sons to replace him as judges. But they are crooked, taking bribes in exchange for unfair rulings. The people call this to Samuel's attention and ask for a king so they can be "like all the other nations" (8:5).

But Israel isn't like other nations. The Israelites are God's people, and he is their king. Even so, God agrees to their request. He chooses a shy man named Saul as the first king. Over the years, Saul becomes vain, disobedient to God, and depressed. For repeated disobedience, God rejects him as king and chooses a shepherd boy named David to become Israel's next king. First Samuel concludes with the tragic death of Saul and three of his sons in a battle against the Philistines.

## Influential People

**Samuel,** a prophet and Israel's spiritual leader, is a model of obedience to God, even when it doesn't seem to make sense. On God's command, he anoints Israel's first king even though he knows it's wrong for the people to demand a king.

**Saul,** Israel's first king, repeatedly disobeys God. He, his family, and the nation suffer the tragic consequences, providing a portrait of how one person's sins affect many others.

**David,** Saul's successor. Even as a teenager, David exhibits such remarkable faith in God's power that he's willing to put his life on the line for it, and battle a giant.

**Eli,** a priest who raises Samuel. His own sons become priests who disrespect God. Eli's refusal to discipline them with more than words leaves God charging that Eli honors them more than he honors God. Eli is a sad example of a man who puts his family above God. Eli and his family suffer the consequences.

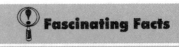

### Fascinating Facts

Samuel wasn't the only Bible kid miraculously born to a previously infertile mother. So were Isaac, Jacob, Samson, and John the Baptist.

First and Second Samuel were originally one book. They fit on one scroll in Hebrew, a language without vowels. But when the book was later translated into Greek, a language with vowels, it took up twice as much space. So it was split into two books, so each could fit on a scroll.

## Key Ideas You Need to Know

**Character flaws.** Each main character in 1 Samuel is flawed. Priest Eli has two sons who show contempt for God by taking for themselves sacrificial meat intended as burnt offerings for God. Eli doesn't stop them, leading God to tell him, "You honor your sons instead of me" (2:29).

Samuel has a similar problem: two sons who become judges on the take.

King Saul begins his reign as a humble and shy person. But he reinvents himself as vain and spiritually defiant. Jealousy leads him to try to kill David. Saul later offers a pre-battle sacrifice that only a priest can rightfully offer. He also consults a medium—a capital offense—to see if he will win the next day's battle.

Even David, described as a man after God's own heart, has an idol in his house (19:13). His wife dresses it up and puts it in bed to convince soldiers who come to arrest him that he's too sick to get up.

Some character flaws are fatal. Saul and Eli's sons die because of their continual disobedience. But Eli, Samuel, and David all seem to retain their faith in God. And there's no indication that David worshiped the idol that likely belonged to his wife.

These people weren't perfect. We're not either. But we don't have to be to stay in God's favor. We do, however, need to love and respect him. If we reject him, he will honor our wishes and leave us—taking his blessings with him.

## Q&A

**Did God really send an evil spirit to trouble Saul?** Perhaps. "The Spirit of the Lord had left Saul, and an evil spirit from the Lord was terrifying him" (16:14). The words for "evil spirit" can also mean "tormenting spirit," which may not refer to a demon. Because of Saul's perpetual disobedience, God's spirit—which in Old Testament times was given to special leaders—was withdrawn. What the Bible means by the tormenting spirit that comes later is unclear. Perhaps it means Saul became depressed and frightened without God's guidance. Or perhaps God allowed Saul to become vulnerable to demonic influences.

## Red Flag Issues

**Psychics.** On the eve of a battle, Saul visits a spirit medium to find out how the battle will end. God had forbidden the Israelites to have anything to do with mediums, psychics, sorcerers or anyone else who tries to tell the future by consulting dead spirits (Deuteronomy 18:10–11). The Bible teaches that there is a spirit world (Ephesians 6:12). There are good and bad spirits. In Saul's case, God sends the spirit of Samuel to deliver the news that Saul will be dead in a few hours. But in other cases, the mediums are either frauds or are probably getting their information from Satan and his evil spirits.

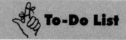

### To-Do List

- "Have I ever cheated any of you? Have I ever oppressed you? Have I ever taken a bribe? Tell me and I will make right whatever I have done wrong" (12:3, New Living Translation). *Samuel's words of farewell to Israel. The people reply by saying Samuel has done nothing wrong.*

- "You're a better person than I am. You treated me with kindness, even though I've been cruel to you" (24:17). *Saul's response to David, who has just spared his life.*

God intends that our channel into the next world should be through Scripture, prayer, and the Holy Spirit—not through mysterious spirits possibly sent from Satan to harm us. (For more on this subject, see "Red Flag Issues: Stay away from psychics," page 43.)

# Bible Scenarios You Can Use

## 1. Hannah prays for a son (1:1–18)

**H**annah is an infertile woman who desperately wants a son. She goes to the worship center, and with tears she prays that if God will give her a son she will let the boy serve him. She is so emotional that priest Eli thinks she's drunk. "Sober up," he tells her. Hannah says she's not drunk, but that she's upset and telling God about her problems. Eli's spirit softens. He says God will answer her prayer. A year later, she has a son: Samuel.

Hannah's infertility had made her life miserable. It was all she could think about. But she took the problem to God. We, too, should talk with God about the problems in our life. He may not answer the way we like, but he will certainly help us.

## 2. God speaks to young Samuel (3:1–21)

**A**s Hannah promised, she takes Samuel while he's still young to live and work at the worship center. Eli will finish raising him, though Hannah and her husband will visit often. One night God's voice awakens young Samuel and says that Eli's sons are evil and won't be allowed to follow their father as Israel's leader. Samuel tells this to Eli, who replies with faith, "He is the Lord, and he will do what's right."

God may not speak to us in an audible voice, but he speaks: through the Bible and the Holy Spirit within us. His voice is recognizable—it's the one forever encouraging us toward goodness. Like Eli, we need to trust God's voice.

## 3. Israel demands a king (8:1–22)

**W**hen Samuel grows old, tribal leaders come to him and ask for a king. Samuel is upset and feels rejected, but he takes their request to God. "Do everything they want you to do," God says, "I am really the one they have rejected as their king." Samuel warns them—at God's direction—that a king will tax them, take their best land and livestock, and force their sons to join the army. But the people insist they know what's best for them.

We can try to run our life on our own, without God's help. But we don't know ourselves as well as God does. And we certainly don't know the future, as he does. When we have to make important decisions, it's wise to consult God and to follow his leading.

## 4. God chooses David as Israel's second king (16:1–13)

**S**aul, Israel's first king, is a dreadful disappointment. He continually disobeys God, by taking spoils of war from defeated people, for instance. When that happened during Joshua's day, the culprit—Achan—died. In this case, Saul's kingship dies. God tells Samuel to go to the house of Jesse in Bethlehem, to secretly anoint one of his sons as the next king. Samuel thinks the oldest son is a perfect choice. But God says, "Don't think Eliab is the one just because he's tall and handsome. He isn't the one I've chosen. People judge others by what they look like, but I judge people by what is in their hearts." God chooses Jesse's youngest son, David.

When we choose leaders, we should follow God's example, focusing less on the person's appearance and resume and more on the inward qualities of character and spirit.

## 5. David fights Goliath (17:1–52)

**G**oliath is a Philistine warrior more than nine feet tall. In a standoff between the armies of Philistia and Israel, Goliath taunts his enemies: "Choose your best soldier to come out and fight me! If he can kill me, our people will be your slaves." All the Israelites cower, except teenage David who is bringing food to his brothers. In one of the Bible's most famous stories, David drops Goliath with a slingshot.

David had said, "the Lord rescued me from the claws of lions and bears, and he will keep me safe from the hands of this Philistine." We gain courage by looking over our shoulder at where we've been, and seeing how God took care of us in the past. We don't fight our battles alone.

## 6. Jealous Saul attacks David (18:1–11)

**D**avid becomes an instant hero. When the army returns home, dancing women welcome them home with the song, "Saul has killed a thousand enemies; David has killed ten thousand enemies!" Saul becomes livid with jealousy. Brooding and deeply depressed, he begins acting crazy. When David tries to calm him with the soothing tones of a lyre, Saul grabs a spear and throws it at the boy, but misses. Later, Saul sends David on a dangerous military mission intended to get him killed, but David survives and gets the promised reward of marriage to Saul's daughter. Saul then sends assassins to kill David in his home—in front of Saul's daughter. But David escapes and becomes a fugitive, with a growing band of followers.

Jealousy can drive us to do terrible things we would never otherwise do.

## 7. David spares Saul (24:1–22)

**S**aul leads his army on a manhunt for David and the men with him, tracking them to an oasis honeycombed with caves. Saul decides to relieve himself in the very cave where David and his men are hiding. David's men whisper that this is the chance they've been waiting for, and they should kill the king. Instead, David sneaks up behind Saul and cuts off a corner of his robe. When Saul leaves, and is a good distance away, David calls him, waves the cloth, and says he would never kill the king. Humiliated, Saul leaves.

When you believe something is wrong—as David believed about killing Saul—don't do it, even if that means standing alone against your colleagues.

## 8. Saul consults a spirit medium (28:1–25)

**T**he Philistines invade Israel, and Saul rushes to stop them. But when he sees their forces, he's terrified. He asks God if Israel will win, but God doesn't answer him in dreams or through prophets because of Saul's long history of disobedience. Samuel, a reliable messenger of God's word, is dead. So Saul visits a nearby medium and asks her to contact Samuel's spirit—a violation of God's law against consulting mediums and psychics. To the medium's horror, Samuel's spirit appears. Saul asks what he should do.

"If the Lord has turned away from you and is your enemy, don't ask me what to do," Samuel says. "Tomorrow the Lord will let the Philistines defeat Israel's army." Saul and his three sons die in the battle.

When we turn from God, we suffer the consequence and spread it around.

# 2 SAMUEL

## Forgiven, But Not Off the Hook

You can describe King David as an adulterer, murderer, and Dysfunctional Father of the Year. Stories in 2 Samuel justify it. But God describes David as "a man after His own heart" (1 Samuel 13:14, New King James Version).

Why would God do that?

David committed some incredibly serious sins. For adultery with Bathsheba, he could have been executed—so says Israelite law. He could have faced the same penalty for ordering Bathsheba's husband killed. And though his sorry performance as a parent wasn't subject to a similar penalty, one son couldn't wait for him to die— and launched a coup.

Despite this, God saw something fundamentally good in David. The flawed king had many of God's best features: patience, generosity, honesty, and dependability—he was true to his word. Stories in 2 Samuel confirm it.

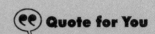 **Quote for You**

"What I did was stupid and terribly wrong. Lord, please forgive me" (24:10). *David's prayer.*

There was yet another character trait that distinguished David. He was quick to repent. And his repentance wasn't the cheap brand that resisted the consequences of his actions. He knew he had a price to pay and that repenting wouldn't get him off the hook. Though David was assured of God's forgiveness, he knew that his actions had set into motion a sad chain of events that wouldn't be stopped. For David's adultery, God warned, "your family will never live in peace" (12:10). Yet, David trusted in God's forgiveness and fairness.

Don't commit adultery, kill someone, or make your kids hate you. But if you do, God will forgive you if you are genuinely sorry. You'll have tough consequences to face, but you can face them forgiven and as a person after God's own heart.

When It Happened

(Dates are approximate)

Abraham 2100 B.C.　Moses 1500 B.C.　Exodus 1440 B.C.　Death of Joshua 1375 B.C.　Death of Saul 1010 B.C.　Death of David 970 B.C.　Ezra 450 B.C.　Jesus born 7/6 B.C.

# Info You Can Use

## Background Notes

**Writer:** The same unidentified person who wrote 1 Samuel, which was originally combined with 2 Samuel as a single book, is likely the author. In it's original language of Hebrew, both books fit onto a single scroll. That's because ancient Hebrew uses only consonants—no vowels. The book's length doubled when it was translated into Greek, sometime between the third to first centuries B.C.

The two books take their name from the first leading character in the history: the prophet Samuel. Whoever compiled the stories into a book likely drew from government records and "the history written by the prophets Samuel, Nathan, and Gad" (1 Chronicles 29:29).

**Time:** The stories cover David's 40-year reign as Israel's king, from about 1010–970 B.C.

**Place:** Most stories take place in Israel. David, however, expands the nation's dominance east into what is now Jordan and north into what is now Syria and Iraq—collecting taxes from the kingdoms in these regions.

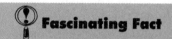

### Fascinating Fact

When David committed adultery with Bathsheba, he already had a large harem. The Bible names eight of David's many wives, and says he left ten in Jerusalem to take care of the palace when he fled during a coup.

**Bottom-Line Summary:** At the beginning of the book, Israel is on the brink of collapse. King Saul and his three sons are all dead—killed in a battle lost to their most feared neighbors, the Philistines.

Though David has been an outlaw in hiding during much of Saul's reign, the giant killer is still a hero to the Israelite people. They proclaim him king, and he sets up the nation's capital and worship center in Jerusalem. He crushes the Philistines, a nation that invaded Canaan about the same time the Israelites did. He also conquers neighboring kingdoms in what are now Jordan, Syria, and Iraq. The taxes he collects from these people pay much of his expenses to maintain his government and army.

Though David's a big success in politics and war, he's a terrible failure on the home front as a husband and a father. His first wife hates him. His stepchildren rape and kill each other. He commits adultery, followed by a cover-up murder of his lover's husband. And one of his sons—the crown prince—leads a nearly successful coup.

## Influential People

**David,** Israel's second king. Though he commits several serious sins during his 40-year reign, he quickly seeks forgiveness and remains loyal to God throughout his life.

**Bathsheba,** wife of an Israelite soldier, commits adultery with David and becomes his wife. Their son, Solomon, becomes one of Israel's greatest kings—a tribute to God's ability to produce something good out of a tragic failure.

**Absalom,** David's oldest surviving son, leads a failed coup against his father. His life and tragic death is a heartbreaking reminder of how unresolved family problems can get out of control and destroy lives.

**Nathan,** a prophet and David's chief advisor, has the courage to confront David about the sin with Bathsheba.

## Q&A

**Why didn't David punish his rapist son?** Amnon was David's oldest surviving son, and considered the crown prince—the man who would inherit David's throne. He fell in love with his half-sister, Tamar, who was David's daughter by another one of David's many wives. Amnon arranged for Tamar to feed him when he pretended to be sick. Alone with her, he asked her to have sex with him. She refused, knowing Israelite law forbade children of the same father to have sex (Leviticus 18:12). So he raped her.

Afterward, "Amnon hated her even more than he had loved her before" (13:15). He ordered a servant to throw her out. Tamar left crying loudly and covering her face with her hands. She later moved from the palace into the home of her full brother, Absalom. The last we hear of her, the Bible says she was always sad and lonely. She probably never married, and as a raped woman lived in a perpetual state of widowhood—rejected by the man who should have married her. By law, a rapist was required to marry his victim and was forbidden to divorce her (Deuteronomy 22:28–29).

### To-Do List

- "You were truly loyal to me, more faithful than a wife to her husband" (1:26). *David's song of lament for his fallen friend, Jonathan, a son of Saul.*

- "I'll be kind to you because Jonathan was your father" (9:7). *David honors the memory of his friend by helping Jonathan's only son.*

- "I keep your laws in mind and never turn away from your teachings" (22:23). *David's song to God.*

"When David heard what had happened to Tamar, he was very angry. But Amnon was his oldest son and also his favorite, and David would not do anything to make Amnon unhappy" (13:21).

**What was so wrong with taking a census that 70,000 Israelites had to die?** Near the end of his reign, David ordered a count of everyone who could serve in the army. The Bible doesn't explain why this was wrong—only that it was wrong, and the leaders knew it. David's commander, Joab, recommended against it (24:3). And afterward, David said it was "stupid and terribly wrong," and asked forgiveness.

One census that Moses took suggests there were certain rituals that needed to be performed in order to prevent a plague (Exodus 30:12). Perhaps David skipped the rituals. Some people in the ancient Middle East also believed that a census drew the attention of demons and invited disaster. But the explanation that may make most sense to people today is that the census could have been an expression of David's pride. He wanted to boast about the size of his army, as though it—and not God—was responsible for Israel's rise to power.

Whatever the sin, the consequences were serious. God gave David the choice of three punishments: seven years of famine, three months of running from invaders, or three days of a plague. David chose the plague, which killed 70,000.

 # Red Flag Issues

**Suicide.** Ahithophel, an advisor of King David who joined Absalom's revolt, is one of only six people in the Bible who committed suicide. He hanged himself after Absalom refused to take his advice (17:23).

Other suicide victims were:

- Samson, who killed himself along with thousands of Philistines by pushing over two support pillars in a temple (Judges 16:30)

- King Saul and his armor-bearer, who both fell on their swords after a lost battle (1 Samuel 31:4–5)

- King Zimri, who set his palace on fire when he saw his city had been captured (1 Kings 16:18)

- Judas, betrayer of Jesus, who hanged himself (Matthew 27:5).

The Bible doesn't say if suicide is sinful. In fact, the Bible doesn't even use the word "suicide," which means "self-murder." The early church, however, soon began teaching that suicide was the same as murder, and was forbidden by the sixth commandment: "Do not murder" (Exodus 20:13). Famous theologians such as Augustine added that the likelihood of repentance and forgiveness for suicide was small.

Centuries later, Christian writers challenged Augustine's position by arguing that it put limits on the mercy of God.

Most Christians today consider suicide wrong. But questions remain about whether God would hold the person responsible, especially in cases of mental illness or stress so high that it's indistinguishable from mental illness.

**Rape.** When David's daughter Tamar was raped, her brother Absalom gave advice many rape victims still hear today: "Don't tell anyone what happened. Just try not to think about it" (13:20).

Absalom thought this was in the best interest of her and the family, especially since her half-brother raped her. But it wasn't. Without understanding the hatred that the rape generated, David didn't punish his rapist son. Two years later, Absalom arranged to have the rapist killed. But for Tamar the damage was beyond repair. In that culture she could never hope for a husband and family.

**Homosexuality.** In David's song of lament over Jonathan's death, David writes, "Oh, how much I loved you! And your love for me was deep, deeper than the love of a woman" (1:26).

Some have suggested this hints of a homosexual relationship between the two men. But the tone of this passage and others about the two reveal they were best friends, not lovers. Homosexuality was forbidden among the Israelites (Leviticus 18:22), and David honored the laws and was rewarded by God for doing so. David's sexual preferences are revealed in his affair with Bathsheba, and in his decision to marry many other women.

# Bible Scenarios You Can Use

## 1. David becomes king (5:1–5)

After Saul's death, his only surviving son becomes king of Israel's northern tribes. But the large tribe of Judah, which dominates southern Canaan, selects as king their tribe's hero: David. Saul's son is a weak leader who's assassinated after a two-year reign. With the continuing Philistine threat, all of Israel's tribal leaders rally behind David, a proven warrior. They anoint him king about 15 years after Samuel secretly anointed him to succeed Saul.

David patiently waited all this time, refusing to take at least two opportunities to kill Saul, who had been trying to kill him. Instead of taking matters into his own hands, David trusted in God's timing. Impatience can lure us to a quick fix—even suggest using methods we know are wrong. But we can't achieve good results through evil methods.

## 2. David dances in a religious parade (6:1–23)

Israel's most sacred object is the ark of the covenant, a chest that holds the Ten Commandments. It has been in hiding for decades, perhaps to protect it from the Philistines who stole it once. David brings it to his newly established capital of Jerusalem, as a symbol of God's presence among the people. Music and shouts of joy fill the streets. David leads the procession with unrestrained enthusiasm. But his wife, Saul's daughter, criticizes him for acting undignified and "dancing around half-naked." She is Michal, whom Saul took from David and gave to another man. David reclaimed her when he became king, though apparently against her will and leaving her husband weeping.

Unresolved anger will destroy a relationship. The only follow-up mention of Michal says she died childless.

## 3. David shows kindness to Saul's grandson (9:1–13)

When a new king takes over, it's common in the ancient Middle East for him to order the execution of the former king's family—to protect against a revolt. But David's best friend was King Saul's son, Jonathan—who died with his father in battle. Because of this friendship, David wants to know if any men from the family are left so he can honor them. Jonathan's son, Mephibosheth, is still alive. But he is crippled—when he was five, his nurse dropped him in a rush to escape the Philistines.

David gives Mephibosheth the land Saul owned, assigns people to work the land, and makes him a permanent guest at palace meals.

The bonds of friendship can overpower evil. It can even outlast your friends, enduring for generations.

## 4. David has an affair with Bathsheba (11:1–26)

**A**fter a nap, David takes a walk on the palace roof. Below he sees a beautiful woman bathing: Bathsheba, the wife of a soldier away at war. David sends for her and has sex with her. She gets pregnant. David orders her husband sent to the front line while the troops are pulled back. The soldier is killed and David marries Bathsheba. The prophet Nathan confronts David about this sin, and David repents. But David and Bathsheba's child dies.

Tragedy waits when we break Commandment number seven: "Be faithful in marriage" (Exodus 20:14). Job had a strategy worth following: "I made a covenant with my eyes not to look with lust upon a young woman" (Job 31:1, New Living Translation).

## 5. David orders land taken from Jonathan's son (16:1–4; 19:24–30)

**D**avid flees Jerusalem during a coup led by his son, Absalom. On the outskirts of town he meets Ziba, the servant in charge of working Mephibosheth's land. Ziba gives him two donkeys loaded with supplies and says his master is staying behind to claim Saul's throne—which is most probably a lie, since crippled Mephibosheth would first have to stop Absalom, something even David's army can't do. Angry, David gives Ziba all Mephibosheth's land.

When David returns after the coup fails, Mephibosheth says Ziba lied and took the donkeys he planned to use to accompany David. Unsure who's telling the truth, David divides the land between the two.

Hasty decisions are often wrong. If you're going to trust your instincts, make sure your instincts are informed with the facts.

## 6. Absalom dies in a coup against his father (18:1–33)

**R**esentment erupts between David and his son Absalom when David fails to punish another of his sons. Amnon—Absalom's half-brother—raped Absalom's sister. Absalom waits two years before taking revenge. He arranges the murder of Amnon, then flees the country. Three years later David calls Absalom home, but refuses to see him for two more years. By then, Absalom has decided to overthrow his elderly father.

The armies of father and son clash in a dense forest. Absalom's long hair gets tangled in tree branches, pulling him off his donkey and leaving him dangling. David's soldiers kill him, against David's orders. David is devastated and wishes he had died instead.

Unresolved family problems feed on silence. Talk. Tackle the problems early, before they tackle you.

# 1 KINGS

## You Reap What You Sow

There are plenty of books in the Bible that teach this lesson. But none teaches it more clearly than the two books of Kings.

In fact, the stories in these books were probably chosen for that one purpose.

We see Israelite kings who devote themselves to God. And we see them reaping the benefits of the ancient agreement their ancestors made with him: rain for the crops, peace in the land, power over enemies. Then we see Israelite kings who abandon God. And we see them reaping the disasters warned about in the ancient agreement: famine, disease, and unstoppable invaders.

Under the leadership of godly King David, the budding nation of Israel blossoms. Life gets even better under Solomon's reign, until his wisdom crashes and he starts worshiping idols. Then come the enemies, followed by a civil war that splits the country.

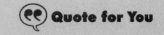 **Quote for You**

"Do what the Lord your God commands and follow his teachings. . . . Then you will be a success, no matter what you do or where you go" (1 Kings 2:3). *King David's dying words to his son, Solomon.*

By book's end, Ahab—one of Israel's worst kings—lies dead in a lost battle. His body is being washed in a pool where prostitutes bathe, and dogs are licking up his blood.

That's not to say the same will happen to us if we abandon God. We may not go to the dogs, literally. But apart from God, we'll miss out on the best that life has to offer—because we'll miss out on God.

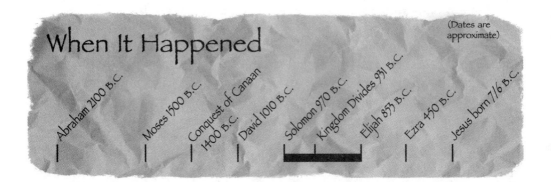

When It Happened

(Dates are approximate)

Abraham 2100 B.C.    Moses 1500 B.C.    Conquest of Canaan 1400 B.C.    David 1010 B.C.    Solomon 970 B.C.    Kingdom Divides 931 B.C.    Elijah 853 B.C.    Ezra 450 B.C.    Jesus born 7/6 B.C.

# Info You Can Use

## Background Notes

**Writer:** Ancient Jewish tradition said Jeremiah wrote 1 and 2 Kings. These two books were originally a single book—like Samuel and Chronicles. Jeremiah was a prophet who lived to see Babylon invade and conquer Israel in 586 B.C., temporarily wiping the nation off the map. In fact, Bible scholars today say the two books of Kings were probably written by someone from Jeremiah's day or later to help explain why God allowed Babylon to wipe out Israel: God was punishing the people for abandoning their agreement to worship him alone, and for turning to the false gods of neighboring nations.

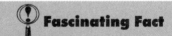

> **Fascinating Fact**
>
> There were prophet schools in Bible times. People singled out by God to become prophets and to deliver his messages to the nation sometimes gathered in groups called "schools of prophets" or "sons of the prophets" (20:35, New International Version). Older prophets taught the younger ones.

Whoever wrote the book, the writer drew from several ancient sources, including three it names: a book about Solomon (11:41) and two books about other kings (14:19, 29). The writer may also have used official kingdom records kept by palace historians (1 Chronicles 29:29).

**Time:** The stories in 1 Kings cover just a little more than a century—from about 970 B.C. until about 850 B.C. The book starts with the last days of David's reign, which ended when he died in about 970 B.C. The history continues with Solomon's reign, and it ends with the nation divided into two: Israel in the north and Judah in the south.

**Place:** Most stories unfold in what is now Israel. But other nations in the Middle East play supporting roles. For example, to get prime cedar for the temple in Jerusalem, Solomon sends loggers to what is now Lebanon. Also, the queen of Sheba visits from what is probably southern Arabia. Solomon opens up trade throughout the region.

**Bottom-Line Summary:** David dies of old age, leaving his son Solomon as the new king. David had secured Israel's borders and dominated surrounding nations, so Solomon rules during a golden age of peace and prosperity. Solomon builds the magnificent temple in Jerusalem, along with a palace and fortresses throughout the country. He starts doing business with neighboring countries, securing peace and trade treaties by marrying royal daughters of the other kingdoms.

In his old age, Solomon starts worshiping the idols of his foreign wives. God says for this he will rip away part of Solomon's kingdom. When Solomon dies, the nation splits in two. Solomon's son rules in the south, and the people in the north appoint Solomon's chief building foreman as their king. The idolatry that Solomon supported grows worse—and so do the troubles for the two nations.

# Influential People

**David,** elderly and dying king of Israel. His final word of advice for his son and successor, Solomon, is to obey God.

**Solomon,** next king of Israel, becomes legendary for his wisdom and for building the nation's first temple. But in old age, he resorts to worshiping idols—a reminder that even the loftiest can fall.

> ## To-Do List
>
> • "Please make me wise and teach me the difference between right and wrong" (3:9). *Solomon's only request of God.*

**Elijah,** a prophet who performs astonishing miracles, flees from Queen Jezebel when she threatens to kill him. In this moment of greatest despair, Elijah's experience becomes a reminder that God never abandons us.

**Ahab,** a king who does "more to make the Lord God of Israel angry than any king of Israel before him" (16:33). Among his sins: he lets his wife, Jezebel, execute prophets and nearly wipe out all traces of Israelite religion in the country.

**Jezebel,** Ahab's evil wife, from what is now Lebanon. She's a prime example of a person who does whatever it takes—murder included—to get what she wants. And she does so without a shred of guilt.

**Rehoboam,** Solomon's son and successor as Israel's king. He lets power go to his head by threatening to make life tougher on the over-taxed, over-worked masses. More than half the kingdom secedes and starts a new nation.

**Jeroboam,** king of the split-off nation of Israel. He builds idols to keep his people from worshiping in Jerusalem, where he fears they might transfer their loyalty back to King David's descendants. In so doing, he sells out his faith to hold onto his power.

# Bible Scenarios You Can Use

## 1. David's dying words for his son (2:1–12)

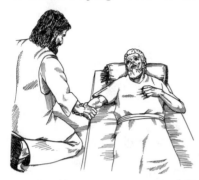

**A**bout 70 years old and dying, David has already relinquished control of Israel to his son Solomon, the new king. On his deathbed, David gives Solomon step-by-step advice about how to deal with certain people—some who had helped David and others who might pose a threat to Solomon's rule. But David's most important advice comes first, before the talk of political strategy: "You and your descendants must always faithfully obey the Lord. If you do, he will keep the solemn promise he made to me that someone from our family will always be king of Israel."

Too often, we ignore the well-seasoned advice of older people. We treat it as words fit for a previous day, but not our day. Solomon knew better. He took his dad's advice, and the entire nation profited from it.

## 2. In a dream, Solomon asks God for wisdom (3:5–14)

**S**hortly after Solomon becomes king, God speaks to him in a dream, inviting him to ask for anything. "Please make me wise," Solomon says. "If you don't, there is no way I could rule this great nation of yours." God commends Solomon, saying the king could have asked for selfish things, such as wealth, power, and long life. Instead he asked for something to help him serve God. Solomon becomes famous for his wisdom.

We, too, can ask God for anything. We don't usually need prodding to ask for more money, the power to make our dreams come true, or the health to enjoy it all. But when we ask for wisdom, we're asking our Father to make us more like him. It must please him to know we love him that much.

## 3. Solomon builds the temple (6:1–38)

**S**olomon builds the first of only three temples the Jews have ever had. He recruits master artisans from throughout the Middle East to erect one of the most beautiful and expensive worship centers in the ancient world—a temple plated with golden ceilings, walls, and floors. It stands for 400 years, until Babylon invades, strips away the gold, and pulls down the white limestone blocks.

We can't afford to build expensive temples to God in every neighborhood. And God probably wouldn't want us to spend such a big hunk of our resources that way. But we can show our respect for God by respecting the place we gather to worship him—whether it's a church, a rented school auditorium, or a friend's house. Wherever it is, God is there. And that makes it a holy place.

## 4. Solomon's thousand wives (11:1–13)

**S**olomon marries 700 wives of royal birth and 300 concubines, or secondary wives. These are mainly political marriages, to seal peace and trade agreements. After all, what foreign king would break his agreement with Israel if he knew his daughter was a wife of Israel's king?

Political marriages are common in the ancient world, but God disapproves. As Moses put it, Israel's ruler "must not have a lot of wives—they might tempt him to be unfaithful to the Lord" (Deuteronomy 17:17). That's what happens to Solomon. In his old age, his foreign wives convince him to worship their gods.

It's hard to resist pressure to do the wrong thing when that pressure comes from those we love most. Though famed for his wisdom, Solomon chose unwisely to marry women who worshiped idols. The company we keep has the potential to rub off on us. That doesn't mean we should isolate ourselves from the ungodly. But we need to surround ourselves with plenty of people who are committed to serving God.

## 5. Israel splits, and the northerners worship idols (12:1–33)

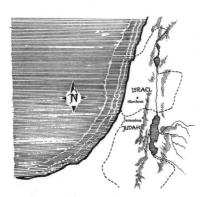

**W**hen Solomon dies, his son Rehoboam becomes king. The people have grown weary of high taxes and of being drafted to help in royal building projects. They ask for relief. Instead, the rookie king decides to show them who's boss. He promises higher taxes and harder work.

The ten Israelite tribes in the north secede and start their own nation, which they call Israel. The southern two tribes become known as Judah, after the biggest tribe. The northerners then appoint their own king: Jeroboam. He worries that his people will go back to the Jerusalem temple to worship (in the south), and that their loyalties may eventually return to David's family of kings. So he sets up shrines with golden calves in the northland, telling the people, "Here are your gods who rescued you from Egypt."

The best leaders are those who serve the people. These two leaders served themselves, and in each case their selfishness backfired. Solomon's son lost half the land in his kingdom. Jeroboam's family endured tragedy, and his dynasty lasted no more than about 25 years. When we decide to serve ourselves at the expense of those we've been entrusted to serve—whether it's on the job or in the home—everyone gets hurt, ourselves included.

## 6. Elijah runs away (19:1–9)

**T**he prophet Elijah challenges Queen Jezebel's 450 prophets of Baal to a showdown to determine who is truly God: Baal, whom Jezebel worships, or the God of Israel. Baal's prophets and Elijah are each to offer a sacrificed bull, laid on a pile of wood. The god who starts the fire on the altar will become the god of Israel.

Baal's prophets pray for hours, even cutting themselves to get Baal's attention. But nothing happens. Elijah prays one short prayer, and fire falls from the sky and consumes the sacrifice. The Israelites kill the prophets of Baal. This suddenly ends a three-year drought.

When Queen Jezebel hears what happened, she sends Elijah the message that she's going to have him killed within 24 hours. Terrified, the miracle worker runs to the desert, where he collapses beneath a small tree, exhausted and depressed. An angel comes and gives him food and lets him sleep. Strengthened, Elijah returns home and remains safe.

Even the godliest among us can get discouraged and depressed. It's nothing to be ashamed of. Sometimes, all we need is a little rest and nourishment. But whatever the remedy, God is there helping us.

## 7. Jezebel murders for a vegetable garden (21:1–16)

**K**ing Ahab wants to buy a vineyard near his summer palace so he can turn it into a vegetable garden. The landowner, Naboth, refuses because Israelite law says the people are supposed to keep the land in their family. Angry and depressed, Ahab "lay on his bed, just staring at the wall and refusing to eat a thing." His wife, Jezebel, quickly hatches a plan. She arranges for two men to publicly accuse Naboth of cursing God and the king. According to Israelite law, two witnesses are all it takes to convict someone. Blasphemy is a capital offense, so the villagers stone Naboth to death. The king confiscates his land.

We can manipulate people to get our own way. We can even manipulate the law to make a sin legal. But it's still sin. And if we get others to do our dirty work for us, all we've managed to do is spread the guilt around.

# 2 KINGS

## Religion Isn't a Private Matter

Do you think your religion is nobody else's business? That it's a private matter between you and your maker?

If you don't discover anything else in the stories of spiritual success and failure in the two books of Kings, discover this: your beliefs will change the history of life on this planet—for better or worse.

Second Kings is full of examples from both sides of that coin. Hezekiah was a godly king. His faith was not only a model that others followed, it protected Jerusalem from being overrun by Assyrian invaders. Then there's his great grandson, Josiah. "No other king before or after Josiah tried as hard as he did to obey the Law of Moses" (23:25). God had already decided to wipe out the Jewish nation because of the people's long centuries of sin. But because of Josiah, God delayed judgment day.

On the flip side of the coin are leaders like Ahab. He and his wife Jezebel led their nation into worshiping idols. Second Kings

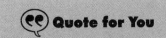

**Quote for You**

"I will rescue you and your city" (20:6, New Living Translation). God's promise to King Hezekiah, in response to the king's prayer. When Assyria later attacks, God repels them because of Hezekiah's faith.

tells how their royal line came to a bloody end. There's a long list of other bad leaders, and the consequences their warped religions had on history. Usually, God sent enemies to raid the nation—one of the punishments that the contract, or covenant, between God and Israel permitted.

You don't have to be a king for your beliefs to influence others and change history. An Israelite slave girl in Syria urged her master—commander of the army—to go to God's prophet for healing of his leprosy. That girl's faith changed the commander's personal history.

Our beliefs make a difference.

(Dates are approximate)

When It Happened

Abraham 2100 B.C.    Moses 1500 B.C.    David 1010 B.C.    Kingdom Divides 931 B.C.    Elijah/Elisha 850 B.C.    Fall of Israel 722 B.C.    Fall of Judah 586 B.C.    Ezra 450 B.C.    Jesus born 7/6 B.C.

# Info You Can Use

## Background Notes

**Writer:** The writer is unnamed, though ancient Jewish tradition says the two books of Kings were written by the prophet Jeremiah, who witnessed the fall of Jerusalem. The stories were compiled by someone after the two Jewish nations of Israel, in the north, and Judah, in the south, were wiped off the map. The writer drew on several ancient sources of history, including books about the kings and probably official palace records.

**Time:** The stories span three centuries, from about 850 B.C., when Ahab's son ruled in the north, to 586 B.C., when Babylon leveled Jerusalem, leaving no semblance of a Jewish nation on the planet.

**Place:** The main events take place in the Jewish nations of Israel, in the north, and Judah, in the south. When Israel falls to the Iraqi-based Assyrian Empire in 722 B.C., the Israelite survivors are taken captive to Assyrian communities. A hundred and fifty years later, when Judah falls to Babylon (the Iraqi-based empire that defeated and displaced Assyria), the survivors are again taken captive and scattered throughout Babylonian communities. The book concludes with the Jews scattered abroad, on foreign soil.

**Bottom-Line Summary:** The story of the split Jewish nations of Israel and Judah picks up where 1 Kings stops. Godless rulers, such as Jezebel, are leading the complacent people into idolatry and other sinful practices, such as having sex with priests and priestesses to entertain and appease Canaanite gods. On God's order, prophets are delivering his message: "Stop doing sinful things and start obeying my laws and teachings!" But the people ignore it. There are isolated pockets of godly rule in this span of history, especially in the southern nation. But most kings don't care about God.

The Israelites have struggled with idolatry since the beginning of their nation, when Moses led them out of Egypt. Now, about 700 years later, God's prophets warn that enough is enough. If the Israelites don't stop, they will lose their nation. They don't believe it, and they don't stop.

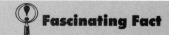

**Fascinating Fact**

Prayer has healing power, according to medical studies. One such study, in 1999 at Kansas City's Mid-America Heart Institute, involved nearly a thousand people with life-threatening heart problems.

About half the patients were assigned to prayer groups. The people praying knew only the patient's first name and that the person was sick. The patients and their doctors didn't know about the study.

According to 35 measurements, such as amount of medicine needed and length of recovery, the patients who were prayed for did better than the patients who were not. This mirrors the results of a smaller study reported in a 1988 issue of *The Southern Medical Journal.*

Hezekiah wouldn't have been surprised. Prayer extended his life by 15 years.

In 722 B.C., Assyria decimates Israel. Judah survives another 150 years, thanks to righteous kings such as Hezekiah and Josiah. But in 586 B.C., it, too, falls victim to centuries of sin. Babylon invades and overruns all the fortified cities, saving the capital of Jerusalem for last. The Jewish nation is gone.

# Influential People

**Elijah,** devoted prophet who doesn't die, but is carried to heaven in a whirlwind. Though he performs dramatic miracles, nothing he does convinces Israel's kings to turn from idolatry. Still, he never gives up hope or thinks of his ministry as a futile effort.

**Elisha,** Elijah's student and successor, learns from his master and follows in his footsteps. He helps the powerful and the poor alike, a reminder that all people are equal in God's eyes.

**Jezebel,** queen of mean, is the murderous bride of King Ahab. Her evil influence over Israel spans the reign of her husband and those of her two sons. Famous for murdering people to get her own way, she herself dies a gruesome death.

**Hezekiah,** a righteous king of Judah. God protects Judah from Assyrian invaders because of Hezekiah's godly leadership.

**Manasseh,** son and successor of Hezekiah, is nothing like his dad. He becomes king at age 12 and turns the nation back to Canaanite gods, even sacrificing his own sons as burnt offerings. Described as the worst king in Jewish history, Manasseh serves as a grim reminder of how swiftly the tide of faith can shift in a nation.

**Josiah,** Manasseh's grandson, is more like his great-grandfather, Hezekiah. He points the nation back to God and restores the neglected, deteriorating temple. For this, God delays the destruction of Judah. But the nation's sinful habits are too deeply engrained, and when the king dies, the people return to their old ways.

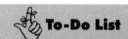 **To-Do List**

- "Stop doing sinful things, and start obeying my laws and teachings" (17:13). *God's message to the Israelites, delivered by prophets.*

- "I will not take anything from you" (5:16). *Elisha's response to a military commander he healed of leprosy. The commander offers Elisha an extravagant gift of 750 pounds of silver, 150 pounds of gold, and ten new outfits. But Elisha refuses to take advantage of the man.*

**Naaman,** a Syrian commander skeptical of God's power to heal him of leprosy. His healing, and subsequent vow to worship only God, is a testimony of hope for the skeptic in all of us.

# Key Ideas You Need to Know

**Punishment for sin doesn't always wait for Judgment Day.** The Bible teaches that when this life is over, we'll all stand before God and be held accountable for our sins (Romans 14:10–12). In the meantime, God sometimes fires warning shots over our bow, to steer us away from danger. For the Israelites, those warning shots came in many forms: prophets predicting disaster if the nation didn't reform, droughts, diseases, raiders, occupying forces that took over the land and milked it for all they could get. Sometimes this approach worked, and the Israelites turned back to God. But usually, they proceeded as though they were doing nothing wrong.

Trouble in our life doesn't always mean we've sinned. The suffering of Job, an innocent man, proves that. And Jesus once said a man was born blind not because of anyone's sin, but to allow others to see God's power—then Jesus healed him (John 9:3).

Even so, troubles in life can prompt us to re-evaluate our relationship with God, to make sure nothing's wrong spiritually. Sin often has some relatively immediate negative consequences. We need to see these as warnings that should prompt us to change our ways. As individuals and a nation, we have a chance to learn from Israel's mistakes and our own.

# Bible Scenarios You Can Use

### 1. Elisha raises a boy from the dead (4:8–37)

**T**he prophet Elisha occasionally travels about the country, sometimes passing through the village of Shunam. There, an elderly couple without children prepare a permanent guest room for him. Whenever he visits the area, he's welcome to stay there and eat. In gratitude, Elisha promises the woman a child. The next year she gives birth to a son. Years later, her young son complains of a terrible headache, then dies. The woman rushes to Elisha at Mount Carmel, about 20 miles away. He returns with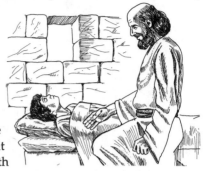

her, stretches his body over the boy "with his mouth on the boy's mouth." The boy sneezes and opens his eyes.

We may not receive miracles for our troubles. But kindness we show can become kindness we receive.

### 2. Syrian general is cured of leprosy (5:1–27)

**N**aaman commands the Syrian army that God is using to punish Israel. But he has a horrible disease: leprosy. An Israelite servant girl in his house tells Naaman's wife that if he would go see Elisha "he would be cured of his leprosy."

Naaman has nothing to lose since leprosy is incurable, so he goes. Elisha tells him to wash seven times in the Jordan River, which Naaman reluctantly does. He is cured, and vows to worship only the God of Israel.

The faith of even a child can produce wonderful results. So think about the needs of people around you. If you know of a godly person who can help—especially if that godly person is you—tell the person in need. Pass along your faith in God and in his people.

### 3. Jezebel, the murderer, is murdered (9:30–37)

**J**ezebel's husband is dead, but her son is now king, and the Queen Mother continues to wield great influence. She leads the nation in worshiping idols, after ordering the slaughter of many Israelite prophets. She once even orchestrated the murder of a farmer so her husband could confiscate the land and use it as a vegetable garden.

Destined to be the new king, an Israelite soldier named Jehu kills her son then rides to the palace. "Why do you come here, you murderer?" she demands, from an upper window. Jehu says if the servants with her are on his side, to throw her from the window. They do, and she falls to her death.

Whether we treat others with contempt or kindness, we can usually expect the same treatment in return.

## 4. God changes his mind and lets Hezekiah live (20:1–11)

**T**he prophet Isaiah stands by the bedside of King Hezekiah and delivers a somber message: "This is what the Lord says: Set your affairs in order, for you are going to die. You will not recover from this illness" (20:1, New Living Translation). With this, Isaiah leaves.

Hezekiah turns his face to the wall and prays, "I have always tried to be faithful to you and do what is pleasing in your sight." Then he breaks down and weeps. Before Isaiah gets out of the palace, God stops him with this new message for the king: "I heard you pray, and I saw you cry. I will heal you. . . . I will let you live 15 more years."

The Bible doesn't explain why God changed his mind. But this story—and others like it—show that prayer makes a difference. Some theologians argue that prayer doesn't change God, who is Goodness perfected. But, instead, it somehow changes us and provides God an opportunity to change his plans for us accordingly. How prayer works is a mystery. That prayer works is a fact.

## 5. Israel is wiped off the map (17:1–41; 25:1–26)

**T**he northern nation of Israel falls first, to Assyria, an empire in what is now northern Iraq. The citizens are deported as slaves, and the ten Israelite tribes that once made up the nation lose track of their tribal identity forever—becoming known as the "Ten Lost Tribes of Israel."

"All this happened," the Bible says, "because the people of Israel had sinned against the Lord their God." For centuries of idolatry, God invokes the punishment clause in his covenant with the Israelites, which allows him to destroy the nation and scatter the survivors to other lands (Deuteronomy 28:15–68).

About 150 years later, the same thing happens to the southern kingdom of Judah, and for the same reason. Babylonian King Nebuchadnezzar overruns all the cities, then makes an example of Jerusalem by tearing it and Solomon's temple to the ground. Survivors are taken captive to Babylon, a Persian Gulf empire that replaces Assyria. The great nation that God promised to make of Abraham's descendants is gone.

Sin leads to tragedy. We can lose everything important to us because of sin—everything except God. He didn't give up on the Jews, and he won't give up on us. He restored Israel, just as he restores broken lives today.

# 1 CHRONICLES

## For Outsiders Who Want to Belong

You know what it's like to stand on the outside—unwanted or ignored. We all do. At one time or another we've all felt left out. Not invited. Overlooked. Politely asked to leave.

The Jews felt unwanted by God. Once, they had been God's chosen people. Now, they feared they were the unchosen.

They had compelling evidence. They lost the promised land. Though they returned after decades of exile in the Persian Gulf, what they came back to was a collection of ghost towns—a nation in ruins. Israel had been founded on an agreement between the Israelite people and God: they would serve him, and he would preserve and bless them. But they shattered the agreement and suffered the curses written into the contract: famines, disease, and in the end a decimated homeland and banishment for the survivors (Deuteronomy 28).

> **Quote for You**
>
> "You belong to the family of Israel . . . you are his chosen ones" (16:13). *The New Testament says, "Everyone who has faith is a child of Abraham"* (Galatians 3:7).

Where did they stand now, in God's eyes?

Were they still the chosen? Was Israel still the promised land? Was the covenant with God still valid? Would God forgive the people and take them back? The two books of Chronicles answer all these questions with a resounding yes.

The Jews had compelling evidence. They were back in the promised land. The temple was rebuilt. The priesthood survived, and so did the royal family of David's descendents. God had not deserted Israel.

We sometimes feel on the outs with God, often because of sin. We tend to feel most alone when we're suffering the consequences of our sin. But even then, God is with us—ready to forgive and lead us home, where we belong.

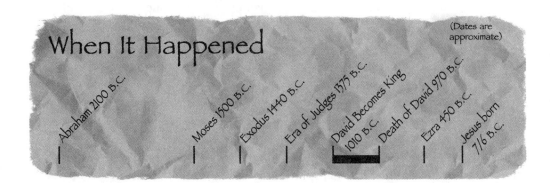

When It Happened
(Dates are approximate)

Abraham 2100 B.C. | Moses 1500 B.C. | Exodus 1440 B.C. | Era of Judges 1375 B.C. | David Becomes King 1010 B.C. | Death of David 970 B.C. | Ezra 450 B.C. | Jesus born 7/6 B.C.

# Info You Can Use

## Background Notes

**Writer:** Ancient Jewish tradition says a priest named Ezra wrote both books of Chronicles, along with the books of Ezra and Nehemiah. In fact, all of these books seem to have been written about the same time—around 450–400 B.C.—about a century after the Jews returned from exile in Babylon.

No one is sure who wrote the books, however, because the writer is never named. Whoever the writer was, he drew from a wealth of written sources—some of which are in the Bible and some of which aren't. About half of 1 Chronicles comes from the books of Samuel and Kings. Other material is plucked from the first five books in the Bible, along with several books of prophets, as well as Psalms. Sources outside the Bible, which are mentioned by name in the books of Chronicles, include history books about the kings and records by prophets.

Like the books of Samuel and Kings, the two books of Chronicles were originally a single book later separated so each would fit on a single scroll. In Hebrew, both books fit on one scroll because Hebrew doesn't use vowels—only consonants. The books doubled in size when translated into Greek a few centuries later, since Greek—like English—uses vowels and consonants.

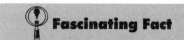

**Fascinating Fact**

There are 39 books in the Old Testament. As many as 23 others—all named in the Old Testament—are lost. Eighteen of the lost books are mentioned in the books of Chronicles (such as the Book of the Kings of Israel, and the Record of the Prophet Nathan). Some names are so similar that scholars suggest they refer to the same book, and that the actual number of lost books is closer to half a dozen.

**Time:** The genealogy in 1 Chronicles starts with Adam and traces the Jewish family tree to what is probably the writer's time—shortly after the Jewish return from Babylonian exile, about 450–400 B.C. The stories that follow the genealogy, however, cover primarily David's reign—about 40 years, from Saul's death in about 1010 B.C. until David's death in about 970 B.C.

**Place:** Most stories take place in what is now Israel, though David's military victories extend the boundaries of the nation into what are now Jordan, Syria, and Lebanon.

**Bottom-Line Summary:** The book begins with nine chapters of names—a genealogy tracing the Jewish family tree from Adam, at creation, through Zerubbabel, King David's descendant and leader of the nation after the exile in Babylon. The point of the genealogy is to show that God has a long history with Israel, and that he hasn't given up on them even though they broke their covenant agreement with him and lost the promised land for a time. God has brought them home and preserved David's family of kings. They have a future.

Israel's story picks up with the death of King Saul, followed by the crowning of the nation's most beloved king: David. The rest of the book spotlights the bright moments in David's reign. Israel's enemies are defeated, including the Philistines who have plagued them for centuries. Israel's most sacred relic, the chest containing the Ten Commandments, is brought out of seclusion in a private shrine and carried—in a parade of singing and dancing—to the worship center in Jerusalem. Plans for construction of Jerusalem's magnificent temple begin.

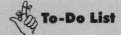

**To-Do List**

- "Get to know the God of your ancestors. Worship and serve him with your whole heart and with a willing mind. . . . If you seek him, you will find him" (28:9, New Living Translation).

- "Tell every nation on earth, 'the Lord is wonderful and does marvelous things!'" (16:24).

## Influential People

**Saul,** Israel's first king, is remembered most for his repeated disobedience to God and for his manic jealousy toward David, which drove him to try to murder the young man. Saul dies on the battlefield, in a tragic end to a tragic life.

**David,** Israel's most celebrated king, devotes himself to God and to God's people by securing the nation's boundaries, bringing to Jerusalem the sacred chest containing the Ten Commandments, and making plans for Israel's first temple. Some people are big talkers—more blow than go. David wasn't that kind of leader. David got things done.

## Key Ideas You Need to Know

**History with a happy spin.** If you've read the books of Samuel and Kings, Chronicles will sound like *déjà vu*. But this isn't a rehash of old stories. The earlier books are written for Jews in exile, to show them how they got there. So Samuel and Kings spend a lot of time talking about Israel's sins. The two books of Chronicles, however, are written for Jews who have come home from exile and are wondering if God is still with them. So Chronicles focuses less on Israel's sinful history and more on their godly heritage.

In retelling David's story, for example, the writer leaves out most of the sad scenes: the conflict with Saul, adultery with Bathsheba, the cover-up murder of her husband, troubles in the royal family that include rape and murder, and the attempted coup by the crown prince.

This isn't whitewashing history. The people of Israel already know these stories painfully well. The writer is simply plucking out scenes that will help the Israelites see God has been with them in the past, and is with them now.

It's an uplifting exercise, even for us today. When we're feeling spiritually low, we count our blessings, and name them one by one.

# Q&A

**Why did God kill someone who was only trying to help out?** God struck dead an oxcart driver named Uzzah when the driver steadied the chest containing the Ten Commandments, to keep it from falling out of the cart. King David had enlisted the drivers to transport the chest—Israel's most sacred object—to Jerusalem. During Moses' day, God had given specific instructions about how to transport this chest. An oxcart was not in the instructions. Priests were supposed to carry it with poles inserted into rings built into the chest. It was never to be touched—by anyone. The penalty was death (Number 4:15).

At this pivotal moment early in Israel's history, God was reminding the people to take his laws seriously.

Though many of the Old Testament laws are no longer relevant today, the most fundamental laws such as the Ten Commandments are. Knowing and obeying these laws can mean the difference between life and death. Though God might not strike us dead for having an affair with another man's wife, her husband might. And even if he didn't, the affair would damage countless lives in both families.

# Bible Scenarios You Can Use

## 1. Israel's family tree (chapters 1—9)

**S**tarting with Adam, the writer of this uniquely tailored history of Israel traces highlights of the Jewish family tree all the way up to his own time: just after the Jewish exile in Babylon. That's thousands of years of history compressed into a nine-chapter list of family names that begins this book.

Sounds like a boring way to start a book. And it is, for most of us today. But for the Jews standing among the ruins of their homeland, this genealogy sends a powerful message: From the beginning, God has been with them. They have a past with God, and a future as well.

God's ancient promise to his people holds true: "No matter what you have done, I am still the Lord your God, and I will never completely reject you" (Leviticus 26:44).

There are times when we, too, feel cut off from God—banished from his presence because of our sin. But we have a past with God. He has been reaching out to us all our lives. Like the Israelites of old, we have a future as well: "God has said, 'Never will I leave you; never will I forsake you'" (Hebrews 13:5, New International Version).

## 2. Saul kills himself when the battle is lost (10:1–14)

**A**fter the family tree, comes Israel's history as a nation—beginning with the tragic death of Israel's first king, Saul. At first, Saul is a humble and shy man. But he lets the power and prestige of his office transform him into a vain and arrogant tyrant who repeatedly ignores God's instructions. For this, God rejects him as king and orders the prophet Samuel to secretly anoint David to become the next king, when Saul dies. Saul and his three sons die in a battle lost to the Philistines. With his three sons dead and himself mortally wounded by an arrow, Saul kills himself by falling on his sword.

This sad story follows immediately after Saul's short genealogy. The point that the writer makes is that our life determines our legacy. This could be unsettling news if you've lived a long time in sin. But turning to God, asking forgiveness, and living your remaining years devoted to God can be part of your legacy, too.

### 3. Three soldiers risk their lives to get water for David (11:10–19)

**W**hile David and his soldiers are preparing for a battle against the Philistines, David mentions in passing that he would enjoy a drink from his hometown well in Bethlehem. David's camp is about 10 miles west of this village. But the Philistines control Bethlehem and have set up camp in the sprawling valley between Bethlehem and David's camp. Even so, three of David's bravest soldiers—known as the Three—take it upon themselves to grant David's wish.

When they return with the water, David is deeply moved. He says, "This water is as precious as the blood of these men who risked their lives to bring it to me" (11:19, New Living Translation). Instead of drinking it, he pours it out in a sacrifice to God. By doing this, David is showing that he is more of a servant than one who expects to be served. He and his men serve each other with selfless devotion—models of how we should all treat each other.

### 4. David prepares for the temple his son will build (chapters 22, 28–29)

**A**fter David and his army secure Israel's borders by defeating the neighboring enemies, David asks God for permission to build a temple where the Israelites can worship. God denies the request, explaining, "You have killed too many people and have fought too many battles." The temple would be built in peacetime, by a peaceful king: David's son, Solomon.

David graciously accepts God's decision. Then with God's blessing, David starts making construction plans for Solomon, and begins stockpiling supplies the builders will need. David even develops a business plan for the temple, setting up a strategy for managing the work of priests and support staff. Among the temple positions he creates are musicians, judges, guards, accountants, and custodians.

Instead of feeling sorry for ourselves about what we aren't able to do, we can make a valuable contribution to God's work by turning our attention to what we can do. You may have limits you think are unfair. Perhaps you're limited physically, intellectually, or socially—and it leaves you frustrated and angry. But you have opportunities, too. Go there and pursue them.

# 2 CHRONICLES

## A Message for the Unraveled

When a rope comes unraveled, it doesn't look like a rope anymore. It looks like a worthless tangle of used twine.

The Jewish nation had become completely unraveled. First, it split into two countries. Next, the nation in the north was destroyed as punishment for centuries of nonstop idolatry. And finally, the southern nation was cleared off the world map, too.

The northern survivors never returned. Instead, they intermarried with their conquerors and were assimilated into other cultures. The southern Jews were allowed to return. But after more than 50 years in exile, only a relatively small remnant was willing to go back and rebuild their nation. Most grew up in the foreign culture, and it became their home. Those few who returned to Israel and were old enough to remember how it used to look must have wept when they saw the stone piles and ashes that was once their home, their city, and their nation.

For these Jews, struggling with doubts about whether God would help them restore their nation—a land God took from them as punishment for centuries of sin—the writer of Chronicles offers a history lesson mingled with a message of hope. He reviews highlights of their long history with God, to assure them they have a long future ahead. Indeed, the Jewish people remain with us today.

What makes the two books of Chronicles a timeless classic is its core message: if there is hope from God for a people who came as unraveled and unrecognizable as the Jews, there's hope for us even when sin or tragedy has torn us apart. God can put us together again.

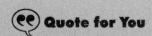 **Quote for You**

"If my people who are called by my name will humble themselves and pray and seek my face and turn from their wicked ways, I will hear from heaven and will forgive their sins" (7:14, New Living Translation). *God's promise to forgive those who repent.*

When It Happened

(Dates are approximate)

Abraham 2100 B.C. | Moses 1500 B.C. | Era of Judges 1375 B.C. | David 1000 B.C. | Solomon 970 B.C. | Kingdom Divides 931 B.C. | Fall of Israel 722 B.C. | Fall of Judah 586 B.C. | Ezra 450 B.C. | Jesus born 7/6 B.C.

# Info You Can Use

## Background Notes

**Writer:** Though the writer is unnamed, ancient Jewish tradition says a priest named Ezra wrote the two books of Chronicles, along with the books of Ezra and Nehemiah.

References in the books (to people and historical events such as the rebuilding of the temple) suggest they were probably written in the 400s B.C., about a century after the Jews returned from exile in Babylon.

**Time:** The stories span roughly 400 years, from Solomon's reign that began about 970 B.C. to the fall of Jerusalem in 586 B.C.

**Place:** Most of the stories take place in what is now Israel. As the book opens, the nation also includes parts of what are now Jordan, Syria, and Lebanon. But after Solomon dies, the nation divides into two nations, with Israel in the north and Judah in the south. Gradually, the nations shrink as their neighbors take away part of the land. Eventually, both Jewish nations are wiped off the map.

**Bottom-Line Summary:** Part two of this version of Israel's history begins with the 40-year reign of Solomon, described as the wisest and wealthiest king who ever lived. During Solomon's reign, Israel enjoys the greatest peace and prosperity in the nation's history. But after Solomon dies, the northern tribes reject his son as king when he vows to draft the people for government building projects and work them harder than Solomon ever did. These tribes start a new nation that survives 200 years, until Assyria wipes them out. Survivors are deported and never return to reestablish their nation. This should have provided a wake-up call for the southern nation of Judah, reminding them that God punishes sin. But Judah has only a few godly kings (which is more than the northern nation had). So about 150 years later, the southern nation of Judah is also destroyed, the people deported. Some of these Jews, however, return to the ruins of their homeland after their exile in Babylon.

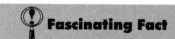

### Fascinating Fact

The Bible says Persian king Cyrus freed the Jews. A clay cylinder from Cyrus' reign confirms that he freed all foreign prisoners so they could go home: "I returned to these sanctuaries on the other side of the Tigris [River]—the sanctuaries which had been ruins for a long time—the images which used to live therein and established for them permanent sanctuaries. I also gathered all their former inhabitants and returned to them their homes."

## Influential People

**Solomon,** famous as Israel's wisest king, builds the temple, opens international trade, and generates the greatest prosperity the nation ever experiences.

Solomon's heyday is an example of the wide-ranging blessings God enjoys showering on his people.

**Hezekiah,** a king whose godliness leads many Jews back to the Lord and prompts God to protect the nation of Judah from Assyrian invaders.

**Manasseh,** son and successor of Hezekiah, is described as the worst king in Jewish history. He turns the nation to idols and sacrifices his own sons to idols. However, he later repents, is forgiven, and turns his people back to God—a tribute to God's amazing grace.

**Josiah,** king of Judah and a religious reformer. After centuries of chronic idol worship in Judah, Josiah's reforms are too little, too late. Because of Josiah's faithfulness, however, God does delay Judah's destruction for about 25 years after Josiah's death. Our faithfulness can help those around us.

**Joash,** king of Judah, leads religious reforms and orders repairs on the neglected temple. But later in life he turns from God and is assassinated by his own people—a warning that a good start in life can be ruined by a sinful finish.

 **Q&A**

**Do God's promises to Israel apply to us?** The broad principles do. For example, when God says if Israel repents of their sins, he will forgive them and life will be better for them—that's a timeless principle that can apply to us individually and as a nation. That's because God has built certain laws into his creation—an automatic cause-and-effect.

Sin wasn't part of God's good creation, so it releases a swarm of problems. Kindness and compassion, on the other hand, keep us in sync with creation and tend to make life go more smoothly.

We can see evidence of this by looking over our shoulder at our own personal history as well as the history of others. The trouble is, we're so focused on getting ahead that we don't often take the time to reflect on the past and how we can learn from it.

**Why were the Jews limited to worshiping God only at the temple in Jerusalem?** Jews could offer sacrifices of worship only at the Jerusalem temple. This was probably to help them resist the temptation of worshiping false gods.

People from other cultures who lived in and around Israel worshiped gods in scattered temples as well as at simple altars built on hilltops. But as long as

> ### 👆 To-Do List
>
> • "If you are good to the people and show them kindness and do your best to please them, they will always be . . . loyal" (10:7, New Living Translation). Sage advice of royal counselors to King Rehoboam. The king ignored the advice and lost half his kingdom when the northern tribes seceded.
>
> • "The Lord will stay with you as long as you stay with him! Whenever you seek him, you will find him" (15:2, New Living Translation). *God's promise to Asa, a king of Judah.*

the Jews worshiped at only one center—a facility directed by trained priests—it was harder for pagan heresies to infiltrate Jewish religion.

Israel's ongoing problem, however, was that they often worshiped at pagan shrines anyhow, sometimes in addition to worshiping at the Jerusalem temple. Some Israelites thought of the Lord as just one of many gods.

# Bible Scenarios You Can Use

### 1. Solomon builds the temple (3:1–17)

**O**n a hilltop overlooking Jerusalem, Solomon builds the first of only three temples the Jews ever had. He assembles a monumental work force of 150,000. Stonecutters quarry massive, white limestone blocks. Lumberjacks travel to Lebanon to harvest the finest wood available: bug-proof, rot-resistant, knot-free cedar. Artisans from throughout the Middle East design furnishings of gold and ivory.

Seven years later, the job is done. Israel has one of the most beautiful and expensive temples in the ancient world—a worship center with golden ceilings, walls, and floors. This is the only place in the world where Jews are allowed to offer sacrifices to God, because this temple represents God's presence among his chosen people.

Today, we can worship God anywhere. As Jesus told a non-Jewish woman who worshiped in Samaria, "The time is coming when it will no longer matter whether you worship the Father here or in Jerusalem. . . . The time is coming and is already here when true worshipers will worship the Father in spirit and in truth" (John 4:21, 23, New Living Translation).

The place we worship isn't especially important. What's important is that wherever we are, we understand we're in the presence of God who loves us.

### 2. The Jewish nation is destroyed (36:9–21)

**A**fter Solomon's reign, the Jewish nations split in two. Judah, in the south, is ruled by descendants of David and Solomon. Israel, in the north, is ruled by an assortment of ungodly kings not associated with David's family. "The Lord sent prophets who warned the people over and over about their sins. But the people only laughed and insulted these prophets." After about 200 years, the northern nation falls to Assyria. The survivors are assimilated into Assyrian cultures. About 150 years later, in 586 B.C., the southern nation falls to Babylon. The survivors are deported to Babylon, where they can be closely watched.

Since Adam and Eve sinned in the Garden of Eden, God has punished people for sinning. Whether the punishment comes from natural consequences of the sinful act or from direct intervention by God, sin produces painful effects and drives us from God. Even so, God is never out of range of our voice. He never abandons us. Though the Jews broke their covenant agreement with God, and according to ancient covenant protocol God had every right to utterly destroy the Jews, he didn't. When they were ready to ask for forgiveness, he was there. And what was true for the Jews then, is true for people of all nations now.

## 3. Persia frees the Jews (36:22–23)

About 50 years after the Jewish nation dies, so does their conqueror, the Babylonians. The Persian empire swallows up Babylon. Persia's ruler, Cyrus, issues an emancipation proclamation: "The Lord God of heaven has made me the ruler of every nation on earth. He has also chosen me to build a temple for him in Jerusalem, which is in Judah. The Lord God will watch over any of his people who want to go back to Judah."

After a generation abroad, many Jews have grown accustomed to their new land. So they decide to stay. But many others return home to rebuild their temple, Jerusalem, and Israel from the ashes. A nation annihilated returns to life.

For the Jews who remembered their homeland, their greatest desire was to go home and rebuild their nation. At times, their greatest desire seemed the most hopeless wish of all. But with God, there's always hope—for any one of us.

# EZRA

## Starting Over

Have you ever had to start all over on something? Your computer crashes, taking with it a project you've been working on for months. You get fired. Or you move to a different town where you don't know anyone.

Imagine having to start over to rebuild a nearly thousand-year-old nation reduced to ashes and rock piles, with wild animals living in the ruins of once thriving cities. That's the monumental task awaiting the Jews, newly released from their 50-year exile in what is now Iraq.

Not since the Exodus and the conquest of Canaan have the Jews faced such a mission of supernatural magnitude. They need God's direct involvement every bit as much as their ancestors did in the days of Moses, when God miraculously freed them from Egypt, blew an escape path across the Red Sea, spouted water from desert rocks, and rained manna from the sky.

This new story is of Israel's second great escape to the promised land. And like before, God gets directly involved in human history. Over the span of about a century, he convinces several Persian kings to let the Jews (and all other foreign exiles, for that matter) return home. Furthermore, the kings send these people away with supplies for the journey and the rebuilding ahead.

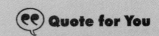 **Quote for You**

"The Lord God has helped me" (7:28). *Ezra's reaction to news that the Persian king is authorizing him to return to Israel to teach God's law to the people.*

Back in Israel, the Jews will face incredible obstacles: alluring women who draw many of the men back into idolatry, descendants of Assyrian pioneers who plot to destroy the rebuilding efforts, and weariness from the decades it takes to rebuild the temple, homes, and cities.

But God is with them, using the righteous as well as the sinners to help them along.

If God is able to help the Jews rebuild a millennium-old nation, he can help us with whatever needs rebuilding in our lives.

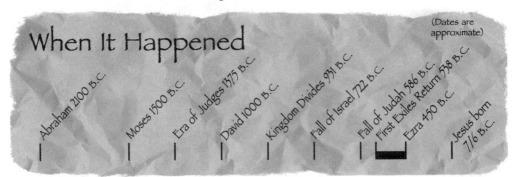

## When It Happened

(Dates are approximate)

Abraham 2100 B.C. | Moses 1500 B.C. | Era of Judges 1375 B.C. | David 1000 B.C. | Kingdom Divides 931 B.C. | Fall of Israel 722 B.C. | Fall of Judah 586 B.C. | First Exiles Return 538 B.C. | Ezra 450 B.C. | Jesus born 7/6 B.C.

# Info You Can Use

## Background Notes

**Writer:** The writer isn't named—as is the case with most books of the Bible. Ancient Jewish tradition said Ezra wrote it, along with writing Nehemiah and the two books of Chronicles. Ezra was a priest as well as a scribe. He was a scholar who studied scripture and taught it to others.

When this story was first written, Ezra and Nehemiah were one book. The first ancient writer to speak of them as separate was Christian scholar Origen, who lived in the A.D. 200s. He called the books 1, 2 Ezra.

The events described in both books suggest they were written sometime shortly after Ezra arrived in Jerusalem, in 458 B.C.

**Time:** The stories in the book cover about 80 years, from the time Persia frees the Jews to return to Israel in 538 B.C. to the time Ezra arrives and begins his teaching ministry in 458 B.C.

**Place:** The story begins in the newly established Persian Empire, centered in what is now Iraq. The Jews return to Israel by following the Euphrates River northwest, and then turning south along the Mediterranean coast. This isn't the most direct route home, and it requires the Jews to travel nearly a thousand miles. But it keeps them near water. The more direct route would have taken them nearly 600 miles directly across the Syrian Desert. Most of the story takes place in Jerusalem, where the Jews begin to rebuild their city, starting with the temple.

**Bottom-Line Summary:** The Babylonian Empire is gone, defeated by the Persian Empire. Persian king Cyrus frees all the people that the Babylonians deported from their homelands. Among these are the Jews, now free to go home and rebuild cities the Babylonians had leveled.

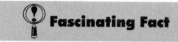

**Fascinating Fact**

Synagogues probably got their start during the Jewish exile in Babylon. With no temple to go to for worship, the Jews gathered on the Sabbath in homes and outdoors, where they sang, prayed, and learned about their traditions.

Not only does Cyrus free the Jews, he returns the temple furnishings confiscated by the Babylonians: thousands of silver dishes, gold bowls, and other sacred objects. In addition, their neighbors help by giving them gifts of gold and silver, supplies for the trip, and livestock to start herds.

Tens of thousands of Jews return in the first wave. Rebuilding begins with the temple. But the work stops abruptly after local descendants of Assyrian pioneers write to the next Persian king and convince him that the Jews are refortifying Jerusalem, perhaps for a rebellion. Work resumes when a third Persian king finds Cyrus' original decree.

Priest Ezra arrives later and teaches the people about the laws of Moses. His sermons put a quick stop to Jewish men marrying non-Jewish women and adopting their wives' foreign religions. Worshiping false gods, Ezra reminds the people, is why God punished them with the exile. It could happen again.

## Influential People

**Ezra,** a priest and a scholar of Scripture (scribe), returns to his homeland to teach the Jews about the laws of Moses. Because Ezra devotes himself to "studying and obeying the Law of the Lord and teaching it to others" (7:10), God is able to use Ezra to help others.

### To-Do List

- "I asked the people to go without eating and to pray" (8:21). *Before the long and dangerous journey home to Jerusalem, Ezra asks the people to fast and pray for safety. Many believers still fast in times of great need.*

**Cyrus,** Persia's first king, and the man who frees the Jews to return home, is a perfect example of why New Testament writers urge believers: "Obey the government, for God is the one who put it there" (Romans 13:1, New Living Translation). God is fully able to work through people, even those who don't worship him.

## Q&A

**Why didn't the exile last as long as predicted?** Bible scholars aren't sure. Jeremiah, a prophet who predicted the fall of Jerusalem and then witnessed it in 586 B.C., said the exile would last 70 years (Jeremiah 29:10). But it lasted only about 50, since the Persians freed the Jews in 538 B.C.

There are several possible explanations for the 20-year difference.

1. Jeremiah was counting from the first deportation of Jews, which took place in about 605 B.C.—about 20 years before Jerusalem's destruction and the final deportation of its citizens.

2. Jeremiah was referring not only to exile from the land, but also from the temple, which wasn't rebuilt until 516 B.C.—70 years after its destruction.

3. The prophet didn't mean 70 literal years, but simply a long time. The number 70 is used this way in other Bible passages (2 Chronicles 36:21; Daniel 9:24).

## Red Flag Issues

**Marrying non-Christians.** Priest Ezra ordered all the Jewish men who married non-Jews to divorce those women and send them away with their children. Ezra knew that the Jews had a long history of marrying unbelievers and then letting those spouses lead them away from God. It even happened to King Solomon, described as the wisest Jew in history.

In New Testament times, Christian leaders such as Paul gave this advice as a general rule to fellow Christians: "Do not be yoked together with unbelievers. For what do righteousness and wickedness have in common? Or what fellowship can light have with darkness?" (2 Corinthians 6:14, New International Version).

Even so, if you're married to an unbeliever, apostle Paul advises against divorce. "If your wife isn't a follower of the Lord, but is willing to stay with you, don't divorce her. If your husband isn't a follower, but is willing to stay with you, don't divorce him. Your husband or wife who isn't a follower is made holy by having you as a mate" (1 Corinthians 7:12–14).

Paul's argument is opposite of Ezra's. Paul says that Christians need not be dragged down by unbelievers, as the Jews were, but that we can lift our mates up to God. Perhaps the difference is that we have something the Jews in ancient times didn't: the spirit of God within us, empowering us with wisdom and persistence.

So if you're thinking of marrying a non-Christian, perhaps Paul's best advice is: don't. But if you're currently married to an unbeliever, Paul's advice is to draw on the power of God within you to love your mate into God's kingdom. If that doesn't work, and "if your husband or wife isn't a follower of the Lord and decides to divorce you, then you should agree to it. You are no longer bound to that person. After all, God chose you and wants you to live at peace" (1 Corinthians 7:15). (For more, see "Should Christians avoid marrying or associating with unbelievers," page 337.)

# Bible Scenarios You Can Use

### 1. The Jews come home (chapters 1—2)

**F**or more than 50 years the Jews live in exile, scattered throughout the Babylonian Empire, in what is now Iraq. But after Persia conquers Babylon, Persian King Cyrus issues an astonishing decree. All foreigners taken from their countries are free to return home. Furthermore, the king decides to let each nation reclaim the temple furnishings that the Babylonians had stolen.

For the Jews—whose culture and worship had revolved around the Jerusalem temple for 400 years—this was the best possible news. Not since the Exodus out of Egypt did the Jewish people have more reason to rejoice. Some 42,000 Jews decide to return to Israel, in the first of many waves of returning exiles. It's a hazardous journey of nearly 1,000 miles.

This is a second chance most Jews probably never expected. Because of their sins, they had lost nearly everything important to them: home, worship center, country. Now they would get it back. Like the Jews, we serve the God of new beginnings. Sin can cost us dearly, but God is willing to forgive and restore us to the life of joy.

### 2. The Jews rebuild their temple (3:7–13; 6:13–18)

**O**nce the Jews arrive in Jerusalem, they take up a collection to start the temple construction. They take in about half a ton of gold and almost three tons of silver—a fraction of the nearly 4,000 tons of gold and 40,000 tons of silver David stockpiled for the earlier temple that Solomon built.

The Jews rebuild the altar first, so they can renew their practice of offering sacrifices to God. Then they start on the temple. When the foundation is finished, the Jews celebrate. But many cry, perhaps because they remember the magnificence of Solomon's temple, and realize this one won't come close in comparison.

Descendants of Assyrian pioneers now living in the region manage to halt the work by writing a letter of complaint to the king of Persia who replaced Cyrus. The letter warns that the Jews are well-known rebels, and are now fortifying the city. The king orders them to stop. For about a decade, the Jews do no more work on the temple. But prophets Haggai and Zechariah later arrive and urge them to finish the job—which they do, with approval from yet another Persian king.

With all the obstacles they face, it takes the Jews nearly 20 years to complete their mission of rebuilding the temple. Today, we're used to fast service and quick results. But God's work often takes a long time and incredible perseverance, and it's worth the patient effort.

## 3. Ezra condemns marriages to idol worshipers (9:1—10:17)

About 80 years after the first wave of Jews arrive home, a priest named Ezra arrives. His assignment, approved by the Persian king, is to make sure the Jews know and are following the laws of Moses. To his horror, Ezra finds that many of the people have broken the very law that led to the exile in the first place. Many of the men have married non-Jewish women. Ezra knows it was Israel's association with non-Jews that led to idolatry, which caused the exile. And he fears that unless he can stop Jews from marrying people of other religions, the Jews are destined to suffer more tragedy.

Ezra goes to the temple courtyard and begins praying and weeping on behalf of the people. One by one, a crowd gathers around him. Within three days a vast crowd gathered there. The date is December 19, 458 B.C., and a chilling rain begins to fall as Ezra speaks.

"You have broken God's Law by marrying foreign women," he says. "Now you must confess your sins to the Lord God of your ancestors and obey him. Divorce your foreign wives and don't have anything to do with the rest of the foreigners who live here."

The crowd agrees.

This isn't entirely a racial issue. In fact, many foreigners in the region are from the same Semitic background. The problem is spiritual. Since the Jews first entered the promised land a thousand years earlier, they had married people who worshiped idols. As a result, the Jews were lured into idolatry. The New Testament says, believers shouldn't "team up with those who are unbelievers" (2 Corinthians 6:14, New Living Translation).

This is wise advice, especially in marriage. When two people marry, they become one. But if your spouse isn't a believer, you may have to compromise some of your beliefs to keep your marriage alive. Faith is a powerful factor to consider when selecting a mate. Don't let passion or emotion keep you from seeing how important it is to marry someone who shares your faith in God. And if you're already married to an unbeliever, hang onto your faith.

# NEHEMIAH

## When Prayer Alone Isn't Enough

Don't expect God to do everything for you. Nehemiah didn't. There are some things God wants us to do for ourselves—just as we want our children to begin doing things for themselves.

Nehemiah was a Jew and a respected palace servant for Persia's king, Artaxerxes. When Nehemiah heard that his people in Jerusalem were defenseless and disgraced because the city walls were still in ruins, he immediately fell into a depression. Jerusalem, for centuries, had been the spiritual and political center of Israel—a glorious symbol of God's presence, protection, and blessing. Yet, without it's walls, Jerusalem remained a symbol of Israel's sin and God's punishment.

Nehemiah took his concern to God, by praying and fasting. He might have stopped there, believing he had done everything he could. But he didn't.

When the king noticed Nehemiah was troubled and asked how he could help, Nehemiah didn't make the king ask twice. Instead, he requested permission to repair the walls. Boldly, he even asked for building supplies, such as timber from the royal forests. Nehemiah got this and more: a military escort and an appointment as governor of Judah.

> ### 🗨 Quote for You
>
> "Don't be dejected and sad, for the joy of the Lord is your strength!" (8:10, New Living Translation).

Later, when Nehemiah heard rumors of a possible attack against his workers at the walls, he again took the double-barreled approach: pray and take action. As he reported in his journal, "We kept on praying to our God, and we also stationed guards day and night. . . . Even the workers who were rebuilding the wall strapped on a sword" (4:9, 18).

Sometimes, prayer is all we can do. But many times, prayer is just the first of many steps we should take. Prayer is a time to quiet ourselves before God and listen for guidance that might come from the common sense we've developed, or from the spirit of the Lord living within us.

When It Happened

(Dates are approximate)

Abraham 2100 B.C. | Moses 1500 B.C. | Era of Judges 1375 B.C. | David 1000 B.C. | Kingdom Divides 931 B.C. | Fall of Israel 722 B.C. | Fall of Judah 586 B.C. | First Exiles Return 538 B.C. | Nehemiah Governs Judah 445 B.C. | Jesus born 7/6 B.C.

# Info You Can Use

## Background Notes

**Writer:** The writer is unidentified, but much of the story is based on the first-person memoirs of Nehemiah, a trusted Jewish servant in the palace of Persia's king. This book was originally combined with the Book of Ezra. Jewish tradition says Ezra, a priest and a scribe, wrote both books along with the two books of Chronicles. In fact, Ezra shows up in later chapters of Nehemiah, reading the law of Moses to the Jews.

**Time:** The story takes place during the 12 years that Nehemiah served as governor of Judah, from about 445 B.C. to 433 B.C. By the time Nehemiah arrived, the Jews had been back from exile for almost a century—returning in 538 B.C.

**Place:** Nehemiah's story begins in the Persian Gulf city of Susa—winter capital of the Persian Empire, located near what is now the border of Iraq and Iran. Here is where Nehemiah serves the Persian king, Artaxerxes, and is granted a leave of absence to go to Jerusalem and repair the city walls.

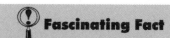

### Fascinating Fact

Jerusalem's wall was made of timber, uncut stone, and dirt. It was about eight feet across at its base and perhaps 20 to 30 feet high, stretching about two miles long and enclosing about 90 acres.

**Bottom-Line Summary:** Nehemiah, a Jew who makes sure the Persian king's wine isn't poisoned, slips into a four-month depression after hearing that the walls of Jerusalem are still in ruins. He prays about the situation and then convinces the king to send him on a mission to repair the walls. Despite opposition from non-Jews living near Jerusalem—including plots to assassinate him—Nehemiah orchestrates an astounding reconstruction that takes only 52 days. His opponents are stunned into silence, recognizing God's hand at work. Afterward, Ezra reads aloud from the books of Moses, while the Jewish crowds listen. At Ezra's request, the people confess their sins and pledge their allegiance to God. Nehemiah leads the people as governor of Judah for 12 years.

## Influential People

**Nehemiah,** a Jewish servant in the Persian palace, returns to Jerusalem and oversees the rebuilding of the city walls in 52 days. The technique he uses to accomplish this—prayer coupled with action—is a model for people tackling tough assignments.

**Ezra,** a priest and scholar of Jewish scripture, is committed to teaching the Jews how to serve God. Though some of his teachings seem extreme—like calling on Jewish men to divorce their non-Jewish wives—his greatest desire is to steer the Jews away from idolatry, which had produced the tragic decimation of Israel and the exile that followed.

**Artaxerxes,** the Persian king, gives Nehemiah permission to rebuild Jerusalem's walls. He's an example of God's ability to use even pagan rulers to accomplish his plans.

**Sanballat,** leader of Nehemiah's non-Jewish opposition, tries to stop the repair of Jerusalem's walls. For all his plotting, intimidation, and bribery, he is no match for Nehemiah, a man whose decisions seem enlightened by God.

# Q&A

**What good is fasting?** When Nehemiah heard that Jerusalem's walls were still in ruins, he mourned for the once great city, and began praying and fasting to express his sorrow to God. Jewish law required Jews to refrain from eating and drinking one day a year on *Yom Kippur,* the national day of repentance. But many people, such as Nehemiah, also fasted when they mourned or sought God's help in a crisis.

Esther asked the Jews of Persia to fast for three days before she went to the king and asked him to stop an ordered holocaust of the Persian Jews. Jesus fasted 40 days before beginning his public ministry that sparked immediate and intense opposition, culminating in his execution.

Fasting doesn't pressure God into doing something he otherwise wouldn't do. But it helps us to pour out our overflowing emotions—rather than deny them—and to say with our actions that the problem we face is immensely serious. Fasting is a spiritual practice that for millennia has helped God's people face trauma and tragedy.

## To-Do List

- "We must honor our God by the way we live, so the Gentiles can't find fault with us" (5:9). *Nehemiah's call for compassion from Jewish leaders who were taking financial advantage of fellow Jews.*

- "We will bring ten percent of our grain harvest to those Levites who are responsible for collecting it in our towns" (10:37). *The Jews agreed to give the tithe—ten percent of their income—to the temple.*

# Red Flag Issue

**Doing business on Sunday.** In Nehemiah's day, one of the vows the Jews made was this: "We won't buy goods or grain on the Sabbath or on any other sacred day, not even from foreigners" (10:31). This was part of their effort to obey the fourth commandment, which prohibited work on the Sabbath—the one day a week set aside for rest and worship.

Early Americans established laws prohibiting work on Sunday, which is the Christian Sabbath. Shops were closed. Buggies remained in the barns—except for the trip to church. Violators could be whipped, put in stocks, even executed for repeat offenses. These laws prohibiting Sunday commerce became known as blue laws, supposedly referring to the blue paper on which Puritan's of the New Haven colony wrote the laws.

Cities and states enacted blue laws that identified what could and couldn't be sold on Sunday. For example, you might be able to buy food but not soap, or a horse but not clothes. In 1961, the Supreme Court ruled that although blue laws came from religion, states have the right to set aside a day of rest. Some communities still prohibit the sale of liquor on Sunday.

Today, many orthodox Jewish communities close their business for the Jewish Sabbath (from sundown on Friday to sundown on Saturday). Many Christians, however, buy and sell on Sunday like it's a holiday instead of a holy day. Other Christians express their conviction that commerce on Sunday should be kept to a minimum, and they vote with their feet by refusing to eat out or go to stores, in the hopes that other Christians will start doing the same, that Sunday business will wane, and that the people forced to work on Sunday will get the day off for rest and worship with their families.

# Bible Scenarios You Can Use

### ━━━ 1. Nehemiah asks permission to repair Jerusalem's walls (1:1—2:10)

**A**bout 70 years after Jerusalem's temple has been rebuilt, the city walls still lay in ruins—a national embarrassment. Nehemiah, a Jew living in Persia and working as a palace servant, hears about this from his brother who visits from Jerusalem.

"I sat down and cried," Nehemiah writes in his memoirs. Then for several days he goes without food and prays. Nehemiah is the king's cupbearer, responsible for protecting the king from being poisoned. Eventually, King Artaxerxes notices something is troubling his servant, so he asks what's the matter.

"I feel sad," Nehemiah replies, "because the city where my ancestors are buried is in ruins, and its gates have been burned down." The king asks how he can help. By this time, Nehemiah has had four months to think about it. He asks for a leave of absence so he can lead the rebuilding project, and he asks for letters to Persian governors in the region to grant him safe passage and to supply building materials. The king grants these requests, gives Nehemiah an armed escort, and apparently names him governor of what used to be Judah (5:14).

When faced with a problem that deeply troubled him, Nehemiah first took his concerns to God through prayer and fasting. But he didn't leave the matter with God. Perhaps during his times of prayer and reflection he realized there where things he could do to help Jerusalem. It's good for us to pray. But when there's something we can do to help solve the problem, we should do it.

### 2. Jews rebuild Jerusalem's walls in 52 days (chapters 3—4; 6:15-16) ━━━

**W**hen leaders of non-Jewish communities in the region hear about the project, they get angry. Perhaps they fear that once the Jews finish rebuilding Jerusalem's defensive walls, the Jews will start taking back the rest of the region. One such non-Jewish leader, a man named Sanballat, secretly plots to kill Nehemiah. Four times Sanballat tries to set up a meeting with him, intending to kill him. But Nehemiah never goes, explaining in his memoirs, "I knew they were planning to harm me."

Fearing an all-out attack, Nehemiah mobilizes men and women alike and urges them to work quickly, carry a weapon at all times, and sleep inside the city instead of returning to their homes outside of town. Astonishingly, the repair is finished in 52 days—with such speed that it terrifies the surrounding communities because they realize God must be helping the Jews.

When you've got an important job to do, ask God to give you the wisdom and strength to overcome your obstacles—whatever, or whoever, they are.

### 3. Nehemiah orders the rich to stop exploiting the poor (5:1–13)

**A**lready, in the re-emerging nation of Israel, there's a sharp divide between the rich and the poor. Some of the poor men and women take their complaints to Nehemiah.

"We have large families, and it takes a lot of grain merely to keep them alive," they say. A recent famine forced many to sell some of their children into slavery and to mortgage their fields, vineyards, and homes to wealthy Jews in order to buy grain and pay the Persian taxes. Rather than help the poor, the rich Jews exploit them by buying their children as slaves and by loaning them money at exorbitant interest rates. Jewish law allows commercial loans but forbids Jews from charging interest to fellow Jews who are poor (Exodus 22:25).

Nehemiah calls together the nobles and officials, points out their wrongdoing, and orders them to give back everything they have taken: land, homes, interest. They agree to do so, and the national crisis ends.

Greed is a source of many problems in our communities. But we can fight this by refusing to exploit the misfortune of others. For example, instead of paying someone an unfairly low wage because we know they'll work for anything, pay them as you would want to be paid. And when you see a poor and helpless person being taken advantage of, speak out on their behalf. Your words may be all the help they need to get them through a crisis.

# ESTHER

## The Risk of Helping Others

Have you ever stood quietly by—afraid to get involved—while someone else got ripped apart with unfair accusations? Maybe the boss was doing the ripping, and you zipped your lips because you wanted to keep your job.

Worse, perhaps you've lived through a scene on the flip side. Maybe you were the one getting ripped up, all the while hoping someone—anyone—would come to your rescue. But no one did.

This scene is a lot like the plot driving Esther. The difference is that it wasn't merely job survival on the line. An entire race was about to get wiped out—all because one Jew refused to bow in the presence of the Persian king's second-in-command. Snubbed, the vain and vindictive official decided to kill not only this one Jew, but also *every Jew in the empire*. Think holocaust!

Only one person could stop it: Queen Esther. But to stop it, she had to appeal to the king, and risk her life in the process. Persian law said that no one—the queen included—could come to the king uninvited. Esther knew the danger, and she was terrified. She asked Jews throughout Persia to fast and pray for her during the three days before she approached the king.

Esther's story is a dramatic reminder that God doesn't plant us somewhere by accident. We're in the right place at the right time. If we stay alert to God's leading, and are willing to take risks to help others, the world will be a better place because of us.

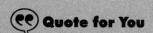 **Quote for You**

"Perhaps you were put in this position so you could use your influence to help others" (4:14, author's paraphrase). *Mordecai's plea for Queen Esther to use her influence to stop a holocaust.*

## When It Happened

(Dates are approximate)

Abraham 2100 B.C.

Moses 1500 B.C.

Era of Judges 1375 B.C.

David 1000 B.C.

Kingdom Divides 931 B.C.

Fall of Israel 722 B.C.

Fall of Judah 586 B.C.

First Exiles Return 538 B.C.

Ezra Returns 458 B.C.

Jesus born 7/6 B.C.

# Info You Can Use

### Background Notes

**Writer:** The writer is unknown. Among the many suggested are Mordecai, Ezra, or Nehemiah—all of whom were alive and living in Persia at the time.

The book's contents suggest the writer was a Jew living in Persia. Among the clues, the writer is familiar with the Jewish festival of Purim and with the fact that the Jews thought of themselves as a distinct people. The writer is also familiar with Persian customs and the names of high-ranking officials. King Xerxes shows up in the ancient records of his enemies, the Greeks. And archaeologists have uncovered the Persian palace in Susa.

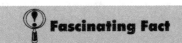
**Fascinating Fact**

Jews and Christians alike argued against including Esther in the Bible because it doesn't mention God and it reads more like a secular story than a religious one.

**Time:** Esther's story takes place sometime during the 21-year reign of Xerxes, who ruled from 486 B.C. to 465 B.C., after his famed father, Darius. Like many other beautiful women, Esther was selected as a possible replacement for Queen Vashti about three years into the king's reign. But Esther had to wait her turn to meet the king. She waited four years. But the king quickly fell in love with her and crowned her the new queen.

**Place:** The dramatic story unfolds in the Persian city of Susa, about 100 miles north of the Persian Gulf. Susa is in Iran, near the border with Iraq. Winter home of the king, Susa was in a warm climate about 300 miles south of the capital in Persepolis.

**Bottom-Line Summary:** Esther, a young and beautiful Jewish woman, marries the king of Persia and manages to save the Persian Jews from an ethnic cleansing massacre.

The king, Xerxes, had divorced his former queen, a strong-willed woman who disobeyed his direct command. His officials realize he misses his queen, so they convince him to let them search the empire for the most beautiful woman, who will become his next queen. The king excitedly agrees. He chooses Esther, an orphan raised by her older cousin Mordecai, a palace servant.

Mordecai refuses to bow before the king's second-in-command, a vicious man named Haman. In retaliation, Haman plots to hang Mordecai and to wipe out all Mordecai's people—the Jews—not realizing the queen is a Jew. Mordecai had told Esther to keep that a secret from everyone.

Haman tells the king there's a troublesome, law-breaking group of people who deserve to die. Easily convinced, the king signs an irrevocable order allowing the Persians, on a set day, to wipe out these people whom Haman apparently never bothers to identify as the Jews.

Esther appeals to the king, who becomes livid when he hears that Haman's plot targets the Jews and that Esther and his trusted servant Mordecai are both Jews. The king executes Haman, and then issues a decree allowing the Jews to defend themselves.

# Influential People

**Esther,** a Jewish orphan, becomes queen of Persia. She risks her life to save the Persian Jews from annihilation.

**Mordecai,** Esther's older cousin, raises her as his own daughter. A palace official, he advises Esther to do the right thing and stand up for her people in spite of the risk.

**Haman,** is Persia's chief official, second only to the king. Vain and vicious, he grows so angry at Mordecai's unwillingness to bow before him that he plots to wipe out Mordecai's entire race. Haman's story is a reminder of how pride can destroy us.

**Xerxes,** king of Persia, naively allows himself to get tricked into ordering the slaughter of his own wife's people.

**Vashti,** former queen of Persia, is divorced for disobeying a direct order of the king. The order is to show off her beauty at a party of drunken men. Though we might sympathize with Vashti's decision to refuse, the king's advisors saw her refusal as a threat to male domination in Persian society.

## To-Do List

- "Go without eating for my sake" (4:16). *Before putting her life on the line in an attempt to prevent a holocaust, Esther asked her fellow Jews to pray and fast for her.*

- "He worked for the good of his people" (10:3, New Living Translation). *A description of Mordecai, a Jew promoted to become Persia's highest ranking official, second only to the king.*

# Key Ideas
# You Need to Know

**Racial hatred is wrong.** Haman, the villain in this story, is a bigot of Hitler proportion. Haman's ancestors and Mordecai's ancestors have been enemies for more than 500 years. Haman is a descendant of King Agag, who fought against Israel's first king, Saul. When Mordecai refuses to bow before Haman, the enraged Haman decides to wipe out all Jews in the empire.

That's an intriguing decision, because God had earlier ordered Saul to wipe out King Agag's nation, the Amalekites—an order Saul ignored. Had Saul done as he was told, there would have been no Haman to threaten the Jews.

At first glance, it looks as though Haman is doing nothing worse than Saul was supposed to do: ethnic cleansing. But there's a big difference. The killing of the Amalekites was God's decision, and was part of God's plan to cleanse the region of idolatry, which featured temple prostitution and human sacrifice. Haman's plot to kill the Jews was based on his hatred of one man—a hatred that Haman unfairly transferred to an entire race.

In New Testament times, when Jesus showed compassion toward a Samaritan woman—a race at odds with the Jews—he taught us that it's wrong to hate people just because they are from a different race or culture. We are all created in God's image, and equally beloved by him.

## Q&A

**Why isn't God mentioned in this book?** No one knows why the writer disguised the religious nature of this book. Perhaps the writer wanted to draw in secular readers, and gently lead them to reach their own conclusion that God helped the Jews.

Though God's name isn't mentioned, he certainly appears to be directing the events through an incredible string of "coincidences."

- A Jew named Esther surprisingly becomes queen of Persia, which puts her in a position to help the Persian Jews.

- Her cousin, Mordecai, overhears an assassination plot against the king and reports it, endearing himself to the king.

- Perhaps months later, the king is unable to sleep, so he reads the royal records and comes across the description of how Mordecai saved his life. The very next day, the king learns that Haman has plotted to kill Mordecai and all the Jews, including the queen.

In another subtle reference to God, Esther calls on the Jewish people to fast on her behalf. There's no mention of prayer, but it's implied. Fasting and prayer are done together, especially in times of crisis.

Also, Mordecai hints of God when he tells Esther that if she doesn't help the Jews, "we will somehow get help" (4:14)—an apparent reference to the fact that God has a long history of helping the Jews.

# Bible Scenarios You Can Use

═══════ **1. Esther, a Jewish orphan, becomes queen of Persia 1:10—2:20)**

**A** bit drunk at the end of a weeklong banquet, Persian King Xerxes calls for his wife, Queen Vashti. He wants to parade her in front of the men at the party to show them how beautiful she is. Vashti refuses the command performance, perhaps because of the dinner party she's giving for the women, or maybe because she has no intention of strutting for the entertainment of drunken men. Furious, the king declares that since she doesn't want to make an appearance, she's never again to show her face in his presence.

Suddenly in the market for a new queen, Xerxes agrees to let his officials conduct an empire-wide search. Many women are added to the king's harem, but only one earns the honored title of queen: a young Jew named Esther. She's an orphan raised by her older cousin, Mordecai, a palace servant. When the king meets her, he falls in love.

Esther had little to do with being chosen queen. She was picked for her good looks and character, and probably didn't have the option of turning down the royal search committee. Sometimes we, too, find ourselves in situations beyond our control. But even there, God can use us in monumental ways. That's because no situation is beyond his control.

## 2. Esther asks the king to stop a Jewish holocaust (4:8—5:8; 7:1-10)

**H**aman is the top-ranking official in Persia, after the king. Whenever he walks by, other palace officials bow—everyone but Mordecai. This so infuriates Haman that he plots to kill Mordecai and wipe out the man's entire Jewish race, not realizing that Esther is also a Jew. Haman convinces the king to sign an irrevocable law that allows Persian citizens to kill the Jews, whom Haman describes only as "some people who . . . refuse to obey your laws." The slaughter is scheduled to take place on March 7, 473 B.C.

Mordecai asks Esther to intercede, saying, "It could be that you were made queen for a time like this." Esther agrees, though she knows that Persian law allows the king to execute anyone who visits him uninvited. The king receives her, and she tells him that Haman's plot is against her people. She explains that this means she could die, as well as Mordecai, who previously saved the king from assassination. Enraged, the king orders Haman hanged, promotes Mordecai to fill the vacant post, and then writes a new decree allowing the Jews to defend themselves from attack.

Esther risked her life to defend her people. In risky situations—where our life, our job, or perhaps our reputation could suffer—our survival instinct often kicks in and urges us to lay low and watch out for Number One. But that's when we need to switch on our spiritual instinct and remind ourselves of God's commission to love our neighbors as much as we love ourselves. Sometimes we have to put ourselves at risk to help another.

## 3. Jews celebrate a holocaust missed (9:1-32)

**F**ighting breaks out between ethnic Persians and Persian Jews, and it extends into a second day. But the Jews prevail, with the help of the Persian military. On the third day, the Jews celebrate their survival with a feast that becomes known as Purim (POR-im), after a Hebrew word for "lots," which is a kind of dice that Haman used to select the holocaust date.

After all these centuries, Jews still celebrate this festival late each winter. In a joyous spirit of a Mardi Gras, they dress the children in costumes, put on plays, share large meals with family and friends, and give gifts to family members and the poor. When Jews read the story aloud during the festival, everyone boos Haman by stomping, jeering, and rattling noisemakers to drown out his name.

Christian annual religious festivals, such as Christmas, Easter, and Pentecost Sunday, help us preserve the memories of what God has done for us. Private anniversaries, such as the day of our conversion or baptism, can do the same.

# JOB

## When Misery Comes Calling

If misery were a houseguest, how should you treat it?

Well, if Job's response is any clue—and the book's happy ending suggests it is—it's okay to pitch a fit.

In fairness to Job, he doesn't start out complaining to high heaven. In fact, it's just the opposite. When he gets the devastating news that all his children have been killed in a windstorm and his herds have been stolen by raiders, he initially takes the blow with resolute grace: "We bring nothing at birth; we take nothing with us at death. The Lord alone gives and takes. Praise the name of the Lord!" (1:21).

Even when he later loses his health to some agonizing, oozing skin disease, and his wife advises him to curse God and die, Job philosophically replies, "If we accept blessings from God, we must accept trouble as well" (2:10).

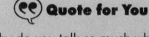 **Quote for You**

Why do you talk so much when you know so little? (38:2). God's question to Job, who makes long speeches about why he doesn't deserve to suffer. Job's embarrassed reply to God: "I have talked about things that are far beyond my understanding" (42:3).

A week into reality, Job changes his tune. Physically hurting, depressed, and confused, he curses the day he was born. He stops shy of cursing God—but he's not shy about blaming him. Job has no idea why he must suffer like this, so he demands an explanation from God.

He never gets one, perhaps because he wouldn't understand it anyhow. What he gets is a reminder of who God is—the Creator who:

- placed the cornerstone of the earth, "while morning stars sang, and angels rejoiced" (38:7)
- set the ocean's boundaries "and wrapped it in blankets of thickest fog" (38:9)
- sends torrents of rain on empty deserts, transforming "barren land to meadows green" (38:27)

When misery comes calling, perhaps it doesn't matter much how we treat it—with grace or fury. Perhaps what matters most is remembering who God is, and trusting him because of it.

When It Happened

(Dates are approximate)

Adam 4000 B.C. · Abraham 2100 B.C. · Job 2000 B.C. · Moses 1500 B.C. · David 1000 B.C. · Ezra 450 B.C. · Jesus born 7/6 B.C.

# Info You Can Use

 ## Background Notes

**Writer:** The writer is unknown. Scholars guess he was an Israelite, since he uses the Hebrew name for God: *Yahweh* (YAH-way), often translated as Lord or Jehovah. Speculation about possible writers makes up a who's who list from the Bible: Moses, Solomon, Isaiah, Hezekiah, or Baruch (the scribe who wrote down Jeremiah's dictated prophecies). Some suggest Job wrote it himself, or at least served as the main source of information for another writer.

It's also unclear when the story was written. It may have been passed down by word of mouth for generations before being com-

Job was considered one of the three most morally upright humans who ever lived, along with Noah and Daniel (Ezekiel 14:14).

mitted to writing in the 900s B.C., which was during the golden age of Israel's wisdom literature. Much of the wisdom writing is said to have come from the mind of King Solomon.

**Time:** Several clues suggest Job lived in the days of Abraham, Isaac, and Jacob—in roughly 2000 B.C. Job was raided by Sabeans and Chaldeans, who lived in Abraham's time. Also, Job—as head of his extended family—served as a priest for the family, as was customary before the time of Moses.

**Place:** Job lived in the mysterious "land of Uz" (1:1). No one knows where that is. Some guess it was in Edom, a region southeast of Israel in what is now Jordan. One of Job's friends is from Teman, an Edomite city. Also, Edomites were famous for their wisdom—and the Book of Job is considered wisdom literature, a style of writing that seeks practical answers to philosophical questions such as "why do good people suffer?"

**Bottom-Line Summary:** Job is truly a good man who lives a rich life. He has a family of ten children, many servants, and thousands of sheep, camels, cattle, and donkeys. Satan meets with God and says it's because Job has such an easy life that he respects God. If life suddenly gets tough, Satan argues, Job will reject God. "All right," God says. "Make Job suffer as much as you want, but just don't kill him" (2:6).

Suddenly, Job's rich life takes a tragic turn. Raiders steal his herds and kill the servants watching them. A windstorm blows down the house where his children are eating, killing all of them. Then Job breaks out with agonizing skin ulcers all over his body.

Three friends arrive to comfort him. They sit in silence for a week, and then open their mouths. That's when the comfort ends. They add to his misery by insisting he must have sinned and that God is punishing him. Job argues that he hasn't sinned, and he complains to God for dumping all this suffering on him. The bulk of the book is Job's debate with his three friends.

By book's end, God enters the conversation. Without explaining why Job is suffering, God rebukes Job for saying it's wrong of God to allow this suffering. God also condemns Job's three friends for their bad advice, and orders them to ask Job's forgiveness. They do so, and give Job some silver and gold. In time, Job builds back his herds to double their original size. And he has ten more children.

## 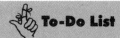 Influential People

**Job,** a good man, tragically loses his riches, children, and health. His story shows that even good people sometimes suffer through no fault of their own. But the story also calls us to hold onto our faith in God during tough times.

**Job's wife** urges her husband to end his misery by cursing God in the hopes God will kill him. She's a sad example of those who give up on God in a crisis.

### To-Do List

- "You respect God and live right, so don't lose hope!" (4:6). *Advice for a discouraged Job, from one of his friends.*

- "Surrender your heart to God, turn to him in prayer, and give up your sins—even those you do in secret" (11:13). *More advice for Job. Though this is generally good advice, the counselor's conclusion isn't always true: "Then you won't be ashamed. . . . Your troubles will go away like water beneath a bridge."*

**Eliphaz, Bildad, and Zophar,** Job's three friends, come to comfort him. By insisting Job sinned and is rightfully being punished for what's happening to him, they illustrate that sometimes the best comfort we can offer is to simply be present and say little or nothing.

## Key Ideas You Need to Know

**Suffering isn't a sure sign of God's anger.** Like many people in ancient times, Job and his friends believe that God rewards good people with prosperity and punishes them with suffering. That's why Job's friends are so quick to accuse him of sin and why Job, bewildered and angry, begins questioning the fairness of God.

The depth of suffering Job experiences is the very reason many people today reject God. They can't understand how any compassionate being—especially a God who supposedly epitomizes love—could stand by and do nothing while good people suffer.

In his moments of deepest despair, Job lashes out at God, criticizing him unfairly by saying that God:

- isn't listening to him (9:16)

- hurts him for no reason (9:17)

- is unjust, making the innocent appear guilty (9:20)

- laughs when a good person dies (9:23)

- causes injustice in the world (9:24).

God knows, however, this isn't what Job really believes. It's the pain talking—perhaps a bit like the tirade of a pregnant woman in the crisis of delivery, blaming her husband for wanting children. In the end, Job adjusts to his tragedy and returns to trusting God, even though God never explains the reason behind the suffering.

Sometimes suffering is God's punishment for sin: he punished Israel for worshiping idols by sending war, famine, and disease (Jeremiah 28:7). Sometimes suffering is to show God's power: Jesus healed a man born blind, explaining "because of his blindness, you will see God work a miracle" (John 9:3). Sometimes suffering is to strengthen our spiritual muscles, to make us stronger: "Suffering helps to endure. And endurance builds character, which gives us a hope that will never disappoint us" (Romans 5:3–4). Sometimes, however, suffering is because someone else's bad choice affects us.

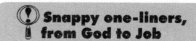

**Snappy one-liners, from Job to God**

"If God has something against me, let him speak up or put it in writing" (31:35).

"I ask you, God, why pick on me?" (14:3).

"You, God, are the reason I am insulted and spit on" (17:6).

In fairness to God, suffering wasn't part of his plan for creation. It entered the world as a side effect of the sinful choices people made. But sin and suffering aren't obstacles too big for God.

Like Job, we may be clueless about why we're suffering. But we can know this: "God is always at work for the good of everyone who loves him" (Romans 8:28). Whether we're suffering or not, God is on our side.

**Snappy one-liners, from God to Job**

"Did you ever tell the sun to rise?" (38:12).

"Did you teach hawks to fly south for the winter?" (39:26).

"Did you set in place the Big Dipper and the Little Dipper?" (38:32).

Job didn't seem to realize that, and it made his suffering harder to bear. We can learn from Job's mistake. Maybe that's why Job suffered: so his story could help us.

# Bible Scenarios You Can Use

### 1. Job loses his family, herds, and health (1:1—2:10)

In a conversation with Satan, God asks, "What do you think of my servant Job? No one on earth is like him—he is a truly good person, who respects me and refuses to do evil."

"Try taking away everything he owns," Satan replies, "and he will curse you to your face."

God accepts the challenge and allows Satan to unleash disasters on Job. Raiders steal Job's vast herds and kill his servants. A windstorm kills all ten of his children. And Job breaks out with festering skin sores.

Conventional wisdom of Job's day said people suffered because they sinned. Period. But Job's story says otherwise: sometimes the innocent suffer. You may never know why you suffer. Perhaps it's to strengthen your faith. Perhaps it's to show God's power, which is why a man that Jesus healed was born blind (John 9:3). Or maybe you suffer because of the effects of someone else's sin. Whatever the reason, God will see you through the suffering. He's also an expert at turning tragedy into blessing. Joseph got sold into slavery—a tragedy. But as a result, Joseph rose to second-in-command of Egypt, and was able to save the Egyptians as well as the Hebrews from a seven-year drought—a blessing.

### 2. Three friends come to comfort Job (2:11-13)

Three of Job's friends arrive. Job's tragedy is so horrifying that the three men sit speechless with him for seven days. Actually, that's probably the best thing they do for Job: sitting with him and keeping their mouths shut. For when they start talking, they accuse him of sinning, and insist that he won't find relief until he confesses.

"Only those who plant seeds of evil harvest trouble," says Eliphaz (4:8). Bildad advises Job to start living right (8:5). And in perhaps the most callous line of the book, Zophar tells the tormented Job who has lost nearly everything, "God has punished you less than you deserve" (11:6).

"Miserable comforters are you all!" Job replies (16:2, New King James Version).

When people are suffering, the last thing they need is criticism. You might as well sucker punch them. What they need is a friend who hurts with them, and who'll help them get through it.

## 3. Job takes his complaints to God (10:1–22)

**"D**on't just condemn me!" an angry Job tells God, "Point out my sin. Why do you take such delight in destroying those you created?"

After a long silence, God speaks, raising questions no human could answer. Questions like:

- "How did I lay the foundation for the earth?" (38:4).

- "Where is the home of light?" (38:19).

God's point is clear: there are some things that humans can't understand. And sometimes suffering is one of them.

Embarrassed, Job apologizes. "I have talked about things that are far beyond my understanding" (42:3). In time, Job raises ten more children and produces herds double the size he had before. He lives long enough to see his great-great-grandchildren.

When you're suffering, take your complaints to God. Don't be afraid of hurting his feelings. If you're mad at him, tell him so. Job did. But hang onto your past experiences with God, letting them remind you that he's with you—and even if he's all you have, he's enough.

# PSALMS

## Honest to God

Take a second. Think about the one concern at the top of your mind. Perhaps you fall asleep pondering it, or wake up to it. Maybe it's an unfulfilled desire, trouble in your marriage, or worries about your finances or your kids.

When have you talked with someone about it? Really talked. Using all the words and emotions necessary to express the depth of your concern.

If you're like many folks in our society, you haven't poured out your feelings to anyone lately—if ever. We specialize in casual conversation, brief exchanges, polite greetings, and goodbyes.

The poets of Psalms do what we wish we could do. In what has become the world's most expressive songbook and prayer manual—which was used in ancient Jewish worship services—poets shoot from the heart. They talk openly, honestly with God about the full range of life's sorrow and joy. Their words reflect anger, sadness, hope, and praise. Words such as these:

"Nothing they say is true! They just want to destroy" (5:9).

"Break my enemies' jaws and shatter their teeth" (3:7).

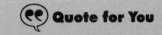 **Quote for You**

"I pray to you, Lord. . . . I tell you all of my worries and my troubles, and whenever I feel low, you are there to guide me" (142:1–3).

"Why are you far away, Lord? Why do you hide yourself when I am in trouble?" (10:1).

Right or wrong, the poets are honest to God about their feelings. Honesty is where help and healing begin. If we don't feel free to tell others about our deepest concerns, we can at least begin where the poets do, by telling God.

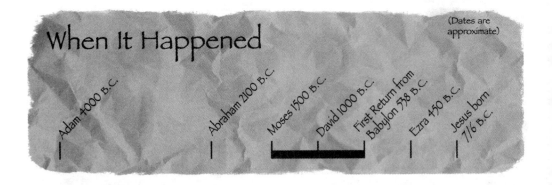

## When It Happened

(Dates are approximate)

Adam 4000 B.C.

Abraham 2100 B.C.

Moses 1500 B.C.

David 1000 B.C.

First Return from Babylon 538 B.C.

Ezra 450 B.C.

Jesus born 7/6 B.C.

# Info You Can Use

 ## Background Notes

**Writer:** There are 150 songs in this book, and scholars aren't sure who wrote any one of them. Seventy-three are described as being written "by David." But the original Hebrew phrase can also mean: "for David," "about David," or "dedicated to David." If David didn't write these songs, at least his life inspired them.

Other songs are attributed to Solomon, Moses, and Asaph, the chief musician during David's reign. Some songs are anonymous.

**Time:** No one knows exactly when the songs were written, but they seem to span almost a millennium. The oldest may have been written during the Exodus, in about 1440 B.C. The latest was written after the exile, when the Jews were banished to Babylon in 586 B.C. If David and Solomon wrote the songs attributed to them, they wrote them in roughly 1000 B.C.

**Place:** The songs are set throughout the ancient Middle East. The songs of David, Solomon, and Asaph take place in Israel—many of them in the capital city of Jerusalem. Psalm 90, attributed to Moses, may have been written in the Sinai Desert. Some songs were written during the exile in Babylon, in what is now Iraq.

**Bottom-Line Summary:** Psalms isn't a story to read. It's a collection of 150 masterfully crafted poems—songs and prayers set to music for God's people to sing and recite. There are traveling songs, for the Jews to sing as they walk to Jerusalem for religious festivals. There are songs for the king's coronation, for weddings, and for worship rituals at the temple. There are prayers praising God for his magnificent creation, asking for forgiveness, and pleading for healing. There are even prayers seeking revenge on enemies.

Surprisingly, the most common songs are complaints: poignant laments about sickness, loneliness, the feeling of being abandoned by God, the treachery of friends, and the threat of enemies.

But there are many songs of praise as well, which is why ancient Jews called the book *Tehillim,* meaning "praises."

## Influential People

**David,** the source or inspiration behind nearly half the 150 psalms. This fact illustrates that a single life devoted to God can influence and encourage more people than we can begin to count.

**Asaph,** a musician in charge of worship music during David's time. Twelve psalms are linked to him—perhaps written by him or in his style.

## Key Ideas You Need to Know

**Poems that repeat thoughts instead of sounds.** Hebrew poetry doesn't rhyme. Instead, it often uses a technique called parallelism. The poet makes a statement in one line, and then says it another way in the next line or two. Sometimes the parallel line simply restates the original line. Other times, the parallel line contrasts with the first line. An example of this:

> "The Lord protects everyone who follows him,
>     but the wicked follow a road that leads to ruin" (1:6).

Sometimes, instead of repeating or contrasting the ideas, the poet builds each line on the one before it. An example:

> "As a deer gets thirsty for streams of water,
>     I truly am thirsty for you, my God" (42:1).

Knowing about this technique can sometimes help us figure out what the writer is talking about. But if you don't know about the technique, the words can become confusing. One classic example is the prophet Zechariah's prediction of Jesus riding into Jerusalem on what could sound like two animals at once:

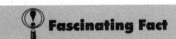

> "He is humble and rides on a donkey;
>     he comes on the colt of a donkey"
>     (Zechariah 9:9).

### Q&A

**Why songs of hatred?** Some of the psalms seem out of place in the Bible. Several call for violent revenge:

> ### Fascinating Fact
>
> "The Bug Bible," as it became known, was an early English version that earned its nickname because of its bizarre translation of one phrase in Psalms. Instead of assuring people that God would protect them from "dangers at night," it calmed them about "bugs by night" (91:5).

> "Babylon, you are doomed! I pray the Lord's blessings
>     on anyone who punishes you for what you did to us.
> May the Lord bless everyone
>     who beats your children against the rocks!" (137:8–9).
> "Rescue me from cruel and violent enemies, Lord!
> . . . Dump flaming coals on them and throw them into pits" (140:1, 10).

These don't sound like songs Jesus would sing. He said, "Love your enemies and pray for anyone who mistreats you" (Matthew 5:44).

Psalms, however, is brimming with the poetry of honest human emotion. It stands as a lasting reminder that it's okay to tell God how we feel, even when we haven't gotten over our hurt and anger. Admitting the pain is the first step to recovery. David, for example, urged God to show no mercy to his enemies. Yet David showed mercy to Saul, who tried to kill him, and to Absalom, who led a doomed coup.

There's another reason for these angry songs. In Old Testament times, cursing the enemy was more a plea for God to bring justice than a plea for personal revenge. It was an emotional prayer for God to stop the wrongs that were being done.

# Red Flag Issue

**Abortion.** Christians who strongly oppose abortion, and call it murder, often support their argument by quoting Psalm 139:13–16.

> "You made all the delicate, inner parts of my body
>      and knit me together in my mother's womb.
> . . . You watched me as I was being formed in utter seclusion,
>      as I was woven together in the dark of the womb.
> You saw me before I was born.
>      Every day of my life was recorded in your book" (New Living
>           Translation).

Other Christians say abortion is too complex to fit into the simple category of murder. Abortion involves more than pregnancies stopped because having the children is inconvenient. Abortion sometimes involves rape, incest, and kids having kids.

Psalm 139 isn't an essay about abortion, or about identifying the moment God put an eternal soul into a human body. If it were, it would need to address why in Exodus 21 the punishment for killing a woman is death, while the punishment for hurting a pregnant woman so badly that the unborn child dies is merely a fine. Psalm 139 is a song about God, thanking him for being involved in every detail of our life from beginning to end.

Christians are divided over the abortion issue. And there will probably never be a consensus on when it is that God puts a soul in a human body. That's because it's not clearly stated in the Bible. Some insist that life begins at conception, since the fetus holds within it all the potentiality that the person may become. Others suggest that if there is one moment when God generally slips a soul into the human form, maybe it's when we take our first breath—when God himself breathes into us: "God formed a man's body from the dust of the ground and breathed into it the breath of life. And the man became a living person" (Genesis 2:7, New Living Translation).

But these are just guesses.

What Christians can agree on is this: life is a sacred gift from God.

For most Christians, it seems wrong to stop a beating heart and all the potential that flows from it merely because it's the convenient thing to do. But to many, it also seems wrong to force a young teen to deliver the child of her rapist. There are no easy answers to this problem, which is why Christians are so sharply divided.

But if the issue rises in our own life, we can turn to God and ask him this question: What is the compassionate and loving thing to do? He will answer.

## To-Do List

- "I trust you, Lord, and I claim you as my God. My life is in your hands" (31:14–15).

- "I will praise you, Lord, with all my heart and tell about the wonders you have worked" (9:1).

- "Shout praises to the Lord. . . . Be joyful and sing as you come in to worship" (100:1–2).

# Bible Scenarios You Can Use

### 1. When you feel abandoned (13:1–6)

**T**he poet sings a sad and lonely song— one that, from time to time, has been our song.

> "How much longer, Lord, will you forget about me?
> Will it be forever? How long will you hide?
> How long must I be confused and miserable all day?
> How long will my enemies keep beating me down?
>
> Please listen, Lord God, and answer my prayers.
> Make my eyes sparkle again."

But the poet refuses to end in a minor key on a sour note. Instead, he remembers God's faithfulness in days past and anticipates more of the same in days ahead.

> "I trust your love, and I feel like celebrating because you rescued me.
> You have been good to me, Lord, and I will sing about you.

We can take our complaints to God—whatever they are. We needn't be concerned about hurting God's feelings. That's because his greatest concern is helping us. The ancient poet certainly understood this. If you're new to faith in God, learn from the testimony of people like this poet. When you walk with God long enough, you get to know and trust him. And you realize that even when it feels like God's nowhere to be found, you know he's working on your behalf. And you know—from his well-established track record in your life—that he's going to see you through your troubles.

## 2. The Lord is my shepherd (23:1–6)

In perhaps the most loved passage in all literature, the poet compares God to a gentle shepherd who tenderly cares for his sheep.

Recited hurriedly in times of life-or-death crisis, or read quietly at funerals, the message and cadence have a strangely calming, healing effect. After all these centuries, the words remain a powerful testimony of this single fact: we can depend on God in every situation—even when we stand face-to-face with death.

"The Lord is my shepherd
  I have everything I need.

He lets me rest in green meadows;
  he leads me beside peaceful streams.
  He renews my strength.
He guides me along right paths.
  bringing honor to his name.

Even when I walk
  through the dark valley of death
I will not be afraid,
  for you are close beside me.
Your rod and your staff
  protect and comfort me.

. . . Surely your goodness and unfailing love will pursue me
  all the days of my life,
and I will live in the house of the Lord
  forever" (New Living Translation).

## 3. A cry for forgiveness (51:1–19)

Adultery and murder are usually considered two of the worst sins on the planet. King David commits them both. He has an affair with Bathsheba, and she becomes pregnant. Then he murders her husband and marries Bathsheba to cover up his sin.

But sin isn't something we need to cover up—especially with another sin. It's something God needs to wash away. When David realizes this, he writes Psalm 51 as a way of seeking God's forgiveness. David's heartfelt plea touches all of us who have ever sinned, and it assures us that God's power to forgive is greater than the guilt we're living with.

"Have mercy on me, O God,
  because of your unfailing love.
Because of your great compassion,
  blot out the stain of my sins.

. . . Purify me from my sins, and I will be clean;
  wash me, and I will be whiter than snow.
Oh, give me back my joy again.

. . . Create in me a clean heart, O God.
  Renew a right spirit within me.

. . . Restore to me again the joy of your salvation,
  and make me willing to obey you.

. . . Forgive me for shedding blood, O God who saves;
  then I will joyfully sing of your forgiveness" (New Living Translation).

## 4. A time to cry (137:1-9)

**M**ost songs in Psalms aren't happy ones, praising God. When you divide the songs by category, the thickest stack is of songs sung blue—people in pain, crying out for God's help.

One of the most heartbreaking is about the Jews exiled in Babylon. Their nation has been destroyed and the survivors dragged away to this foreign country in what is now Iraq. The Jews, famous for their beautiful music, are asked to sing for their captors. But there's no music left in their hearts. This is the day the music died.

"Beside the rivers of Babylon we thought about Jerusalem,
  and we sat down and cried.
We hung our small harps on the willow trees.
Our enemies had brought us here as their prisoners,
  and now they wanted us to sing and entertain them.
They insulted us and shouted, 'Sing about Zion!'
Here in a foreign land,
How can we sing about the Lord?"

When the music dies in our life, we can bring our sorrow and grief to God. It's not just the therapeutic thing to do. God is the one person who can bring back the music.

## 5. God watches over us (139:1–24)

**A**s loving parents keep careful watch over their newborn, God watches over each one of us. That's the reassuring message of this song—we are precious in God's eyes. Some folks might not like us at all. We might not even like ourselves at times. But the one who knows us best loves us.

"You have looked deep into my heart, Lord,
    and you know all about me.
You know when I am resting or when I am
        working,
    and from heaven you discover my thoughts.

You notice everything I do and everywhere I go.
Before I even speak a word,
    you know what I will say,
And with your powerful arm
    you protect me from every side.

. . . Where could I go to escape
    from your Spirit or from your sight?
If I were to climb up to the highest heavens,
    you would be there."

## 6. How to praise God (150:1–6)

**F**or all God has done for them, the Jews praise God. Gathering in groups on the Sabbath or during religious holidays, they retell the stories of God's work in their lives, and they sing and dance to express their joy.

We, too, have stories to tell, songs to sing, and every reason to kick up our heels for joy.

"Shout praises to the Lord! Praise God in his
        temple.
    Praise him in heaven, his mighty fortress.
Praise our God!
    His deeds are wonderful, too marvelous to
        describe.

Praise God with trumpets and all kinds of harps.
Praise him with tambourines and dancing,
    with stringed instruments and woodwinds.
Praise God with cymbals, with clashing cymbals.
Let every living creature praise the Lord.
    Shout praises to the Lord!"

# PROVERBS

## Why Learn the Hard Way?

Imagine a high school or college class: "Advice from Your Elders."

Course description: "A panel of respected older adults in your community give you practical tips for living. Hundreds of life-tested insights about everyday experiences you face."

Wouldn't sell, would it?

We're not a people who take advice well—especially advice from old folks. We figure their advice doesn't apply to us—that it might have worked for their generation, but not for life in this decade. Whether or not we listen, older folks who love us keep talking. That's because they know that most of their advice is timeless. And they know that what they learned the hard way, we don't have to.

That's Proverbs—advice from wise and loving elders, packaged into snappy one-liners and two-liners for the quickly bored.

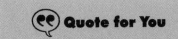 **Quote for You**

"Respect and obey the Lord! This is the beginning of knowledge. Only a fool rejects wisdom and good advice" (1:7).

The advice was intended for young men, but most of it applies to women as well.

Lots of great topics: How to handle seduction. What to do with spoiled kids. How to succeed in business. Etiquette at dinner meetings. The danger of co-signing loans. Learning to control your temper.

The writer who compiled the wise sayings promised a lot. "Proverbs will teach you wisdom and self-control," he says. "You will learn what is right and honest and fair. From these, an ordinary person can learn to be smart, and young people can gain knowledge and good sense" (1:2–4).

Or, we could learn the hard way.

When It Happened

(Dates are approximate)

Adam 4000+ B.C.  Abraham 2100 B.C.  Moses 1500 B.C.  David 1000 B.C.  Solomon 970 B.C.  Hezekiah 700 B.C.  Ezra 450 B.C.  Jesus born 7/6 B.C.

# Info You Can Use

 **Background Notes**

**Writer:** Solomon wrote most of it. He's the Israelite king about whom God said, "I'll make you wiser than anyone who has ever lived or ever will live" (1 Kings 3:12). Solomon wasn't just a king, he was a writer: "Solomon wrote three thousand wise sayings" (1 Kings 4:32).

Two otherwise unknown contributors to Proverbs are Agur (30:1) and a king named Lemuel (31:1), who said he was passing along his mother's advice. Additional proverbs come from a group of sages simply identified as "people with wisdom" (22:17). Sages served as consultants to kings and as teachers to young men, offering practical and philosophical advice.

**Time:** Solomon probably wrote his proverbs during his reign, from about 970–930 B.C. Writers working for King Hezekiah, about 250 years later, began compiling these proverbs (25:1). Other proverbs were probably added as the centuries went by, though the timeframe from which they came is unknown. Scholars guess that the work of collecting the Proverbs may have continued as late as the 300s B.C.

**Place:** Proverbs by Solomon would likely have been written in Jerusalem, the capital of Israel. Others could have come from anywhere in the Middle East. Similar collections of wise sayings have been discovered in Egypt and Iraq.

**Bottom-Line Summary:** Solomon and other wise men offer practical advice on a wide array of everyday issues, including family life, business, and spiritual matters. The purpose is to teach young people wisdom and discipline in all facets of life, so they'll learn right from wrong and common sense from nonsense.

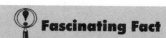 **Fascinating Fact**

Some of the wise sayings may have been adapted from other ancient writings, such as an Egyptian collection called "the Wisdom of Amenemope," a sage who taught sometime between 1200–1000 B.C.

For example, here's how the Bible's proverbs of a group of unnamed wise men begins:

"Don't take advantage of the poor
or cheat them in court" (22:22).

Here's how the Egyptian book begins:

"Do not steal from the poor nor cheat the cripple."

## Influential People

**Solomon,** described in the Bible as the wisest man who ever lived. His decision to write his proverbs serves as a reminder that God wants us to use our talents to help others.

## Key Ideas You Need to Know

**Don't read proverbs like promises.** Some of the proverbs sound like promises you can take to the bank, literally.

- "Giving to the poor will keep you from poverty" (28:27).

- "My teachings and instructions . . . will help you live a long and prosperous life" (3:1–2).

Yet good and generous people often die young and broke. The wise sayings of Proverbs don't offer full-proof promises. Instead, they merely lay out general principles based on the writer's observations over many years. And the main principle they're plugging is that people who live godly lives usually get along better with others and make fewer foolish choices that can hurt them.

For exceptions to the rule, you can scan the story of Job, a righteous man who suffered terribly through no fault of his own.

### Q&A

**Why do women get a bad rap in Proverbs?** This is a book for young men. The older men offering the advice know how susceptible young men are to lust. So they warn against it, using powerful images.

"Let's go there [to my bed] and make love all night," the sage quotes an immoral woman. "My husband is traveling."

How does the foolish young man handle the woman's invitation? "Right away he followed her like an ox on the way to be slaughtered" (7:18, 22).

Not all the words about women are negative. The sages advise the young men to remain faithful to their wives, and to praise them for their love and devotion.

### Red Flag Issue

**Drinking alcoholic beverages.** "Drinking makes a fool of you and leads to fights" (20:1). Bible verses like this, coupled with personal observation on the harm alcohol can do, has led many Christians to take a strong stand against alcohol. Some denominations order their members to abstain from liquor.

For 13 years, from 1920–1933 during Prohibition, liquor was outlawed in the United States. Evangelist Billy Sunday championed Prohibition by touring the country and promoting two replacement drinks: water and buttermilk.

### To-Do List

- "Trust in the Lord with all your heart; do not depend on your own understanding. Seek his will in all you do, and he will direct your paths" (3:5–6, New Living Translation).

- "Never tell lies or be deceitful in what you say" (4:24).

- "To have understanding, you must know the Holy God" (9:10).

- "It's stupid to say bad things about your neighbors. If you are sensible, you will keep quiet" (11:12).

- "Generosity will be rewarded: Give a cup of water, and you will receive a cup of water in return" (11:25).

- "Drawing straws is one way to settle a difficult case" (18:18).

- "If you do your job well, you will work for a ruler and never be a slave" (22:29).

- "Don't fail to correct your children. You won't kill them by being firm, and it may even save their lives" (23:13).

Some Christians refuse to drink liquor not because of what the Bible has to say about it, but because they've seen its power to wreck lives. They've seen people easily addicted, who aren't able to drink in moderation. And they've seen others party too hearty, and end up unintentionally drunk—hurting themselves and others.

Though many Christians refuse to drink liquor, others argue that liquor is okay if used in moderation. In fact, the Bible doesn't teach that drinking is sinful, only that abusive drinking is hazardous. Wine was the most popular drink in the ancient Middle East because it was safer than the water. Apostle Paul once advised a friend, "Stop drinking only water. Take a little wine to help your stomach trouble" (1 Timothy 5:23). Jesus' first recorded miracle was to turn water into wine during a wedding feast.

The wine in Bible times, however, was low in alcohol and was often diluted. Its punch was nothing close to the wallop from distilled liquors available today.

## For the Record: Proverbs Abused

**Spanking children.** "He who spares the rod hates his son, but he who loves him is careful to discipline him" (13:24, New International Version). This single verse, perhaps more than any other in the Bible, has made some parents feel they not only have a right to beat disobedient children—but that they have God's command to do it.

A rod is a stick shepherds use to beat off attacking critters, not to club the sheep under their care. When a sheep strayed in the wrong direction, the shepherd used a rod or a staff (which was longer) to gently nudge the sheep back.

The reason parents are supposed to discipline children is to teach them right from wrong—a lesson of love, intended to help them. Next time you see a parent spanking a child, look in the parent's eyes. Do you see love? Or do you see anger?

# Bible Scenarios You Can Use

## 1. Stay away from bad company (1:10–19)

In a collection of practical advice targeted especially to young men, the life-savvy sage offers a piece of advice that parents throughout the ages have been giving their children: steer clear of any kid whose middle name is Trouble. It's one thing to help out troubled people, but it's quite another to hang out with them and open yourself up to the same temptations that turned them bad. If they want to change, help them. If they want to change you, stay away.

> "Don't be tempted by sinners or listen when they say,
>    'Come on! Let's gang up and kill somebody,
>       just for the fun of it!
>    They're well and healthy now,
>       but we'll finish them off once and for all.
>    We'll take their valuables
>       and fill our homes with stolen goods.
>    If you join our gang, you'll get your share.'"

## 2. Stay faithful to your wife (5:1–23)

The sage knows that sexual excitement in marriage can dry up a bit, and that it's tempting for men to quench their thirst for sexual pleasure with another partner. But it's a horrible idea, the sage says. "Drink water from your own well—share your love only with your wife."

The sage adds the following advice about women who would try to sweet-talk you into adultery. His advice applies equally to sweet-talking men.

> "The words of an immoral woman may be as sweet as honey
>    and as smooth as olive oil.
> But all that you really get from being with her is bitter poison and pain.
>
> Save yourself for your wife
>    and don't have sex with other women."

## 3. Don't co-sign a loan (11:15; 6:1–5)

**M**oney, like sex, causes a heaping helping of trouble in people's lives. That's why Proverbs is full of advice about money matters. In these short verses, the sage doesn't advise against generosity, but against jumping in over your head in debt—especially the debt of someone else, whose credit may be so damaged or such an unknown commodity that they can't get a loan.

"It's a dangerous thing
   to guarantee payment for someone's debts.
   Don't do it."
"My child, suppose you agree to pay the debt of someone,
   who cannot repay a loan.
Then you are trapped by your own words,
   and you are now in the power of someone else.
Here is what you should do:
   Go and beg for permission to call off the agreement."

## 4. Honesty is the best policy (11:1–3)

**I**n the short run, lying and cheating might seem like a fine idea. They certainly can generate a quick buck. But life is a marathon. Most of us hope to be around for a while.

If we earn for ourselves the reputation of a crook, we'll eventually get fewer takers and a whole lot of leavers. But if we earn for ourselves the reputation of an honest person, we'll usually do quite well because on this planet there's a shortage of honest folks—so they're in demand.

"If you do the right thing, honesty will be
      your guide.
   But if you are crooked,
      you will be trapped by your own dishonesty."

## 5. Teach your kids right from wrong (22:6)

**T**he proverb sounds like a promise:

"Teach your children right from wrong,
　　and when they are grown they will still do right."

But it's not a guarantee. Instead, it's an observation from a lifetime of experience. In general, children who are taught to do the right thing will grow into adults who do the right thing. But as long as people have the freedom to make their own choices, some will choose unwisely—even tragically.

If you're a parent whose grown child chooses badly, skip the blame. God doesn't blame himself when we—his children—do wrong. Instead, he reaches out in love and offers help. You can do the same with your child.

## 6. Don't be lazy (24:30–34)

**T**he sage has no patience for lazy people. He would certainly have said "Amen" had he lived long enough to hear the apostle Paul suggest this as a rule to live by: "If you don't work, you don't eat" (2 Thessalonians 3:10).

Exempt are those who can't work, and who deserve our compassion and help (Proverbs 19:17). The lazy are those who can work, but won't. People like this man, observed by the sage:

"I once walked by the field and the vineyard of a lazy fool.
Thorns and weeds were everywhere,
　　and the stone wall had fallen down.
When I saw this, it taught me a lesson:
Sleep a little. Doze a little.
　　Fold your hands and twiddle your thumbs.
Suddenly poverty hits you and everything is gone!"

## 7. Don't gossip (26:20–22)

**"T**here is nothing so delicious as the taste
　　of gossip!
　　It melts in your mouth."

That's the sage talking. Sounds like he has chewed on a morsel of gossip once or twice in his life. We all have. We human beings are naturally curious, and we love a good story. But when fact becomes fiction or when unimportant minutia get blown out of proportion and these stories get passed on, wildfires break out and people get hurt.

"When there is no fuel a fire goes out;
　　where there is no gossip arguments come to an end."

That's the sage's advice. Don't pass gossip on to another. Cut the fuel line and let the fire die.

## 8. Don't nag (27:15–16)

"The steady dripping of rain and the
        nagging of a wife
    are one and the same.
It's easier to catch the wind or hold olive oil in your
        hand
    than to stop a nagging wife."

The sage targets women, but we know better. Men nag, too.

We nag when we think we're not getting through to someone—that they don't agree with us or that they're tuning us out.

Nagging might work for a while, but its effectiveness quickly wears off. And even when it is effective, it's torment—like the Chinese water torture test. Drip. Drip. Drip. Nag. Nag. Nag. It's not healthy.

If you're a nag, explore other ways of getting your point across. Let the person experience the consequences you've been warning them about. Try a polite and loving talk about the underlying problem. Or contact a counselor—it's not a sin.

## 9. Treasure your wife (31:10–31)

In Proverbs, a woman gets the last word. She's the mother of a king, and she paints for her son a picture of the ideal wife. Oddly—especially in our culture, where looks are so important—there's not a hint of how she looks. The portrait is of a woman's single most important trait: her character.

"A truly good wife is the most precious treasure
    a man can find.
Her husband depends on her,
    and she never lets him down.
She takes good care of her family and is never
    lazy.
Her children praise her,
    and with great pride her husband says,
'There are many good women, but you are the best!'"

Of all the sages represented in Proverbs, Mother knows best. Treat your good wife like the treasure she is.

# ECCLESIASTES

## When You Can't Find Meaning in Life

Call it a mid-life crisis if you like, though it can also hit you as a young adult or an older adult. It's a stage of disappointed reflection when you look over your shoulder at where you've been and what you've done with your life, and you don't like what you see. Worse, as you turn your gaze ahead, you see more of the same. And in that moment of awareness, your spirit sinks.

"Nothing makes sense!" complains the writer of Ecclesiastes, who is thought to be the wise King Solomon. "What is there to show for all of our hard work?" (1:2–3).

Solomon, however, didn't seem to be focusing just on his own personal crisis. He broadened the crisis to all of humanity. As far as he could tell, the human race makes no difference. "People come, and people go, but still the world never changes" (1:4).

Being a wise man, Solomon sets out to analyze the affects of humanity on creation, in an attempt to understand why humans exist. His mental experiment is a bust. He can't figure out why we're here. We make no lasting difference. We may tweak the landscape, but with or without us, the sun keeps rising and the rivers keep flowing. Furthermore, all our endeavors are "as senseless as chasing the wind" (1:14).

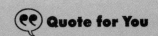 **Quote for You**

"Everything you were taught can be put into a few words: Respect and obey God! This is what life is all about" (12:13).

Though Solomon finds no answer to the question he's asking, he reaches a conclusion. Life is God's gift to us. We should enjoy the gift, and show our gratitude to the Giver.

When It Happened

(Dates are approximate)

Adam 4000+ B.C.

Abraham 2100 B.C.

Moses 1500 B.C.

David 1000 B.C.
Solomon 970 B.C.

Ezra 450 B.C.

Jesus born 7/6 B.C.

# Info You Can Use

## Background Notes

**Writer:** Solomon seems to be the writer, though many scholars doubt this. There are plenty of clues that point to Solomon. The writer identifies himself as:

- "the son of David"

- "king in Jerusalem"

- "known to be very wise"

- recipient of "silver, gold, and precious treasures" from foreign rulers

- having "many wives" (Solomon had a thousand).

But many Bible experts say the style of the Hebrew words—some that seem borrowed from Persia—suggests the book was written many centuries after Solomon, perhaps as late as 300 B.C. That could mean Solomon's work was revised for later Hebrews, the way we revised English Bible translations from the days of King James. Or it could mean someone else wrote it, approaching the perplexing issue in the spirit of wise King Solomon, and in tribute to him.

One clue that someone else wrote it, or at least added to it, is that the writer blames the king for overtaxing the poor (5:8–9).

> ### Fascinating Fact
>
> "Ecclesiastes" comes from the word the writer uses to identify himself. In English, the word is "teacher." But in Greek, it's *ekklesiastes*.

**Time:** If Solomon wrote it, he did so during his 40-year reign that started in about 970 B.C. Whenever it was written, Ecclesiastes became respected as an important Jewish work by 150 B.C. We know this because fragments of the book from that date were found among the Dead Sea scrolls, about 14 miles from Jerusalem.

**Place:** If Solomon wrote the book, he probably did so at his palace in Jerusalem, the capital of Israel.

**Bottom-Line Summary:** The writer performs an experiment in logic to search for meaning in life. His findings are depressing. He concludes that everything humans do is meaningless. Our attempts to become wise get sidetracked by foolishness. Our ambitious work isn't worth the trouble, since nothing we do will last. Our wealth does little more than make us lose sleep at night—and besides, we can't take it with us. When we're gone, someone else will spend it.

Despite the writer's pessimism, he points us to God. "How can anyone explain what God does?" (11:5), he asks. His implication is that though we can't find the meaning to life, we should find consolation in the fact that God is the source of life. "After all, he created everything."

The writer ends his experiment with the advice that we accept and enjoy life as God's unexplainable gift to us.

# Influential People

**Solomon,** wisest and richest king of Israel, and traditionally considered the writer of Ecclesiastes. His candid struggles with doubt, disillusionment, and despair reveal that such struggles are natural and that they don't inevitably drive us away from God. In fact, an honest search for truth leads to God.

# Key Ideas You Need to Know

**God gives meaning to life.** Solomon—described in the Bible as the wisest man who would ever live—wants to know why humans exist. So he puts his gifted mind to work on a solution. He finds that our every endeavor "under the sun" is meaningless. Bible experts debate what that phrase means, but many say that in the context of Solomon's conclusion, the phrase is another way of saying "all human endeavor apart from God."

We can build great cities, but sand will one day cover them. We can live a long time and stockpile a fortune, but we'll eventually die and leave our pile of money behind. We can go to the best schools and make ourselves smart, but the same thing that happens to fools will happen to us: we'll die and people will forget us. (Point in fact: Scholars aren't even sure who wrote this book.)

Apart from God, that's the best we could expect of life. Fortunately, we're not apart from God. He's the reason for the season of life. He invented life, and gave it to us. We honor him by enjoying that gift—even if what we enjoy about it is building things that won't last, making money that we'll leave for others, or getting smart enough to know how ignorant we really are.

## To-Do List

- "The best thing we can do is to always enjoy life, because God's gift to us is the happiness we get from our food and drink and from the work we do" (3:12).

- "Do what you want and find pleasure in what you see. But don't forget that God will judge you for everything you do" (11:9).

# Bible Scenarios You Can Use

## 1. What difference does our life make? [1:1–18]

**A**pparently late in his life, Solomon looks over his shoulder at all he has seen and done. He's unimpressed—even though his reign will be considered the most prosperous in Israel's history. He may have built Jerusalem's magnificent temple and fortress cities throughout his nation. He may have opened up lucrative international trade relations. And he may have organized Israel into a well-run country. But that's not enough to satisfy him.

Solomon knows nothing will last forever. In fact, invaders would eventually tear down his temple. Trade agreements would fall apart. Israel would split, and then disappear from the world map.

"I have seen it all—nothing makes sense!
What is there to show for all of our hard work
here on earth?
People come, and people go,
but still the world never changes."

It's easy to feel discouraged and unfulfilled. Solomon had wealth, fame, and power. Yet even he grew discouraged. That's because an enduring sense of worth doesn't come from what we're able to accomplish. It comes from who we are: children of God, cherished by him.

## 2. Life goes on (3:1–22)

"**E**verything on earth has its own time and
its own season.
There is a time for birth and death,
planting and reaping,
for killing and healing, destroying and
building,
for crying and laughing, weeping and
dancing,
for throwing stones and gathering
stones,
embracing and parting."

God's in control of the life cycle. Everything in the human experience has its appointed time. That includes the big moments of birth and death, as well as the mundane moments of picking crops and collecting stones to build a wall. These kinds of experiences are inevitable for all of us, in due time. Nothing we can do can change it.

Rather than complaining about it and resisting the season of life that's upon us, Solomon implies that we should work on accepting it as a fact of life—and trust God as our scheduler: "God makes everything happen at the right time."

## 3. Wealth won't make you happy (5:10–20)

**M**oney doesn't satisfy us, says King Solomon. He ought to know. "He was the richest and wisest king in the world" (1 Kings 10:23).

"People get rich, but it does them no good," Solomon explains. "If you love money and wealth, you will never be satisfied with what you have." The king adds that at least the poor folks who work hard for a living get a good night's sleep because of their weariness. "But if you are rich, you can't even sleep. . . . Besides all this, they are always gloomy at mealtime, and they are troubled, sick, and bitter."

We come into the world naked, Solomon says, and we leave just as naked. We take nothing with us. So the king advises us not to target money as our goal. Instead, "enjoy working hard—this is God's gift to you."

## 4. Life is short, so enjoy it while you can (9:7–9; 12:13)

**S**olomon knows luxury. His annual income is about 25 tons of gold (1 Kings 10:14). He has so much gold that during his reign, "silver was almost worthless" (1 Kings 10:21). Yet he concludes that it's the simple things in life that matter most.

"Enjoy eating and drinking," he says. "Life is short, and you love your wife, so enjoy being with her. This is what you are supposed to do as you struggle through life on this earth."

After searching for a rational explanation about why humans exist—and coming up empty—Solomon offers this suggestion. "Here is my final conclusion: Fear God and obey his commands, for this is the duty of every person."

Life remains an unfolding mystery. We may not know exactly what God plans for our life, or when the seasons of crying and laughing will come. But we can trust in the one who does. And we can enjoy the gift of life he has given us.

# SONG OF SONGS

## Spicing Up Your Love Life

This poem is about sex.

If that makes you feel uncomfortable, you're in great company. Some of the finest minds in early Jewish history tried to convince folks that the poem was a kind of parable about God's love for Israel. Early Christians said it symbolized Christ's love for the church.

Imagine, however, God saying this to Israel, or Jesus saying this to the church: "My darling, you are perfume between my breasts" (1:13).

Doesn't work, does it?

This is a poem about sex, as most modern scholars agree. But the poem isn't just about the physical act of sex—though it certainly gets physical. It's about the kind of sex we're not used to seeing portrayed in the movies: sanctified sex, as God intended it—sincere, expressive, committed, and fun.

You've got a woman and a man in love, graphically praising the physical features of each other and revealing their shared fantasy about making love. Their words aren't crude or vulgar, but they are unashamedly sensual and intimate.

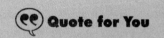 **Quote for You**

"I am my beloved's" (7:10, King James Version).

This isn't a peep show. It's a portrait of true love. It's a stunning reminder that love feeds on tender words of endearment, whether poetic or plain, and that it blossoms into sexual intimacy uniting two people, body and soul.

When It Happened

(Dates are approximate)

Adam 4000+ B.C.  Abraham 2100 B.C.  Moses 1500 B.C.  David 1000 B.C.  Solomon 970 B.C.  Ezra 450 B.C.  Jesus born 7/6 B.C.

# Info You Can Use

## Background Notes

**Writer:** At first glance, it looks like Solomon wrote it. But we can't be so sure. "This is Solomon's most beautiful song" (1:1). So begins the poem. That's why the book is sometimes called the Song of Solomon. King Solomon did write over a thousand songs (1 Kings 4:32), and since this is said to be his best one, it's sometimes called the Song of Songs, in the manner that Jesus is called the King of kings. But it's possible Solomon didn't write this poem at all.

The Hebrew phrase that attributes the song to Solomon can mean it was written by him, for him, about him, or dedicated to him.

It's quite possible the poem was originally a wedding song written by a professional musician to entertain King Solomon during one of his thousand weddings. Or perhaps it was a song popular at many weddings, just as certain love songs are popular at weddings today.

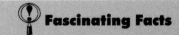

Rabbis in ancient times didn't allow Jews to read Solomon's erotic song until they reached age 30.

Like Esther, this book never once mentions God or religion. Yet it praises two of God's greatest gifts to humanity: love and sexuality.

**Time:** The setting for the love story is uncertain. If Solomon wrote it, or if it was about him and one of his wives, the story probably took place during his 40-year reign, from 970 to 930 B.C.

**Place:** The setting is Israel, perhaps in the capital city of Jerusalem. One clue is that the bride has a series of conversations with her friends, "young women of Jerusalem." Also, the bride and groom occasionally refer to Israelite landmarks. The woman describes her love as "flower blossoms from the gardens of En-Gedi," an oasis south of Jerusalem. And the man says of his bride, "Your head is held high like Mount Carmel."

**Bottom-Line Summary:** This is a passionate, erotic celebration of love between a man and a woman. Neither the man nor the woman feels the least bit inhibited about expressing their most intimate feelings and sexual desires. And express them they do.

Bible experts can't agree on the story line that drives the poem. There's not enough background in the dialogue to set the scene. There's lots of talk about ravenous desire, alluring body parts, and scented love nests. But there's nothing definite about who these lovers are and what they do for a living.

Scholars suggest a variety of possible story lines. Here are three of the most popular:

- King Solomon chooses a country girl for his bride, but she turns him down in favor of her country lover.

- Solomon and the country lover are the same person, loved by the country girl.

- The country lover is the only man in the story, and when he comes to his lady, she thinks of him as the glorious "King Solomon carried on a throne" (3:7)—a kind of knight in shining armor.

## Influential People

**An unnamed woman,** from the countryside of Israel. Without a hint of embarrassment, she praises the physical features of her husband and offers her body for his pleasure. She also asks for his faithfulness, a reminder that love requires devotion for its survival.

**An unnamed man,** the woman's true love. He matches the woman compliment for compliment, desire for desire. His words are an encouragement to husbands who hesitate to tell their wives how much they love them.

## Key Ideas You Need to Know

**Love talk.** Sparks of romance shower every chapter in this book. The couple in love are constantly praising each other and speaking of their desire to make love. Granted, these are newlyweds. So we expect love talk. Yet, their story is for everyone in love. It's a reminder that all of us want and need to hear that we are loved. Husbands and wives may express their love for each other by doing their share of the chores needed to keep the family afloat, and through unexpected acts of affection: a surprise gift, or a weekend date. But words say it best. "I love you." "You have brought joy to my life."

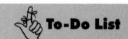 **To-Do List**

- "Always keep me in your heart and wear this bracelet to remember me by" (8:6). *As we wear a wedding band to remind us of our spouse, the woman in this song asks her husband to always think of her.*

We may not be a poet, but what poet could compete with a simple and sincere "I love you" exchanged between two people who mean it?

## Q&A

**Are the lovers married?** By the time they have sex they are. However, the poem never uses the word "husband" or "wife." The poet prefers "lover." Other favorites are "darling," "dearest," and "my love." In our day—as in many ancient cultures—"lover" could refer to an unmarried couple who have intimate relations. But that's not the case in ancient Hebrew culture. For Jews in Bible times, sex outside of marriage is considered sin.

# Bible Scenarios You Can Use

### 1. True love is sweeter than wine (1:1–17)

**"K**iss me again and again, for your love is sweeter than wine," says a beautiful young farm girl to the man in her life (New Living Translation).

Without shame or embarrassment, the man matches her endearing passion. "My darling," he replies, "you are lovely, so very lovely—your eyes are those of a dove."

"My love," the woman answers, "you are handsome, truly handsome—the fresh green grass will be our wedding bed in the shade of cedar and cypress trees."

Though this exchange may have been only a wedding song to entertain a bride and groom and their guests, it conveys an important message about the facts of life. If you want to keep the sparks of romance alive, express your love in tender words. It's fine to give flowers, cards, and candy (sugar-free if your beloved is diabetic). But they're no substitute for your own words, spoken heart to heart, expressing your love and sexual desire.

## 2. Passionate pillow talk (4:1–16; 7:1–13)

**A**fter the wedding, the bride and groom boldly and passionately praise each other's body, and express their shared desire to make love. The man speaks first, praising his wife's eyes, hair, teeth, lips, mouth, and neck. Then he tells her how beautiful her breasts are, declaring, "I will hasten to those hills sprinkled with sweet perfume and stay there till sunrise."

"Let the north wind blow, the south wind too!" his wife replies. "Let them spread the aroma of my garden, so the one I love may enter and taste its delicious fruits."

She then praises his body, from his raven hair to his strong legs and feet.

He answers, "You are tall and slender like a palm tree, and your breasts are full. I will climb that tree and cling to its branches. I will discover that your breasts are clusters of grapes and that your breath is the aroma of apples. Kissing you is more delicious than drinking the finest wine. How wonderful and tasty!"

"My darling," she replies, "I am yours."

Merely reading the words can become intoxicating. Imagine the power they would have when spoken by the one you love. Most of us aren't poets, so we can't express our love nearly as creatively and erotically as the person who wrote this song. But the feelings of love and desire are there. And we nurture those feelings by talking about them and acting on them. A husband doesn't need fancy poetry to tell his wife she's a beautiful human being, that he loves her, and that he enjoys the time he spends in her arms. Nor does a wife need a thesaurus to praise her husband, speak of her love, and invite him to bed.

Sexuality is a gift from God for us to enjoy. But it's not a gift we can enjoy to its fullest if it's just a physical act, apart from intimate and heartfelt words shared.

## 3. Love is powerful and priceless (8:6–7)

**I**t's the woman who delivers the song's most passionate moment. It's a moment beyond sex, for it speaks of commitment and of the power and price of love. This woman isn't just beautiful and romantic; she's got the wisdom to match.

"Always keep me in your heart and wear this bracelet to remember me by," she says. "The passion of love bursting into flame is more powerful than death, stronger than the grave. Love cannot be drowned by oceans or floods; it cannot be bought, no matter what is offered."

Love can, however, die of neglect. Don't let it. Nurture it with honest words and gentle caresses.

# ISAIAH

## God Would Rather Forgive

God doesn't like to punish. He has a long history of trying to avoid punishing people.

If you have children you dearly love, you know how much it hurts you when you have to punish them. You want them to be happy. But even more than that, you want them to be safe and to learn how to make wise decisions. So you warn them. And when they ignore your warnings and put themselves in danger or make bad choices, you punish them in an attempt to steer them back toward safety and wisdom.

The prophet Isaiah is an example of God's warning to the Israelites. By the time Isaiah began his ministry, the Israelites had been in the promised land of Israel for about 700 years. Most of that time, they'd been breaking God's most basic laws. They worshiped idols, took part in pagan sex rituals, abused the poor, and shelved the Ten Commandments. They were in breach of their contract to obey God in return for the promised land and protection.

The contract itself, preserved near the close of Deuteronomy, stipulates that if the

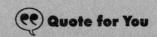 **Quote for You**

"I, the Lord, invite you to come and talk it over. Your sins are scarlet red, but they will be whiter than snow" (1:18).

Hebrews broke their agreement, they would lose their land and be scattered abroad. God tried to remind them. He even sent lesser punishments to get their attention: plagues, famines, and bully empires who demanded high taxes. Finally, God "sent prophets who warned them to turn back to him. The people refused to listen" (2 Chronicles 24:19).

Enter Isaiah. His message was as blunt and clear as a parent's emotional warning to a rebellious teenager. Unfortunately, it was just as futile. But it wasn't worthless. As teens grow up and come to their senses, they remember their parent's warnings as evidence of loving concern. Israel will do the same. But first they'll suffer. It's their choice, not God's.

## When It Happened

(Dates are approximate)

Adam 4000+ B.C. | Abraham 2100 B.C. | Moses 1500 B.C. | David 1000 B.C. | Fall of Israel 722 B.C. | Fall of Judah 586 B.C. | Ezra 450 B.C. | Jesus born 7/6 B.C.

# Info You Can Use

## Background Notes

**Writer:** "I am Isaiah, the son of Amoz," the book begins. Ancient Jewish tradition says the prophet Isaiah wrote the entire book. But many scholars today doubt it. The reason is that the book covers material well past Isaiah's lifetime—more than a century beyond.

The book has 66 chapters. The first 39 are from Isaiah's day, in the 700s B.C. But chapters 40–55 seem set in Babylon, when the Jews were exiled there about 100 years after Isaiah died. And chapters 56–66 seem set in Israel again, after the Jews returned home and started rebuilding the country. Many scholars say one or two people who lived during those later times probably wrote the last two sections.

Others argue that Isaiah probably wrote the entire book, predicting the future in chapters 40 and beyond. In fact, the oldest copy of Isaiah—a scroll written in about 100 B.C. and found among the famous Dead Sea Scrolls—shows no break between chapters 39 and 40. This suggests the book was considered a single work by a single writer.

**Time:** The prophecy spans about 200 years of Israel's Old Testament history, not counting Isaiah's prophecies believed to refer to Jesus, who came 700 years later.

The ministry of Isaiah started in about 740 B.C. and spanned at least the last four decades of that century and perhaps beyond. His ministry outlasted four kings: Uzziah, Jotham, Ahaz, and Hezekiah.

The prophet apparently lived another 20 years, because he mentioned the assassination of Assyrian King Sennacherib, who was murdered by his sons in 681 B.C.

How and when Isaiah died isn't reported in the Bible. But Jewish tradition says he was sawn in half at the order of Hezekiah's son and successor, Manasseh, who reigned from 696 to 642 B.C.

**Place:** Isaiah lived and ministered in the southern Israelite nation of Judah, and probably stayed in the capital city of Jerusalem. The setting changes to Babylon later in the book, when the prophecies speak about the people being exiled there.

**Bottom-Line Summary:** A young man named Isaiah has a dramatic vision of God seated on heaven's throne, surrounded by angelic beings. There, God commissions Isaiah to become a prophet. Isaiah's job is to deliver God's messages to the Israelites. Most of his messages are warnings to stop sinning or suffer the consequences: invasion and national annihilation.

This is a critical time in Middle Eastern history. It's the closing half of the 700s B.C., when Assyria has emerged as the strongest power in the region.

By 722 B.C., Assyria wipes the northern Israelite nation off the map, scattering the survivors abroad—never to return or restore their nation. Isaiah lives in the southern Israelite nation of Judah, which is one of many small nations that do as they are told by the Assyrians—including paying heavy taxes. Isaiah says the fall of the northern nation of Israel should serve as a spiritual wake-up call for the Judeans, who are in danger of suffering a similar fate.

Isaiah predicts the inevitable fall of the southern nation, which comes at the hands of Babylonian invaders in 586 B.C. But Isaiah also predicts that God won't punish the Jews forever, but will return them to their homeland. In addition, Isaiah predicts what appear to be parallel events on a massive and global scale: God will punish the entire world, and then make a new creation for the people who have been faithful. These prophecies sound a lot like the New Testament promises of the end times.

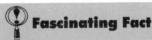

**Fascinating Fact**

In a graphic object lesson, Isaiah goes naked for three years to show that Egyptians rebelling against Assyria will be stripped and led away as slaves. Isaiah warns the Jews not to join Egypt in the revolt (20:1–6).

## Influential People

**Isaiah,** a young man who volunteers to serve God in the thankless job of delivering an unpopular message: repent, or else. His story is a reminder that we need to speak out against sin and try to help move our nation toward godly principles.

**Hezekiah,** a Judean king who seeks God's help in times of need, whether it's personal health concerns or a national crisis. That's an example God wants us to follow.

## Key Ideas You Need to Know

**God's holiness.** God is absolute goodness, with no trace of sin. Humans, on the other hand, live in a world that makes it nearly impossible to avoid sinning. Even Isaiah, considered one of Israel's greatest prophets, feels thoroughly sinful when he stands before God's throne in a vision. "My destruction is sealed," he says, "for I am a sinful man and a member of a sinful race. Yet I have seen the King, the Lord Almighty!" (6:5, New Living Translation).

If religion were science, he'd be describing something similar to a meeting between matter and anti-matter, which can't co-exist.

God sets Isaiah's mind at ease by saying, "Your sins are forgiven and you are no longer guilty" (6:7).

On this planet, we can't hope to be as perfect as God intended us to be when he created the human race in his image. But he can forgive us of our sins, cleanse away our guilt, and set us at ease in his presence. Until we ask him to do that for us, however, we'll treat him the way Adam and Eve did after they committed the world's first sin by eating the forbidden fruit—as someone to avoid.

**Punishment for sin.** God is patient. But sooner or later, he punishes people for their sins. That's the prevailing theme in Isaiah because that's the main problem in ancient Israel. Like people today who charge up their credit cards with no thought of the coming bill, the people of Isaiah's day sin with no regard to the results. Isaiah simply says, "The bill is coming."

His point is that the people had better file for spiritual bankruptcy, clean their slate, and start doing business the right way. In other words, they should ask God to forgive them and live the rest of their lives as spiritually responsible people.

**A deliverer is coming.** God promises that he won't abandon his people to their sins. He is sending a deliverer, a messiah, who will come and set up a kingdom and rule with righteousness and justice. Jesus later claims to fulfill these prophecies, but explains that his kingdom is not of this world. It's of the world to come.

## Q&A

**What's a prophet?** A prophet is a person who receives God's messages—often through dreams, visions, or spoken words—and delivers them in person or in writing.

Priests, on the other hand, took messages in the opposite direction: from the people to God. Priests delivered the people's requests to God in prayer and led the community in worship rituals. Unlike priests, prophets didn't inherit their assignments. God personally selected prophets—and included women among them, such as Miriam (sister of Moses) and Deborah (one of Israel's famous judges).

> ## 👉 To-Do List
>
> - "See that justice is done. Defend widows and orphans and help those in need" (1:16).
>
> - "Our Lord . . . because of your wonderful deeds we will sing your praises everywhere on earth" (12:4–5).
>
> - "I chose you to bring justice . . . I selected and sent you to bring light and my promise of hope to the nations" (42:6). *From the Suffering Servant chapter. Many Jews say these words describe their mission. Many Christians, however, say these words point to the mission of Jesus and his followers. In either case, God's desire for the world is justice, spiritual enlightenment, and hope.*
>
> - "Don't be discouraged when others insult you and say hurtful things" (51:7).

There were a lot of false prophets. And since anyone could claim to be a prophet, it could be hard to tell the genuine from the fake.

After the exile, prophets seemed to fade from the scene, perhaps because priests were able to deliver God's message revealed in Scriptures. The New Testament lists prophecy among the spiritual gifts, but as in Old Testament times, prophecy faded as Scripture became more available.

The recurring message of the prophets was that the Israelites had broken their agreement with God and that if they didn't repent, God would punish them—as the agreement permitted. Israel's main sins, according to the prophets, included worshiping idols, immorality (often sex rituals associated with pagan worship), and oppressing the poor.

**Why don't Jews see the connection between Jesus and Isaiah's prophecies?**
New Testament writers clearly saw Jesus in the prophecies of Isaiah. In fact, so
did Jesus. When he announced the beginning of his ministry, he did so by reading
from Isaiah 61 and proclaiming, "What you have just heard me read has come
true today" (Luke 4:21).

Many Jewish people, however, say the promised messiah hasn't come yet.
When he does, they argue, he will rule the world in heavenly peace: "Leopards
will lie down with young goats, and wolves will rest with lambs" (11:6). Many
Christians suggest that these prophecies will be fulfilled with Christ's Second
Coming.

**Why wouldn't God forgive the people?** "I won't forgive them for this," God
says of the rebellious Jews, "not as long as they live" (22:14). This wasn't because
the Jews had committed some mysterious, unpardonable sin. It's because they
wouldn't repent. No repentance, no forgiveness.

If God forgave them without requiring them to repent and stop their serial
sinning, he would have been condoning their behavior.

**Why did God change his mind and heal Hezekiah?** The Bible doesn't say.
What it does say is that God told Isaiah to tell the sick king that he wouldn't
recover, so he'd better get his affairs in order (38:1). The king prayed and wept,
and God said, "I will let you live 15 years more" (38:6).

Some theologians say it's impossible for God, who knows everything, to
change his mind. Instead, they claim he intended to heal Hezekiah all along. If
so, it would appear God is a liar who misled Hezekiah. Other theologians say
Hezekiah's prayer didn't change God, who is Goodness perfected. But, instead, it
somehow changed Hezekiah. So, God changed his plans for the king accordingly.

It's a mystery how prayers like Hezekiah's work. But this much is clear:
prayer changes things. It added 15 years to Hezekiah's life. It spared the people
of Nineveh from destruction (Jonah 3:10). And it kept God from destroying the
Israelites of the Exodus after they worshiped a golden calf (Exodus 39:9–14).

**Does God hear the prayers of sinners?** "Your sins have cut you off from
God. Because of your sin, he has turned away and will not listen anymore" (59:2,
New Living Translation).

Does this mean God refuses to listen to the prayers of sinners? Not a chance.

God isn't listening to these particular sinners, but that's because there's not
a spark of sincerity in their prayers. "Your talk is filled with lies and plans for
violence. . . . All you think about is sin; you leave ruin and destruction wherever
you go. You don't know how to live in peace or to be fair with others" (59:3, 7–8).

God isn't deaf. He hears the prayers of everyone—even the prayers of sinners.
The fact is, the sincere prayers of repentant sinners are those that especially
interest him. As Jesus put it, "I didn't come to invite good people to turn to God.
I came to invite sinners" (Luke 5:32).

# Bible Scenarios You Can Use

### 1. God is sick of pretend worship (1:4–17)

"Israel, you are a sinful nation," God says through his prophet Isaiah. "Your sacrifices mean nothing to me. I am sick of your offerings of rams and choice cattle. . . . Stay out of my temple!"

The Israelites observe the Sabbath and all the religious holidays. They bring the offerings required by law. They pray to God, praise him in songs, and recite Scripture. But their hearts aren't in it. Their worship is out of habit, or just for show.

"I am disgusted with your filthy deeds," God says. "Stop doing wrong, and learn to live right. See that justice is done. Defend the widows and orphans and help those in need."

Honoring God doesn't start at the threshold of the church. And it doesn't have anything to do with going through the motions of worship rituals. We honor God by the way we live day in and day out—by observing his most basic laws, which includes loving your neighbor as yourself.

### 2. Isaiah's doomed job assignment (6:1–13)

Israel is headed for trouble. Most people have abandoned their devotion to God. They worship idols (often in addition to worshiping God) and they treat the Ten Commandments like they're the Ten Suggestions. In a vision, Isaiah sees God in heaven asking whom he can send to warn Israel that if they don't turn from their sin, they will suffer horrible consequences.

"Send me," Isaiah replies.

God agrees, but warns that the people won't listen. When Isaiah asks how long their stubbornness will last, God's reply is shocking: "Until their towns are destroyed and their houses are deserted, until their fields are empty, and I have sent them far away, leaving their land in ruins."

Astonishingly enough, even with this promise of failure, Isaiah begins his life's work.

Some jobs God gives us are difficult and painful, but they are part of his plan to save humanity from the tragic effects of sin. Some assignments—like Isaiah's—seem a hopeless waste of time. An example would be offering help to a friend who refuses to admit he has a problem, such as an addiction. Even though we'll often fail to get through thick skulls, our efforts can touch hearts and remind people that God cares enough to send needed help even when it's not welcome.

### 3. "A child is born" (9:2–7)

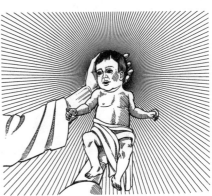

**A** bit like the ghost of Christmas future in the tale about Ebenezer Scrooge, Isaiah warns of horrors ahead: invasions, starvation, and slavery. Yet alongside this sobering message is a word of hope—a prophecy that New Testament writers say points to the birth of Jesus.

"A child has been born for us. We have been given a son who will be our ruler. His names will be Wonderful Advisor and Mighty God, Eternal Father and Prince of Peace. His power will never end; peace will last forever."

The Prince of Peace has come. When heartache and tragedy come calling, as it inevitably will from time to time, we can turn to him for peace that calms the storm. "I give you peace," Jesus told his followers. "It isn't like the peace that this world can give. So don't be worried or afraid" (John 14:27). The world can rob us of many things, but not of God's peace that will last forever.

### 4. The end of human history (24:1–23)

**N**ot only will Israel suffer God's punishment for sin; someday the entire world will suffer. Chapter 24 begins a horrifying four-chapter prophecy that Bible experts call the Apocalypse of Isaiah.

"The Lord is going to twist the earth out of shape and turn it into a desert," Isaiah says.

How or when this will happen is unknown. Volcanoes, earthquakes, droughts, and meteorites could devastate the planet this way. But so could a single word from God. Whatever happens, the destruction is so complete that it looks as though God is wiping out his creation and starting over, much like he did with the Flood of Noah. Many experts, in fact, think Isaiah is talking about the end of human history, when God defeats evil once and for all. Afterward, however, comes a new creation—perhaps the kingdom that Jesus told his disciples he was preparing (John 14:2–3).

Sin will have no place in God's new kingdom. Though sin still runs rampant in our world, with God's help we can be a living example of the kingdom to come.

## 5. "Your sins are forgiven" (40:1–31)

Isaiah suddenly shifts 200 years into the future, to a time when Israel's punishment for sin is over. Their exile in Babylon is history. Isaiah's tone makes a radical switch, from doom to comfort.

"Comfort my people," God says. "Tell her that her sad days are gone and that her sins are pardoned" (New Living Translation).

The message of forgiveness is one that John the Baptist will pick up and use to announce the arrival of Jesus. Quoting this chapter, John will describe himself as a voice in the desert shouting for people to get ready for the Lord's arrival.

Like Israel, when we sin we can expect sad consequences. But when we repent, we can expect the Lord to come, bringing forgiveness with him.

## 6. The Suffering Servant (53:1–12)

In one of the most intriguing and moving prophecies in the Old Testament, Isaiah tells about a mysterious servant who suffered terribly. Many Jews think the prophecy refers to their people, who suffered near annihilation several times in history. But New Testament writers see this as a portrait of Jesus.

"He was wounded and crushed because of our sins, by taking our punishment, he made us completely well. . . . He was condemned to death without a fair trial. . . . The Lord will reward him with honor and power for sacrificing his life."

In Old Testament times, people had to sacrifice animals for sin—as a graphic reminder that sin is deadly serious. But Jesus became that sacrifice for us—a graphic example that God's love can overpower sin and resurrect us to a new life, in this physical world and beyond. As the apostle Paul put it in a letter, "Our Lord Jesus Christ . . . died for us so that we can live with him forever" (1 Thessalonians 5:9–10).

# JEREMIAH

## When Your World Falls Apart

In sadness or horror, have you ever watched the end of something or someone you loved?

Perhaps you watched a family member die slowly of disease. Maybe you saw your company struggle and finally fold. Or maybe you watched the dissolution of your marriage, while feeling like you were witnessing a tragic scene from someone else's life.

If so, you might be able to understand a bit about what the prophet Jeremiah suffered. He lost his country. He watched it slip slowly away over 40 years, while he tried exhaustively to save it.

He spoke the desperate words of warning God gave him, urging the people to change their evil ways or suffer the punishment that's written into Israel's agreement with God: national annihilation. He spoke with dramatic actions: wearing a yoke to symbolize Babylon's enslavement of the Jews, and refusing to marry to show that the nation would be no place to raise a family. He spoke, too, in written prophecies, which the king, Jehoiakim, burned.

When the Jewish world fell apart—and Babylon leveled Jerusalem—Jeremiah was there to see it. Perhaps he felt like a failure, since this was the very tragedy he had tried to prevent. But he wasn't a failure. For though his message was lost on his own generation, it wasn't lost on the apostle Paul, who wrote, "the wages of sin is death" (Romans 6:23). Nor is it lost on any of us who have chosen life.

> ## (ee) Quote for You
>
> "My power will make you strong" (1:18). God's promise to Jeremiah, at the beginning of the prophet's long and difficult ministry.

## When It Happened

(Dates are approximate)

Adam 4000+ B.C.　　　Abraham 2100 B.C.　Moses 1500 B.C.　David 1000 B.C.　Fall of Israel 722 B.C.　Josiah 640 B.C.　Fall of Judah 586 B.C.　Ezra 450 B.C.　Jesus born 7/6 B.C.

# Info You Can Use

 ## Background Notes

**Writer:** "My name is Jeremiah," the book begins. "I am a priest. . . . This book contains the things that the Lord told me to say."

Jeremiah dictated the prophecies to a scribe named Baruch, who wrote them on a scroll (36:4). In most Bible translations, these prophecies appear indented, as poetry. The rest of the book is prose—stories that report on the life and times of Jeremiah. Bible experts say that Jeremiah might have written these sections, or that Baruch or other writers could have added them later.

**Time:** Jeremiah prophesied for 40 years, from 626 B.C. to 586 B.C., when Babylon defeated the Jewish nation and exiled most of the survivors. His ministry started during Josiah's reign, and extended through the reigns of four subsequent kings: Jehoahaz, Jehoiakim, Jehoiachin, and Zedekiah.

**Place:** Before he became a prophet, Jeremiah worked as a temple priest in Judah's capital city of Jerusalem. He was raised in a village three miles away, and may have lived there. But it was in Jerusalem that he delivered his prophecies. By book's end, Judah fell and most Jewish survivors were taken as exiles to Babylon, in what is now Iraq. But because Jeremiah urged the Jews to surrender to Babylon, he was released. Other Jews left behind forced him to go with them to Egypt, where he got lost in history.

**Bottom-Line Summary:** God calls a young priest, Jeremiah, to become a prophet who will deliver the Lord's messages to the Jewish nation. God's main message is this: repent or invaders from the north will annihilate you.

Jeremiah's message seems to make a difference at first. He begins his ministry during the reign of King Josiah, who is remembered for making religious reforms, such as tearing down pagan shrines around the country. But the reforms are too little, too late. When Josiah dies, the people go back to worshiping idols and disregarding God's other laws.

For 40 years, Jeremiah warns the Jews that their judgment day is coming. But the people ignore him, just as they usually ignore all prophets God sends. Judgment day arrives in 586 B.C. when Babylonian soldiers storm into Judah. They capture every major city in the country, then surround and destroy the capital, Jerusalem. Soldiers take most of the survivors with them, in exile to Babylon.

Jeremiah said this would happen. But he also said that God would eventually allow the Jews to return home and rebuild their nation. Just as the sinful Hebrews of the Exodus had been sentenced to wander for a generation in the wilderness, the sinful Jews of Jeremiah's day would spend a generation banished to Babylon.

## Influential People

**Jeremiah,** a prophet who predicts the end of the Jewish nation and lives to see it. His long ministry is filled with emotional and physical hardship, but God helps him through it. His life is a reminder that godly people sometimes face tough times, but that God is a reliable helper.

**Baruch,** a scribe who writes the prophecies Jeremiah dictates. His loyalty to Jeremiah—a prophet generally despised among the Jews of his day—serves as a model to those who stand by their friends and associates in hard times.

**Jehoiakim,** the king who burns Jeremiah's prophecies, represents everyone who rejects God's word.

**Zedekiah,** last king of Judah. When invaders surround Jerusalem, he takes his soldiers and tries to sneak away, abandoning his people. His action epitomizes selfishness. Captured, the last thing he sees is the execution of his sons. He is then blinded and taken with other exiles to Babylon.

## Key Ideas You Need to Know

**A new agreement with God.** The Jews and God have a formal agreement—a covenant. In return for the promised land and God's protection, the Jews are to obey God's laws, which are based on the Ten Commandments. If the Jews fail to live up to their end of the agreement, they will lose God's protection and their homeland. The agreement, which is as binding as a contract, is outlined in Deuteronomy 27—29.

The Jews break the agreement, and are eventually driven from their homeland. But God makes another promise:

"The day will come," God says, "when I will make a new covenant with the people of Israel and Judah. This covenant will not be like the one I made with their ancestors when I took them by the hand and brought them out of the land of Egypt. They broke that covenant." God describes his new covenant this way: "I will put my laws in their minds, and I will write them on their hearts" (31:31–33, New Living Translation).

Hours before his crucifixion, Jesus held up a cup of wine symbolizing the blood he was about to shed. He told his disciples, "This is my blood. It is poured out for you, and with it God makes his new agreement" (Luke 22:20).

---

### ⚡ Fascinating Facts

In 1975, a clay impression of a seal was discovered, and it seems to have belonged to Jeremiah's scribe, Baruch. Written documents were often sealed shut with a small glob of soft clay or hot wax, impressed with the writer's personal seal. This particular seal impression says, "Belonging to Baruch son of Neriah the scribe." This is exactly how the Bible describes Jeremiah's associate (32:12). The clay was scorched, indicating it may have been burned in the fire that destroyed Jerusalem.

Some of the most famous prophets didn't want the job, knowing it was a frightening and dangerous responsibility. Moses tried five times to excuse himself, arguing he was a nobody, didn't know God's name, and was a poor speaker. Jeremiah said he was too young. And Jonah ran away, taking a ship headed in the opposite direction of where God told him to go. A storm and a large fish turned Jonah in the right direction.

The old system of staying in God's good graces by carefully observing hundreds of laws and offering sacrifices is over. It has become obsolete (Hebrews 8:13). God has put his spirit in each of us, so we know right from wrong without having to consult a manual. And when we choose wrong, forgiveness sincerely sought is only a prayer away.

## Q&A

**Why does God punish kids for the sins of the parents?** In a prayer, Jeremiah complains to God, saying, "You show kindness for a thousand generations, but you also punish people for the sins of their parents" (32:18).

It's true that when God sent the Babylonians to wipe out the Jewish nation, children died. Others were raised in exile, through no fault of their own. But it's not fair to blame God for that. Blame the people who chose to sin, ignoring God's warnings. Sin produces damaging consequences that often hurt more than just the sinner.

If God is just, as the Bible claims, then the children will be treated fairly—even in death. Though it's hard to grasp in our world of physics, death isn't the end.

As Paul explained in a letter to Christians in Corinth, "Our bodies are like tents that we live in here on earth. But when these tents are destroyed, we know that God will give each of us a place to live. These homes will not be buildings that someone has made, but they are in heaven and will last forever" (2 Corinthians 5:1).

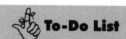

**To-Do List**

- "Be fair and honest with each other. Stop taking advantage of foreigners, orphans, and widows" (7:5–6).

- "Do not do your work on the Sabbath, but make it a holy day" (17:22, New Living Translation).

## Red Flag Issues

**Abortion.** Christians who oppose abortion, calling it murder, sometimes turn to Jeremiah 1:5. In this verse, God calls Jeremiah to become a prophet: "Jeremiah, I am your Creator, and before you were born, I chose you to speak for me to the nations" (1:5).

Many Christians see in this an indication that God has a plan for every unborn child. And they say that if you kill that unborn life, you're taking a stand against God.

Other Christians see poetry in the passage, not a statement on the ethics of abortion. They see the verse as a beautiful way of expressing God's plan for Jeremiah, and for each of us. But they also remind us that God knows which children will survive birth, and which won't. (For more on this controversial topic, see "Abortion" in the "Red Flag Issues" of Psalms and Exodus, pages 144 and 34.)

## For the Record: Jeremiah Abused

**Racism, a bestseller.** At the beginning of the 1900s, a line from Jeremiah inspired the title of a minister's racist novel that demeans black people and delivered a savage counterpunch to Harriet Beecher Stowe's anti-slavery book, *Uncle Tom's Cabin.*

Jeremiah's line: "Can an Ethiopian change the color of his skin? Can a leopard take away its spots? Neither can you start doing good" (13:23, New Living Translation).

The racist book: *The Leopard's Spots,* by Rev. Thomas Dixon, published by Doubleday in 1902.

Dixon, a North Carolina native, wrote the book after seeing a play based on Stowe's book. He explained his motive: "It may shock the prejudice of those who have idealized or worshipped the negro as canonized in 'Uncle Tom.' Is it not time they heard the whole truth? They have heard only one side for forty years."

Dixon's novel tried to legitimize the hatred of blacks, which was already mainline thinking in America at the time. The book sold 200,000 copies the first year and led to two other novels that became part of the "Klan Trilogy." The *Atlanta Journal* called Dixon's first book "a worthy successor to *Uncle Tom's Cabin.*"

Jeremiah's line in no way demeans black people. The prophet was simply saying it was as impossible for the Israelite nation to change its evil ways as it is for, say, a white man to change the color of his skin. One of Christianity's first converts was a man from the African nation of Ethiopia (Acts 8:26–38). (See also the "Slavery" feature in Genesis, page 24.)

## Jeremiah Well Used

**Helping the oppressed.** Godly people throughout history have found support in Jeremiah for helping refugees and other oppressed people, such as the Jews during World War II, blacks during South Africa's Apartheid, and poor people in our own nation today.

God's order:

"You have been allowing people to cheat, rob, and take advantage of widows, orphans, and foreigners who live here. Innocent people have become victims of violence, and some of them have even been killed. But now I command you to do what is right and see that justice is done. Rescue everyone who has suffered from injustice" (22:3).

In the United States, the Statue of Liberty has been a shining beacon of welcome to arriving refugees. Inscribed upon Lady Liberty are words that read like a reply to God's command:

> "Give me your tired, your poor,
> Your huddled masses yearning to breathe free,
> The wretched refuse of your teeming shore,
> Send these, the homeless, tempest-tost to me:
> I lift my lamp beside the golden door."

These are fine words. But each generation must adopt them as their own, or abandon them as hopeless.

# Bible Scenarios You Can Use

## 1. God calls a reluctant Jeremiah to be his prophet (1:1–10)

**J**eremiah is a young priest who serves in the Jerusalem temple. He expects he will work as a priest all his life, as his father has done. But God has other plans.

"Jeremiah," God says, "I am your Creator, and before you were born, I chose you to speak for me to the nations."

The young priest, perhaps still in his 20s, immediately resists. "I'm not a good speaker, Lord," he replies. "And I'm too young."

"Don't say you're too young," God answers. "If I tell you to go and speak to someone, then go! And when I tell you what to say, don't leave out a word! I promise to be with you and keep you safe, so don't be afraid." God then reaches out and touches Jeremiah's mouth, as a symbol of the words the young man would deliver on God's behalf.

For most of us, God doesn't suddenly appear and tell us what to do with our life. But he shouldn't have to. His word is preserved in the Bible, and our mission is clear. It's a mission that if the Jews had accepted, God wouldn't have needed to send a prophet to them. The mission is to devote ourselves to God.

If you are one of the people God uniquely calls for a specific job, discover from the story of Jeremiah that God can use the most reluctant and inexperienced people in dramatic ways.

## 2. The hypocrite nation (3:1–10)

**T**he Jews go through the motions of worshiping God at his temple, but they treat the Lord as just one of many gods.

"Have you seen what fickle Israel does?" God asks. "Like a wife who commits adultery, Israel has worshiped other gods on every hill and under every green tree" (New Living Translation). This adultery is both spiritual and physical, because in addition to being unfaithful to God the Jews are sometimes having sex with pagan priests and priestesses as part of the worship rituals.

"Worst of all," God adds, "the people of Judah pretended to come back to me. Even the people of Israel [the northern Jewish nation destroyed by Assyria 100 years earlier] were honest enough not to pretend."

Hypocrisy is portrayed in the Bible as one of the worst sins, perhaps because when we pretend to follow God, others follow us. And the damage multiplies.

### 3. The sentence: 70 years in exile (25:1–14)

"**C**hange your ways! If you stop doing evil, I will let you stay forever in this land that I gave your ancestors." That has been God's patiently repeated message to the Israelites for some 800 years—since they first entered the promised land and began worshiping local idols (7:25).

Now their time is up.

"You refused to listen to me, and now I will let you be attacked by nations from the north," God says. "This country will be as empty as a desert, because I will make all of you the slaves of the king of Babylonia for seventy years."

God didn't ignore the nation's sins for 800 years. He fired the equivalent of warning shots over the bow, trying to stop the sin by sending prophets, along with punishing disease, famine, and invaders. But for blatant and perpetual sin, God eventually has to take drastic action. God's attitude about sin hasn't changed. If we persist in sinning, we face punishment—perhaps even extreme measures in this lifetime. But when we come to him in sorrow—as the Jews later did—he'll forgive us and help us pick up the pieces of our life.

### 4. The king burns Jeremiah's prophecies (36:1–32)

**A**t God's instruction, Jeremiah dictates all his prophecies while an associate, a scribe named Baruch, writes them on a scroll. Jeremiah then has the scribe take the prophecies to the temple and read them to the people. Officials confiscate the scroll and read it to King Jehoiakim, who reacts angrily at the message that Babylon will destroy his country. As the reader finishes each section, the king reaches over with a knife, cuts off that part of the scroll, and tosses it into a fire he's using to warm himself on the winter day.

When Jeremiah hears this, he dictates a second, longer version, which becomes the core of this Bible book. He also warns that since the king threw away God's word, the king himself would be discarded. Several years later the king dies of an unknown cause, perhaps assassination.

We can reject God's word, just as the king did, but we can't silence God. He'll get his message across one way or another because it's a message designed to save us. Would you ever stop trying to save a loved one in danger? Neither would God.

# LAMENTATIONS

## Crying Till You Can Cry No More

This is the saddest book in the Bible. Turn here if you're depressed and want company or want to know what you can possibly say to God in your time of greatest sorrow.

Lamentations is made up entirely of five heartbreaking songs of sorrow. The Jewish nation is dissolved. It's capital, Jerusalem, is leveled. Many of the people are dead, and most survivors are exiled and suffering in a foreign land. Lamentations is the song of one of these survivors—an eye-witness to the freshly imprinted horror.

This poet masterfully expresses his peo-ple's grief by starting each verse with a letter of the Hebrew alphabet, beginning with *alpha*, then *beth*, and working his way through all 22 letters. He does this for three of the five songs. The exceptions are chapter three, which starts every third verse with a new Hebrew letter, and chapter five, which doesn't start the verses with ordered letters but at least follows the 22-verse format. The point is clear, yet softly subtle: the people have suffered everything from A to Z.

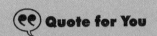 **Quote for You**

"Deep in my heart I say, 'The Lord is all I need; I can depend on him!'" (3:24).

The scenes that the poet describes are jarring:

- "Is it right for mothers to eat their children?" (2:20). This is probably a reference to how the Jews inside the surrounded Jerusalem dealt with starvation.

- "A child begs its mother for food and drink, then blacks out. . . . The child slowly dies in its mother's arms" (2:12).

- "I have cried until the tears no longer come" (2:11, New Living Translation).

The suffering poet talks to God frankly, honestly, holding back nothing. Some-where during the talk, though, he finds a glimmer of hope from past experience. His hope is in God, of whom he pens a line that will live on in a famous Christian hymn: "Great is thy faithfulness" (3:23, King James Version).

When It Happened

(Dates are approximate)

Adam 4000+ B.C.    Abraham 2100 B.C.    Moses 1500 B.C.    David 1000 B.C.    Fall of Israel 722 B.C.    Fall of Judah 586 B.C.    Ezra 450 B.C.    Jesus born 7/6 B.C.

# Info You Can Use

## Background Notes

**Writer:** The writer is unknown. Jewish tradition, from before the time of Jesus, says Jeremiah wrote the book. That's why Lamentations follows the Book of Jeremiah. There's some evidence supporting the belief that Jeremiah wrote the book. The writing style and word choices of both books are similar. Also, the writer of Chronicles said Jeremiah knew how to write laments such as this, since he wrote one when King Josiah died (2 Chronicles 35:25). In addition, Jeremiah lived to see the fall of Jerusalem and the exile that followed. Lamentations, with its throbbing emotion and graphic scenes, reads like such an eyewitness wrote it.

**Time:** The fresh pain of the songs suggests they were written shortly after the fall of Jerusalem and the exile of the survivors in 586 B.C., but before the Jews began returning home about 50 years later.

**Place:** Some of the sad songs take place in Jerusalem, during Babylon's siege of the city. Others take place in a foreign land, as the homesick poet grieves over his once glorious homeland that's now in ruins. If Jeremiah wrote the book, he may have done so in Egypt. The Babylonians freed him because he advised Judah's king to surrender. A group of Jews forced him to go with them to Egypt, to get away from the Babylonians. If a Jewish exile wrote it, he probably did so in Babylon, now Iraq. That's where most of the Jewish survivors were taken.

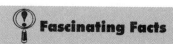

### Fascinating Facts

Many Jews read Lamentations at Jerusalem's Wailing Wall, where they still lament the temple's destruction and pray for the day it will be rebuilt. This famous wall is part of an ancient retaining wall, and all that remains of the Jewish temple. A 1,400-year old mosque, the Dome of the Rock, now sits on the former temple site (which is why the temple hasn't been rebuilt). The mosque marks the place where Muhammad, founder of Islam, is said to have ascended to heaven.

When Jeremiah predicted that the Babylonians who were besieging Jerusalem would burn down the city, officials had him thrown into a muddy cistern and left to die. One official later convinced the king to rescue him.

**Bottom-Line Summary:** Lamentations is a collection of five songs of sorrow—laments—about the worst tragedy in Jewish history. Babylon invades from the north and wipes out all the major cities of the Jewish nation of Judah, saving the Jerusalem capital for last. Babylon surrounds the city and stays there for a year and a half, not allowing anyone in or out. When the residents start dying of starvation and of disease caused by sanitation problems, the invaders break through the walls, level the city, slaughter many of the people, and take most of the survivors away in exile to Babylon. At least temporarily, the Jewish nation no longer exists.

The first song paints the horrifying scenes inside Jerusalem during and after the siege: starving mothers eating their children, corpses lying on the streets, priests massacred in the temple. Song two laments God's anger that allowed this to happen. Song three speaks of the writer's personal suffering and of his hope for the future. Song four again laments God's punishment of Jerusalem. And song five is the writer's stirring plea for God to have mercy on the survivors.

### Influential People

**Jeremiah,** the prophet who predicted the fall of the Jewish nation and who lived to see it. Traditionally considered the writer of Lamentations, he is known as the "weeping prophet." His songs show us how to talk to God in tragic times (speak freely) and how to deal with hurting people (show compassion)—even if some of those people have mistreated us.

> **To-Do List**
>
> - "It is good to wait patiently for the Lord to save us" (3:26).
>
> - "Being rubbed in the dirt can teach us a lesson; we can also learn from insults and hard knocks" (3:29–30).

# Bible Scenarios You Can Use

## 1. Weeping over lost Jerusalem, (2:1–22)

From somewhere in exile, far from Jerusalem, the poet weeps as he remembers the day the glorious city fell—wiping the Jewish nation from the map.

"My eyes are red from crying, my stomach is in knots, and I feel sick all over," he writes. "My people, both young and old, lie dead in the streets. . . . Enemies killed my children, my own little children."

Sin brought down the capital city and the entire nation. The poet understands that: "Jerusalem's horrible sins have made the city a joke. . . . Her sins made her filthy, but she wasn't worried about what could happen."

Sin can still break hearts and destroy lives, cities, and nations. When we sin, others cry because they get hurt too. Sin is no more private than a tidal wave, and is sometimes no less destructive.

## 2. "You rescued me and saved my life" (3:1–66)

Deep in depression, the poet complains to God—even blaming him: "God took careful aim and shot his arrows straight through my heart."

But as the poet's bitterness and sorrow pour out, something dramatic and unexpected happens—a sudden moment of awareness.

"I remember something that fills me with hope," he says. "The Lord's kindness never fails! If he had not been merciful, we would have been destroyed." Turning to the Lord, the poet says, "You rescued me and saved my life."

This transforms the poet's spirit, filling him with hope. Instead of telling himself, "I am finished! I can't count on the Lord to do anything for me," he starts reminding himself, "The Lord is all I need."

The song never explains why the sudden change. But those of us who've hit the bottom a time or two know what's happening. It suddenly dawns on us that God has always been there for us—and always will be. We'll probably face hard times in the days ahead, even tragedy. But the God who has been with us through good times will stay with us in the bad. As the poet put it, "I can depend on him."

# EZEKIEL

## Getting a Second Chance at Life

Ezekiel has two messages for the Jewish people of his day.

1. They're doomed.

2. But they'll get a second chance.

God's word hasn't gone out of date. It still applies, to each one of us. If we, like the Jews of Ezekiel's generation, insist on living a sinful life—persistently choosing wrong over right—we're doomed to suffer the consequences of our choices.

The Jews suffered in many ways: famine, disease, attacks by wild animals, invasion, starvation, and finally the loss of their national sovereignty—they were erased from the world map. We suffer for our sins in many ways as well. We can lose our job, our marriage, our children, our closest friends, our confidence and self-respect. We can even lose our freedom if we commit a crime.

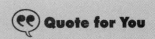 **Quote for You**

"My Spirit will give you breath, and you will live again" (37:14).

No matter what our sin or its consequences, God offers us a second chance. That doesn't mean we can skip the punishment. Sin often has unavoidable costs. But punishment doesn't have to be the closing act of your story.

God makes his point in a remarkable vision—the most famous scene in the Book of Ezekiel. He transports Ezekiel to a valley filled with scattered bones of humans. Right before Ezekiel's eyes, the bones start rattling, and then snap into place. Muscles, skin, and organs encase them. Breath fills the corpses, and they stand, resurrected.

The message: God will revive the Jewish nation that sin destroyed. God can also restore lives destroyed by sin today.

## When It Happened

(Dates are approximate)

Adam 4000+ B.C.

Abraham 2100 B.C.

Moses 1500 B.C.

David 1000 B.C.

Fall of Judah 586 B.C.

Ezra 450 B.C.

Jesus born 7/6 B.C.

# Info You Can Use

## Background Notes

**Writer:** "I am Ezekiel—a priest and the son of Buzi," the book begins. This book is a personal record of Ezekiel's ministry to the Jews exiled in Babylon.

**Time:** Ezekiel, age 25, was among the first wave of Jewish exiles deported from Jerusalem to Babylon in 597 B.C. His ministry as a prophet began five years later, when God called him into service through an astonishing vision. Just a few years after that, Babylon destroyed Jerusalem and temporarily brought an end to the Jewish nation. Ezekiel's ministry lasted a little more than 20 years, until 571 B.C.

**Place:** As a priest, Ezekiel ministered in Jerusalem until he was deported to Babylon, in what is now Iraq. In Babylon, he lived near an irrigation channel known as the Chebar River, which connected with the Euphrates River. He lived among a colony of fellow Jews who settled near the Babylonian Empire's capital city of Babylon, which was about 50 miles south of the modern Iraqi capital of Baghdad.

**Bottom-Line Summary:** Ezekiel is a Jerusalem priest deported to Babylon with about 10,000 other upper-class Jews, including the king. They are hostages to insure Judah doesn't rebel against the Babylonian Empire.

After five years in exile, Ezekiel experiences a vision in which God calls him into service as a prophet. Ezekiel's assignment is to deliver God's message to the Jews in exile. For the next 22 years, Ezekiel does just that. First, he warns the people that their beloved nation will fall: "Israel will soon come to an end! Your whole country is about to be destroyed as punishment for your disgusting sins" (7:2–3).

When the end comes, about eight years after Ezekiel started predicting it, the prophet radically changes his message. He switches from doom to hope, assuring the exiles that God will eventually let them return to their homeland and rebuild their cities.

> ## Fascinating Facts
>
> Many people in ancient times believed they could tell the future by studying the markings on the liver of a sacrificed animal. Ezekiel 21:21 is the only place in the Bible that mentions this practice, reporting that a Babylonian king did this to determine his next military move.
>
> Israel had been addicted to worshiping idols for nearly a thousand years—in spite of their agreement with God to worship only him. The exile, as harsh as it was, broke this national addiction. Some Jews would worship idols later, but it never again became the persistent national problem it had been throughout Israel's early history.

## Influential People

**Ezekiel,** a Jewish priest exiled to Babylon, where God calls him to become a prophet to his fellow captives. God puts him there to assure the people that though their nation is being punished for sin, God won't abandon them. Through Ezekiel, God is able to console the people and begin the process of healing the damage caused by sin.

## Q&A

**Why did Ezekiel act so bizarrely?** Ezekiel became famous for his bizarre behavior. But his actions were intended to demonstrate prophecies that he hoped would reach the Jewish people. Here are a few examples.

- He shaved his head and beard. Some of the hair he burned, some he cut with the sword, some he tossed to the wind, and a few strands he saved. This, he explained, is what would happen to the Jewish people when Babylon invaded to suppress a rebellion.

- He didn't mourn when his wife died. He didn't cry, or put on torn clothing, or throw dirt on himself—all of which were mourning customs in the ancient Middle East. When asked why he didn't mourn, he said the Jews were about to suffer a loss so terrible that it would leave them stunned and unable to mourn.

- He lay on his right side for 40 days to symbolize that the Jews had 40 more years to suffer the consequences of their sin.

Demonstrations such as these certainly seem bizarre. Many people must have thought Ezekiel was crazy—at least until the prophecies came true. But afterward, his actions would have reinforced the people's memory of what happened. The Jews would have both words and actions as reminders that God had warned them.

## Red Flag Issues

**Modern Israel as God's people.** Christians are divided over whether God considers the modern nation of Israel his chosen people. Ezekiel and other prophets speak of God restoring the nation (36:33–38). In fact, the national sovereignty of the Jewish race has been restored several times in history—most recently in 1948.

God promised he would never abandon the descendants of Abraham. But New Testament Jewish writers declared that the church has become the spiritual descendants of Abraham. Paul wrote to Christians: "Everyone who has faith is a child of Abraham" (Galatians 3:7). The apostle Peter echoes this, telling Christians scattered throughout what is now western Turkey: "You are God's chosen and special people. You are a group of royal priests and a holy nation. . . . Once you were nobody. Now you are God's people" (1 Peter 2:9–10).

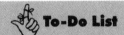
**To-Do List**

- "He never cheats or robs anyone and always returns anything taken as security for a loan; he gives food and clothes to the poor and doesn't charge interest when lending money. He refuses to do anything evil; he is fair to everyone and faithfully obeys my laws and teachings" (18:7–9). *God's description of a truly good man.*

As far as the New Testament writers were concerned, God's new covenant agreement wasn't with just the Jewish race—as the first covenant had been—it was with the human race. "That's why God told Abraham the good news that all nations would be blessed because of him," Paul explained (Galatians 3:8).

**Rebuilding a Jewish temple.** Ezekiel spends several chapters talking about a new temple that God will allow the Jews to build (40—44). It's unclear what temple Ezekiel is talking about: the temple the Jews rebuilt after the exile, a temple to be built when Jesus returns, or a figurative temple to symbolize the people's devotion to God.

Currently, the Jews have no temple in Jerusalem. Many pray for the day they can rebuild it. Others don't want one because they don't want to return to the ancient rituals of animal sacrifice. Some of the violence in Israel has been sparked over this issue. The hill on which the temple once stood is a sacred worship site for Muslims, where Jews aren't welcome. On this hilltop sits the 1,400-year-old Dome of the Rock, built around a rock from which the prophet Muhammad is said to have ascended to heaven. It seems that the Jewish temple can't be rebuilt here without destroying the Muslim worship center.

New Testament writers say the sacrifice of Jesus made the ancient sacrificial system obsolete (Hebrew 8:13). Still, some Christians argue that Ezekiel's temple will be rebuilt one day as a memorial to Jesus' sacrifice.

# Bible Scenarios You Can Use

## 1. Ezekiel sees God in a vision (1:1–28)

**E**zekiel is a 30-year-old priest living in exile in Babylon when he sees a fantastic vision of God in heaven.

The heavens open. Then, in the middle of a blazing cloud, Ezekiel catches sight of four celestial beings, each with four heads and four wings. Suddenly, a jeweled throne appears. Ezekiel describes the scene this way: "Sitting on the throne was a figure in the shape of a human. From the waist up, it was glowing like metal in a hot furnace, and from the waist down it looked like the flames of a fire. . . . I realized I was seeing the brightness of the Lord's glory! So I bowed with my face to the ground."

Most of us won't encounter God the way Ezekiel did. But we can meet with God in moments of solitude. As we grow to understand more about his holiness and majesty, we will find ourselves filling with awe and respect for him. And as it was for Ezekiel, so it is for us: bowing before God and obeying him seems natural.

## 2. God leaves the temple (10:1–22)

**I**n another dramatic vision, Ezekiel is transported back to the Jerusalem temple where he once ministered. There, he witnesses a tragic event in the spiritual world that will affect the physical. He sees the dazzling light of God's presence leave the temple.

For the Jews, the temple is God's earthly home. The temple's back room, which contains the golden chest that holds the Ten Commandments, is considered God's earthly throne. After all, when Solomon dedicated the temple 300 years earlier, "the Lord's dazzling glory then filled the temple" (2 Chronicles 7:3). For this reason, many Jews think Jerusalem and the ancient temple are indestructible—that God himself will protect them.

They are wrong. Ezekiel's vision shows that God left because sin made it an unfit place for him. Sin ran the country. There was no room for God. When we let sin run our lives, God leaves. He's always willing to return. But we have to want God more than we want the freedom to sin.

## 3. Valley of the dry bones (37:1–14)

(37:1-14)

**A**fter God gives Ezekiel visions that predict Judah's doom and a punishing exile, God offers a vision of hope. In the book's most famous scene, Ezekiel stands in a valley full of human bones. At God's command, Ezekiel tells the bones that God will wrap them with muscle and skin, and breathe life back into them. While the prophet is still talking, the bones begin to rattle. They snap together and spontaneously grow muscles and skin. Wind blows from every direction, and the bodies fill with breath, come back to life, and then stand up in testimony to God's power.

"The people of Israel are like dead bones . . . they have no hope for the future," God explains. But God has this message for them: "You will live again. I will bring you home."

No matter how spiritually dead we are, God can restore our life. He did it for Israel, when the people asked. He'll do it for us, too.

# DANIEL

## Trusting God When the Lions Arrive

Ask someone who doesn't believe in God why they don't believe. The answer you'll likely get more than any other is this: If a loving God existed, he wouldn't stand by and do nothing when people are hurting.

Unbelievers can read you their evidence from the headlines in today's newspaper.

- Six-year-old boy run over by tractor-trailer
- Teen girl raped and killed by American soldier
- Drunk driver kills family of five
- Government leader backs ethnic cleansing

Frankly, it doesn't even make sense to believers. We know if we had the power to stop these things from happening, we would. And if the God we believe in exists, he has the power to stop them. Yet, he doesn't.

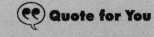 **Quote for You**

"Our God, your name will be praised forever and forever. You are all-powerful, and you know everything. You control human events—you give rulers their power and take it away" (2:20–21).

The Book of Daniel offers evidence to the contrary. It tells about times when God steps into human history. And it gives a hint about why he doesn't step in at other times.

When Daniel's three friends were ordered to worship an idol or face execution by burning in a furnace, they chose the furnace. God saved them. When Daniel was thrown to the lions for praying, God protected him. When a king saw a disembodied hand writing on the palace wall, Daniel interpreted the writing by saying, "God has numbered the days of your kingdom" (5:26).

The point: God's in control.

The clue about why he allows tragedy: "Those who lie in the ground will rise from death" (12:2). Our life doesn't end on this planet. How an agonizing death figures into God's plan remains a mystery. But Daniel and his friends were willing to trust God with that mystery.

When we face the lions—whatever or whoever they are—we can have that same trust in God, just like Daniel.

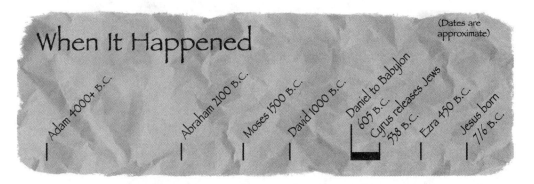

When It Happened

(Dates are approximate)

Adam 4000+ B.C.

Abraham 2100 B.C.

Moses 1500 B.C.

David 1000 B.C.

Daniel to Babylon 605 B.C.

Cyrus releases Jews 538 B.C.

Ezra 450 B.C.

Jesus born 7/6 B.C.

# Info You Can Use

## Background Notes

**Writer:** It's uncertain who wrote this book. Many scholars say Daniel wrote it, or at least parts of it. Others argue that someone else compiled the material, drawing from Daniel's prophecies and from stories about him. Daniel's visions are written in the first person, as though he is personally reporting them. But the stories are in the third person, as though reported by someone else.

Some prophecies are so close to historical events that took place almost 500 years after Daniel that many scholars suggest the book was written after those events, not before. If so, the "prophecies" are actually history disguised as prophecies. One example is that Daniel's description of a war between a northern and a southern king (chapter 11) matches history's account of what happened after Alexander the Great died: the Ptolemies of Egypt fought with the Seleucids of Syria for control of the Middle East.

Still, many Bible experts insist the prophecies are real and that God is able to predict the future.

**Time:** Daniel's story starts in 605 B.C., when he is taken captive to Babylon, and it continues for more than 60 years. He serves as a palace official first for the Babylonians and then for their successors, the Persians.

**Place:** The stories and visions are set in Babylon, capital city of the Babylonian Empire and later part of the Persian Empire. This is in what is now Iraq.

**Bottom-Line Summary:** Babylon becomes the new Middle Eastern superpower, replacing Assyria. To discourage rebellion among lesser nations and to build up their own empire, they take the brightest people

## Fascinating Facts

The famous saying, "I could see the handwriting on the wall," comes from a story in Daniel. A terrified Babylonian king watches as a disembodied hand writes a message on the palace wall, warning that the empire is about to fall.

Nebuchadnezzar—the vicious Babylonian king who decimates the Jewish nation and levels Jerusalem—wrote part of the Bible. After personally witnessing how God saves Daniel's three friends from the blazing furnace, he makes a royal proclamation praising God. It's preserved in Daniel 3:28–29. He also tells of a miraculous dream God gave him (4:1–18).

In an ancient Jewish legend, Daniel kills a Babylonian god with a hairball. The god, called a "dragon," is probably a snake. To prove it's mortal, Daniel feeds it cakes made of tar, fat, and hair. Inside the creature, the hairball expands and makes the animal burst.

Jesus' favorite phrase for describing himself was "Son of Man." Though the title can mean "human," as it does in the Book of Ezekiel, scholars say Jesus probably also has in mind the celestial person mentioned in Daniel: "I saw what looked like a son of man coming with the clouds. . . . He was crowned king and given power and glory so that all people of every nation and race would serve him. He will rule forever, and his kingdom is eternal, never to be destroyed" (7:13–14). Many Christians believe this is a description of Jesus at the Second Coming, sometime in the unknown future.

from surrounding nations and force them to serve in the king's palace. A young nobleman named Daniel and three of his friends are among those taken from the Jewish nation. After a three-year training program, they become royal advisors.

Though the men serve with devotion and excellence, they refuse to worship anyone but God. Daniel's three friends refuse to worship an idol, and are thrown into a furnace to be burned alive. Later, during Persian rule, when Daniel refuses to pray to the king, he is punished by being thrown into a lion's den. God protects each of the men, which prompts the kings involved to free the men and grant them the right to worship as they please.

In the second half of the book, Daniel records his visions about what appears to be the end of human history. These visions conclude with the Bible's first mention of life after death, promising that the faithful will have eternal life.

# Influential People

**Daniel,** a young Jewish nobleman who becomes God's prophet in Babylonian exile. His courage in the face of danger and his visions of hope for the persecuted show that God can use faithful people wherever they are—even in hostile situations.

**Shadrach, Meshach, Abednego,** three wise Jews taken to Babylon to serve the king. Their friendship and their shared religious convictions give these three men the courage to put their lives on the line and disobey the king's order to worship an idol. Their story reminds us of the importance of godly friends. It also offers a model of supreme confidence in God, since the men vow to worship only God even if he doesn't deliver them from execution.

**Nebuchadnezzar,** Babylon's most powerful king, and an evil man who slaughters thousands for his own glory. God uses even the likes of him: to punish sinful Judah, and to show his power to deliver Shadrach, Meshach, and Abednego from the execution furnace.

**Belshazzar,** Babylonian king who sees God's handwriting on the wall, which predicts the end of Babylon. The king's story is a reminder that earthly rulers are subject to God—even government and business leaders today.

# Key Ideas You Need to Know

**God's in charge.** If the book has one main take-home message for us today, that's it. No matter who thinks they're in control, God's the final word. An iron-fisted dictator might think he's in charge of his nation. And from the flip side of the coin, where people feel helpless, even free citizens might think they have no substantial power—living in a nation run by the rich, for the rich.

But it's not true, because God is in control. That doesn't mean he'll always stop the evil folks in their tracks, though sometimes that's exactly what he does. Babylonian King Belshazzar is throwing a palace party when he sees handwriting on the wall warning that his empire is about to fall. That very night, Medes and Persians storm the capital and kill the king. The Babylonian Empire dies and the Persian Empire is born.

God's in charge not only of human beings, but of all creation—animals and elements as well. He protects Daniel from hungry lions. And he protects Daniel's three friends from the flames of what may have been a large kiln furnace heated to well over 1,500 degrees Fahrenheit.

Life might not go as we want or as we would expect with God in charge, but he's in charge nonetheless. He can protect us from evil. He can find creative ways to use evil people to help us. When we suffer, he suffers with us. And when we die, he ushers us into a new life where suffering and death are unknown.

## Q&A

**Does God still talk to us in dreams?** Daniel became famous for his ability to interpret dreams as messages from God, much as Joseph did about a thousand years earlier. The Bible has many stories—from Genesis through Revelation—of God speaking in dreams to both the good and the evil: Jacob, Pharaoh, King Nebuchadnezzar, Pilate's wife, and John the writer of Revelation.

Many people in ancient times believed that vivid dreams were messages from the spirit world. Some people even sought these dreams by sleeping in holy places such as temples, in an attempt to get an answer to a question troubling them. Professional dream interpreters had manuals to help them explain the symbolism in dreams.

In Bible times, God spoke to people in many ways: dreams, wakeful visions, angels, a talking donkey, prophets, and Scripture.

God can still communicate in any way he chooses. Many Christians believe that even today he occasionally talks through dreams, visions, angelic messengers, and modern-day prophets. Others say these types of revelations stopped, or at least grew less common, beginning in New Testament times, when every Christian began to be guided by the Holy Spirit and the Bible.

**If God's in charge of the planet, why do we have so many evil rulers?** We might expect a loving and all-powerful God to put saintly people in charge of our governments. But you know that's not what happens. God lets us make our own choices.

Yet, whether we choose good leaders or bad ones, God can use both. He used the vain Nebuchadnezzar to discipline the Jews. He used the oppressive Romans to strengthen the church and to build roads that paved the way for the spread of Christianity. And Hitler's efforts to wipe out the Jewish race, ironically, became the jolt that resurrected the Jewish nation in 1948—after it had been dead for some 2,000 years.

---

**To-Do List**

- "Go about your business" (12:8). *An angel's instruction after Daniel asks when the end times will come. Instead of getting distracted by trying to solve mysteries about the end of human history, Daniel is to focus on his work in this life. What that means to us: spend less time on theories about when Jesus is coming back, and more time helping others.*

# Bible Scenarios You Can Use

━━━━━━━━━━━━━━━━━━━━━━━━━ **1. Daniel's friends in the fiery furnace (3:1–30)**

**W**hen the Babylonians swallow up Assyria, to become the world's new superpower, they set out to dominate the entire Middle East. After taking control of Jerusalem in 605 B.C., Babylonian king Nebuchadnezzar orders one of his officials to select the wisest Jews to serve in his palace. Four young men are chosen and deported to Babylon: Daniel, along with three of his friends—Hananiah, Mishael, and Azariah. We know them by their Babylonian names: Shadrach, Meshach, and Abednego.

The king has a 90-foot-high idol built and orders his officials to attend the dedication and worship it. Daniel's three friends refuse to comply. (Daniel isn't mentioned, and is probably not available.) Other officials report this to the king, who becomes livid. He orders the three to report to him and he demands that they worship the idol or be burned alive—a common form of execution in Babylon.

"The God we worship can save us from you and your flaming furnace," the men reply. "But even if he doesn't, we still won't worship your gods."

Nebuchadnezzar has the three thrown into what may have been a large kiln furnace. The fire is so hot that it kills the soldiers who throw the men in. Yet the three walk around inside the furnace, unharmed. The king looks in and sees a fourth man who "looks like a god." Jumping up, Nebuchadnezzar calls the men back out, and then vows to protect their right to worship God.

When we take a stand for God, we never stand alone. God stands with us. That doesn't mean he'll always keep us from getting hurt. The Bible is full of stories about people who suffered doing God's work—people such as Paul who was beaten and imprisoned, and Stephen who was stoned to death. But God will never abandon his faithful people, not in this life nor in the life to come.

## 2. Daniel in the lion's den (6:1–28)

**W**hen Persia bumps aside Babylon, to become the next superpower, King Darius puts Daniel in charge of running a third of the empire. Daniel does so well that he is put in charge of the entire empire. Jealous officials, perhaps those demoted, plot to get rid of their competition. Knowing Daniel's devotion to God, they convince Darius to order everyone to pray only to the king for the next month, or face the lions.

Daniel, however, continues his routine of praying three times a day. When the officials report him, the king is upset and tries to find a way to save his favorite servant. But the law he signed is irrevocable. Daniel spends the night in a lion's den.

At daybreak and after a sleepless night, the king rushes to the lion's den, calling out to Daniel and asking if his God was able to save him. "He sent an angel," Daniel replies, "to keep the lions from eating me." The king orders Daniel released and his accusers thrown in, where they get the execution they planned for Daniel.

God isn't a spectator, simply watching our world play out its scenes. He's very much involved in his creation, and quite willing and able to step into human history. He has in the past, and he will in the future. So don't stop praying. He's listening, and he'll prove it.

## 3. Resurrection is coming (12:1–13)

**I**n Old Testament times, the Jews rarely talk about life after death. That's probably because most of them don't realize there's any such thing. Daniel is the first Jewish writer to speak clearly about dead people being resurrected.

In a prophecy about the end times, he says there will be a period of suffering like never before. Afterward, "Many of those who lie dead in the ground will rise from death," Daniel says. "Some of them will be given eternal life, and others will receive nothing but eternal shame and disgrace."

When Daniel asks an angel when this will happen, the angel answers in riddles that he says can be solved only at the end of time. The angel advises Daniel to "go about your business," instead of trying to solve the riddles. And he assures the prophet that if he stays faithful, though death will come, "you will rise from death to receive your reward."

There are two clear messages for us today. First, we shouldn't spend a lot of time and energy seeking answers about the end times, or the Second Coming of Jesus. Second, we should find comfort in the teaching that if we remain true to our faith, we will one day reap the reward of a place in God's never-ending kingdom.

# HOSEA

## Cheating on God

"Sin" wasn't a strong enough word to describe what was going on in Israel. So God chose some other words: adultery and prostitution.

Even that wasn't enough. So he brought the words to life. He had his prophet, Hosea, marry a prostitute who would cheat on him and eventually leave him for a lover. Why would God do such a thing?

"Israel has betrayed me like an unfaithful wife," God explained to Hosea. "No one is faithful or loyal or truly cares about God. Cursing, dishonesty, murder, robbery, unfaithfulness—these happen all the time. Violence is everywhere" (1:2; 4:1–2).

Sounds like here and now.

So what did God do about it? He warned the Israelites of punishment if they didn't change their ways, but he offered forgiveness if they did change. Again, bringing his words to life, he had Hosea seek out his runaway wife and bring her home.

The spirit of God's offer to Israel—and to all sinners, for that matter—is captured in a tender story from the New Testament. Some men caught a woman in adultery. So they dragged her to Jesus and asked what they should do with her, reminding him that the law says they should kill her.

Jesus paused, then answered, "If any of you have never sinned, then go ahead and throw the first stone" (John 8:7). Not a stone was hurled, and the men left. Alone with the woman, Jesus asked, "Isn't there anyone left to accuse you?" "No, sir," she answered. "I am not going to accuse you either," Jesus said. "You may go now, but don't sin anymore."

Sin is so horrible that God sometimes has to take extreme measures to remind us of it. But as horrible as sin is, it can't compete with God's forgiveness. The thing is, we've got to want the forgiveness more than the sin.

> ### 💬 Quote for You
>
> "Sow the wind, and reap the whirlwind" (8:7, New International Version). *God's warning that you'll reap what you sow. If you plant trouble, you'll get trouble—and lots of it.*

## When It Happened

(Dates are approximate)

Adam 4000+ B.C.    Abraham 2100 B.C.    Moses 1500 B.C.    David 1000 B.C.    Fall of Israel 722 B.C.    Fall of Judah 586 B.C.    Ezra 450 B.C.    Jesus born 7/6 B.C.

# Info You Can Use

## Background Notes

**Writer:** "I am Hosea son of Beeri," the book begins. Very little is revealed about Hosea, as is the case with most Bible prophets.

Hosea says he has a wife and three children, but even that is up for debate. Many Christians and Jews throughout the centuries have suggested that the story of Hosea's marriage to a prostitute is a kind of parable—a make-believe morality story that symbolizes Israel's spiritual adultery.

Among the famous Christian leaders who've said God would not order a prophet to actually marry a prostitute are Martin Luther, who's the father of the Protestants, and John Calvin, theological father of many Presbyterians and Southern Baptists.

Ancient Jewish commentators, however, had no trouble accepting the story as a fact of history. As far as they were concerned, it showed the extremes to which God was willing to go to turn Israel away from sin. This was, after all, the God who took Abraham to the brink of sacrificing his son—and the God who sacrificed his own son.

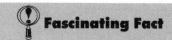

**Fascinating Fact**

The northern Jewish nation of Israel had only one prophet whose work appears in the Bible: Hosea. All others are from the southern nation of Judah, where Jerusalem and the temple were located. Israel was more ungodly than Judah, and for that reason was wiped out 150 years before Judah.

**Time:** Hosea said he was called to be God's prophet sometime late in the 40-year reign of King Jeroboam II (786-746 B.C.). Hosea prophesied during the last 20 years or more of Israel's existence—just before Assyria invaded in 722 B.C., exiled many of the survivors, and resettled the land with Assyrian pioneers. His ministry followed that of Amos, a prophet from the southern Jewish nation of Judah. Amos came as a prophet missionary to condemn the Israelites for worshiping idols and oppressing the poor.

**Place:** Hosea's story takes place in the northern Jewish nation of Israel. The united Jewish nation that existed under David and Solomon split in two during the reign of Solomon's son—with Israel in the north and Judah in the south. The two competing nations had been separated for about 200 years by the time Hosea began his ministry.

**Bottom-Line Summary:** God tells his prophet Hosea to marry a prostitute. The marriage is a kind of walking, talking parable—a living reminder to all of Israel that the people have committed spiritual adultery. They have abandoned God and goodness and have taken up with idols and wickedness.

Hosea gives his three children symbolic names that warn of what God is going to do with the Israelites if they don't honor the vows they took to be faithful to the Lord: "God Scatters," "No Mercy," and "Not My People."

Hosea's wife leaves him and takes a lover. But at God's command, Hosea brings her home—a living example of how God wants to bring Israel back. If the people will only return to him, God says, "I will heal you and love you without limit" (14:4).

# Influential People

**Hosea,** prophet to the northern Jewish nation of Israel. His willingness to marry an adulteress—as a symbol of Israel's spiritual adultery—is a model of total devotion to God. Hosea sacrifices what most of us would consider a normal life—and does so in an attempt to turn others away from sin and back to God.

**Gomer,** Hosea's wife. She's a prostitute when Hosea marries her, and she eventually leaves him for a lover. She symbolizes not only Israel's sin of abandoning God. She symbolizes us when we do the same—when we know what is right, and do what is wrong.

# Key Ideas You Need to Know

**Temptation can be a fatal attraction.** Israel's underlying problem in Hosea's time is that they can't resist temptation—and it was the death of them. When the Israelites first arrived from Egypt, after the Exodus, the most popular religion in the land was worship of Baal, a god who promised fertility in family, flocks, and field.

It's bad enough that the Israelites start worshiping Baal, thereby breaking the first of the Ten Commandments, which calls them to worship only God. But they also take part in sex rituals that are a part of Baal worship.

Bible experts say that in Hosea's day, many Baal shrines and temples—especially in the northern nation of Israel—have prostitutes for sexual fertility rites. The Baal worshiper has sex with a temple prostitute as a way of requesting Baal to grant them many children, large flocks, and an abundant harvest.

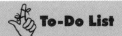 **To-Do List**

- "Worship me, the Lord, and I will send my saving power down like rain" (10:12).

- "Return to your God. Patiently trust him, and show love and justice" (12:6).

- "If you obey me [the Lord], we will walk together, but if you are wicked, you will stumble" (14:9).

Hosea preaches against this. "Having sex at pagan shrines won't produce children," he argues. Hosea puts the blame squarely on the men of Israel. "You men are to blame, because you go to prostitutes and offer sacrifices with them at pagan shrines. Your own foolishness will lead to your ruin" (4:10, 14).

Perhaps some Israelites are tempted because of their desperate need: an infertile marriage, diseased livestock, or a string of bad harvests. Some, likely, are tempted by nothing more than the sex.

There's two ways to deal with temptation. You run to it, or from it. The Israelites of Hosea's day run to it. Their forefather, Joseph, did the opposite. When his master's wife grabbed him and asked him to make love to her, "Joseph ran out of the house, leaving her hanging onto his coat" (Genesis 39:12).

 **Q&A**

**Does God sometimes hide from us?** "You offer sheep and cattle as sacrifices to me," God tells the Israelites, "but I have turned away and refuse to be found" (5:6). If God hides from the Israelites, wouldn't he hide from us as well?

Actually, God doesn't hide from anyone. It's the other way around, though the effect is the same: separation from God. The Israelites abandoned the spirit of God's teachings, yet thought they could appease God by going through the motions of their religion—by offering sacrifices for their sins, without being sorry for what they had done and without committing themselves to better living.

If we seek God, we will find him. Moses put it this way, when he predicted that the Israelites would someday worship idols and that God would have to scatter them to other nations. "From there you will search again for the Lord your God. And if you search for him with all your heart and soul, you will find him" (Deuteronomy 4:29, New Living Translation).

**Why is Hosea called one of the "Minor Prophets"?** It's not because he's less important than the "major" prophets of Isaiah, Jeremiah, and Ezekiel are. He's "minor" because his book is shorter.

There are 12 books called the Minor Prophets—the last section in the Old Testament. Hosea is the first of these 12. Jews in ancient times called these books "The Twelve." The books were compiled into a single collection because, according to early Jewish teachings, "as they are small, they might be lost."

# Bible Scenarios You Can Use

### 1. Hosea marries a prostitute (1:1–11)

God makes a shocking request of his prophet. "Hosea," God says, "Israel has betrayed me like an unfaithful wife. Marry such a woman and have children by her."

"So I married Gomer," Hosea writes, "and we had a son."

The Hebrew words used to describe Gomer suggest she had made her living walking the streets in what has been called the world's oldest profession. Hosea and Gomer eventually have three children, two sons and a daughter. But Hosea's phrasing suggests that someone else fathered the second and third children. For instead of saying "we" had a daughter and another son, Hosea says "Gomer had a daughter," and "she had another son."

Hosea's marriage and children all serve as living symbols—like a walking, talking morality play in real life. Gomer symbolizes Israel's broken vow to remain faithful to God—the vow to worship only him. The children symbolize God's warning—the punishment clause written into the agreement that's preserved in Deuteronomy 28. For breach of contract, God has the right to disown the Israelites and punish them in any number of ways. Among the most devastating punishments: he can dissolve their national sovereignty, kill them, and scatter the survivors abroad as slaves. To accent these warnings, in an effort to convince the Israelites to honor their vows, God instructs Hosea to name his children Jezreel, meaning "God Scatters," Lo-Ruhamah, meaning "No Mercy," and Lo-Ammi, meaning "Not My People."

Gomer and her children aren't just symbols for an ancient and dead society. They're symbols for us as well. We're unfaithful to God anytime we know something is wrong, but do it anyway. If we lie to make a bigger profit, then money becomes our idol. If we walk on others to get our way, then pride becomes our idol. For our sins, we might not end up as strangers in a foreign land, but we can end up as strangers with God.

## 2. Hosea buys back his wife (2:1—3:5)

**G**omer leaves her husband and family, apparently to return to prostitution. Hosea writes a song of mourning, directed to his children. The song has a double meaning, referring not only to Gomer, but to the nation of Israel as well.

"Accuse! Accuse your mother!" the song begins. "She is no longer my wife, and now I, the Lord, am not her husband. Beg her to give up prostitution and stop being unfaithful."

God gives Hosea a second startling command. "Hosea," God says, "fall in love with an unfaithful woman who has a lover. Do this to show that I love the people of Israel, even though they worship idols." The Bible never identifies this woman, but many experts say that the context points to Gomer. She apparently returned to her old ways, and is now living with another man.

Hosea has to buy her back, perhaps because her lover feels he owns her. Hosea pays 15 silver coins and about 10 bushels of grain, which is roughly half the price of a female slave.

Homer's graciousness toward Gomer, in taking her back and offering to forgive her, is like God's offer to the Israelite people. In spite of their repeated sins, God loves them and wants them back. Gomer's return is a living symbol of what God wants to see from Israel. As God puts it later in the book, "Israel, I can't let you go. I can't give you up" (11:8).

No matter how deeply we wander into sin, God loves us and is willing to forgive us. That's hard for some people to believe because sin is just about all they've ever known. By the time Hosea arrived with his message, the northern nation of Israel had been worshiping idols—almost exclusively—for about 200 years. Yet God didn't give up on them, and he won't give up on us.

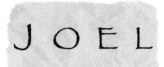

# JOEL

## A Wakeup Call from God

Israel woke up one morning to find out it was still night. At least it seemed that way with billions of locusts in the sky.

A prophet named Joel reported the ancient event. We know a bit about how terrified the Jews must have been because locust plagues still occasionally happen in the Middle East, with devastating results. In 1915, billions of these aggressive grasshoppers swarmed into Israel, darkening the sky for five days and devouring the plants.

After a similar swarm in Joel's day, God had a message for the Jews: "Wake up" (1:5, New Living Translation). What the locusts had started, an invading army would finish.

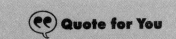 **Quote for You**

"Anyone who calls on the name of the Lord will be saved" (2:32, New Living Translation).

The locusts were an ominous wakeup call—a warning for the Jews to remember their promise to serve God in return for him bringing them into the promised land and protecting them there.

The army would come soon. But it didn't have to come at all. "I don't like to punish," God said. "It isn't too late. You can still return to me" (2:12, 13).

With the buzzing locusts gone, Israel rolled over and went back to sleep.

In all fairness to Israel, it's a bit hypocritical of us to blame them completely. We've all turned a deaf ear to God at one time or another. Some of us have been around long enough to realize that whenever we do, we regret it later. But even then—in the painful reality of "later"—there's good news: we don't have to face the consequences alone. When we call on God, he's there for us. Always.

## When It Happened

(Dates are approximate)

Adam 4000+ B.C.   Abraham 2100 B.C.   Moses 1500 B.C.   David 1000 B.C.   Fall of Israel 722 B.C.   Ezra 450 B.C.   Jesus born 7/6 B.C.

# Info You Can Use

 **Background Notes**

**Writer:** The book starts by identifying the writer: "I am Joel the son of Pethuel." Unfortunately, that's not much help, because that's all we're told about him. His father is never mentioned again, and Joel is mentioned only once, when the apostle Peter quotes part of his book during a sermon (Acts 2:16). Bible writers do, however, refer to about half a dozen other men by this popular name.

**Time:** Joel may have lived in the 700s B.C., shortly before Assyria defeated the northern Jewish nation of Israel. This is a guess based partly on the book's location in the Bible: between Hosea and Amos, two other prophets from that century.

Joel warns of an invasion force "from the north" (2:20). But there were several important invasions from the north. Assyria wiped out the northern Jewish nation in 722 B.C. Babylon wiped out the southern Jewish nation of Judah in 586 B.C. And Alexander the Great captured the Middle East in the 330s B.C. Joel doesn't identify which invasion he's talking about. In fact, his prophecy could refer to both of the invasions that destroyed the two Jewish nations.

**Place:** Joel may have lived in the southern Jewish nation of Judah. He mentions Judah half a dozen times. But he also mentions Israel, in the north, three times. The references to Israel, however, could refer to the entire Jewish race.

> ## Fascinating Facts
>
> Locusts, a type of grasshopper, thrive in the desert where there are few birds and other predators. But when their numbers swell into the millions and billions, they swarm into neighboring farmlands and devour the plants. They lay their eggs in the soil, but plowing can destroy the eggs.
>
> John the Baptist, who lived in the desert, survived on a diet of locusts and wild honey (Matthew 3:4).

**Bottom-Line Summary:** Billions of hungry locusts invade Israel, probably from the desert. They devour the crops and wild plants, setting off an economic catastrophe that causes widespread starvation. Even the trees are completely stripped. Without shade, streams and ponds evaporate. Herds wander aimlessly in search of pasture and water.

The prophet Joel says this is just a sampling of the disaster that's coming if the people don't stop sinning and turn back to God. Joel doesn't say what sins the people committed, but other prophets fill in the gaps. The Jewish people are worshiping idols and abusing the poor. Justice is for sale.

If the people don't repent, God vows to lead an invading army from the north and wipe out the Jewish nation.

Repent or not, God promises that one day—after Israel's punishment, if necessary—his people will once again prosper. They will know that the Lord is their

God and that there are no other gods. In that day, the Lord will give his Spirit to everyone as a spiritual counselor and guide who teaches us right from wrong.

## Influential People

**Joel,** a prophet, warns of coming disaster if the people don't stop their chronic sinning. His frank message wrapped in a compassionate offer for reconciliation is a model for how to approach tough issues today: state the problem, but offer a solution.

## Key Ideas You Need to Know

**The day of the Lord.** This is a Bible phrase for an event we might call judgment day. But in the Bible it's more than one day at the end of time, when Jesus comes back to earth to reward the good people and punish the bad. It's any day God steps into human history to set things right.

Jews in the early centuries think of it as a good day because it's the day when God comes to deliver them from their enemies, such as Pharaoh and the Egyptians who enslaved them.

Joel and other prophets, however, use the phrase another way. They portray the Jews as the enemy—God's enemy. So the phrase "the day of the Lord" becomes a Jewish doomsday. When the Assyrians and Babylonians later storm into the two Jewish nations and blot them off the world map, those certainly are doomsdays.

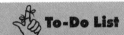 **To-Do List**

- "Turn to me now, while there is time! Give me your hearts. Come with fasting, weeping, and mourning. Don't tear your clothing in your grief; instead, tear your hearts" (2:12–13, New Living Translation).

- "Be glad now and rejoice because the Lord has done great things" (2:21, New Living Translation).

Yet even with the prophets, "the day of the Lord" means more than doom. It points to the dawning of a new and glorious age, when God's people will find peace. In Old Testament times, that happens when the Jews return to their homeland. But the New Testament speaks of yet another judgment day of the Lord, which will be followed by everlasting peace in a heavenly kingdom ruled by God (Revelation 21).

Whether judgment day is good or bad depends on us. If we're God's enemy, it's bad. If we're God's people, it's good.

## Q&A

**Why fast?** Joel tells the Jewish people to repent of their sins and "to go without eating and to pray sincerely" (1:14). There's only one day a year that the Bible says Jews have to go without eating and drinking: the Day of Atonement, an autumn holy day also known by its Hebrew name of *Yom Kippur*. This is a national day of repentance for sins committed that year. Joel's request, tied to a call for national repentance, is like a special *Yom Kippur*.

Some Jews fasted for other reasons, too. They would fast during a crisis, as a way to express their deep concern. And they would fast after the death of a loved one, to express their grief.

In New Testament times, some Jewish leaders got in the habit of fasting every Tuesday and Thursday, often dressing in ragged clothes. Jesus said many of these people were hypocrites concerned only with showing everyone how religious they were. Jesus approved of sincere fasting, and practiced it himself. He fasted just before starting his ministry.

**Why does God tell the people to tear their hearts in grief instead of tearing their clothes?** People in Bible times sometimes ripped their clothes when they heard tragic news, such as the death of a family member or the approach of an invading army. The act was a dramatic way of showing their deep grief and venting their emotions.

Joel gives the entire Jewish nation horrifying news: the end is near. But God tells the Jews they have the power to rewrite their future, if they repent. Upon hearing about the looming invasion, it would have been customary for the people to show remorse for their sins by tearing their clothes. But God wanted more than a mere showing—more than a physically demonstrated ritual. He wanted heartfelt sorrow. He wanted the people to be broken-hearted over their sins, just as he was broken-hearted over their disobedience. Pretend repentance wouldn't be good enough because it wouldn't change them. Genuine repentance changes us from the inside out.

**How would God give his Spirit to everyone?** In Old Testament times, God's presence seemed available only to a select few: kings, prophets, and spiritual leaders. When young David was anointed as Israel's future king, "at that moment, the Spirit of the Lord took control of David and stayed with him from then on" (1 Samuel 16:13).

But Joel said the day would come when God would give his Spirit to everybody (2:28). The prophet Ezekiel also predicted a day when God would pour out his Spirit (Ezekiel 39:29).

This day came after Jesus returned to heaven. In one of his last commands, Jesus told his disciples to wait in Jerusalem for the Holy Spirit. When the Spirit arrived, the room filled with the sound of a rushing wind. Above each disciple's head hovered a flame, perhaps symbolizing God's presence.

Until then, God had communicated with humanity only through select people. But on this day, God's Spirit became available to everyone—as Joel predicted.

# Bible Scenarios You Can Use

## 1. Locusts invade (1:1–20)

**S**tarving for food, locusts swarm in from the Arabian Desert. Thick enough in flight to darken the sky, they descend on the Jewish homeland and decimate every crop that grows: wheat, barley, grapes, olives, figs, pomegranates, and apples. Even the trees are stripped to their naked branches.

As catastrophic as this is, it's only a warning of what's ahead if the people don't stop their serial sinning. The agreement that their ancestors made with God allows him to send disasters—and to wipe out the nation if all else fails. God has been patient for centuries, sending comparatively mild calamities as well as prophets to warn the people. But the Jews ignore the warnings.

Sometimes we get so focused on ourselves and our physical desires in life—for money, pleasure, or power—that we abandon all things spiritual, such as compassion and justice. It can take a tragedy to wake us up to the facts. And even that might not work.

## 2. Soldiers invade (2:1–16)

**"I**t isn't too late," God tells his people. "You can still return to me with all your heart."

But soon, it will be too late. God will pass judgment on the nation, and he'll have no choice but to find them guilty.

"Troops will cover the mountains like thunderclouds . . . even arrows and spears cannot make them retreat." These invaders from the north will deliver God's death sentence on the Jewish nation.

God doesn't want this to happen. "I don't like to punish," he says. But for the sake of future generations, to show the seriousness of sin and to curb its practice, he will punish if he must.

Today, God is still patient and slow to punish. He gives us every opportunity to stop hurting others and ourselves, and to start living the kind of life that we know in our heart is right.

## 3. Young men and women prophesy (2:17—3:21)

Judgment day will come and go. Israel will ignore God's repeated warnings, reject his offer of forgiveness, and be erased from the world map. But the survivors scattered abroad will learn from this horror that sin is deadly serious. And they will commit themselves to God with an enduring depth of devotion unlike any in their history.

Just as children grow up to realize that the punishment they received from loving parents was to steer them toward safety, the Jews do the same with God, and grow in their love and respect for him. In return, God vows that the years ahead will more than make up for the suffering they experienced.

"There will be survivors on Mount Zion and in Jerusalem." These Jewish survivors will have their land again. They will have the food and shelter they need. And they will have the presence of God—not in a sacred room in the temple of stone, but within the temple of the human body: "I will give my Spirit to everyone."

The apostle Peter, in New Testament times, saw in these words a prediction of the Holy Spirit's arrival after Jesus left (Acts 2:16). In a way we can't begin to understand, God is inside us. He talks to us, guiding us, giving us insight, pointing out problems we need to address, and praising us for jobs well done. That was God's promise through Joel, now fulfilled. We're all the better for it, if we listen.

# AMOS

## When We Don't Care About the Poor

Here's a shocker—a 2,700-year-old description of Israel that sounds like our nation today!

"You rich people lounge around on beds with ivory posts, while dining on the meat of your lambs and calves. You sing foolish songs to the music of harps, and you make up new tunes, just as David used to do. You drink all the wine you want and wear expensive perfume, but you don't care about the ruin of your nation" (6:4–6). By "ruin", the writer means spiritual and physical poverty.

Granted, ivory bedposts are politically incorrect today, and harps are obsolete. But substitute solid oak bedposts and electric guitars, and you have a disturbingly accurate portrait of suburbia, U.S.A.

> (ꞔꞔ) **Quote for You**
>
> "Let justice and fairness flow like a river that never runs dry" (5:24).

It's disturbing because of what follows in verse seven: "So you will be the first to be dragged off as captives; your good times will end."

Long before American civil rights leaders and advocacy groups, there was a sheepherder named Amos. To a prosperous nation where the rich got richer and the poor picked up the tab, Amos delivered God's message: "This is the end for my people Israel. I won't forgive them again" (8:2).

Nobody had reason to believe Amos. Life was good; Israel was at the peak of prosperity. Amos was a nobody—a sheepherder who suddenly appeared on Israel's doorstep, coming from their neighbor Jewish nation in the south. Maybe God chose Amos for that very reason—he was one nobody who represented all nobodies.

Amos called for fairness, for a stop to exploitation of the poor, and for an end of letting money do the talking in court.

Israelite leaders had two words for Amos: "Get out!" (7:12). With those words, they sentenced themselves. Assyria would invade Israel and drag the wealthy away as prized slaves.

The message was clear: No one abuses God's poor and gets away with it.

When It Happened

(Dates are approximate)

Adam 4000+ B.C.    Abraham 2100 B.C.    Moses 1500 B.C.    David 1000 B.C.    Fall of Israel 722 B.C.    Ezra 450 B.C.    Jesus born 7/6 B.C.

# Info You Can Use

## Background Notes

**Writer:** "I am Amos," the book begins (1:1). "I'm not a prophet! And I wasn't trained to be a prophet. I am a shepherd, and I take care of fig trees. But the Lord told me to leave my herds and preach to the people of Israel" (7:14–15).

The book's eloquent prose and poetry suggest Amos was more than a hired hand. He was an educated man who probably owned his herds and fig grove.

**Time:** Amos says he lived when "Jeroboam son of Jehoash was king of Israel" (1:1). Jeroboam II, as he's also known, ruled for about 41 years, from 786–746 B.C. The prosperity Amos describes fits the closing third of Jeroboam's reign, beginning in 760 B.C. That's why some Bible experts roughly date the prophecy to that year. The destruction Amos predicts comes later, in 722 B.C.

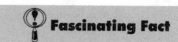

**Fascinating Fact**

Amos' prediction came true about 40 years later when Assyria invaded from the north and conquered Israel.

**Place:** Amos lives in Tekoa, a village ten miles south of Jerusalem, near the edge of a harsh and rocky badlands called the Judean Wilderness. Tekoa and Jerusalem are border towns in the southern Jewish nation of Judah. God orders Amos to cross the border, into the northern Jewish nation of Israel. Amos delivers his message in Bethel, a worship center about 20 miles north of his village.

**Bottom-Line Summary:** At God's command, a shepherd named Amos leaves the southern Jewish nation of Judah, travels across the border and into the northern Jewish nation of Israel, which is enjoying great prosperity. There, Amos delivers messages from God. He calls attention to some of the nation's most blatant sins:

- Rich people exploit the poor.

- In court, bribe-accepting judges rule for the litigant with the most money.

- Father and son sleep with the same woman—probably temple prostitutes engaging in pagan rituals.

- People go through the motions of worship, sinning one day and offering sacrifices the next, as though paying for the privilege of sinning makes it acceptable.

"I will crush you, just as a wagon full of grain crushes the ground," God says (2:13). Israel's prosperity will be their undoing, for it will lure Assyria to come and take everything they want.

Furious, an Israelite priest orders Amos to go back to Judah. Amos leaves, but not before predicting that the priest's children will die in war, his wife will become a prostitute, and the priest will die in a foreign country. As for Israel, Amos promises that one day God will restore the Jewish nation he has been forced to destroy.

# Influential People

**Amos,** a shepherd and fig grower whom God calls to deliver a prophetic message. The courage and boldness Amos shows in confronting national leaders with their sins is a model for Christians today. When we see injustice flow like a river, it's time to build a dam.

**Amaziah,** a priest who chases Amos away, is a perfect symbol of people so caught up in a sinful way of living that they've convinced themselves they're doing nothing wrong.

# Key Ideas You Need to Know

**Prosperity doesn't mean God is happy with us.** If we're doing well, and making a good living, it's tempting to think it's because God has blessed us. In fact, at times in early Jewish history, God promised to enrich the people if they obeyed his laws. For example, Moses told the Israelites on their way to the promised land, "Stay on the path that the Lord your God has commanded you to follow. Then you will live long and prosperous lives in the land" (Deuteronomy 5:33).

Some Jews in Bible times—like many religious people today—take that as an eternal promise for all godly people, a rightful privilege of God's royal family.

But if you think wealth is a measure of God's acceptance, read the story of Job, a righteous man who lost all his wealth. Read about Jesus describing himself as homeless (Matthew 8:20) and about him saying it's nearly impossible for rich people to please God (Matthew 19:24).

As for the Jews that Amos condemns, God's approval has nothing to do with their wave of prosperity: "They have become rich from violence and robbery" (3:10).

**The day of the Lord.** Like Joel, Amos reverses this once-positive phrase and turns it into something for Israel to fear. Popular preaching of the day said Israel was enjoying the rich fruits of God's favor, and that life would get even better on the day of the Lord, when God passes judgment on their enemies.

"You look forward to the day when the Lord comes to judge," Amos says. "But you are in for trouble! It won't be a time for sunshine; all will be darkness" (5:18). Anytime God passes judgment, it's bad news for bad people. Only those who live at peace with God have reason to eagerly await the day of the Lord— whether it's one of the many days when God steps into human history to set things right, or the final Judgment Day at the end of human history.

**Going through the motions of religion.** "Sin all you want!" Amos says sarcastically. That's exactly what the people of Israel people do. "Offer sacrifices the next morning and bring a tenth of your crops. . . . Bring offerings to show me how thankful you are. Gladly bring more offerings than I have demanded. You really love to do this" (4:4–5).

These Jews are an ancient variation on modern-day crooks who think, "We can't wait to cheat and charge high prices" (8:5):

- Builders who charge inflated prices for crackerjack box homes with cardboard ductwork, plastic water pipes and faucets, and warped siding.

- Lawyers who help themselves to 40 percent of what's awarded to their client.

- Utility company owners who run government-sanctioned regional monopolies that price-gouge everyone, including the elderly and frail whose meager and fixed income forces them to live in frigid temperatures in the winter and sweltering, air-conditionless heat in the summer.

- Political leaders whose goal above all else is to stay in office.

This list goes on and on because it draws from a seemingly bottomless well: a prosperous society permeated with greed. If we're caught up in the selfish lifestyle that's so prevalent, we think all we have to do is go to worship services every weekend. But that's not enough to undo the harm we cause the rest of the week.

To cheaters and crooks throughout the ages, Amos offers this riveting one-liner: "Get ready to face your God!" (4:12).

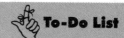

**To-Do List**

- "Do what is good and run from evil" (5:14, New Living Translation).

## Red Flag Issues

**Welfare.** Many people say it's a handout—giving people what they didn't earn and don't deserve.

God, on the other hand, created a welfare system. His was specially suited to the agricultural world of Bible times.

- Farmers were not to completely harvest their fields and vineyards, but were to leave the edges and other gleaning areas for the needy (Leviticus 23:22).

- Temple tithes—including crops, meat, and money—were used partly to help needy people: the widowed, orphaned, old, disabled, or strangers in the land (Deuteronomy 14:28–29).

- Every seventh year, farmers were to let the fields grow wild and allow the needy to take whatever they needed (Exodus 23:11).

- Every seventh year, all debts were erased—to keep debt from becoming a lifelong burden (Deuteronomy 15:1–2).

- "If there are any poor people in your towns," God tells the Israelites, "do not be hard-hearted or tightfisted toward them. Instead, be generous and lend them whatever they need" (Deuteronomy 15:7–8, New Living Translation).

Believing that poverty is unacceptable and unjust, many have sought to fight it through charity, welfare systems, and social change. John Wesley, theological father of many denominations including the United Methodist Church and the Church of the Nazarene, advocated a personal solution: earn all you can, save all you can, and give all you can. Though he earned a wealth of money through his preaching and writing, he gave most of it away throughout his life.

The point isn't to give people a free ride, but to help those who can't help themselves. Some people—those who pretend to be needy—will abuse the gift. But those truly in need are in no position to do so.

Perhaps the place to start is with a localized version of the goal Moses stated for his people: "No one in Israel should ever be poor" (Deuteronomy 15:4).

## Amos Well Used

**Helping the poor.** Civil rights leaders and advocates for the needy often draw from Amos and other prophets in pleading for justice. In his most famous speech, Martin Luther King, Jr. drew from Amos' prevailing theme of justice for the oppressed by saying, "I have a dream that one day even the state of Mississippi, a state sweltering with the heat of oppression, will be transformed into an oasis of freedom and justice."

Peruvian priest Gustavo Gutierrez, writing in the book *A Theology of Liberation*, says, "Poverty is not caused by fate; it is caused by the actions of those whom the prophet condemns," pointing to Amos 2:6–7. These two verses condemn rich people who crush the poor and make it impossible for them to break out of the cycle of poverty. For example, the rich loaned money to the poor by:

- demanding even the clothes off their back as security deposits,

- charging loan shark fines,

- and then selling the poor into slavery to cover the principal, interest, and fines for even the tiniest loan—equal to the price of a few loaves of bread.

# Bible Scenarios You Can Use

## 1. Rich people exploit the poor (2:6–7; 4:1–3; 8:4–6)

**"I** will punish Israel for countless crimes," God says. Israelite people with some wealth "smear the poor in the dirt and push aside those who are helpless." Poor folks who can't pay their debts—even small debts that amount to the price of sandals—are sold as slaves so the money lender can get back the principal and an excessive profit.

"We can't wait to cheat and charge high prices," Amos quotes the rich.

Amos calls the women of Samaria, the capital city, "fat cows." A more literal translation is "cows of Bashan." In Bible times, cattle from Bashan, in southern Syria, are famous as pampered prime stock, well bred and well fed. "You mistreat and abuse the poor and needy," Amos says, "then you say to your husbands, 'Bring us more drinks!'"

For this nationally condoned exploitation and abuse of the needy, God vows to crush Israel.

As people of God, we have a responsibility to treat others fairly and to defend the rights of those who can't defend themselves. This may mean contributing money, speaking out in city government meetings, and writing letters to our national policymakers. But if we see the abuse and do nothing, we stand with the abuser.

## 2. Judges are bought and paid for (5:7, 10–13)

**"Y**ou twist the truth and stomp on justice," Amos says.

"How you hate honest judges! How you despise people who tell the truth. . . . You oppress good people by taking bribes and deprive the poor of justice in the courts" (5:10, 12, New Living Translation).

Israel's wealthy often have enough money to bribe the judges when a case goes to trial. So the poor, no matter how right their cause, often lose.

Though the rich today can't usually bribe a judge or a jury, they often can and do have the best 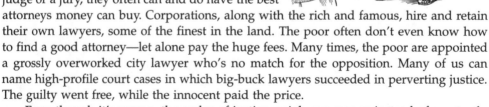 attorneys money can buy. Corporations, along with the rich and famous, hire and retain their own lawyers, some of the finest in the land. The poor often don't even know how to find a good attorney—let alone pay the huge fees. Many times, the poor are appointed a grossly overworked city lawyer who's no match for the opposition. Many of us can name high-profile court cases in which big-buck lawyers succeeded in perverting justice. The guilty went free, while the innocent paid the price.

Even though it's wrong, the scales of justice weigh our money instead of our truth. As Christians, God urges us to become champions of justice for all. In the end, we're going to win. Jesus said, "God blesses those who are hungry and thirsty for justice, for they will receive it in full" (Matthew 5:6, New Living Translation).

## 3. Israel is crooked (7:7–9)

"**T**he Lord showed me a vision of himself standing beside a wall and holding a string with a weight tied to the end of it," Amos says. "The string and weight had been used to measure the straightness of the wall."

When God asks Amos what he sees, the prophet answers, "a measuring line." In builder's terms, it's a plumb line. Bricklayers use it to make sure the wall they are building is perfectly vertical.

"I'm using this measuring line to show that my people Israel don't measure up," God says, "and I won't forgive them any more."

Like a crooked wall, Israel is weak and will be torn down.

God doesn't ignore our sins. He checks to see if we measure up. That may seem unnerving, especially given what he did to the crooked Jewish nation. But God has given us the ability to check ourselves, and the opportunity to make the necessary repairs. Our plumb line is the Bible and God's Spirit within us. We know when something about us is crooked, and we generally know how to fix it. If the problem is more complicated, and we don't know how to fix it, help is available and waiting.

# OBADIAH

## When You Can't Get Even

Imagine this modern version of Obadiah's story.

Burglars break into your house and kill your family. You escape to your neighbors—distant cousins with whom you don't get along. There, you find, to your horror, that they were in on the burglary. They march you back home, where the burglars tie you up and start loading your family's valuables into a rental truck. Your neighbors take what the burglars don't want, then cheer as the burglars set fire to your house and drive away with you.

So, how would you feel about your neighbors?

That's exactly how the Jews felt about the people of Edom.

Babylon invaded the southern Jewish nation of Judah. The northern Jewish nation of Israel had been wiped out about 150 years

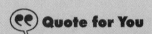
earlier, so Judah was all that was left. Babylon leveled city after city, saving Jerusalem for last. Many Jewish refugees escaped south to Edom, homeland of their distant relatives. Jews descended from Jacob, while the people of Edom descended from his twin brother, Esau. That means both nations were children of Abraham and Isaac. But they didn't get along any better than the twins did. The people of Edom arrested the Jews and gave them to the Babylonians. Then the Edomites joined in the Babylonian victory party in Jerusalem and scavenged Judah's ruins for anything the invaders didn't take.

Most of us haven't suffered anything this horrifying, but we've been wronged many times in our lives. Bullies spit in our face. Teachers falsely accuse us. Employers cheat us. Colleagues lie about us. Mechanics fix what isn't broken. Robbers break what can't be fixed.

At times, it seems like justice extends beyond our reach. Obadiah reminds us that it's always within God's reach. In due time, justice will prevail.

## When It Happened

(Dates are approximate)

Adam 4000+ B.C.    Abraham 2100 B.C.    Moses 1500 B.C.    David 1000 B.C.    Fall of Israel 722 B.C.    Ezra 450 B.C.    Jesus born 7/6 B.C.

# Info You Can Use

 **Background Notes**

**Writer:** "The Lord God gave Obadiah a message about Edom," the book begins. We know nothing else about Obadiah, except that his name means "servant (or worshiper) of the Lord." Some Bible experts guess that "Obadiah" isn't the writer's name, but simply a description of an unidentified prophet. But it certainly could have been his name, since Obadiah was a common name shared by about a dozen people in the Old Testament.

**Time:** Because Obadiah talks about how Edom helped invaders destroy Judah, he probably delivered his prophecy sometime after 586 B.C., when Babylon defeated Judah and exiled the survivors.

**Place:** Edom was the dry and rocky region south of the Dead Sea. The country's name means "red," perhaps referring to the cinnamon-colored sandstone hills. One famous Edomite city—Petra—was carved into the face of these hills. Located in Jordan, about 100 miles southeast of Jerusalem, Petra's ruins are a tourist attraction today.

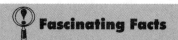 **Fascinating Facts**

With only 29 verses, Obadiah is the shortest book in the Bible.

"Indiana Jones and the Last Crusade," a movie starring Harrison Ford as an archaeologist racing with the Nazis to find the cup Jesus used in the Last Supper (the Holy Grail), went on location in what used to be Edom. To represent the secret location of the Holy Grail, the director chose a huge temple-like façade carved into the cliffs at Petra. In reality, the façade extends only a few feet into the cliff wall.

**Bottom-Line Summary:** The Babylonian Empire invades and destroys the southern Jewish nation of Judah—the last remnant of the once powerful Israel. Soldiers plunder all the nation's valuables, including the luxurious temple decorated in gold and silver. Jewish survivors are rounded up as prisoners of war, doomed to become slaves in what is now Iraq.

The people of Edom, Judah's neighbors to the south, are delighted. They round up Jewish refugees who cross their border, and return them to the Babylonians. Then they raid the Jewish ruins to steal anything the Babylonians missed.

For their cruelty, Obadiah says, Edom will "vanish without a trace" (16). And he quickly adds that the Jewish nation will be restored.

This is exactly what happened. The Jews start returning home about 50 years later, in 538 B.C. Within about a century of that, the nation of Edom was gone, possibly driven out by Arabs. Ironically, many of Edom's refugees fled to Israel, where they lived and became assimilated into the Jewish culture. King Herod the Great, who lived in Christ's time, was a descendant of the Edomites. That's one reason the Jews hated him so much.

# Influential People

**Obadiah,** a prophet who predicts the end of Edom and the restoration of Israel. His message, delivered during the darkest days of Jewish history, is a stirring portrait of unshakable confidence in God.

# Key Ideas You Need to Know

**Pride is a shortcut to destruction.** "You are proud because you live in a rock fortress and make your home high in the mountains," God says to the people of Edom. "Though you soar as high as eagles and build your nest among the stars, I will bring you crashing down" (3–4, New Living Translation).

Edom's sole surviving ruins is the seemingly impenetrable rock city of Petra, accessible only through a narrow and sheer vertical canyon. The canyon is so narrow that in places it would be difficult for two charging horsemen to ride side-by-side. Tourists today walk or ride horses through the canyon pass. Once tourists clear the canyon they see a plateau surrounded by steep rock hills. The sight of those hills is breathtaking, for out of the solid stone cliffs, master artisans carved homes and temples—many that are several stories high, with majestic columns and ornate designs.

Edom was once known for its wise men. One of Job's comforters—a thoughtful and highly educated man—came from a city in Edom. But God vowed that a day was coming when "not a single wise person will be left in the whole land of Edom" (8, New Living Translation).

As a sage once put it, "Too much pride will destroy you" (Proverbs 16:18). The people of Edom could testify to that, but they're gone.

# Bible Scenario You Can Use

### 1. Obadiah's promise: Edom will fall, the Jews will rise again (1:1–21) ━━━━

**B**abylonian invaders overrun the Jewish nation, leveling one city after another, including Jerusalem. Jewish refugees run for their lives. Many escape to Edom, their neighbor to the south. Edom is anything but a good neighbor. They arrest the refugees, turn them over to the Babylonians, and then join the invaders in celebrating the death of the Jewish nation. Afterward, the people of Edom rummage through the Jewish ruins, "sneering and stealing."

Though it's true God is punishing the Jews for their centuries of sin, that doesn't give the people of Edom any right to intensify the Jewish tragedy. "Edom," God says, "you will pay in full for what you have done." The Jews will one day return home. And when they do, "Israel will be a fire and Edom will be straw going up in flames."

As Obadiah predicts, the Jews are released to come home a few decades later. Edom mysteriously dies the next century. Archaeologists guess they were driven from their homes by Arab invaders.

When someone does us wrongly, we want to retaliate. It's a very human response. The Mosaic law put some limits on the retaliation, to make the response match the offense. Later, Jesus taught his followers to break the cycle of violence by not retaliating personally. Often, retaliation is the worst thing to do because it prolongs and aggravates our suffering. Believers today are God's people, as surely as the Jews were in ancient times. We can count on God to settle the score for us, too. That means we can walk away from deep wrongs and take with us our peace of mind, assured of God's justice.

# JONAH

## Mercy for the Mean

Who can blame Jonah for running away from God? What God asked of him was a lot like asking a Polish Jew during the Second World War to go to Berlin and tell the Germans they were doomed.

That was the message God told Jonah to deliver to the Assyrians, Israel's mortal enemies who had a maniacal fetish for cruelty. For entertainment, Assyrian soldiers cut open the stomach of live prisoners, inserted a live cat, quickly stitched up the stomach, and then watched the cat claw itself free.

Why deliver a death threat to people like this? Jonah could die trying. Why not just wipe out the Assyrians and be done with it? The sooner the better—for the Jews and everyone else in the ancient Middle East.

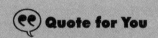

**Quote for You**

"You are a kind and merciful God, and you don't get angry very easily. You always show love, and you don't like to punish anyone" (4:2).

There have been times when God wiped out entire cities—Sodom and Gomorrah, for example. In fact, Nineveh eventually got sacked by invaders and became a sheep pasture. That happened about 150 years after Jonah. Archaeologists discovered the ruins in 1845.

But in Jonah's lifetime, God had a chance to turn a corner in history—to dramatically show that his love and salvation weren't just for the Jews. They were for everyone, including the ruthless but repentant Assyrians.

It took a few miracles and one very large fish to convince Jonah to deliver God's message. But once delivered, the message helped human beings catch a glimpse of the enormous heart of a God who shows the greatest of mercy to the meanest of people.

When It Happened

(Dates are approximate)

Adam 4000+ B.C.

Abraham 2100 B.C.

Moses 1500 B.C.

David 1000 B.C.

Divided Kingdom 931 B.C.

Fall of Israel 722 B.C.

Ezra 450 B.C.

Jesus born 7/6 B.C.

# Info You Can Use

## Background Notes

**Writer:** Bible experts can't tell if Jonah wrote the book himself, or if someone else wrote about him, perhaps after his story had been passed on by word of mouth for generations. Many experts prefer the theory that someone else wrote it because the book says Nineveh "was" a great city, as though its glory days were over (3:3). Whoever wrote the book, the story is about "Jonah, the son of Amittai."

**Time:** This same "Jonah, son of Amittai" is identified in 2 Kings 14:25 as a prophet who assured King Jeroboam II of success in expanding Israel's borders. Jeroboam ruled for about 40 years, from 786–746 B.C. Other famous prophets living about this time included Amos, Hosea, Micah, and Isaiah.

**Place:** Jonah lived in the northern Jewish nation of Israel, in the tiny Galilean village of Gath-Hepher, about three miles north of Nazareth. Jonah's story takes him first to the Mediterranean Sea, as he tries to run away from God. The story ends in Nineveh, a leading Assyrian city (sometimes its capital), in what is now northern Iraq.

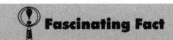
**Fascinating Fact**

Many Jews today read the Book of Jonah on *Yom Kippur* (the Day of Atonement), an annual Jewish holy day for seeking forgiveness.

**Bottom-Line Summary:** God tells the prophet Jonah to go to Nineveh, a city deep inside the Assyrian empire, which is Israel's most feared enemy. Jonah's assignment is to tell the Assyrians that God will destroy Nineveh in 40 days.

Though Nineveh is east of Israel, in what is now Iraq, Jonah heads in the opposite direction. He boards a ship that sets sail on the Mediterranean Sea. God produces a storm that nearly sinks the ship. At Jonah's instruction, the crewmen throw him overboard. The storm stops and a large fish swallows Jonah. Three days later, the fish vomits Jonah onto the shore.

Jonah goes to Nineveh and delivers the message. Terrified, the Assyrian king orders his people to stop sinning and to pray for God's mercy. God spares Nineveh. This infuriates Jonah, who lived through a whale of a nightmare to deliver a message that didn't come true. While Jonah sits outside the city and pouts, God explains that he has a right to show mercy on the 120,000 people of Nineveh.

## Influential People

**Jonah,** a Jewish prophet whom God compels to deliver a message that ends up saving 120,000 people. Jonah repeatedly comes across as a man who's more concerned about himself than others. As a result, one of the main points of the story seems to be this: don't be like Jonah. Even so, God uses Jonah for important work and continues teaching him how to mature into a compassionate person.

Jonah is a reminder that even if we're selfish, God can use us as we are and teach us to become better.

#  Key Ideas You Need to Know

**God cares about everyone—not just those who love him.** Some people think God loves only those who love him, or at least he loves them best. In Bible times, many Jews think God cares only about them, since he chose them as his special people and proved it with miracles.

Jonah's story, however, is just one of many in the Bible that prove otherwise. Though the Assyrians are Israel's most feared enemy in Jonah's day, God loves them enough to send Jonah to warn them they are on the brink of disaster—an endeavor that requires several miracles.

More Bible examples of God's love for everyone:

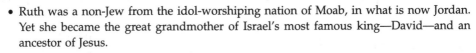

**To-Do List**

- "Pray to the Lord God with all your heart and stop being sinful" (3:8).

- When God chose Abraham to become the father of the Jews, God explained that instead of enjoying a monopoly on divine love and salvation, the Jews were to spread the wealth: "I have placed you here as a light for other nations; you must take my saving power to everyone on earth" (Isaiah 49:6).

- Ruth was a non-Jew from the idol-worshiping nation of Moab, in what is now Jordan. Yet she became the great grandmother of Israel's most famous king—David—and an ancestor of Jesus.

- In Jesus' parable of the prodigal son, the loving father (who represents God) eagerly welcomes home his wayward son (who symbolizes all sinful people).

God certainly doesn't approve of our sins, but he doesn't stop loving us because of them—anymore than a parent stops loving a child who makes a long string of bad decisions.

**Love your enemies.** Jonah wanted nothing to do with Assyria, Israel's most threatening enemy. God had to take extreme measures to convince Jonah to go there. And even after Jonah's message convinced the citizens to repent, Jonah preferred them dead.

God's wish for Jonah—and for all of us—is well expressed by Jesus, several centuries later: "Love your enemies and pray for anyone who mistreats you" (Matthew 5:44).

#  Q&A

**Why did Jonah believe he could run away from God?** You'd think a prophet would know better. But people in Jonah's day had a limited understanding of God, compared to what we know today through the Bible. Many Jews seemed to believe that God lived with his people in the promised land, much as he had traveled with their ancestors during the exodus out of Egypt (leading them in a pillar of fire and smoke). Jews considered the temple as God's earthly home.

Jonah may have thought that by leaving Israel he could get away from God who ruled Israel.

The point of the story is to prove otherwise—that the Lord is God of all, and that there's no limit to the range of his power and compassion.

**Why would Assyrians listen to a Jewish prophet when the Jews didn't?** The Bible doesn't say. The Jews habitually ignored warnings from the prophets, and suffered the consequences. The Assyrians of Nineveh, however, immediately believed the message of a foreign stranger.

Perhaps the answer to the puzzle lies in a comment Jesus made when the people of his hometown—Nazareth—rejected his message: "Prophets are honored by everyone, except the people of their hometown" (Matthew 13:57). Though prophets of God were common in Israel, they may have been as rare in Nineveh as a solar eclipse—and just as foreboding.

It could also be that Jonah looked the part of an apocalyptic messenger, bearing the effects of living three days in the fish's acidic stomach.

**Is Jonah a true story or a fictional parable?** Bible experts debate the matter. The story sounds a lot like a short, action-packed parable. It grabs and holds your attention with a short 48 verses brimming with drama and miracles. And it ends suddenly, as soon as the moral is delivered—just like a parable. Also, archaeologists have uncovered a lot of records from the ruins of Nineveh, but nothing confirming Jonah's story.

On the other hand, 2 Kings 14:25 says there was a prophet named Jonah who lived during the Assyrian era. Jesus also spoke of Jonah, comparing his three days in the grave with Jonah's three days inside the fish.

History or parable, the message doesn't change: God cares about everyone, and he wants us to do the same.

# Bible Scenarios You Can Use

### 1. Man overboard (1:1—2:10)

**G**od orders a Jewish prophet named Jonah to go to Israel's most feared enemy—the Assyrian Empire, in what is now Iraq. The prophet's mission: tell the people of Nineveh they're doomed.

Jonah promptly books passage on a ship headed in the opposite direction. After all, Jonah had correctly predicted that Israel would reclaim territory lost to Assyria (2 Kings 14:25). So the Assyrians might be steamed. They're an insatiably violent people even without provocation. Fine art displayed on their palace walls include foreign landscapes—with the locals impaled on stakes.

With Jonah's getaway ship sailing in the Mediterranean Sea, God churns up a perfect storm. The crew jettisons the cargo and then turns to prayer. Jonah confesses he's the problem, and he says that to calm the storm the crew needs to throw him overboard. At first they refuse, and try rowing to shore. But with the ship in danger of sinking, the seamen do as Jonah instructed, and the seas calm down.

Some kind of huge, unidentified fish swallows Jonah. The Bible doesn't say it was a whale, perhaps because even Jonah never knew. Inside the fish's stomach, Jonah prays a bewildered prayer thanking God for rescuing him. Three days later, the fish vomits Jonah onto a beach.

God may not pursue us as persistently as he did Jonah, whose ministry saved 120,000 people, but God never stops reaching out to us. Like the father in Jesus' parable of the prodigal son, God may not pursue us at all—but instead may wait patiently for us to come home, wiser and more devoted than ever. When we do, God's arms are open. Meanwhile, his love is always tugging at our heart, reminding us where home is.

## 2. Jonah preaches and Assyrians repent (3:1–10)

From the Mediterranean coast, Jonah travels to Nineveh—about a thousand miles away, following the trade routes along the rivers. There, before a crowd, Jonah delivers his prophecy: "Forty days from now, Nineveh will be destroyed."

The people believe him. The king orders citizens of Nineveh to stop doing evil things, to wear ragged clothes like those that people in mourning wear, and to pray for God's forgiveness. "Maybe God will change his mind and have mercy on us," the king says.

God sees the Assyrian transformation, so he changes his plans for them accordingly. He forgives them and lets them live.

Some people feel they've sinned so horribly that God would never forgive them. But the Assyrians had an earned reputation as one of the most violent cultures in history. They burned surrendering cities, smashed children's heads on rocks, and impaled living victims on stakes. Their kings glorified war. Yet, God forgave the likes of these people when they asked. He'll forgive the likes of us, too.

## 3. Jonah gets mad about God's mercy (4:1–10)

Jonah is furious. He told the people they were doomed, and now God changes his mind.

"Let me die," Jonah prays. "I'd be better off dead."

Jonah considers himself a discredited failure because his prophecy didn't come true, and Israel's mortal enemy survived God's judgment. Actually, Jonah didn't fail. He is one of the few Bible prophets who succeed in convincing people to stop sinning.

While Jonah pouts in the hot sun outside the city walls, God lets a vine grow to shade him. Then God kills the vine, which upsets Jonah again. "You feel sorry about the plant," God says. "And a plant is only, at best, short lived. But Nineveh has more than 120,000 people living in spiritual darkness. . . . Shouldn't I feel sorry for such a great city?" (4:10–11, New Living Translation).

We all want to see the bad guys get what's coming to them. But God wants to see the bad guys become the good guys. That's what he created them to be. When evil people we know turn their lives around, we need to work on releasing our anger about their past offenses and start seeing them as God does: forgiven.

# MICAH

## What God Hates

Some of us would prefer to think of God as pure love—unable to hate. Maybe that's because we know if he can hate, he might hate us.

Well, there's good news and bad news. First the bad: though God is pure love, he also hates. The good news is he doesn't hate us.

Micah paints a picture of the two sides of God—the love and the hate. God's love is goodness, and nothing but. That means there's only one thing he can hate: evil.

God hates the evil we do, but he doesn't hate us for committing the sin. In other words, he hates the sin, not the sinner. How's that possible? We can see an example of it in the loving family relationships around us. We see parents disciplining, supporting, and loving their wayward children—even visiting a child on death row for murder admitted. Parents will passionately hate the drugs, guns, gangs, or anything else that contributed to the evil in their child's life. But they will tenaciously love their child.

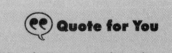 **Quote for You**

"See that justice is done, let mercy be your first concern" (6:8).

In Micah's day, Israel was an evil place. God hated what was happening there. Micah rattled off a litany of the nation's sins: greed, fraud, extortion, robbery, corruption among judges and rulers, immorality, oppression, witchcraft, injustice, murder. God hated it all. Since the people wouldn't put a stop to it, God said he would. He vowed to dismantle the Jewish nation and start over. If he had hated the people along with the sin, he would have left out the part about starting over.

What God did for the Jews, he does for all people. Because he loves us, he hates the sin that hurts us. And he takes his stand against the sin.

## When It Happened

(Dates are approximate)

Adam 4000+ B.C.    Abraham 2100 B.C.    Moses 1500 B.C.    David 1000 B.C.    Fall of Israel 722 B.C.    Fall of Judah 586 B.C.    Ezra 450 B.C.    Jesus born 7/6 B.C.

# Info You Can Use

## Background Notes

**Writer:** The book was written by Micah, a prophet from a rural village a hard day's walk from Jerusalem. He didn't have the political savvy of aristocratic prophets such as Isaiah, so he didn't give advice about international matters. But Micah was well acquainted with problems of the common folks, who were losing their limited resources to corrupt rulers, judges, and nobles.

**Time:** Micah said he delivered God's messages during the reigns of three kings: Jotham, Ahaz, and Hezekiah. The reigns of these three kings covered about 55 years, from 742–687 B.C.

**Place:** The prophet said he lived in Moresheth, a tiny village in the Judean hills, about 25 miles southwest of Jerusalem.

**Bottom-Line Summary:** Micah, a hill-country prophet, takes on the upper crust of both Jewish nations, Israel and Judah. In graphic and gruesome imagery directed at the two capital cities, Samaria and Jerusalem, he accuses the rich of butchering and cannibalizing the poor. Greed drives the two nations; judges take bribes, priests teach God's law only for money, and prophets tell fortunes for a fee. Rulers and other rich landowners abuse the poor with price-gouging and excessive interest rates. In desperation, the masses pray to idols for relief.

Micah warns that God will punish both nations, and the prophet lives to see it. Assyria destroys Israel in 722 B.C. About 20 years later, Assyria overruns Judah and turns it into a vassal nation forced to pay high taxes to the empire. Babylon will later finish fulfilling the prophecy by destroying Judah in 586 B.C.

### Fascinating Fact

After a Jewish revolt in A.D. 135, the Romans replaced Jewish and Christian shrines with ones devoted to Roman gods. Over a Bethlehem cave stable thought to have been Jesus' birthplace, they built a shrine to Adonis—a god known for his death and resurrection. Roman myth says that Adonis goes to the place of the dead during winter and he returns in the spring. The shrine was replaced by a church two centuries later—the Church of the Nativity, a popular tourist attraction.

Though doom is Micah's prediction, that's not the final word. Micah promises that God will one day restore the Jewish nation, and that the people will again love the Lord.

## Influential People

**Micah,** a rural prophet who's not intimidated by royalty, criticizes the sins of Jewish rulers. His boldness is a reminder that we serve the King of kings, and we don't have to be shy about taking a stand against evil—even evil supported by powerful institutions.

# Q&A

**Does God sometimes ignore our cry for mercy?** "Someday you will beg the Lord to help you," Micah says, "but he will turn away because of your sins" (3:4).

Would God do to us what he did to the Jews? If necessary. The Jews took their sins too far, and ignored God's warnings for too long. When invaders crossed their borders and the Jews cried for help, God knew that if he stopped the invasion the Jews would just return to business as usual. Mercy wouldn't change them. But judgment would help future generations see the connection between sin and consequences. That's exactly what happened. The restored nation of Israel became more devoted to God than past generations had ever been.

With repeat offenders who have no intention of changing their evil way of living, God may withdraw his mercy—which would only have been trampled on anyhow. But for those who call for mercy and are

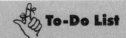 **To-Do List**

- "Humbly obey your God" (6:8).

- "I trust the Lord God to save me, and I will wait for him to answer my prayer" (7:7).

willing to accept the godly changes it produces, there's more mercy than we could ever need. "God is so rich in mercy, and he loved us so very much" the apostle Paul said, "that even while we were dead because of our sins, he gave us life when he raised Christ from the dead" (Ephesians 2:4–5, New Living Translation).

# Red Flag Issues

**Fortune-telling.** Just like many people today, some folks in Bible times experimented with ways to look into the future. They went to mediums, sorcerers, and the prophets of various gods. Some even tried sleeping at shrines and temples, hoping the spirit world would contact them in a dream.

Some religious people today see nothing wrong with consulting psychics, arguing that some people have the gift of opening channels to the dead. Though many psychics today are frauds, some may have this gift. But it's a dark gift that God wants his people to avoid. Conjuring up the dead, or asking someone else to do it for you, drew the death penalty in the days of Moses. Micah repeats God's disapproval by quoting the Lord: "I will stop you from telling fortunes and practicing witchcraft" (5:12).

The Bible never explains what's wrong with consulting psychics. Some Bible experts say that it may be because there are good spirits and bad spirits, and unless we're consulting God, we can't know we're dealing with a spirit who wants to help us.

The apostle Paul refers to this in one of his letters: "We are not fighting against humans. We are fighting against forces and authorities and against rulers of darkness and powers in the spiritual world" (Ephesians 6:12). In another letter

Paul adds: "In the last times some will turn away from what we believe; they will follow lying spirits and teachings that come from demons" (1 Timothy 4:1, New Living Translation).

If we want to know what lies ahead, God wants us to turn to him. And if the answers don't come, he wants us to trust him with the future. (For more, see "Stay away from psychics," Leviticus, page 43.)

## Micah Well Used

**Liberating the poor.** Christians in parts of Central and South America have taken their cue from the prophet Micah, and have started finding practical ways to help the poor. In many regions, wealthy landowners and military leaders lay claim to all the land—entire villages and surrounding forests. The rural masses often live in huts of scrap metal and wood, and pay rent by working for the landowners at wages that will never free them from the cycle of poverty. In many places the villagers can't even gather firewood from the forest without paying for the wood.

For these reasons, many church leaders have associated rich landowners with the wealthy people Micah condemned: "You grab any field or house that you want; you cheat families out of homes and land" (2:2).

In response, church leaders have organized efforts to provide the masses with basic services, such as water and sewage. Some even buy land at high prices and give it to villagers so these families can own their home and have a little plot of ground for a garden. Churches have also gotten involved in the political arena, as advocates for the poor.

The principle that generated these efforts became known as liberation theology. Critics quickly linked the idea with communism. But with the collapse of communism in Europe, many onlookers are feeling less threatened, and are seeing the work as a grassroots effort to give millions of poor people a chance to break free from poverty.

# Bible Scenarios You Can Use

## 1. Leaders take bribes (3:1–12)

**A** rural prophet from the countryside, Micah criticizes Jewish leaders who abuse the poor. "Listen to me, you rulers of Israel!" he says. "You know right from wrong, but you prefer to do evil instead of what is right. You skin my people alive. You strip off their flesh, break their bones, cook it all in a pot, and gulp it down." This is graphic, poetic imagery of the rich taking the poor for everything they can get—and in any way they can get it.

"You leaders accept bribes for dishonest decisions. You priests and prophets teach and preach, but only for money." For this and many other sins against God and each other, Micah says, the Lord is going to turn the greatest Jewish cities into rubble and plowed fields.

It's no secret that we can get rich and powerful by cheating others out of their money, taking bribes, and concentrating most of our efforts on increasing our wealth. But there's a price to pay. We invite tragedy: retaliation from those we hurt; robbery and murder from those who want what we have; God's judgment for sin—which can leave us as bankrupt as it did the Jewish leaders.

Jesus said, "Don't store up treasures on earth! Moths and rust can destroy them, and thieves can break in and steal them. Instead, store up your treasures in heaven" (Matthew 6:19–20). Among heavens treasures are justice and mercy (6:8). We can't accumulate these when we're cheating the daylights out of our neighbors. Nor can we accumulate them when we silently stand by and watch our leaders do this to others.

## 2. A ruler will be born in Bethlehem (5:2–5)

**T**hough God vows to destroy the two Jewish nations for their sins, he promises that annihilation won't be his last act. He will restore Israel and send a leader unlike any of the self-obsessed, bribe-taking leaders from Micah's day.

"Like a shepherd taking care of his sheep," Micah prophesies, "this ruler will lead and care for his people by the power and glorious name of the Lord his God. His people will live securely, and the whole earth will know his true greatness, because he will bring peace."

Micah says this ruler will come from the tiny village of Bethlehem, near Jerusalem. New Testament writers said this ruler was Jesus, the Prince of Peace.

Jesus is the perfect model for any of us in a position of leadership, whether we're ruling a country, managing employees, or taking care of kids. When we deal with others, God wants us to deal fairly, compassionately, and lovingly. We're to take all the bad examples of leadership that we read about in Micah, and go in exactly the opposite direction.

## 3. Looking for one who does right (7:1–9)

**M**icah says that finding good and honest people is like trying to find figs or grapes after the harvest—there aren't any.

"No one is loyal to God; no one does right. Everyone is brutal and eager to deceive everyone else. People cooperate to commit crime. Judges and leaders demand bribes, and rulers cheat in courts."

Sin is contagious, spreading quickly. Before we know it, corruption, dishonesty, and greed are so prevalent that we talk ourselves into using the same tactics just so we can survive. The government taxes us nearly to death and then squanders much of it on luxurious offices and perks for the

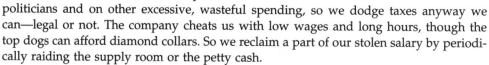

politicians and on other excessive, wasteful spending, so we dodge taxes anyway we can—legal or not. The company cheats us with low wages and long hours, though the top dogs can afford diamond collars. So we reclaim a part of our stolen salary by periodically raiding the supply room or the petty cash.

When we do that, we become part of the very landscape Micah condemns: "No one does right." God calls for us to live in honesty and fairness, instead of making excuses for our sins. For though evil is contagious, so is goodness. Spread it around.

# NAHUM

## Victims Anonymous

Remember that school bully who used to shove you up against the lockers just to hear the sound of your head clanging into the steel?

Or how about that builder who gave you a mere one-year warranty on that cheaply built house? Remember how you felt when the builder refused to honor even that paltry warranty, and then the lawyer you contacted said his fees wouldn't make a lawsuit worth the trouble?

It's natural to want justice—to see our victimizers get nothing less than they deserve. To see the bully stuffed in a locker. To see the builder sentenced to live 30 years in a house he built for someone else.

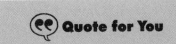
Unfortunately, we can't usually control justice. Sometimes, it eludes us entirely. The bully moves away. The builder gets rich.

Nahum is the Bible book for the victim in all of us. It's all about being victimized, and about one victimizer in particular: the Assyrians. This brutal empire headquartered in what is now northern Iraq was hated from the Persian Gulf to Egypt. Along this swath they had slaughtered entire cities, subjugated countless kingdoms, and wiped the northern Jewish nation of Israel off the map. Nahum told the southern Jewish nation of Judah, which was forced to pay exorbitant taxes to avoid Israel's fate, that God was about to settle the score with Assyria.

At one time or another we've all been victimized: lied to, cheated, robbed, raped, beaten, shot. We want justice. But we can't always find it. Nahum points us toward peace of mind. And he does it by reminding us that the matter is in God's hands. "The Lord is powerful," Nahum says, "he makes sure that the guilty are always punished" (1:3).

When we accept this, we can get on with our life.

## When It Happened

(Dates are approximate)

Adam 4000+ B.C.

Abraham 2100 B.C.

Moses 1500 B.C.

David 1000 B.C.

Fall of Israel 722 B.C.

Fall of Nineveh 612 B.C.

Fall of Judah 586 B.C.

Ezra 450 B.C.

Jesus born 7/6 B.C.

# Info You Can Use

## Background Notes

**Writer:** "I am Nahum from Elkosh," the book begins. Nahum is never again mentioned in the Bible. We don't even know where Elkosh was.

**Time:** Nahum probably delivered his message sometime between 663 and 612 B.C. This is a guess based on two facts. First, Nahum said the city of Thebes, in Egypt, had already fallen (3:8–10); Assyria captured Thebes in 663 B.C. Second, Nahum predicted the fall of Assyria; it fell to the Babylonians and Medes in 612 B.C. This means Nahum lived and ministered about the time of two other prophets: young Jeremiah along with Zephaniah.

**Place:** No one knows exactly where Nahum's hometown of Elkosh was. But it was probably somewhere in the southern Jewish nation of Judah, since Assyria wiped out the northern nation of Israel in 722 B.C. The Assyrian Empire, which Nahum said would soon collapse, extended from the Persian Gulf to Egypt. It's capital, Nineveh, was in northern Iraq.

**Bottom-Line Summary:** About 100 years after Assyria wipes out the northern Jewish nation of Israel, and while it continues terrorizing Judah and other kingdoms throughout the Middle East, the prophet Nahum delivers a welcome message to his Judean countrymen: the monster is about to be slain. Nineveh, Assyria's capital, will be destroyed. The king will be killed, and his empire will fall.

"I will send you to the grave," Nahum says, quoting God. "You will never again make victims of others" (1:14; 2:13).

Probably within 50 years of this prophecy, perhaps much less, Nahum's prediction comes true. Combined armies of the Babylonians and Medes overrun the Assyrians.

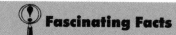

### Fascinating Facts

About a century before Nahum, God sent Jonah to the Assyrian capital to tell them their city was about to fall. At the king's command, they repented and God spared them. Unfortunately, they eventually returned to their sinful living.

The name Nahum means "comfort." That's an odd coincidence since his message sounds almost entirely vindictive. Yet his promise that God would soon destroy evil Assyria would have brought comfort and hope to the many nations Assyria victimized.

## Influential People

**Nahum,** a Jewish prophet who promises his fellow countrymen that God will punish Assyria for its cruelty. Nahum's message is a reminder that victimized people need to know that justice will prevail—even if settling the score is something they have to entrust to God.

## Key Ideas You Need to Know

**No power is stronger than God.** Assyria was the strongest power on the face of the earth during Nahum's day, much like the United States today. The Jews felt as helpless against the Assyrians as tiny nations do today when confronted by major nations that can impose sanctions or embargoes to force compliance. But no power is stronger than God, who pursues justice. If we live in a land that does not honor justice, our future will likely repeat Assyria's history. We'll be dished up what we dish out.

**Vicious Assyria.** The Jews and other cultures throughout the ancient Middle East hated Assyria for good reason. Archaeologists have confirmed what the Bible reports: the Assyrians were merciless invaders. Storming into captured cities, they would slaughter the citizens, young and old. They'd set up rows of stakes as thick as fence posts, and then impale the bodies of the living and the dead. Grabbing babies by the ankles, they would swing them like clubs and dash their heads against stone walls.

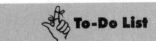

**To-Do List**

• "The Lord God demands loyalty" (1:2).

One Assyrian king, Shalmaneser III, had the citizens of a defeated city decapitated, and then used the heads to build a grisly pyramid. Royalty, nobles, and other survivors were auctioned off to the highest bidder, or tortured for the entertainment of the soldiers.

Assyrian kings were so proud of their empire's violent reputation that they hired artists to recreate gruesome battle scenes in stone carvings that were mounted on the palace walls.

Assyria's defeat sparked rejoicing throughout the known world.

## Q&A

**Why does God punish?** If you've been brutally victimized, you're more likely to ask why God doesn't punish sooner. In fact, the two questions are closely related. God was incredibly slow at punishing the Assyrians. Nahum explains it this way: "The Lord is powerful, yet patient" (1:3). On the brink of destroying Assyria's capital 100 years before Nahum, God mercifully relented when the people asked for forgiveness. But the Assyrians later rejected God's mercy. That's when God determined that the time had come for them to receive the sentence they had imposed on others: death. Sometimes, the most loving and merciful thing to do is to put an end to cruelty—especially when there's no more chance that the cruel ones will have a change of heart.

# Bible Scenario You Can Use

## 1. Assyria will fall (1:12—2:13)

"**A**ssyria, no matter how strong you are, you are doomed!" says the prophet Nahum, quoting God. "Your name will be forgotten. I will destroy every idol in your temple, and I will send you to the grave, because you are worthless."

For nearly as long as the Jewish nation has existed, Assyria has been terrorizing the Middle East—some 700 years. A vicious superpower, Assyria has at one time or another pillaged almost every nation in the region, from the Persian Gulf to Egypt. Their specialty is collecting protection money. They invade a country, take whatever and whomever they want, then order the survivors to pay oppressive taxes as an insurance against invasion. Kingdoms that rebel are punished as an example to others considering rebellion. That's what happens when the king of the northern Jewish nation of Israel refuses to make his insurance payment. Assyrian soldiers swarm in, level the cities, exile the survivors, and repopulate Israel with Assyrian pioneers. Israel ceases to exist.

Judah, the southern Jewish nation, makes the payments and survives—but only as hostages who continually pay their own ransom.

About a century after wiping out Israel, the Assyrians themselves are overrun by a coalition army of Babylonians and Medes. Assyria's capital city of Nineveh is so utterly destroyed that its ruins aren't discovered until 1845.

Citizens of the thriving and prosperous Assyria must have felt like nothing could stop their nation. Many of us today may harbor that same false sense of security. So we overlook any oppressive policies of our nation—as long as we're not the oppressed. One lesson to learn from Assyria is that God holds citizens accountable for the evils of their nation. If we see our leaders setting up policies that oppress others, inside or outside our country, we have a responsibility to express our disapproval and work toward compassionate policies. It's a matter of life or death—ours. As the Assyrians found out, "sin pays off with death" (Romans 6:23).

# HABAKKUK

## Why Does God Let the Wicked Win?

Whoever said crime doesn't pay isn't paying attention. It pays quite well in any nation on this planet—especially in our nation, driven by profit.

We can make mega-bucks:

- cheating people with inferior products
- charging for services we don't perform
- price-gouging customers at our mercy
- denying medical treatment (as in: healthcare insurance providers)
- skipping our corporate taxes, skipping the country, and then giving comparatively cheap gifts to our politicians in anticipation of a presidential pardon
- helping injured clients sue, and then taking 40 percent of the court's award, plus expenses
- rewriting the laws to legalize certain crimes that enrich the wealthy and suck the life out of everyone else

Habakkuk put together a list of crimes going on in his country: violence, injustice, cruelty, and laws that couldn't be enforced. "Justice is always the loser," he said, taking his complaint directly to God (1:4).

The two—prophet and God—talk back and forth in a frank and enlightening conversation. The last word is this: winning by sinning is an optical illusion. It only looks like we've won. We can't keep anything. We might lose it all in this life, as the Judeans did when Babylon invaded and as Babylon did when the Persians invaded. Or we'll lose it all at the end of our life when we stand empty-handed before our maker.

After his talk with God, Habakkuk reaches the conclusion that he can afford to lose anything and everything as long as he doesn't lose God—his strength and salvation.

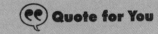 **Quote for You**

"The Sovereign Lord is my strength! He will make me as surefooted as a deer and bring me safely over the mountains" (3:19, New Living Translation).

## When It Happened

(Dates are approximate)

Adam 4000+ B.C. — Abraham 2100 B.C. — Moses 1500 B.C. — David 1000 B.C. — Fall of Israel 722 B.C. — Fall of Nineveh 612 B.C. — Fall of Judah 586 B.C. — Ezra 450 B.C. — Jesus born 7/6 B.C.

# Info You Can Use

## Background Notes

**Writer:** "I am Habakkuk the prophet," the book begins. We know nothing else about him. No other books of the Bible mention him.

**Time:** Habakkuk said God was "sending the Babylonians" to punish the southern Jewish nation of Judah (1:6). That suggests Habakkuk ministered sometime during the 26-year span between the time Babylon overran Assyria in 612 B.C. to become the Middle Eastern superpower, and before it destroyed Jerusalem in 586 B.C.

**Place:** The story seems to take place in the southern Jewish nation of Judah, since the northern Jewish nation of Israel had fallen to Assyria in 722 B.C. Part of the story unfolds on a "watchtower" (2:1), perhaps one of the many guard towers on the walls protecting Jerusalem. The Babylonians, God said, "laugh at fortresses" (1:10). They built dirt ramps against the walls and charged up them to capture cities. The Babylonian Empire, which dominated the Middle East from 612–539 B.C., extended from the Persian Gulf to Egypt.

**Bottom-Line Summary:** A Jewish prophet named Habakkuk boldly asks God to explain why he does nothing about the injustice and cruelty that has thoroughly polluted Judah. "Why do you allow violence, lawlessness, crime, and cruelty to spread everywhere?" the prophet demands (1:3).

"Look and be amazed," God replies (1:5). In a vision, God reveals that he will send Babylonian invaders to punish Judah. Habakkuk is appalled. The Jews are only petty crooks next to the Babylonians, who are vicious murderers. So in a follow-up question Habakkuk asks God why he's using the godless nation of Babylon to punish Judah.

God doesn't answer the question directly. Instead, he assures Habakkuk that the Babylonians will be punished for their sins, too. That's enough to satisfy the prophet, who responds with a majestic prayer of absolute trust in God—a prayer so beautiful that it's later set to music and sung in worship.

> ### Fascinating Fact
>
> An ancient Jewish legend says Habakkuk survived the Babylonian invasion and that about 60 years later an angel miraculously transported him from Judah to the Persian Gulf region, where he delivered food to Daniel in the lion's den. This story is in the apocryphal book *Bel and the Dragon*. The Apocrypha is a collection of ancient Jewish writings from before the time of Christ. They aren't included in Jewish or Protestant Bibles, but many of these writings are included in Bibles of the Catholic and Orthodox churches.

## Influential People

**Habakkuk,** a Jewish prophet who asks God why he's not punishing the wicked. Habakkuk's story is a reminder that we can talk to God about anything—

even to complain about God himself. When we keep the communication channels open, our faith grows.

## Key Ideas You Need to Know

**In God we trust, no matter what.** That's the conclusion Habakkuk reaches for himself. After hearing the horrifying news that God is going to allow Judah to be conquered, the prophet essentially says, "God knows best."

But that's not where Habakkuk started. He started by asking what amounts to this: "What do you think you're doing?"

The trust level that Habakkuk finally reaches doesn't come easy, or naturally. He has to nurture it by talking with God.

Like Habakkuk, most of us will face some tragic times in our life—lost jobs, lost love ones, lost health. We might get as upset with God as the prophet did. We might complain with words that make Habakkuk sound polite. But in time we, too, can reach a level of extraordinary trust in God. And instead of complaining, we can say with the prophet, "Let all the world be silent—the Lord is present" (2:20).

## Q&A

**Is it okay to argue with God?** Habakkuk certainly did. And he's in good company. The Bible has many examples of people trying to talk God out of something that seemed to them like a bad idea. Some people succeeded in changing God's mind. But most didn't.

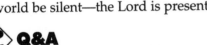

### To-Do List

- "Only those who live by faith are acceptable to me" (2:4).

- "Olive trees may be fruitless, and harvest time a failure; sheep pens may be empty, and cattle stalls vacant—but I will still celebrate because the Lord God saves me. The Lord gives me strength" (3:17–19).

When God told Moses to go to Egypt and free the Hebrews, Moses argued that he wasn't a good enough public speaker to debate Pharaoh, the Egyptian king. Gideon couldn't believe God wanted him to lead an army to fight off raiders, so he demanded—and got—miracles to convince him that God would help him. Job accused God of unfairly punishing him by taking away his children, herds, and health. And when God called Jeremiah to become a prophet, Jeremiah insisted he was too young.

On occasion, people talked God out of something. When the Hebrews worshiped a golden calf while Moses was up on a mountain getting the Ten Commandments, God told Moses he would wipe out all of them and start a new Hebrew nation through him. Moses convinced God to spare the people. King Hezekiah, on his deathbed, got news from a prophet that his time was up. But Hezekiah prayed for mercy, and God healed him. Citizens of Nineveh were told by Jonah that their city would fall in 40 days because of the people's sin. But they prayed for forgiveness and mercy, and God spared them.

God is not an unapproachable know-it-all. It's true that he knows it all and sees it all. But he hears it all, too. If we talk, he listens. Sometimes he responds with an inner assurance that everything will be okay because he's in control—that's what happened with Habakkuk. But sometimes our conversation with him changes us—as it did the citizens of Nineveh—so he changes his plans for us accordingly.

Arguing with God can be a good thing. It's much better than ignoring him.

**Why does God use evil to make good things happen?** Perhaps because there's a whole lot more evil to work with than good. Habakkuk didn't understand why God would punish evil Judah by sending invaders from an even more evil nation. We might wonder the same thing—why would God stoop to using the Babylonians when he could punish Judah without using some evil force in the world. In the past, he used floods, earthquakes, and firestorms to punish sin. Why not this time?

We don't know. All we know is that it worked. The Jews who returned from Babylonian exile a generation later were more devoted to God than ever.

God wants to help humanity, especially to protect them from the deadly effects of sin. God uses a wide variety of resources to accomplish that goal. In the Bible there's another excellent example of God using evil to accomplish good. When Joseph's brothers sold him to slave traders, that was evil. But Joseph ended up as second in command in Egypt, where he prevented the Egyptians as well as his own people from starving during a famine. As Joseph explained to his brothers, "You tried to harm me, but God made it turn out for the best, so that he could save all these people" (Genesis 50:20).

God doesn't cause the evil. But he can use it for good.

In a more modern example, known by the author, there's a retired man in his 60s who recently suffered through a bitter divorce. Alone, the man was able to help his older sister in another state take care of her dying husband—help that the sister desperately needed. God didn't cause the divorce or want the man and his family to suffer the pain that resulted. But God used the divorced man—who was suddenly released from many responsibilities—in a way that he couldn't have used him before the divorce.

## Habakkuk Well Used

**Living by faith.** "The just shall live by his faith" (2:4, King James Version). This verse, as paraphrased in Romans 1:17, convinced Martin Luther to break from the Catholic Church and launch the Protestant movement. In Luther's day, most Christians believed they were saved by obeying the Catholic Church's rules and by observing rituals approved by church leaders. Luther argued, with the apostle Paul, "It is through faith that a righteous person has life" (Romans 1:17, New Living Translation).

# Bible Scenarios You Can Use

## 1. The wicked thrive and the righteous suffer (1:1–4)

**H**abakkuk is fed up with the wickedness in his country of Judah—and with God not answering his prayers to do something about it.

"How long must I beg for your help before you listen?" the prophet complains. "Why do you allow violence, lawlessness, crime, and cruelty to spread everywhere? Laws cannot be enforced; justice is always the loser; criminals crowd out honest people and twist the laws around."

Habakkuk's complaint sounds impatient, brash, and even disrespectful. But as the verses that follow reveal, God doesn't take them that way. He takes them seriously—as the honest plea of a good man who's deeply upset by what he sees around him.

It's okay to complain to God—even about our anger and disappointment in him. If we don't talk to him about our concerns, we can grow cynical and even begin thinking he doesn't care about us. But if we raise the tough questions, he gives us answers that reassure. We may not get the answers we want—Habakkuk certainly didn't. But we get the answers we need.

## 2. God uses horrible sinners to punish mild sinners (1:5–17)

**G**od's answer to Habakkuk is a shocker. He vows to stop the injustice and cruelty in Judah, all right. But he's going to do it by sending invaders: Babylon—the cruelest and most unjust nation on the planet at the time. God himself acknowledges it: "They are fierce and cruel . . . their only laws and rules are the ones they make up."

Habakkuk is stunned. "Will you, who cannot allow sin in any form, stand idly by while they swallow us up?" the prophet asks. "Should you be silent while the wicked destroy people who are more righteous than they?" (New Living Translation).

It makes no sense at all, as far as Habakkuk's concerned. And he says so.

There are plenty of things that don't make sense to us. We get rid of Hitler, but megalomaniacs continue to rule nations with a sadistically iron fist. We replace monarchies and dictatorships with democracy, but the rich elite keep living like royalty—buying their way into high position and then fostering policies that favor their own kind, while the poor and the middle class suffer. If Habakkuk can question God's fairness, so can we. It's allowed. In fact, it's necessary if we want to maintain a healthy relationship with God and pursue justice in our world.

## 3. Trusting God no matter what (2:1—3:19)

**G**od never explains why he's going to use the likes of vicious Babylon to punish Judah. But he makes it clear that Babylon won't escape the punishment it deserves either. Without actually naming Babylon, God describes that nation in detail: arrogant, greedy, robbers, murderers, above the law, filthy rich, and getting richer at the expense of the poor. God has two words for them: "You're doomed!"

Habakkuk knows Judah is doomed as well. He knows, too, that invaders often decimate the target nation. And with this in mind, he writes one of the most beautiful affirmations of faith in God anywhere in the Bible:

"Even though the fig trees have no blossoms, and there are no grapes on the vine; even though the olive crop fails, and the fields lie empty and barren; even though the flocks die in the fields, and the cattle barns are empty, yet will I rejoice in the Lord! I will be joyful in the God of my salvation. The Sovereign Lord is my strength! He will make me as surefooted as a deer and bring me safely over the mountains" (New Living Translation).

Habakkuk came to the place in his spiritual understanding where he realized that he needed one thing more than security, possessions, and even a homeland. He needed God. And if that's all he had, it would be enough. No matter how bleak our situation, we can depend on God's help.

# ZEPHANIAH

## The End of the World

It's not as hard as it used to be to imagine Armageddon—the end of life on this planet. With Hollywood's help, we've already seen it. Asteroids arrive. Or alien invaders. Or we pollute ourselves to death. Or we blow up civilization and then radiate the planet in a nuke duke-out.

Remember any of the story lines that emerged when people realized they were about to die? Sin was the first casualty. Nobody was counting stolen money, swindling the elderly, or abusing their kids. Instead, feuding daughter and father re-united. Self-absorbed grown men called Mom. Husband and wife huddled with their children, choosing to die in each other's arms.

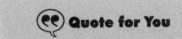 **Quote for You**

"Walk humbly and do what is right" (2:3, New Living Translation).

You don't have to go to the movies to see that sort of thing. We each have our personal Armageddon from time to time. Someone we dearly love gets the news they'll die soon. Or we get that news ourselves. Suddenly, the way of living according to the Bible takes over, as though it's the natural way to live—the way we were created to live. Money, power, and prestige mean nothing. Truth, compassion, and loving relationships mean everything.

We say, "I'm sorry" and "I love you." From the deathbed we plead with loved ones to be kind to the rebel child and to forgive that child even before forgiveness is sought.

These values surface naturally. They're right there with us. Actually, they were there all the time, suppressed. We'd been living the unnatural life and didn't realize it until we looked eyeball to dust ball at our own mortality.

We don't have to wait for Armageddon—planetary or personal—to start living the way we know in our heart is right.

## When It Happened

(Dates are approximate)

Adam 4000+ B.C.    Abraham 2100 B.C.    Moses 1500 B.C.    David 1000 B.C.    Fall of Israel 722 B.C.    Josiah 640 B.C.    Fall of Judah 586 B.C.    Ezra 450 B.C.    Jesus born 7/6 B.C.

# Info You Can Use

 ## Background Notes

**Writer:** "I am Zephaniah," the book begins. Then, in an unusual move, Zephaniah briefly traces his family tree through four generations—ending with his great-great grandfather: Hezekiah. Zephaniah stops short of saying he's a prince and that his great-great grandfather was King Hezekiah of Judah. In fact, Hezekiah was a popular name, so it's possible the prophet wasn't related to the godly and revered king. But the unusual genealogy hints he was. And Zephaniah lived at the right time for that—when Hezekiah's great grandson reigned as king.

**Time:** Zephaniah said he received God's message when Josiah was king of Judah. Josiah, great grandson of Hezekiah, ruled for 31 years—from 640–609 B.C. Josiah assumed the throne at the tender age of eight, after his father was murdered. His father and grandfather, Amon and Manasseh, had been wicked kings who worshiped idols and built shrines throughout the country. But when Josiah reached age 20, he started leading the people back to God and tore down pagan altars.

Because Zephaniah said idolatry was running rampant in Judah, it's possible that he issued his warning of global disaster early in Josiah's reign, prodding the king to make the religious reforms.

**Place:** Zephaniah delivers his message in the southern Jewish nation of Judah, perhaps in the capital city of Jerusalem. By this time, the northern Jewish nation of Israel had been gone nearly a century—wiped out by the Assyrians in 722 B.C.

### Fascinating Fact

One clue that at least part of Zephaniah's prophecy is literal, and not symbolic, appears in the way he describes earth's destruction. It reads as a reversal of the Creation story. God created fish, birds, land animals, and humans—in that order. But now, says Zephaniah, God is going to destroy all life: "people and animals, birds and fish" (1:3). God used the same reverse listing—excluding fish—when he warned Noah about the coming flood (Genesis 6:7).

**Bottom-Line Summary:** In a short, horrifying three chapters—written as poetry—the prophet Zephaniah warns the Jews that God is so sick of watching sinful humanity that he's going to wipe out all life: "people and animals, birds and fish" (1:2–3). This message is reminiscent of the one delivered before the flood in Noah's day: God saw how wicked humans were and declared, "I'll destroy every living creature on earth! I'll wipe out people, animals, birds, and reptiles. I'm sorry I ever made them" (Genesis 6:7).

Surprisingly, the end of life on earth isn't the end of the story. Zephaniah says God will gather righteous survivors and return them home to live in peace. It's unclear if the prophet is talking about the exiled Jews returning to their homeland, or to a heavenly home, or both.

## Influential People

**Zephaniah,** a prophet who predicts that rampant sin will force God to destroy Judah and the rest of the earth. Though we don't need to carry a sign saying the end is near, we can take a page from Zephaniah's life by encouraging goodness in our communities.

## Key Ideas You Need to Know

**The end of what?** Bible experts wonder if Zephaniah uses exaggerated and figurative images to describe Judah's fall to the Babylonians a few decades later, or if he's talking literally about the end of the world.

It could be both. Bible prophecies sometimes have two meanings: one points to the immediate future, and another refers to the distant future. Jesus used this technique when he gave signs about "the end of the world" (Matthew 24:3). Parts of his prophecy were fulfilled 40 years later, when Rome destroyed Jerusalem. Other aspects remain unfulfilled, and many believe they will unfold only at the Second Coming of Christ.

> **To-Do List**
>
> - "If you humbly obey the Lord, then come and worship him" (2:3).

Zephaniah says "the great day of the Lord is coming soon, very soon" (1:14). That might refer to Judah's fall in 586 B.C. But he also talks about a coming era when God will "bring together the lame and the outcasts, then they will be praised, instead of despised" (3:19), perhaps a reference to an idyllic life in heaven.

# Bible Scenario You Can Use

### 1. Life on earth ends (1:1–18)

**N**o previous punishment from God compares to what's about to happen—not the firestorm that incinerated Sodom and Gomorrah nor the flood that wiped out civilization, sparing only Noah's family and the animals on the ark.

"I, the Lord, now promise to destroy everything on this earth—people and animals, birds and fish . . . I will wipe out the entire human race. . . . My anger will flare up like a furious fire scorching the earth and everyone on it."

Yet somehow, in a way that God doesn't explain, his true worshipers will survive to enjoy a new age in which people "will live right and refuse to tell lies. They will eat and rest with nothing to fear" (3:13). Perhaps this is an early portrait of life in heaven, when humanity gives way to a higher form of existence.

This much is clear: God will punish the unrepentant for their sins.

In a day when the rich could buy their way out of trouble through bribery, God gave this warning: "not even your silver or gold can save you on that day when I, the Lord, am angry." The Judeans let prosperity and good times lure them into a false sense of security in spite of their sins. Their world came to an end when Babylon invaded. We don't want to repeat Judah's mistake, because all the money and military muscle in our nation won't protect us from the unavoidable consequences of sin.

On the other hand, if we hold tight to godly living, "nothing can separate us from God's love—not life or death" (Romans 8:38).

# HAGGAI

## When God Gets Squeezed Out

Like most prophets, Haggai didn't mince words. Quoting God, he summed up a touchy situation: "Is it right for you to live in expensive houses, while my temple is a pile of ruins?" (1:4).

Eighteen years earlier, the Jews had come home from exile in Babylon. Their nation was a wasteland of burned out cities, with the walls and stone buildings in scattered heaps. Still, the Jews were so grateful that God brought them home that their first order of business was to rebuild their place of worship, the Jerusalem temple.

The priority changed quickly. It started when the non-Jewish locals who had moved into the area filed a formal complaint with the Persians, the superpower that defeated Babylon. The locals said the Jews would rebuild their city and then rebel, just as they had against the Babylonians and Assyrians. The Persian king checked the ancient records and found that the Jews did have a history of rebelling, so he ordered the work stopped. The Jews offered no effective argument, and for the next 18 years, turned to their own needs: restoring their houses, farms, and herds. Then, Haggai arrived with his blunt message.

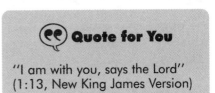

**Quote for You**

"I am with you, says the Lord"
(1:13, New King James Version)

Today, nobody orders us away from God—to stop building churches, to skip worship services, or to put a lid on the Bible reading and prayer. Instead, they order us to do so many other things that God gets squeezed out of our schedule. And, truth be told, sometimes we don't put up much resistance. Our kids are scheduled for sports events on Sunday morning, and we raise no question. So the schedule-makers see no problem. Or the boss is convinced our world spins around the job. And then there are the bills, which don't leave much money for offerings.

Before we know it, our relationship with God can crumble into ruins.

## When It Happened

(Dates are approximate)

Adam 4000+ B.C. | Abraham 2100 B.C. | Moses 1500 B.C. | David 1000 B.C. | Fall of Judah 586 B.C. | Decree of Cyrus 538 B.C. | Ezra 450 B.C. | Jesus born 7/6 B.C.

# Info You Can Use

## Background Notes

**Writer:** Haggai delivered this prophecy. Another prophet from the same time, Ezra, confirmed that Haggai urged the Jews to rebuild the temple (Ezra 6:14).

**Time:** Haggai is quite specific about when his ministry took place. He delivered three prophecies from late August through December in 520 B.C., beginning shortly after harvest time in "the second year that Darius was king of Persia" (1:1). Darius reigned from 522–486 B.C. The dating is unusually precise because Haggai reported the month and day of each prophecy, as well as the date the Jews resumed work on the temple. Prophecy 1: August 29. Work resumes on the temple: September 21. Prophecy 2: October 17. Prophecy 3: December 18.

Haggai's ministry came about 66 years after Babylon defeated Judah and destroyed the cities in 586 B.C., and 18 years after the first wave of exiled Jews returned to their homeland in 538 B.C.

**Place:** The events took place in Jerusalem, former capital of the southern Jewish nation of Judah. The Jewish nation is now, however, just a small province in the Persian Empire.

**Bottom-Line Summary:** Eighteen years after the Jews return from exile in Babylon to rebuild their demolished homeland, they're struggling. They've had a string of bad harvests. And after yet another pitiful crop, the prophet Haggai explains what's wrong: the people haven't bothered to rebuild the Lord's temple.

To get their attention, God has sent mildew, mold, and hail to damage the crops. But the Jews didn't associate these farming disasters with their spiritual negligence. So now God sends Haggai with a clear message: the harvests will continue to fail until the people rebuild the temple.

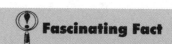

**Fascinating Fact**

With only two chapters, Haggai is the second shortest book in the Old Testament—after the one-chapter book of Obadiah.

Under the leadership of the high priest as well as the Persian-appointed governor of Judah, the Jews quickly organize themselves and start the construction. They have the foundation done by mid-December. Because of this quick progress, Haggai promises a good harvest the next season. Haggai doesn't report what happens next, but Ezra says the entire project takes about three and a half years (Ezra 6:15). The new temple is dedicated in the spring of 516 B.C., 70 years after the Babylonians destroyed the temple Solomon built.

## Influential People

**Haggai,** a Jewish prophet, criticizes the Jews of Jerusalem for living in nice homes while the Lord's temple lay in ruins. His words are a reminder that we sometimes have to send a strong message to motivate people to do the right thing.

**Zerubbabel,** a descendant of King David, is appointed governor of Judah by the Persian king. A competent leader, once he realizes what the problem is, he immediately gets to work on it.

**Joshua,** a high priest, works with Zerubbabel to rally the people behind the building project. The two of them working together show that government and religious leaders can accomplish plenty when they join forces.

# Q&A

**Does God send misfortune to get our attention?** He did in Bible times, and probably still does on occasion. The crop failure in Haggai's day was God's attempt to prod the Jews to rebuild the temple. On other occasions, God sent illness, droughts, and earthquakes to turn the people away from their sin.

This doesn't mean that all our misfortune comes from God, to steer us away from sin. Some hard times are intended to make us stronger (James 1:2–4). Others are the result of sinful choices someone else makes—such as the choice to drink and drive, which can have deadly consequences.

Anytime misfortune strikes, it's appropriate to turn to God and ask for his insight and guidance.

# Red Flag Issues

**Prosperity for all believers?** Some Christians teach that prosperity is our royal right, as children of the Heavenly King. Many Jews in Bible times also believed God would grant them prosperity if they obeyed him. Haggai helps fuel that interpretation because after the Jews start rebuilding the temple he quotes God as saying, "Although you have not yet harvested any grain, grapes, figs, pomegranates, or olives, I will richly bless you in the days ahead" (2:19).

The Psalms and many other Bible passages abound with promises that the righteous will prosper (Psalm 106:5). But there are also complaints of the wicked prospering (Psalm 73:3). And there are plenty of good people who aren't prosperous. Job loses all his wealth. Jesus says he doesn't even have a place to rest his head at night (Matthew 8:20). He also says we shouldn't store up treasures on earth, but should store them in heaven—a graphic way of illustrating the value of helping others in need (Matthew 6:19–20).

For reasons such as these, most Christians don't believe financial prosperity is their spiritual birthright. (For more, see "Prosperity doesn't mean God is happy with us," Amos, page 215.)

# Bible Scenario You Can Use

### 1. Haggai tells the Jews to rebuild the temple (1:1–2:23)

The exile is over. Jews taken prisoner to Babylon have been freed by Persia, the new superpower of the Middle East. Many of these Jews return to Israel and start rebuilding their nation, which had been left in ruins. Eighteen years have passed—long enough for the people to rebuild their homes, herds, farms, and parts of their cities. But not long enough to rebuild their place of worship—the Jerusalem temple. Actually, they had started the temple project almost as soon as they returned, but opposition from non-Jewish locals who had moved into the region forced them to put the project on hold.

For this spiritual negligence, Haggai reports, God has punished the people by devastating their crops with mildew, mold, and hail. Haggai delivers this message in late summer, after a terrible harvest. The Jews respond immediately, laying the temple's foundation before winter. Haggai, pleased with the progress, promises abundant harvests in the years ahead.

Because we're pulled in so many directions, it's tempting to tell God to take a number and wait his turn. We have a house to maintain, a job that takes too much time, and endless obligations to family and friends. Spending time with God—in worship, prayer, or service—seems like just another chore on the to-do list. But God isn't a chore that saps our time and energy. He's our source. He makes our time worthwhile. He gives us strength. He doesn't hurt us—he helps us.

Creation needs its Creator, thriving in his presence and withering in his absence.

# ZECHARIAH

## Filling God's Tall Order

Have you ever felt as though God wanted you to do something, and you felt you couldn't possibly do it?

Maybe it was to teach a Sunday school class, though you're terrified of public speaking. Maybe it was to befriend a neighbor, though you're not the social type. Or maybe it was to start a Good Samaritan savings account devoted to helping others, though your expertise is spending.

What was God thinking, to ask such a thing?

The Book of Zechariah is about filling tall orders from God. Jewish refugees, exiled from their homeland for about 50 years, were finally allowed to return home. Many didn't bother, since the nation was in ruins. Those who did go home struggled for almost 20 years just to survive—to keep a roof over their head and food in their stomach. It seemed a losing battle because they suffered many setbacks, including crop failures and opposition from non-Jewish settlers who had moved into the land during their absence.

> **Quote for You**
>
> "Don't depend on your own power or strength, but on my Spirit" (4:6).

Imagine their shock when the prophets Zechariah and Haggai said God wanted them to rebuild the Jerusalem temple, and then the entire city. To build the first temple, Solomon needed a work crew of nearly 200,000 to work for seven years. How could a few thousand returned refugees rebuild the temple, let alone the entire city?

They couldn't.

But God could. "Not by force nor by strength," God said, "but by my Spirit" (4:6, New Living Translation).

It's a mystery how God works through human beings to accomplish what seems impossible, but he does. He's been doing it for thousands of years. And he promises to do it until kingdom come—his kingdom come.

"I am the Lord All-Powerful!" he said. "So don't give up" (8:9).

When It Happened

(Dates are approximate)

Adam 4000+ B.C.  Abraham 2100 B.C.  Moses 1500 B.C.  David 1000 B.C.  Fall of Judah 586 B.C.  Decree of Cyrus 538 B.C.  Ezra 450 B.C.  Jesus born 7/6 B.C.

# Info You Can Use

## Background Notes

**Writer:** The 14-chapter book begins by identifying the author: "I am the prophet Zechariah, the son of Berechiah and the grandson of Iddo." Many Bible experts say Zechariah was probably also a priest, since a priest named Iddo is listed among the Jews who returned from exile in Babylon.

Most experts agree that Zechariah wrote the first eight chapters, but many say that others—perhaps one or more students of Zechariah's writings—wrote chapters 9–14, which scholars call Second Zechariah. These later chapters are radically different in writing style, word choice, and message. Also, these later chapters mention the Greeks, though Zechariah lived about 200 years before the Greeks defeated the Persians.

Whether or not Zechariah wrote the entire book, Jesus and New Testament writers cited passages from both sections of the book as authentic messages from God.

**Time:** Zechariah said he received his first message from God in the autumn of 520 B.C., "the eighth month of the second year that Darius was king of Persia" (1:1). Darius' reign started in 522 B.C. The "eighth" month refers to the Jewish lunar calendar, and corresponds with the last part of October and the first part of November on today's calendar. This means Zechariah's ministry overlapped with Haggai's, who delivered three prophecies between August and December of 520 B.C.

The ministries of Zechariah and Haggai came about 66 years after Babylon defeated Judah and destroyed the cities in 586 B.C. That was 18 years after the first wave of exiled Jews returned to their homeland in 538 B.C.

Zechariah's ministry continued for at least two years. We know this because the last date he mentioned is December 7, 518 B.C.—the day he received another message from God (7:1).

Messages in later chapters aren't dated, but are simply identified as messages (more literally "oracles") from God. This is another reason many scholars think later prophets added to Zechariah's work.

> ### 💡 Fascinating Fact
>
> Predicting what appears to be the beginning of eternal life with God, Zechariah says, "On that day the sources of light will no longer shine, yet there will be continuous day! Only the Lord knows how this could happen!" (14:6–7, New Living Translation). This sounds much like the New Testament writer's description of heaven's light: "There will be no night there—no need for lamps, or sun—for the Lord God will shine" (Revelation 22:4).

**Place:** Zechariah ministered in Jerusalem, the former capital of Judah. Though Judah was once a Jewish nation, in Zechariah's day it was just a small province in the Persian Empire. A Jewish governor appointed by the Persian king ruled Judah.

**Bottom-Line Summary:** Eighteen years after the first Jews return to Jerusalem from exile in Babylon, the people are finally getting around to rebuilding the temple that the Babylonians had destroyed. Actually, the Jews had started the project when they first returned, with the Persian king's blessing and contributions. But they abandoned it after non-Jewish locals convinced the next Persian king that if the Jews rebuilt Jerusalem they would rebel. The king ordered all construction stopped. The Jews started the project again, at the urging of the prophet Haggai, and with the approval of yet another Persian king. The work resumes on September 21, 520 B.C. About a month later, Zechariah begins his ministry.

Zechariah knows it looks impossible for a group of returned refugees to rebuild the temple and the entire city. But he encourages the people with God's promise: "I will have pity on Jerusalem. The city will be completely rebuilt, and my temple will stand again" (1:16). Furthermore, God vows that the entire nation will again prosper.

Prophecies in the first section of the book—chapters 1–8—deal mostly with the rebuilding of the temple and Jerusalem. Chapters 9–14 are messages that promise God will punish the ungodly and save the faithful. Zechariah's final prophecy looks to the end-time age when God defeats evil once and for all, then reigns unopposed as King of creation.

## 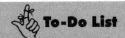 Influential People

**Zechariah,** a Jewish prophet likely born in Babylonian exile, but among the first Jews freed to return home. He understands human nature, and how people can feel completely overwhelmed by life's obstacles. But he reminds us all that "the Lord All-Powerful" will help us.

## Key Ideas You Need to Know

**A savior is coming.** This book talks more about the coming savior, or Messiah, than any other Old Testament book, with the exception of the much longer Book of Isaiah. Jesus and New Testament writers often quoted Zechariah to show that Jesus fulfilled these predictions.

Some of the more memorable prophecies that point to Jesus include the following:

---

**To-Do List**

- "Return to me, and I will return to you, says the Lord Almighty" (1:3, New Living Translation).

- "Sing and celebrate! The Lord has promised to come and live with you" (2:10). *Reminiscent of Jesus' last words to his disciples: "I will be with you always, even until the end of the world"* (Matthew 28:20).

- "See that justice is done and be kind and merciful to one another! Don't mistreat widows or orphans or foreigners or anyone who is poor, and stop making plans to hurt each other" (7:9).

- "Be truthful with each other, and in court you must give fair decisions that lead to peace" (8:16).

- He will ride into Jerusalem on a donkey, while the crowds cheer (9:2–10, fulfilled in Matthew 21:4–5)

- He will be betrayed for 30 pieces of silver (11:12–13, fulfilled in Matthew 26:14–15)

- His body will be pierced by a spear (12:10, fulfilled in John 19:34, 37)

- Described as a Good Shepherd, he will be killed and his sheep will scatter (13:6–7, fulfilled in Matthew 26:31).

These prophecies are important to the New Testament community, initially made up mostly of Jews, because they help show that Jesus didn't start a new religion. He was continuing God's plan for saving humanity.

 **Q&A**

**What should we do when religious rituals become mere habits?** Change the rituals, or change our way of thinking about them.

Through Zechariah, God accused the Jews: "During those seventy years of exile, when you fasted and mourned in the summer and at the festival in early autumn, was it really for me that you were fasting? And even now in your holy festivals, you don't think about me, but only of pleasing yourselves" (7:5–6, New Living Translation).

In other words, the Jews went through the motions of worshiping God, but it wasn't sincere. They weren't thinking about their sins when they fasted or about their gratitude for God during harvest festivals. Fasting was probably just a routine—an obligation required by religious leaders. Festivals were party time, for reunions and food.

We have no room to criticize the Jews if we go to church out of habit—as a chore or as a social event. If we take communion or repeat the Lord's Prayer in worship services, and don't think about the meaning behind the actions and words, we're just as guilty as the ancient Jews.

**When will the Lord reign over the earth?** In the final prophecy of his book, Zechariah says "the Lord will be king over all the earth" (14:9, New Living Translation). Bible experts aren't sure what this means.

Some Christians say this refers to a thousand-year period called the Millennium, when one New Testament writer says Satan will be locked up and Jesus will reign on earth (Revelation 20:1–6). But many Christians read this as mysterious symbolism common in apocalyptic literature, and not as a literal event.

Another view sees Zechariah's prophecy as a reference to the end of human history, when God creates a new heaven and a new earth and lives forever with his people (Revelation 21:1–3).

Yet another view sees God already reigning over the earth, through the work of the church that now reaches all around the world.

# Bible Scenarios You Can Use

## 1. Rebuilding the temple, (1:1–17; 4:6–10)

**E**ighteen years after returning from exile in Babylon, the Jews still haven't rebuilt their Jerusalem temple. Such a massive project probably seems impossible to this rag-tag community struggling on the brink of poverty and suffering a string of bad harvests. The first temple, destroyed by the Babylonians, took Solomon's construction crews seven years to build. But Zechariah rallies the people behind the project with eight captivating visions from God.

"My temple will stand again," God reveals in the first vision. And Jerusalem will grow so large that people will have to start living outside the walls. "I am the Lord All-Powerful. So don't depend on your own power or strength, but on my Spirit."

The people continue working on the new temple, and then dedicate it about three and a half years after they started. Though it's not as elegant as Solomon's temple, King Herod later remodels and expands it into a much larger and more lavish worship center.

Some responsibilities in life seem more than we can handle: raising kids, caring for a dying relative, moving to a new job in an unfamiliar place. But we don't have to handle the work alone. Our greatest accomplishments will come not by our own strength and perseverance, but by God's Spirit at work through us. For God is the source of our strength.

## 2. A prophet's message: be honest and fair (5, 1–4; 7:8–14)

**Z**echariah sees a vision of a flying scroll that puts a curse on everyone who lies and steals. "I am sending this scroll into the house of everyone who is a robber or tells lies," God says. "It will remain there until every piece of wood and stone in that house crumbles."

In a related message later, God orders the people to show justice, kindness, and mercy. More specifically, he tells them, "Don't mistreat widows or orphans or foreigners or anyone who is poor."

These are some of the most basic laws of God—laws that the Jews' ancestors failed to obey. That failure, God says, is why "I came with a whirlwind and scattered them among foreign nations, leaving their lovely country empty of people and in ruins."

Life is complicated, and we don't always know how to respond to situations that spring up in front of us. But when in doubt, we can do the kind thing. We generally know what that is because it comes natural—as though our Creator programmed kindness into us.

## 3. The king of peace comes (9:9–17)

**T**o inspire the Jews and encourage them to continue rebuilding their broken nation, Zechariah looks deep into the future. What he sees is a land and a people thriving. The word picture he paints is one that New Testament writers say predicted the arrival of Jesus into Jerusalem on Palm Sunday.

"Everyone in Jerusalem, celebrate and shout! Your king has won a victory, and he is coming to you. He is humble and rides on a donkey. . . . I will bring peace to nations, and your king will rule from sea to sea."

Though God's kingdom of peace isn't completely established, Jesus gave it a big boost when he came preaching peace among humanity and with God.

Just as the Jews finished the temple they started, God will finish the kingdom of peace he has started. We can count on that. The kingdom may not be on earth, or part of the physical realm. Jesus said as much during his trial before Pilate (John 18:36). But God's kingdom of peace will be as real as God.

# MALACHI

## Pretend Worship

"Don't strain yourself!" Maybe you've used that expression when someone is doing something for you but their heart is clearly not in it.

That's what God thinks of half-hearted worship. "I wish someone would lock the doors of my temple, so you would stop wasting time building fires on my altar" (1:10).

A modern version of that quote would call for someone to lock the churches so we'd stop wasting time in worship services.

The Jews were merely going through the motions of worship, as though God wanted the motions instead of the worship. The sacrificial animals they brought to God were livestock no one would want: diseased, crippled, blind, or stolen. The offerings fell far short of the 10 percent tithe they were supposed to bring. And their lifestyle included infidelity, lying in court, cheating employees out of wages, and mistreating widows, orphans, and refugees.

Worship is a time to honor God. We can't honor God when we're giving him leftovers (which too often mean nothing) and when we're ignoring his most basic laws about how to treat others. Under these conditions, worship is a waste of time. We might as well lock the church doors and stay home. That way we can save time and money.

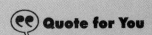 **Quote for You**

"The day of judgment is certain to come. And it will be like a red-hot furnace with flames that burn up proud and sinful people. . . . But for you that honor my name, victory will shine like the sun with healing in its rays, and you will jump around like calves at play" (4:1–2).

But that's all we'd save. It would pretty much negate our role as a community that's supposed to be helping God save the world.

## When It Happened

(Dates are approximate)

Adam 4000 B.C.

Abraham 2100 B.C.

Moses 1500 B.C.

David 1000 B.C.

Ezra 450 B.C.

Jesus born 7/6 B.C.

# Info You Can Use

## Background Notes

**Writer:** This is a message from God, delivered by Malachi, as indicated in the introduction. But many Bible experts suggest Malachi wasn't a person's name, but a descriptive title for the prophecy. *Malachi* means "my messenger," which was a common title for a prophet. The first translation of the Old Testament—into Greek in about 250 B.C.—used the term as part of a title for the book, calling the prophecy that followed "the word of the Lord to Israel by my messenger." The book became know as "my messenger" (Malachi), for short.

The writer may have chosen this title to identify himself only as a prophet, without revealing his name. It's possible that Malachi was the writer's name, but nothing else is known about him.

Whatever the author's name, Jesus and New Testament writers felt free to quote the book as a God-given source of information.

**Time:** Malachi talked about the rebuilt temple in Jerusalem, which was dedicated in 516 B.C., so the book was written after that. Malachi's description of the nation's weakening spiritual condition—especially the lack of respect for sacrificial offerings—fits well with the mid-400s B.C., during the time of Ezra and Nehemiah. Ezra called for spiritual reform, and Nehemiah led the people in rebuilding the city walls. This means the people of Malachi's day probably lived about 100 years after the Jews returned from exile in Babylon.

**Place:** Malachi addressed Jews in Judah—probably those living in and around the city of Jerusalem, where the temple was located.

**Bottom-Line Summary:** About a century after the Jews have returned to their homeland from exile in Babylon, their respect for God has dropped. The masses haven't gone so far as to abandon God and start worshiping idols—the prominent sin that sparked the destruction of the Jewish nation and the exile that followed. But like sheep that gradually wander away from the shepherd and into danger, the people are moving away from God.

Instead of offering the best animals for sacrifice, as Jewish law requires, the people offer the worst animals in the herd—the sick and crippled. They've stopped giving the required 10 percent tithe to the temple. And they're playing fast and loose with other im-

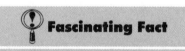

**Fascinating Fact**

Tithing among Christians started as a tax, when, in A.D. 585, landlords of the Saone Valley in France gave bishops the right to levy and collect a compulsory tax called the decimum, meaning "tenth." King Pepin the Short made this a kingdom-wide law in A.D. 765.

portant laws, ignoring God's commands to stay faithful in marriage, tell the truth in court, help the poor, and treat everyone fairly.

Judgment day is coming, the prophet says. On that day, the sinful will suffer, but those who honor God "will shine like the sun" and "jump around like calves at play" (4:2).

# Influential People

**Malachi,** a prophet, condemns insincere worship in Judah. He delivers God's truth with boldness and clarity, while softening blunt criticism with promises of hope. Malachi does what the apostle Paul says we should all do: speak the truth in love (Ephesians 4:15).

# Q&A

**Do we need to obey all the laws of Moses?** Malachi said the Jews did: "Remember to obey the instructions of my servant Moses," Malachi quotes God, "all the laws and regulations that I gave him on Mount Sinai for all Israel" (4:4, New Living Translation).

Malachi was talking about the hundreds of laws that God gave Moses to set up and run the nation of Israel. Many laws are about crime and punishment. Many are about sacrificial rituals. And many are about moral issues, such as worshiping only God and being honest.

Christians consider the legislative and ritual laws obsolete, since the ancient nation of Israel no longer exists and the sacrificial system ended when Romans destroyed the temple in A.D. 70. Jesus and New Testament writers confirmed this, explaining that God fulfilled the old agreement with Israel and established a new agreement with the entire human race (Hebrews 8:13; Matthew 5:17).

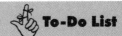

**To-Do List**

- "Don't ever be unfaithful to your wife" (2:15).

- "I will quickly condemn all who practice witchcraft or cheat in marriage or tell lies in court or rob workers of their pay or mistreat widows and orphans or steal the property of foreigners or refuse to respect me" (3:5).

Though most laws of Moses are now outdated, the moral laws are timeless— be kind to others, don't lie, don't cheat, and don't seek revenge. Jesus repeated such teachings throughout his ministry.

**Did Elijah come back from the dead?** "I am sending you the prophet Elijah before the great and dreadful day of the Lord arrives," God said. "His preaching will turn the hearts of parents to their children, and the hearts of children to their parents. Otherwise I will come and strike the land with a curse" (4:5–6, New Living Translation).

That's the end of the Old Testament and, for many Jews, the beginning of their search for a messiah. Many expected Elijah to appear as a forerunner of the Lord's arrival—to prepare the Lord's way. Even today, when Jews eat the annual Passover meal many leave the door cracked open and set out an extra glass of wine called the "Elijah cup." They do this in anticipation that Elijah will return to announce the Lord's coming.

Elijah did return—along with Moses—to talk with Jesus shortly before the

Crucifixion. This miracle took place on a hilltop that became known as the Mount of Transfiguration, where Jesus was temporarily transfigured into a glowing being (Matthew 17:1–3). But New Testament writers indicate this wasn't the appearance Malachi was talking about. Instead, John the Baptist fulfilled the prophecy.

John led many to salvation, by urging them to repent and stop sinning. Even though he said he was preparing the way for someone whose sandals he wasn't worthy to untie, when priests asked him if he was the promised Elijah, he replied, "No, I am not!" (John 1:21).

Jesus knew better. He said, "John is Elijah, the prophet you are waiting for" (Matthew 11:14). Elijah was a great prophet, and Jesus interpreted Malachi's prophecy as meaning God would send another great prophet (John the Baptist) of the caliber of Elijah.

## Red Flag Issue

**Should Christians give 10 percent of their income to the church?** The New Testament doesn't say. In New Testament times, there weren't any church buildings. Groups of Christians met in homes or other locations. They took offerings, especially for the needy among them. But there's no mention of Christians giving a tithe—a word that means "tenth."

Many denominations teach that Christians should give a tenth of all their income to the local church. Some call it "storehouse tithing," in recognition of Malachi's command: "Bring the entire ten percent into the storehouse," (3:10), meaning the temple in Jerusalem—the only worship center for the Jews.

In Old Testament times, Jews were expected to annually donate to the temple 10 percent of their harvest, new livestock, and other profits. This was a law of Moses (Leviticus 14:22–23). Most of the offering supported the priests and other temple workers, who didn't own any land and whose survival depended on offerings from the people. But much of the income was also donated to the needy, such as widows, orphans, and people from other countries.

With the destruction of the temple in A.D. 70 and the recognition that God had made a new agreement with humanity, through Jesus, early church leaders rejected the Old Testament idea of a tithe. Christians didn't tithe, they gave. In fact, not one Christian preacher from the first century through the early 1800s left behind a single sermon on tithing.

In the United States, the First Amendment to the Constitution made compulsory tithes illegal. Most Americans rejected tithing as legalism, and as an effort to earn salvation. But in the early 1800s, as churches began vastly expanding their work—erecting church buildings, supporting missionaries, educating children, helping the poor—Christian leaders started teaching that the Old Testament tithe is a moral obligation intended to support God's work through the worship center, which is now the local church.

Some denominations still reject the idea that God demands tithes today. But all need the financial support of Christians to pay the bills that allow the ministry to continue.

# Bible Scenarios You Can Use

### 1. Giving God damaged offerings (1:6–14)

The Jews insult God. They bring animal sacrifices to express their gratitude and to seek forgiveness, but the animals they bring are an embarrassment. Jewish law says "there must be nothing wrong with the animal" (Leviticus 22:18). But the Jews are bringing animals that are blind, crippled, sick, or stolen.

"Just try giving those animals to your governor," God says. "That certainly wouldn't please him or make him want to help you. I am the Lord God All-Powerful, and you had better try to please me. You have sinned."

The Jews apparently think what God wants most is sacrifice. But that's not true. What God wants most is something that a sacrifice can only illustrate: that the people love, honor, and obey him. The prophet Samuel put it this way, when King Saul disobeyed God by stealing enemy livestock for use as sacrifices: "Does the Lord really want sacrifices and offerings? No! He doesn't want your sacrifices. He wants you to obey him" (1 Samuel 15:22).

We don't observe ritual sacrifice anymore. But we observe worship rituals. We go to church, recite the Lord's Prayer, take communion, give donations, and help in some of the church work. But that's not what God wants most. What God wants most is what those rituals can only illustrate: that we love, honor, and obey him. He doesn't want the motions of worship; he wants the worship.

## 2. Priests mislead the people (2:1–9)

The Jewish people aren't acting alone. The priests are letting the people get by with insincere worship.

"You priests should be eager to spread knowledge, and everyone should come to you for instruction, because you speak for me," God says. "But you have turned your backs on me. Your teachings have led others to do sinful things."

Religious leaders aren't infallible. We've seen ministers of national acclaim plummet into sin. And many of us have seen the same thing happen in churches closer to home. Though church leaders can occasionally make sinful choices like the rest of us, and have the same access to God's forgiveness, the general path of their life should be toward God. They should show their goodness by the way they live and lead. If they don't, we should find leaders who do.

### 3. Bringing a tenth of the income to the temple (3:8-12)

To fund the Jerusalem temple—the only approved worship center where the Jews could offer sacrifices—the people are supposed to donate 10 percent of their annual harvest, new livestock, and other goods. This provides support for the priests and other temple workers, upkeep of the temple facility, and charitable causes such as caring for widows, orphans, and refugees.

But the Jews aren't paying.

"You people are robbing me," God says. "You are robbing me of the offering and of the ten percent that belongs to me" (3:8). God says that's why the entire nation is suffering.

"Bring the entire ten percent into the storehouse," God says. "Then I will open up the windows of heaven and flood you with blessing after blessing." God says he will also stop the locusts from eating the crops, and that all the surrounding nations will take notice of how God has blessed the Jews.

Today, the temple is gone, as are animal sacrifices. But God's work continues, through the local churches, charitable organizations, and compassionate individuals. Our offerings support this work.

# MATTHEW

## God Sends the Cavalry to Calvary

If you've watched some of the early westerns, you know that when everything looked hopeless, the cavalry arrived. Soldiers charging on horseback got there just in time to save the:

- wagon train from hostile Native Americans.
- city folk from a terrorizing gang of dirty-faced outlaws.
- innocent, dark-haired hero from being hung by a mob.

What if the army had sent General George Armstrong Custer, by way of the Little Bighorn? Nobody would have gotten saved.

To the Jews, the story of Jesus must have seemed like that kind of tragic ending. They had been waiting hundreds of years for their promised deliverer—the Messiah sent from God. Dominated by one invader after another—Rome, at the moment—the Jews expected their Messiah to ride in and free Israel, then restore the glory of King David's day.

Matthew's Gospel, more than any of the other three Gospels, presents Jesus as that promised savior. That's why it's first in the New Testament—it's a natural progression from the Old Testament prophecies that spoke of him.

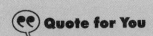 **Quote for You**

"Treat others as you want them to treat you" (7:12). *The Golden Rule, from Jesus' most famous sermon: The Sermon on the Mount.*

The savior, however, died. He was crucified on a Jerusalem hill called Calvary.

But in so doing, he became more of a savior than anyone had hoped for. And he started a kingdom more glorious than David's.

He came to save us all, for a kingdom that will never end. His resurrection gives us a peek at what "forever" means. And his teachings show us how to live in this life as citizens of God's kingdom to come.

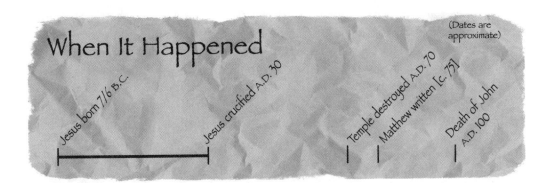

When It Happened

(Dates are approximate)

Jesus born 7/6 B.C.

Jesus crucified A.D. 30

Temple destroyed A.D. 70

Matthew written [c. 75]

Death of John A.D. 100

# Info You Can Use

## Background Notes

**Writer:** The writer isn't named. Christian leaders writing in the second century, however, said the book was written by Matthew, a tax collector who became one of Jesus' 12 original disciples.

**Time:** The events in the book cover the life and ministry of Jesus, from about 6 B.C. to about A.D. 30. Although December 25, 1 B.C. was considered Jesus' birthday when the Gregorian calendar was created in A.D. 325, most scholars today say Jesus was probably born between 6–4 B.C. That's because King Herod died in 4 B.C., and he was the king who ordered all Bethlehem infants age two and younger killed, in an effort to stop the baby Jesus from growing up and stealing his throne.

It's unclear when the Gospel was written. Clues in the story suggest it was late in the first century, sometime after Roman soldiers destroyed the Jerusalem temple in A.D. 70. For one thing, Matthew emphasized the role of the Pharisees, who were Jewish scholars. They rose in influence after the temple fell, because without a place to offer sacrifices, there was no need for priests.

Another clue is that the book seems targeted to a Christian Jewish community trying to define and defend itself against traditional Judaism that, before the century was over, formally declared that any Jews who accepted Jesus as Messiah would be excommunicated from the synagogues. In Matthew 23:34, Jesus predicted the Jews would beat and kill God's people in the synagogues and chase them from town to town. Perhaps Matthew took care to preserve this prophecy because it was currently being fulfilled.

**Place:** The story of Jesus takes place in what is now the general area of Israel. Jesus was raised in northern Israel, in a region still called Galilee. And he was executed in southern Israel, at the capital city of Jerusalem.

**Bottom-Line Summary:** With the Romans occupying and oppressing Israel, many Jews are fervently praying for God to send the Messiah—a deliverer whom the Old Testament prophets said would come from King David's family and start a never-ending kingdom of peace.

Jesus is that deliverer, Matthew reports. To start proving it, Matthew begins with a genealogy that traces Jesus' family back to King David and beyond. Next, Matthew reports Jesus is born to a virgin, conceived by the Holy Spirit. In addition, Matthew says stargazers from a foreign country follow a new star to Jesus' birthplace in Bethlehem and conclude that Jesus must be the future king of the Jews. (Many who studied the sky—especially those in what is now Iraq and Iran—taught that celestial wonders announced the birth of a great ruler.) When King Herod hears of this, he orders what is known as the "Massacre of the Innocents"—the slaughter of all infants, two years and younger, in Bethlehem. But Jesus and his family escape to Egypt, where they stay until Herod dies.

At about age 30, Jesus begins his ministry. He selects 12 disciples, and for about three or four years he teaches and heals people throughout his home region of Galilee, where he gains a large following.

Then, predicting his death, he travels to Jerusalem, which is crowded with Jewish pilgrims getting ready to celebrate the springtime festival of Passover. There, Jesus confronts Jewish leaders who envy his popularity and despise his teachings that sometimes challenge Jewish traditions. The Jewish leaders also fear Jesus may start a freedom movement that will cause Rome to clamp down even harder on the Jews. So they plot to kill him.

To avoid stirring up Jesus' supporters, the Jews secretly arrest him on Thursday night while he's praying with his disciples. The Jews are tipped off about the prayer location—the Garden of Gethsemane—by one disciple: Judas, whose motivation for betraying Jesus remains a mystery. During and after this arrest, the other disciples run for their lives.

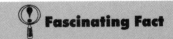

### Fascinating Fact

Jesus never traveled more than about 70 miles from his hometown in Nazareth. But he told his followers to take his teachings everywhere. Christianity now spans the globe.

Jesus is interrogated all night during an emergency session of the 70-member Jewish high council. By daybreak, the council condemns him of blasphemy for saying he will sit at the right hand of God. The council immediately calls for his death. Judas, hearing this, hangs himself.

By early morning, the council takes Jesus to Pilate, the Roman governor who has to approve any such executions. Pilate tries to talk the Jews out of the execution, but reluctantly gives in. The execution is carried out immediately. Jesus is nailed to a cross on a hill just outside Jerusalem's city walls, and is dead before sundown.

His body is rushed to a grave, since Jews aren't supposed to work on the Sabbath, which begins at sunset on Friday. On Sunday morning, women go to the tomb to finish preparing his body for burial—but he has risen. He later meets with his disciples and tells them to go to every nation and make the people his disciples.

## Influential People

**Jesus,** God's son in a human body, and the Messiah that prophets said God would send to save the people. His life and teachings not only show what God is like, but how God wants us to live.

**12 apostles,** working-class men Jesus recruits to become his main disciples. Jesus entrusts the future of Christianity to the likes of these men—fishermen and tax collectors. Today, he entrusts Christianity to the likes of us.

**Pilate,** Roman governor of the Jewish homeland and a politician gifted at surviving through compromise. Though he's opposed to executing Jesus, he makes the politically expedient decision to give the crowd the blood it demands. He's a classic example of going with the crowd instead of taking a stand for what he believes.

**Caiaphas,** a high priest in charge of the Jewish council that condemns Jesus to death. Like many Jews of his day, Caiaphas is so blinded by religious traditions and rituals that he doesn't recognize the Messiah that God himself sends. Though religious habits can help us be better people, they can sometimes get in the way—as when a weekly prayer meeting keeps us from helping one of our children in emotional crisis who needs that time with us.

## Key Ideas You Need to Know

**Messiah.** Old Testament prophets said God would one day send a messiah, or deliverer, from King David's family to free the people from oppression and set up a never-ending kingdom of peace. In Jesus' time, the Jews hope that such a leader will drive out the Romans and reestablish Israel as an independent nation.

That's why many don't recognize Jesus as the Messiah, in spite of all his miracles. He doesn't meet their expectations. He came to free all people, not just the Jews, from the oppression of sin and death. And his never-ending kingdom isn't part of the physical dimension, but of the spiritual.

**Kingdom of heaven.** This isn't just heaven, but anywhere God rules—including the human heart. Other Gospel writers call it the "kingdom of God," but Matthew, like many Jews of his day, prefers to show respect for God's name by using it sparingly.

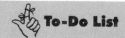

**To-Do List**

- "Love the Lord your God will all your heart, soul, and mind. This is the first and most important commandment. The second most important commandment is like this one. And it is, 'Love others as much as you love yourself'" (22:37–39).

- "Go to the people of all nations and make them my disciples" (28:19). *Called the Great Commission, this is the assignment Jesus gives to his apostles.*

- "Love your enemies and pray for anyone who mistreats you" (5:44).

- "When you pray, don't talk on and on" (6:7).

- "Stop judging others, and you will not be judged. For others will treat you as you treat them" (7:1, New Living Translation).

**Parables.** Jesus often uses simple stories from everyday life to help people understand how they should live by God's standards, as citizens of God's kingdom. Called parables, these symbolic stories often feature farmers, shepherds, rich landowners, and others in Jesus' audience. There are more than 40 parables in the New Testament.

The most famous parable—the Good Samaritan—is Jesus' practical answer to a question about who is the "neighbor" we're supposed to love as much as we love ourselves. The story of a stranger from Samaria helping a man beaten by robbers shows that everyone we come into contact with is our neighbor.

**Beatitudes.** Jesus' most famous sermon, the Sermon on the Mount, starts with a list of what is called the Beatitudes, a word that means "blessings." In this list, Jesus highlights the kind of people God will bless with a deep sense of peace and spiritual well-being—the very people many in society pity. This includes the humble, the mistreated, and the grieving. (For more about this, see "Sermon on the Mount" on pages 9–15.)

## Q&A

**Why a virgin birth?** The Bible never explains why God decided that Jesus should be born to a virgin. Matthew simply reports it as a miraculous fact, not unlike the many other miracles that follow in Jesus' life.

Matthew considers the virgin birth as more than an isolated miracle, however. He sees it connected to Isaiah's prophecy, which he quotes: "A virgin will have a baby boy, and he will be called Immanuel" (1:23, from Isaiah 7:14).

Whatever reasons God may have had for planning the virgin birth, this miraculous event introduces Jesus as someone more than human—as the divinely conceived Son of God who has come to fulfill God's ancient promise to save the human race from itself.

**Why would Jesus tell us to be perfect, when he knows it's impossible?** He probably didn't—it only sounds that way. To the crowd gathered for the Sermon on the Mount, Jesus said, "You are to be perfect, even as your Father in heaven is perfect" (5:48, New Living Translation). But what he said immediately before that suggests he's not talking about moral perfection. He's talking about taking our cue from God and loving people—even people who don't like us.

As Jesus put it a few verses earlier, "Love your enemies and pray for anyone who mistreats you. Then you will be acting like your Father in heaven" (5:44).

Learning to love our enemies usually takes a lot of time, and it doesn't come easy. But practice makes perfect.

**What's the unforgivable sin Jesus mentioned?** If you're worried about it, you haven't committed it.

Jesus' short statement that has needlessly worried Christians for some 2,000 years was directed to a group of Jewish religious leaders who had just witnessed a miracle from God, but attributed it to the dark power of Satan. Jesus healed a demon-possessed man who was blind and mute, and the religious leaders said, "No wonder he can cast out demons. He gets his power from Satan, the prince of demons" (12:24, New Living Translation).

Jesus responded by saying, "Every sin or blasphemy can be forgiven—except blasphemy against the Holy Spirit, which can never be forgiven" (12:31, New Living Translation).

Those words probably didn't trouble the religious leaders, but they've certainly terrorized people throughout the ages who feared they committed the unpardonable sin by swearing at God or venting their anger in other ways. Ministers say this is a common worry among their parishioners.

Sin against the Holy Spirit isn't unforgivable because it's an industrial strength stain that the blood of Jesus can't wash away. It's unforgivable because it's unconfessed. After a lifetime of hypocrisy, the religious leaders were so spiritually callous that they couldn't tell God from the devil. Protecting their turf was Job One. Repentance was the last thing on their mind.

## Red Flag Issues

**War and capital punishment.** Many Christians—and some entire denominations—teach that war and capital punishment are not compatible with the teachings of Jesus.

Jesus, after all, said:

- "Love your enemies and pray for anyone who mistreats you" (5:44).

- "When someone slaps your right cheek, turn and let that person slap your other cheek" (5:39).

In Old Testament times, however, God himself led Israel into battles. And many of God's laws demanded the death penalty for certain offenses, such as murder.

Perhaps Jesus wasn't giving us a principle that we're to apply in every situation, no matter the unique circumstances. For though he dealt with soldiers, there's no mention of him ever asking any of them to leave military service. Perhaps Jesus was showing us how to break the cycle of retaliation that's so common among feuding individuals and nations.

It would seem unreasonable for God to give us a survival instinct only to tell us not to protect ourselves when attacked. Yet it would seem just as unreasonable to rush into war and executions now that we've seen enough of life to know that wars can be prompted by politically self-serving reasons and that people can be unjustly convicted and executed. At the very least, Jesus calls us to seek alternatives to war and execution. (For more, see "Capital Punishment" in Genesis, page 24.)

## For the Record: Matthew Abused

**Divorce.** Throughout the centuries, many religious leaders have argued that adultery is the only acceptable reason to get a divorce. They've taken this firm stance because of something Jesus said: "I tell you not to divorce your wife unless she has committed some terrible sexual sin" (Matthew 5:32).

The result of this uncompromising position has been that many men and women stayed in torturous marriages—with spouses who beat them, who physically and emotionally abused their children, or who abandoned them.

Would Jesus have condoned a lifetime of torture like that, insisting that the marriage vow is more important than the suffering it's causing?

Many Christians believe not. In fact, Jesus said as much when he acknowledged that God allowed divorce in Moses' day because sin had the power to destroy a marriage. It still does.

Jesus wasn't establishing a new and rigid law about divorce. He was addressing a specific group of men who had been debating divorce. Some argued a man could get a divorce for any reason, while others argued that adultery was the only acceptable reason for getting a divorce. Jesus sided with the position that sought to conserve marriage, perhaps because he was surrounded by chauvinistic men from the other camp who wanted the freedom to end their marriage the moment another woman caught their eye. Jesus reminded them that God's plan is for marriage to last a lifetime. Divorce isn't God's idea. It's only a last resort he permitted in worst-case situations, which in Bible times was best illustrated by adultery.

The apostle Paul showed that adultery wasn't the only worst-case scenario when he assured women abandoned by their husbands that they had the church's blessing to end the marriage: "If the husband or wife who isn't a Christian insists on leaving, let them go. In such cases the Christian husband or wife is not required to stay with them, for God wants his children to live in peace" (1 Corinthians 7:15, New Living Translation).

Marriage is supposed to be a lifetime commitment. But sin sometimes destroys the marriage. Today, however, many people may be giving up too soon on their marriage, when the damage can be healed and the sins forgiven. As far as Jesus was concerned, even adultery is forgivable—as one woman discovered when no one could cast the first stone at her (John 8:3–11).

# Bible Scenarios You Can Use

## 1. Joseph takes pregnant Mary as his wife (1:18–24).

**A** young virgin named Mary becomes engaged to Joseph, a descendant of King David. Joseph finds out, to his shock, that Mary is pregnant though he hasn't slept with her. A compassionate man, he decides to break off the engagement quietly, rather than make a big scene.

In a dream, however, an angel comes to Joseph with startling news: "The baby that Mary will have is from the Holy Spirit. Go ahead and marry her. Then after her baby is born, name him Jesus, because he will save his people from their sins."

Joseph soon married his fiancée. His willingness to go ahead with the wedding would have signaled he was the father of this child conceived out of wedlock. If Joseph's main concern was to protect his reputation, he made the wrong decision. But he was more concerned about obeying God than worrying what others think—a good rule to live by.

## 2. Wise men visit Jesus (2:1–12)

**W**ise men who study the stars follow an unusual star to Bethlehem, where Jesus is born. Many stargazers at the time believe that an unusual event in the heavens, such as a comet, is a sign that a great leader has been born. The wise men from an unnamed country in the east—perhaps in what is now Iraq or Iran, where stargazing is an honored profession—arrive with expensive gifts for Jesus.

Jewish leaders must have hated this story. They would have preferred God to involve the religious elite in this grand event—not pagan foreigners. But God doesn't allow human expectations and prejudice to limit the good things he does for us. The wise men foreshadowed Jesus' message that salvation is for everyone—a message that shocked many Jewish elders. God will sometimes surprise us by the way he helps people. We can count on it, and learn from it.

## 3. Satan tempts Jesus (4:1–11)

**A**fter his baptism, and before starting his public ministry that will end in his death, Jesus goes into the desert-like Judean badlands to fast and pray. There, Satan tempts him. First temptation: turn stones into bread. Second: prove his deity by jumping from a high place. Final: worship Satan in exchange for world domination. Each time, Jesus resists by quoting the Bible.

Knowledge of the Bible can help us overcome temptation, too. For example, if someone seduces us, we can remember how Joseph in the Old Testament handled it. When the wife of Joseph's master ordered Joseph to have sex with her, he ran in the opposite direction.

## 4. Jesus' most famous sermon (5:1—7:29)

**O**n a grassy hillside Jesus delivers his most famous sermon of all: the Sermon on the Mount. It's a thoughtful masterpiece of godly teaching that captures the essence of Jesus' entire ministry. In this message, Jesus calls people to humility, nonjudgmental attitudes, faithfulness in marriage, compassion for the poor, devotion to their marriage partner, and love for God.

Instead of giving detailed rules, he offers broad principles that make it hard to find loopholes—as the Jews are so skilled at doing with Old Testament laws. When in doubt about what to do, Jesus says, "Act like your Father in heaven." And to help us know how God acts, Jesus shows us. (For more, see "Sermon on the Mount," page 9.)

## 5. Jesus heals a soldier's servant (8:5–13)

**W**hen Jesus arrives in the fishing village of Capernaum, on the shores of the Sea of Galilee, a Roman officer kneels before him and asks for help. "Lord, my servant is at home in such terrible pain that he can't even move."

Jesus agrees to go with him. Astonishingly, the soldier says that's unnecessary. He explains that he gives commands and people obey, and that Jesus can do the same: "Just give the order, and my servant will get well."

Jesus says no one has shown this much faith. He sends the officer home to the healed servant saying, "Your faith has made it happen."

In ways we don't understand, faith in God can produce miracles. We don't always get what we request, but faith is believing that God can give it.

## 6. Jesus eats with sinners (9:9–13)

Jesus goes to the home of Matthew, a tax collector, and eats a meal with him and his friends. Jewish religious leaders are furious that an influential rabbi like Jesus would mingle with such scum. Tax collectors are Jews who collaborate with the Roman occupying force by collecting taxes for Rome. They get rich by overtaxing and keeping the extra. Many Jews consider tax collectors ritually unclean, meaning Jews who touch them have to bathe before they can worship in the temple.

When asked why he's keeping such bad company, Jesus says, "Healthy people don't need a doctor, but sick people do."

As Christians, we usually gravitate to our own kind. That's natural. But we shouldn't isolate ourselves from the people who most need to see Jesus in us and through us.

## 7. Jesus sends out his disciples (10:1–42)

In what looks like a training mission, Jesus tells his 12 disciples to go throughout the countryside teaching and healing, just as he has done, and as they will do on their own after he's gone.

They're to go to the Jews, since it's the Jews who've been anxiously waiting for the Messiah to come. "If someone won't welcome you or listen to your message," Jesus says, "leave their home or town."

Some Christians try to cram their religion and morality down the throat of people who are wailing and flailing in resistance. But it's not Jesus' style to force religion on anyone. His style—one we should emulate—is to be a friend to sinners and to teach those who are willing to listen.

## 8. Jesus feeds 5,000 (14:13–21)

In a memorable story reported in all four Gospels, Jesus gets word that his beloved relative John the Baptist has been executed. Jesus leaves the crowd and sails with his disciples across the Sea of Galilee to a remote area. But the masses follow him along the shore. Moved with compassion, Jesus heals the sick and instructs his disciples to feed the people. But there are 5,000 men, not counting the women and children. And all the disciples can round up is one boy's lunch: five pieces of bread and two small fish.

Jesus takes the small lunch, blesses it, and then hands it to the disciples to distribute. The people eat their fill, and the disciples collect 12 baskets of leftovers.

Sometimes we think we have too little to offer God. But God multiplies our gift.

## 9. Disciples argue about who is greatest (18:1–6)

**O**ther Gospels report that the disciples begin arguing about who will be greatest in God's kingdom. In fact, elsewhere in the Gospels the brothers James and John ask to sit at the right and left of Jesus in his new kingdom. But here, the story picks up with the disciples coming to Jesus and asking him to settle their dispute about who is greatest.

Jesus calls over a child and says, "If you are as humble as this child, you are the greatest in the kingdom of heaven."

That must have silenced the men, for they likely realized that a humble person wouldn't even ask the question they were so bold to ask. Pride may be a desirable attribute on Planet Earth, but not in the kingdom of God. Pride is self-serving. Humility is self-giving.

## 10. How to treat a believer who does you wrong (18:15–20)

**J**esus tells his disciples how Christians should settle disputes among themselves. First, the wronged person should privately confront the other person. If the offender refuses to listen, the wronged person should try again, but with one or two witnesses. If that fails, the wronged person and the witnesses should present the problem to church leaders. If the leaders agree that an offense has been committed and the offender refuses to settle the matter, the offender should be treated like an outsider.

The purpose isn't to make the offender suffer, but to help that person see the seriousness of the problem and to straighten things out.

Instead of doing what Jesus recommends, we often let the problem fester inside us, or we tell others who spread the news as gossip—which only inflames the issue. Though it's hard to confront the person, that's the best first step in solving the problem.

## 11. Jesus teaches about divorce (19:1–12)

**J**ewish leaders debate when divorce is acceptable, and some argue it's acceptable for any reason. When they ask Jesus for his opinion, he says marriage is a lifetime commitment and that people shouldn't even consider divorce for any reason less than adultery. And the implication in his other teachings is that even adultery is forgivable.

Instead of approaching marriage as an experiment that may or may not work out, we should enter marriage with the intent of doing everything we can to keep it healthy. The alternative—divorce—creates shock waves that hurt many people for the rest of their lives.

## 12. Jesus disappoints a rich man (19:16–30)

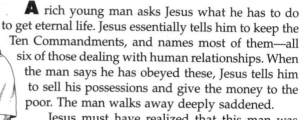

**A** rich young man asks Jesus what he has to do to get eternal life. Jesus essentially tells him to keep the Ten Commandments, and names most of them—all six of those dealing with human relationships. When the man says he has obeyed these, Jesus tells him to sell his possessions and give the money to the poor. The man walks away deeply saddened.

Jesus must have realized that this man was breaking the first and most important commandment: instead of worshiping God, the man worshiped his money as an idol.

If we care more about our money than about God's laws of goodness, which includes generosity toward the poor, we care too much. Money is dangerously seductive, which is why Jesus said, "It's terribly hard for rich people to get into the kingdom of heaven!"

## 13. Parable of invested money (25:14–30)

**J**esus tells a story of a man who gives money to three of his servants, asking them to invest it for him. The employer gives each man an amount equal to the person's ability, so none of them feels overwhelmed. One man gets 5,000 coins. Another gets 2,000. And the third man gets 1,000.

When it comes time to return the principle and profit, the first two men had doubled their money. But the third man wasted his opportunity by burying the money, fearing he would

lose the principle. The employer gave that man's money to the first investor.

In the story, the employer represents God. We are the servants. The point is that God gives everyone some resources: time, talent, and money. He wants us to use them to enlarge his kingdom, and not to let fear of failure paralyze us.

## 14. Jesus dies and rises from the grave (27:33–28:30)

**J**ewish leaders arrest and condemn Jesus for blasphemy because he implies he is God's equal. Pilate, the Roman governor, reluctantly agrees to the demand to execute Jesus. On Friday morning, Jesus is nailed to a cross. Before sundown, he is dead and placed in a nearby tomb. On Sunday morning, after the Jewish day of rest, women go to his tomb to finish preparing his body for burial, but they find the tomb empty. Jesus later meets with his disciples and gives them his final instruction: "Go to the people of all nations and make them my disciples."

The disciples, who ran for their lives after Jesus' arrest, are transformed. They no longer fear death, because Jesus conquered it. Combining this fearlessness with their love for Jesus, they minister to the people and lay the foundation for church planting. We don't have to fear death, either. We only have to live and serve in a way that allows others to see the love of Jesus in us.

# MARK

## Suffering to Help Another

More than any other Gospel, Mark throws the spotlight on how much Jesus suffered for us.

Nearly half of this shortest Gospel lays out the grim details of the final, traumatic week of Jesus' life. But even in the early half of the story, there's perpetual anguish from the very beginning of Jesus' ministry:

- Confrontation with evil spiritual forces,

- Clashes with religious leaders plotting to discredit him and, when unsuccessful, to kill him,

- Rejection by his family, who apparently thought he had gone mad.

The rigged trial, beating, carrying the cross till he collapsed, and then getting nailed to it was only one day in a lifetime of suffering.

Frankly, it seems God could have worked out a better plan for his only son, and a less gruesome way for saving humanity.

We don't know why he didn't.

But we know this: "God loved the people of this world so much that he gave his only Son, so that everyone who has faith in him will have eternal life and never really die. God did not send his Son into the world to condemn its people. He sent him to save them!" (John 3:16–17).

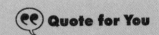 **Quote for You**

"I, the Son of Man, came here not to be served, but to serve others, and to give my life as a ransom for many" (10:45, New Living Translation).

We sinned and Jesus suffered. Perhaps God planned this tragic response because he knew we wouldn't miss the point: "The greatest way to show love for friends is to die for them" (John 15:13).

We won't likely be put to a test that extreme. But we'll occasionally suffer on behalf of someone we care about. And when we do, we'll be in the greatest company.

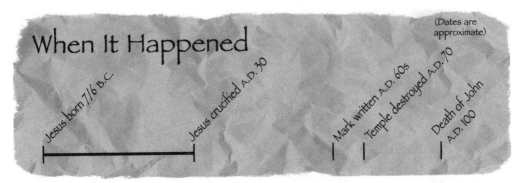

## When It Happened

(Dates are approximate)

Jesus born 7/6 B.C.

Jesus crucified A.D. 30

Mark written A.D. 60s

Temple destroyed A.D. 70

Death of John A.D. 100

# Info You Can Use

 **Background Notes**

**Writer:** The writer never identifies himself. But Christian leaders in the early second century—a few decades after the Gospel was written—say John Mark wrote it in Rome, and based it on the memories of Peter.

John Mark wasn't one of the 12 disciples, though his apparent source was leader of the 12. It's unclear if John Mark even knew Jesus. Early Christian writers, however, say John Mark was with Jesus and the disciples when the Jews arrested Jesus. John Mark, the writers claim, was the unidentified young man who was grabbed by an arresting officer, but who escaped naked, leaving his robe in the hands of the officer (14:51–52).

John was his Jewish name, and Mark was his Roman name. The early church history book, Acts of the Apostles, reports that John Mark traveled with Peter and Paul on various trips. It also reports that after an angel released Peter from the Jerusalem prison, Peter went to the home of John Mark's mother, a widow, where Christians had gathered to pray for him (Acts 12:12).

**Time:** Mark's story covers just the three or four years of Jesus' public ministry, from perhaps A.D. 26 to 30.

It's unclear when the Gospel was written. Many Bible experts say Mark was the first Gospel, and that Matthew and Luke drew heavily from it. The experts also guess Mark was written sometime in the A.D. 60s, possibly after Rome started persecuting Christians in A.D. 64, but before Rome destroyed the Jerusalem temple in A.D. 70.

One reason experts suggest the mid to late 60s is because it helps explain why Mark focused so much on Jesus' sufferings. Many Christians—especially in Rome—were being persecuted at the time. They would have found courage in the sufferings of Jesus. The reason experts date the book before A.D. 70 is because there's no reference to the temple's destruction—a monumental disaster among Jews—or to any conditions that prevailed afterward.

**Place:** Mark's story of Jesus takes place mainly in what is now Israel. Jesus' early ministry is in the northern region: Galilee. But the second half of the book, covering the final week of his life, takes place in the Jerusalem area.

**Bottom-Line Summary:** In the Bible's fastest-paced, most action-packed account of Jesus' life, Mark skips the miraculous birth in Bethlehem. Instead, he jumps to the start of Jesus' ministry, with the baptism in the Jordan River, and the Lord's voice calling from heaven: "You are my own dear Son, and I am pleased with you" (1:11).

Jesus retreats to the Judean desert for 40 days. There, he overcomes several temptations of Satan and prepares for his three- to four-year teaching and healing ministry that will lead to his execution. Jesus returns to his home region of Galilee, in northern Israel, where he chooses 12 disciples, beginning with four fishermen.

Then a flurry of miracles occurs, including casting out demons, walking on water, and healing the sick.

These healings, along with his new insights into ancient Scripture, captivate the Galilean crowds. Each day they gather around him by the thousands. Word spreads to Jewish religious leaders in Jerusalem, in southern Israel, and they send representatives to check him out. These inves-
tigators don't appreciate his non-traditional interpretations of Scripture, so they repeat-edly try to discredit and humiliate him with trick questions designed to get him in trou-ble no matter how he answers. Each attempt fails, and they walk away embarrassed. By chapter three in this 16-chapter book, the Jews start plotting to kill him.

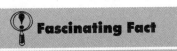

**Fascinating Fact**

Mark is the shortest Gospel, and was probably the main source for the Gospels of Matthew and Luke, which quote all but 31 verses from Mark.

When Jesus takes his ministry south, into the heart of Jewish opposition, he knows his execution is near. He tries explaining this to his disciples, but they can't conceive of a suffering Messiah. They've grown up hearing about a promised deliverer from King David's family who would restore Israel's glory, peace, and prosperity.

Jesus arrives in Jerusalem on what becomes known as Palm Sunday. He rides into town on a donkey while crowds cheer him with a king's welcome. Jewish leaders circumvent his supporting crowds by arresting him Thursday night and trying him all night long. By 9 A.M. the next morning, he is nailed to a cross. And by 3 P.M., he is dead. Sunday morning, however, his tomb is empty and an angel dressed in white declares that he's alive and preparing to meet his disciples.

## Influential People

**Jesus,** God's son, comes to earth in human form to save humanity. We may not understand exactly how or why his suffering and death saves us, but we can understand the love that drives him. And we can follow his lead by striving to be more loving and self-giving toward others.

**12 apostles,** working-class men Jesus invites to join his ministry as disciples. Mark emphasizes how slow the disciples are to realize that Jesus isn't the Messiah of conventional wisdom, with an earthly kingdom for his destiny. Only after Jesus' death and resurrection do the disciples begin to grasp it. We're sometimes a bit like the disciples: seeing in Jesus what we want to see instead of what's really there.

## Key Ideas You Need to Know

**Son of man.** This was Jesus' favorite title for himself. The title sounds odd at first, but as we examine how Old Testament prophets used it, we can understand why Jesus chose it.

"Son of man" works on two levels, pointing to humanity and to God, which makes it a perfect way to describe God who has come in the flesh. On the first level, Ezekiel used "son of man" to mean "human." God often called Ezekiel by this title.

On the second level, Daniel used the title to refer to a mysterious person from heaven: "I saw what looked like a son of man coming with the clouds. . . . He was crowned king and given power and glory so that all people of every nation and race would serve him. He will rule forever, and his kingdom is eternal, never to be destroyed" (Daniel 7:13–14). Many Christians believe this is a description of Jesus at the Second Coming, sometime in the unknown future.

## Q&A

**Is there a devil and evil spirits?** It might surprise you to hear that many Christians doubt it. They read "Satan" and "demon" in the Bible and they don't think of personal, spiritual beings who are every bit as real as God, Gabriel, or us. They interpret the words as a kind of shorthand for evil at its most potent—as a way to help us grasp a very real force in this world that would otherwise be impossible to understand.

Disembodied evil would certainly be hard to visualize. So these Christians take the position that Satan is a symbol—a face to help us see the enemy.

One big concern of these Christians is that we too often blame Satan for evil that we come up with by ourselves and are capable of stopping. It shifts our responsibilities by allowing us to say, "The devil made me do it."

Most Christians, however, believe there's nothing symbolic about the devil and his army of spirits. They exist as sentient beings. As Methodist founder John Wesley once put it, "No devil, no God."

The Roman Catholic Church is so convinced demons exist that priests have rituals to exorcize the demon-possessed. Jesus performed exorcisms, too, and often talked with the demons—even getting their names (Mark 5:9). And the apostle Paul said we are fighting "against rulers of darkness and powers in the spiritual world" (Ephesians 6:12).

**Should Christians fast?** Jesus did. He fasted after his baptism, just before starting the arduous work of his ministry. Yet his disciples didn't fast because Jesus said their time with him was to enjoy and celebrate. He said they would fast after he was gone (2:19–20).

Christians throughout the ages have fasted—skipping some or all meals for a time—as a way of helping them turn their attention to God. Instead of eating, they'll pray. Or they'll think about the special concern that is troubling them. Maybe they're worried about their health, a financial problem, or a loved one in trouble. So they set aside a time to fast—perhaps a meal a day—to bring the matter to God.

The fast can sharpen our concentration and sensitivity to God's leading. It was during a time of prayer and fasting that a group of early Christians decided to commission Paul and Barnabas as the first missionaries (Acts 13:2). (For more see "Why fast?" in Joel, page 209.)

## Red Flag Issues

**A day of rest.** Christians have long debated what activities should be allowed on Sunday, their Sabbath. The word *Sabbath* is Hebrew meaning "rest." Jews celebrate the Sabbath from sundown on Friday through sundown on Saturday.

The Sabbath dates clear back to Creation. After creating the universe in six days, God rested on the seventh. One of the laws he gave Moses was this: "You have six days to do your work, but the Sabbath is mine, and it must remain a day of rest" (Exodus 31:15).

The Bible stopped short of defining what was and wasn't work, but Jewish teachers created a long and complicated list—to make sure people didn't accidentally break the law. For instance, there was no cooking on the Sabbath—meals were prepared the day before. And the people could walk only about a thousand yards.

In Israel today, many businesses are closed on the Jewish Sabbath. Even elevators in many hotels stop automatically at every floor, so observant Jews don't have to push the buttons. In our country, which is predominately Christian, many businesses are closed on Sunday—though this isn't as common as it was in past generations.

Sunday has, for many, become an extra Saturday—a time for catching up on the shopping, errands, and household chores. Many of these activities require that others work

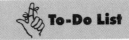

### To-Do List

- "Give to Caesar what is Caesar's and to God what is God's" (12:17, New International Version). *Jesus' reply when asked if Jews should pay taxes to Rome.*

- "Go home to your friends, and tell them what wonderful things the Lord has done for you" (5:19, New Living Translation).

- "If any of you wants to be my follower," Jesus says, "you must put aside your selfish ambition" (8:34, New Living Translation).

- "If you want a place of honor [in God's kingdom], you must become a slave and serve others!" (9:35).

- "You must forgive what others have done to you. Then your Father in heaven will forgive your sins" (11:25).

on Sunday—to serve us at checkout counters, restaurants, and gas stations. For this reason, some Christians limit their activities on Sunday, hoping others will do the same so businesses won't require as many people to work on Sunday.

The Bible doesn't give us a strict list of dos and don'ts for the Sabbath. On the contrary, Jesus said the Sabbath was made to help us, not to restrict us (2:27). So perhaps a list is a bad idea. But this much is clear: in the bustle of our busy week, God has given us the gift of a day off to refresh our body and spirit.

## For the Record: Mark Abused

**End-time predictions.** End-time specialists jump into the spotlight from time to time making end-time predictions that captivate millions before fizzling unfulfilled.

The specialists take cryptic phrases from scattered Bible passages and piece them together into messages they present as code-broken for the current generation.

One of the passages they draw from is Jesus' prediction of future events, described in Mark 13. There, Jesus talked about what most Bible experts believe is the fall of Jerusalem in A.D. 70. But there also appear to be references to events at the end of human history—including a period of great suffering (which some call the Tribulation) before Jesus returns in power and glory.

Though Jesus said no one knows when the end will come, there are signs. "So when you see all these things happening, you will know that the time has almost come" (13:29). Some Christians have taken this as a kind of Second Great Commission—to spend our energy examining the signs and making predictions about the end.

Self-taught Bible student, William Miller, drew from vague numbers and references in the Bible to calculate that Jesus would return on October 22, 1844. Some 50,000 people—many of whom sold their property and dressed themselves in white robes—waited for what became known as "the Great Disappointment." Miller pushed the date back a year, but Jesus was a no-show.

Author Hal Lindsey made many predictions in his best-selling 1976 book *The Late Great Planet Earth,* including that the Jewish temple would be rebuilt within a generation of Israel's establishment as a nation. Israel became a nation in 1948—well beyond the 40-year generation marker.

Edgar Whisenant caused quite a stir when he published *88 Reasons Why the Rapture Will Be in 1988.* Of course, 88 reasons weren't enough.

Even in New Testament times, some folks were preoccupied with Jesus' return. But the apostles urged those people to get busy with the Lord's work instead (1 Corinthians 15:58). Perhaps the best advice came from angels talking to the disciples immediately after Jesus ascended into heaven: "Why are you men from Galilee standing here and looking up into the sky?" (Acts 1:11). They had work to do—and it wasn't to calculate the date of Jesus' return. It was to teach others what Jesus had taught them about living in the here and now.

**Snake handling in church.** When Jesus told his disciples to preach to all people, he said he would give them power to do wonderful things, such as healing people, casting out demons, and speaking in new languages. He also said his disciples "will handle snakes and will drink poison and not be hurt" (16:18).

Some churches, especially in Appalachia, take this verse as an invitation to test their faith and God's power. Some worshipers will hold the snakes—usually rattlesnakes or copperheads—as a show of their faith and God's power.

The practice started in 1909 when an evangelist named "Little" George Hensley quoted the passage from Mark, took out a rattlesnake, and challenged the people to pick it up as a test of faith. Though the practice is outlawed, some churches continue to observe this bizarre ritual.

What Jesus intended by the statement is that God would protect his disciples from danger they encountered—not danger they invited. There's no mention in the New Testament of Christians being forced to drink poison. Paul, however, was bitten by a poisonous snake during a missionary journey. He survived, to the astonishment of the witnesses (Acts 28:6).

# Bible Scenarios You Can Use

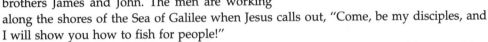

### 1. Jesus invites fishermen to join him (1:14–20)

**F**or centuries, the Jews have been waiting for God to send a deliverer who will set up a godly kingdom. The prophets promised it would happen. Jesus begins his ministry with this startling announcement: "The time has come! God's kingdom will soon be here. Turn back to God and believe the good news."

Jesus assembles a group of 12 men to work with him and learn from him. The first four are professional fishermen: brothers Andrew and Simon (whom Jesus later renames Peter), and brothers James and John. The men are working along the shores of the Sea of Galilee when Jesus calls out, "Come, be my disciples, and I will show you how to fish for people!"

The men join him immediately, perhaps because they've already heard his preaching and witnessed his miraculous power.

At least five of the disciples are fishermen, and one is a tax collector. The jobs of the others are never mentioned, probably because there's nothing unusual about their work.

We may think we're in no position to make much of a difference in our world, but common folks can make an uncommon difference. God sees to it.

### 2. Picking grain on the Sabbath (2:23–3:6)

**O**ne Sabbath—the Jewish day of rest—Jesus' disciples pick a snack of grain while walking through a field. A group of Pharisees, a strict Jewish sect, sees it and demands to know why Jesus let his disciples break the Sabbath laws.

God had told the Jews not to work on the Sabbath, but he stopped short of defining "work." The Pharisees took it upon themselves to do this, so people wouldn't accidentally break the law. The Pharisees taught that picking grain—even just a few heads for a snack—was harvesting, which is work.

Jesus disagrees. "People were not made for the good of the Sabbath," Jesus replies. "The Sabbath was made for the good of people."

Later, Jesus further angers the Pharisees when he breaks another Sabbath rule by curing a man with a crippled hand. Practicing the healing arts is on the Pharisees' "work" list, and is allowed on the Sabbath only in life or death cases.

God's laws are to make life better for us, not more difficult. If fellow believers try to impose oppressive rules on us, we're in good company when we resist.

### 3. Parable of a farmer sowing seeds (4:1-20)

Jesus tells a parable—a symbolic story with a message—to crowds gathered by the Sea of Galilee. A farmer sows his springtime seeds by scattering them on the ground. Some fall on packed footpaths and are snatched up by birds. Some fall in shallow dirt on rocks, sprouting fast but dying quickly. Some fall among weeds and get choked. But some fall in good soil and produce a great harvest.

The seeds, Jesus says, represents his message. The packed soil represents people who hear the message but do nothing, and Satan takes it away. Shallow dirt represents people who accept the message at first, but don't let it sink in. Weedy soil represents people who accept the message but get sidetracked by making money or other distractions. The good soil represents people who accept the message and share it.

Not everyone we talk to about Jesus will accept our message, but we shouldn't let that discourage us from spreading the word.

### 4. Jesus criticizes hypocrites (7:1-23)

Pharisees come to Jesus and complain that his disciples aren't following the Jewish custom of ritual hand washing before meals.

"You hypocrites!" Jesus replies. "You ignore God's specific laws and substitute your own traditions" (7:6, 8, New Living Translation). Jesus goes on to say that they can wash their hands all they want to show off their religion, but it won't clean their dirty minds or evil hearts.

God wants religion that starts inside us, and works its way out—not pretend religion that has memorized the Dance of the Pious.

### 5. Jesus blesses the children (10:13-16)

While Jesus is teaching and healing people, some parents come forward hoping to have Jesus put his hands on their children and bless them. The ancients believe that spoken blessings, like prayers, have power to make good things happen.

The disciples turn back the parents, saying Jesus can't be bothered. But Jesus overhears this and says, "Let the children come to me!" Then he takes them in his arms and blesses them.

Everyone is important to Jesus—even those who ancient society doesn't consider especially important, such as children, widows, and tax collectors. Likewise, everyone should be important to those of us who follow Jesus. That includes the poorest of the poor and the worst of sinners.

## 6. Asking for anything in prayer (11:20–25)

**O**n a morning walk to the temple, Jesus and the disciples pass a fig tree that Jesus checked for fruit the day before. When he found it empty, he said no one would eat from it again. The disciples are amazed to see that the tree has already died.

The fig tree episode may have been an acted out parable to show the disciples the power of prayer, for Jesus responds by saying, "Have faith in God! If you have faith in God and don't doubt, you can tell this mountain to get up and jump into the sea, and it will. Everything you ask for in prayer will be yours, if you only have faith."

That doesn't mean if you're a road construction foreman that you can pray a highway through the Rockies. Jesus' point is that God can do things that seem as impossible as mountain lifting. We can ask him for anything, and if it's in the best interest of his kingdom, he'll do it. Sometimes God answers our prayer by saying no, as he did when Paul asked for relief from some unspecified suffering (1 Corinthians 12:7). But that doesn't diminish the fact that prayer has the power to change reality.

## 7. Jesus' advice on paying taxes (12:13–17)

**J**ewish religious leaders who want to get rid of Jesus bring him a question designed to hurt his reputation. They ask if it's right for Jews to pay Roman taxes—the taxes that support Rome's oppressive occupation, pagan temples, and the rich lifestyle of Roman leaders. If Jesus says yes, the leaders figure he'll drop in the popularity polls. If he says no, he could be arrested for treason against Rome.

"Whom are you trying to fool with your trick questions?" he asks. "Show me a Roman coin, and I'll tell you" (12:15, New Living Translation). When handed the coin he asks, "Whose picture and title are stamped on it?"

"Caesar's," they reply.

"Well, then, give to Caesar what belongs to him. But everything that belongs to God must be given to God."

Most of us hate taxes. We think they're oppressive, wasted, and used to fund programs we believe are wrong-headed and even sinful. But as citizens of our nation, we should pay the taxes we owe. We can work to change the tax laws, but until the laws are changed, our responsibility is to pay them.

## 8. The two greatest commandments (12:28–34)

**"W**hat is the most important commandment?" a Jewish teacher asks Jesus.

"The most important one says: 'People of Israel, you have only one Lord and God. You must love him with all your heart, soul, mind, and strength. The second most important commandment says: 'Love others as much as you love yourself.' No other commandment is more important than these."

If we love God and cultivate loving compassion and respect for the people in our circle of influence, everything else in our spiritual life will fall into place. For as Jesus said elsewhere, "All the Laws of Moses and the Books of the Prophets are based on these two commandments" (Matthew 22:40).

## 9. Our big assignment (16:15–18)

**J**ewish leaders secretly arrest Jesus and convince the Roman governor to execute him for claiming to be the Messiah and the Son of God. Jesus dies on Friday, but rises from the dead on Sunday. He meets with his followers on several occasions over 40 days, and then one last time before he ascends into the sky.

In his final words, Jesus gives his disciples an assignment that becomes known as the Great Commission: "Go and preach the good news to everyone in the world."

In the years that followed, the church blossomed in Jerusalem. Then when Jewish leaders started persecuting and killing Christians, the believers scattered to neighboring regions and nations, taking their faith with them. Paul and Barnabas became the first missionaries, sent abroad specifically to take the teachings of Jesus to people in other nations (Acts 13). Since then, Christianity has spanned the globe, becoming one of the dominant religions on earth. And as long as new generations are born, the mission continues.

# LUKE

## Salvation: You Can Take It With You

A Kansas City pastor spent time with a dying man who had lived a life of wealth, power, and prestige. The pastor asked this thoroughly secular man if he had given any thought to what awaits him on the other side.

"Not one item of my life matters now," he replied, in a confession that gave way to conversion.

It didn't matter that he had lots of money, or that he owned thriving businesses, or that people looked up to him as a model of success. He couldn't take any of that with him.

This man was a modern version of Jesus' parable about a rich landowner who had a bumper crop and decided to build bigger barns to hoard it. Wealthy beyond his dreams, the landowner decided to kick back and enjoy himself. He died first.

Jesus said of this man, "A person is a fool to store up earthly wealth but not have a rich relationship with God" (12:21, New Living Translation).

We can't take it with us. Not the money. Not the home. Not the toys.

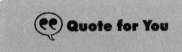 **Quote for You**

"A Savior was born for you. He is Christ the Lord" (2:11).

Yet there are treasures we can take to heaven. Jesus said so (18:22). We can take ourselves. Jesus is called Savior throughout Luke's Gospel because saving us for eternity is why he came. We can also take our goodness: the love we have, the compassion we show, the encouragement we give. Jesus never explains how we take them or what they'll look like when we get to where we're going, but his teachings are clear that each of us, along with the goodness we express, are the treasures of heaven.

Perhaps when we walk in eternity with someone we helped, we'll understand what Jesus meant by "treasures in heaven."

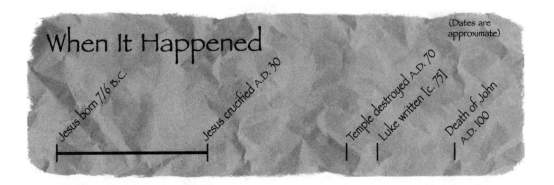

When It Happened

(Dates are approximate)

Jesus born 7/6 B.C.

Jesus crucified A.D. 30

Temple destroyed A.D. 70

Luke written [c. 75]

Death of John A.D. 100

# Info You Can Use

## Background Notes

**Writer:** Luke and its sequel—Acts—were written by the same person. But who this person was remains a mystery. Christian leaders in the second century said the writer was a non-Jewish Christian physician whom the apostle Paul called "dear doctor Luke" (Colossians 4:14). Paul also described Luke as a colleague in ministry, and the only one who stayed with him during his imprisonment in Rome (2 Timothy 4:11).

There are clues that a physician wrote this Gospel. We see in Luke the most complete and dramatic account of Jesus' birth. We also see more healing miracles than in any other Gospel.

Both books are addressed to "Honorable Theophilus," perhaps a Roman official who asked for information about the controversial and rapidly growing Christian religion. In response, the writer drew from a variety of sources that may have included eyewitnesses, the Gospel of Mark, and a collection of Jesus' teachings sometimes called "Q," for *quelle,* a German word meaning "source."

**Time:** The story spans the life and ministry of Jesus, from about 6 B.C. to A.D. 30—beginning with his birth and ending with his ascension into heaven 40 days after his resurrection.

We don't know when Luke and Acts were written. Some guess it was as early as the late 50s or early 60s, before the execution of Luke's colleague and helpful source of information, Paul. But emphasis on Jesus' prophecy about the fall of Jerusalem, which was fulfilled when Rome leveled the city in A.D. 70, suggests the book was written afterward, in the last decades of the first century.

**Place:** The story about Jesus took place mainly in what is now Israel. Most of Jesus' ministry was in his home region of Galilee, in northern Israel. The last, dramatic week of his life took place in Jerusalem.

**Bottom-Line Summary:** Gabriel, one of God's chief angels, arrives in the Jerusalem temple to tell the elderly and childless priest, Zechariah, that he will soon have a son. This child will become known as John the Baptist, who will announce the coming of the promised Messiah.

A month later, Gabriel appears to Mary, a young virgin, and tells her she will miraculously give birth to a son conceived by the Holy Spirit. "His name will be Jesus," Gabriel says of the child, "He will be great and will be called the Son of God Most High" (1:31–32).

Both boys are born and grow up. John doesn't become a priest like his father, but a prophet who calls the people to repentance and announces that God's special messenger is coming soon. That messenger, Jesus, begins his public ministry at about age 30. For three or four years Jesus travels throughout his home region of Galilee, healing the sick and teaching people how to live godly lives. He builds a large and devoted following, but he gives special attention to teaching his 12 handpicked disciples who are to continue his ministry when he is gone.

Jewish religious leaders grow to hate Jesus because he challenges their hypocrisy and many of their traditional teachings—some of which needlessly oppress the people, and others that create loopholes through God's commandments.

One night, while Jesus and his disciples are in Jerusalem, the Jewish leaders secretly arrest him. After an all-night trial, they condemn him to death and convince the Roman governor, Pilate, to execute him immediately. By about 9 A.M., Jesus is hanging from a cross. By about 3 P.M., he is dead. Sunday morning, on what is now celebrated as Easter, he raises from the dead.

Over the next 40 days, he appears to his disciples, calming them, eating with them, and teaching them. He shows them, in the Scripture, prophecies that said the Messiah would be killed and resurrected. And he commissions his followers to tell people of all nations about everything they have seen and heard so the people can find God's forgiveness for sin and be assured of living forever in God's heavenly kingdom.

Afterward, on the slopes of the Mount of Olives near where he had been arrested, Jesus ascends into the sky. The disciples return to Jerusalem, praising God.

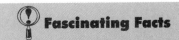

## Fascinating Facts

Many Jewish Christians living in Jerusalem fled before Roman soldiers destroyed it in A.D. 70. They left because they remembered what Jesus said in his prophecy of Jerusalem's fall: "Run to the mountains. If you are in the city, leave it" (21:21).

Luke is the only Gospel that has a sequel. The Book of Acts picks up where Luke leaves off, with the ascension of Jesus into heaven followed by the birth of the church. Together, the books form about a fourth of the New Testament.

Among all the writers believed to have contributed to the Bible, Luke is the only one not a Jew.

## Influential People

**Jesus,** God's son who comes to earth as humanity's Savior, shows us how to find God's forgiveness and assures us of an eternal home with God.

**12 apostles,** working-class men Jesus invites to join his ministry as disciples. It's with common folks like fishermen, taxmen—and us—that Jesus entrusts the mission of telling the world about God's love and salvation.

## Key Ideas You Need to Know

**Jesus is our Savior.** The Gospels of Matthew and Mark don't even use the word "Savior," though they present the idea. The Gospel of John uses the word once. But in Luke, the salvation that Jesus offers is clear from the very beginning. As an angel puts it for some startled shepherds in Bethlehem: "A Savior was born for you. He is Christ the Lord" (2:11).

On the eve of Jesus launching his ministry, John the Baptist repeats the angelic message by announcing the Lord's imminent arrival and declaring, "then everyone will see the saving power of God" (3:6).

Everything Luke reports—stories, miracles, and teachings—point to the single truth that Jesus is the savior of the human race.

## Q&A

**How important is it that we believe in Jesus' resurrection?** "If Christ wasn't raised to life," the apostle Paul said, "our message is worthless, and so is your faith" (1 Corinthians 15:14).

If Jesus had died and stayed dead, there would be no compelling reason to believe he was God's Son. The miracles he did were much like those other prophets performed. Moses didn't walk on water like Jesus did, but God used him to part the Red Sea. Elijah raised a widow's dead son to life (1 Kings 17:17–22). Elisha cured a soldier of leprosy (2 Kings 4:1–19).

Only Jesus came back from the dead, as he promised he would do. Only he gave us reason to believe in life after death.

**What kind of body did Jesus have after the resurrection?** His body had physical features, yet with abilities beyond what physical bodies can do. It was also immortal—like our bodies will be in heaven (1 Corinthians 15:42).

Jesus' resurrected body wasn't merely a restored physical body, like Lazarus had after Jesus raised him from the dead. Yet it was physical—though Jesus had to prove it to his terrified disciples.

"Why are you so frightened?" Jesus asked. "Look at my hands and my feet and see who I am! Touch me and find out for yourselves. Ghosts don't have flesh and bones as you see I have" (24:38–39). Jesus even ate some cooked fish to convince them he wasn't a disembodied spirit.

### To-Do List

- "Love your enemies, and be good to everyone who hates you" (6:27).

- "Don't be hard on others, and God won't be hard on you. Forgive others, and God will forgive you" (6:37).

- "Sell what you have and give the money to the poor" (12:33). *Not necessarily a call to give away everything, but certainly a call to give away something—enough to be considered generous.*

- "To those who use well what they are given, even more will be given" (19:26, New Living Translation).

- "Eat this as a way of remembering me" (22:19). *Jesus' instruction to his disciples at the Last Supper, when they ate bread representing Christ's body and drank wine representing his blood.*

- "With my authority, take this message of repentance to all the nations, beginning in Jerusalem: 'There is forgiveness of sins for all who turn to me'" (24:47, New Living Translation).

Unlike a purely physical body, Jesus' new body was able to suddenly appear in locked rooms, disappear as quickly, and ascend into the sky. He also appeared able to disguise his looks, since two believers on the road to Emmaus didn't recognize him until a moment before he disappeared (24:31).

Years later, the apostle Paul described the enhanced bodies of heaven as "spiritual" (1 Corinthians 15:44). Yet by "spiritual" he didn't mean something invisible and untouchable. He said our spiritual body would be every bit as real as a physical body—but a lot better.

**Why did Jesus have to die?** The Bible doesn't say why God's plan to save humanity required the death of Jesus. But Bible scholars speculate on possible answers.

- As far as the Jews of Jesus' day were concerned, only a sacrifice could erase a person's sins. The Old Testament teaches that the punishment for sin is death. "Life is in the blood," God told Moses, "and I have given you the blood of animals to sacrifice in place of your own" (Leviticus 17:11). Jesus, however, rendered the sacrificial system obsolete: "By this one sacrifice," a New Testament writer explains, "he [Jesus] has forever set free from sin the people he brings to God" (Hebrews 10:14; see also Hebrews 8:10–13).

- Christ's death shows how much he loves us.

- Christ's willingness to die shows that he was completely devoted to his Father—as we should be. Though we may not be called upon to die for our religious beliefs, we may have to make sacrifices.

- Christ's death gave way to the resurrection and ascension into heaven, which gave the disciples solid proof of life after death. This eyewitness proof filled the disciples with courage to spread Jesus' teachings even under the threat of death. In fact, most of the disciples are believed to have died as martyrs.

# Red Flag Issues

**Once saved, always saved?** Many Christians, especially some Baptists, Presbyterians, and Lutherans, teach that once you become a Christian you can never lose your assurance of heaven—no matter what sins you commit. The belief is called eternal security. It's based on several Bible passages, including Jesus' teaching that to those who follow him, "I give them eternal life, so that they will never be lost. No one can snatch them out of my hand" (John 10:28).

Other passages suggest believers can abandon the faith—a position held by denominations such as United Methodists, the Salvation Army, and Nazarenes. In the parable of the farmer sowing seeds, Jesus said the rocky soil represents "people who gladly hear the message [of salvation] and accept it. But they don't have deep roots, and they believe only for a little while. As soon as life gets hard, they give up" (8:13).

Some Christians who argue for eternal security say these shallow-rooted believers never had true faith in the first place.

The debate continues.

# Bible Scenarios You Can Use

## 1. Shepherds at the manger (2:1–20)

**M**ary is nearing her delivery date for the birth of Jesus when the Roman emperor orders a census, perhaps to collect tax. Men take their families and register at their hometowns. Joseph, now living in Nazareth, goes with his fiancée, Mary, to Bethlehem—about 70 miles south. This tiny village near Jerusalem is considered his family's traditional hometown, and is where his most famous ancestor, King David, was born.

Bethlehem's inn is full, but Joseph finds shelter in a stable—perhaps a small cave. Jesus is born here, and is laid in a manger, which is a feeding trough for livestock.

On the rolling hills near Bethlehem, shepherds are watching over their sheep. Suddenly, an angel bathed in brilliant light appears and announces, "This very day in King David's hometown a Savior was born for you. He is Christ the Lord." The shepherds rush into the village and find Jesus lying on a bed of hay.

And so it is that God's Son is born to an unwed mother, in a stable, with a birth announcement sent to sheepherders. We expect God to marvel us with extravagance, but he often prefers to marvel us with simplicity—choosing unexpected people and unlikely places for moments of great joy. Sometimes he even chooses us, right where we are.

## 2. Hometown folks reject Jesus (4:16–30)

**A**t about age 30, Jesus starts his public ministry of teaching about God and healing the sick. He announces his mission one Sabbath day in a synagogue in his hometown of Nazareth. Opening a scroll of Isaiah, he reads a prophecy: "The Lord's Spirit has come to me, because he has chosen me to tell the good news to the poor. The Lord has sent me to announce freedom for prisoners, to give sight to the blind, to free everyone who suffers."

Jesus closes the scroll and says, "What you have just heard me read has come true today."

The people are shocked. They know that Isaiah's words refer to the Messiah, and that Jesus is just Joseph's boy. Their shock churns into anger and they try to kill him, but he slips away.

As we serve God, some people will reject our efforts and perhaps even try to block them. Some of our most powerful opposition may come from the very people we love most. But if we're clear about what God wants us to do—as we usually are when it involves helping others—we shouldn't let rejection and opposition stop us.

## 3. A sinful woman weeps on Jesus (7:36–50)

**A** religious scholar invites Jesus home to dinner. A woman in town who has a bad reputation hears Jesus is there, so she goes into the house uninvited. She has probably heard Jesus teaching about God's forgiveness. In what appears to be an act of deep gratitude, she kneels beside him and weeps as she pours expensive perfume on his feet.

The scholar is disgusted. "If this man really were a prophet," he thinks, "he would know what kind of woman is touching him!"

Jesus knows what the scholar is thinking, and replies with a parable. Two people owe money. One person owes 50 coins, and the other owes 500. Both debts are forgiven. Who is most grateful?

"The one who owed more?" the scholar replies.

Jesus turns to the woman and says, "All her sins are forgiven, and that is why she has shown great love."

Those of us who have experienced God's forgiveness know the joy this woman must have felt. For this reason, we should celebrate with repentant people instead of looking down on them because of the bad things they've done in the past. If God has forgiven them, so should we.

## 4. Jesus calms the storm (8:22–25)

**"L**et's cross the lake," Jesus tells his disciples one day. The freshwater lake is the Sea of Galilee, which rests in a deep basin 700 feet below sea level, almost completely surrounded by hills. Sudden storms erupt when hot air trapped in the basin rises and collides with cool air rolling in from the Mediterranean Sea, funneling down the ravines.

Exhausted, Jesus falls into such a deep sleep that when a fierce storm threatens to sink the small boat, his disciples have to wake him. "Master, Master! We're about to drown!"

Jesus wakes up and tells the wind and waves to stop. They obey, and the lake falls placid.

The Lord has power over nature, so it's okay to ask him for help with such problems. He can also calm the storms in our lives. It's easy to be afraid as the storm approaches—just as the disciples were afraid. And like the disciples, it's even easier to let our faith slip by questioning God's protection over us.

Jesus asked his disciples, "Don't you have any faith?" (8:25)

Even if the storms rage on—whether outside us or inside us—he sails with us. And we can trust that he'll take good care of us.

## 5. Jesus heals a bleeding woman (8:40-48)

**W**hile walking through a crowd Jesus feels healing power moving from him to someone who touches him. He stops. "Who touched me?" he asks.

Everyone denies it, and the disciples remind him that he's in a crowd and people are jostling him from all sides. But Jesus insists healing power went into someone.

Terrified and trembling, a woman kneels before Jesus and admits she touched the fringe of his robe. She has suffered from bleeding, probably a menstrual period, for 12 years and had spent all her money on doctors who weren't able to help her. By Jewish law, she shouldn't have been in the crowd. Women in their period were ritually unclean, and anyone who touched them had to go through cleansing rituals before worshiping in the temple.

"You are now well because of your faith," Jesus says, "May God give you peace!"

Jesus didn't single her out to embarrass her. He likely wanted her to know there was no magic in his robe, but that the power was in her faith in him. There's nothing magical about faith, either. The power rests with God. Our faith is the confidence that God can use that power to help us, either with healing or with coping.

## 6. The Good Samaritan (10:30-37)

**A**fter Jesus tells a Jewish scholar that the two most important commandments are to love God and to love your neighbor, the scholar asks who is our neighbor. Jesus responds with a now-famous parable reported only in Luke.

A Jewish man walking the 15-mile desert trail from Jerusalem to Jericho is attacked, beaten, robbed, and left for dead. Later in the day, a priest arrives and sees the man, but keeps on walking. Then another temple worker does the same. Finally, a Samaritan arrives. Jews and Samaritans are bitter rivals, because the Samaritans are a mixed race. Centuries earlier, Jews in northern Israel intermarried with Assyrian invaders and then added to their Jewish faith some elements of pagan religions. These people became known as Samaritans, after the region of Samaria in which they lived.

The Samaritan treats the Jew, takes him to an inn, and pays the innkeeper to take care of him until he recovers.

"Which one of these three people was a real neighbor?" Jesus asks.

"The one who showed pity," the scholar replies.

"Go and do the same," Jesus says.

Our neighbor is anyone we come into contact with who needs our help. And helping that person is one of the two most important commandments God has given us.

## 7. How to pray (11:1–13)

**A**fter Jesus returns from praying alone, his disciples ask him to teach them how to pray.

He gives them an example that has become known as the Lord's Prayer. Instead of being a long, eloquent speech like those that Jewish leaders pray publicly as a proud testimony of their godliness, the Lord's Prayer is short and simple.

"Father, help us honor your name. Come and set up your kingdom. Give us each day the food we need. Forgive our sins, as we forgive everyone who has done wrong to us. And keep us from being tempted."

Jesus then adds a couple of parables—one about a man who grudgingly gives in to a neighbor's late-night request for bread to feed guests, and another about a father who wouldn't even think of giving a snake to his child who has asked for a fish. Jesus says that God, who dearly loves us, is far more eager to help than is this neighbor or father.

When we need something, we should ask God for it. He will give us what we need, or show us the difference between what we need and what we want.

## 8. Parable of a greedy rich man (12:13–21)

**"T**eacher," a man calls out to Jesus from a crowd, "tell my brother to give me my share of what our father left us when he died."

Jesus asks what right he has to settle the legal dispute, and then he promptly shifts into a parable that gets at the heart of the problem.

A rich man has a bumper crop that his barns can't contain. Instead of selling the excess or giving some away, he builds bigger barns. Then he says to himself, "You have stored up enough good things to last for years to come. Live it up! Eat, drink, and enjoy yourself."

The man dies that night.

Jesus says, "This is what happens to people who store up everything for themselves, but are poor in the sight of God."

To the brothers squabbling over their inheritance—and to any of us preoccupied with money and possessions—Jesus shows it's more important to become rich in the things of God, such as compassion, honesty, and love for your family.

## 9. Parable of the prodigal son (15:11–32)

Jesus associates with notorious sinners. This sets off grumbling among Jewish leaders, who say godly people—especially rabbis—shouldn't keep such bad company.

To explain himself, Jesus tells what has become one of the most famous parables of all.

A son asks for his share of the family inheritance, which his father graciously gives him. The son promptly leaves home and spends all the money on wild living. Broke, he takes a job working for a pig farmer. Pigs are non-kosher animals that are forbidden for Jews to touch or eat. Life gets tough enough that the young man resorts to eating some of the pods he feeds the pigs. He finally comes to his senses and realizes that even the workers at his father's house are better off than he is. So he heads home to ask for a job.

On the last road home, his father spots him in the distance and takes off running, arms wide open to hug him.

That's why Jesus associates with sinners. He and his followers are making people feel welcome in God's family. No matter where we go or what we do, God is always reaching out to us like a loving father who desperately wants his runaway child to come home.

## 10. Jesus helps Zacchaeus the tax man (19:1–26)

Jesus arrives in the Jordan River village of Jericho, on his way to Jerusalem. An eager crowd greets him, while one man runs ahead and climbs a tree along the path, hoping to at least catch sight of him as he walks by. The man is Zacchaeus, a Jewish tax official. The people hate him for collaborating with the Romans by collecting the empire's taxes, and for getting rich by overcharging the people.

When Jesus reaches the tree he stops, looks up, and says he'd like to stay the night at Zacchaeus' house. The crowds are disgusted, but Zacchaeus is overjoyed.

By the time Jesus leaves Jericho, Zacchaeus is a changed man. He vows to give half his money to the poor and to repay everyone he has cheated by giving back four times as much as he took.

"Today you and your family have been saved," Jesus says. "The Son of Man came to look for and to save people who are lost."

As followers of Jesus, that's our job, too. We shouldn't let criticism stop us from reaching out to help the people who need God most. The most hated people in our society may be the very ones with whom we should be sharing a meal.

## 11. A widow donates her last pennies (21:1–4)

**W**hen Jesus arrives in Jerusalem, he goes to the worship center that dominates the hilltop city: the temple. There, he stands near the collection box and watches people drop in their offerings. Some contributors are rich, as the size of their offerings show. Then along comes a poor widow. Without a husband, she's like a minor under Jewish law: she can't own property or conduct business. She's completely dependent on the charity of others—for food, shelter, and her existence. She drops in two of the smallest coins in circulation.

"I tell you," Jesus says to his disciples, "this poor woman has put in more than all the others. Everyone else gave what they didn't need. But she is very poor and gave everything she had."

The size of our gift to God isn't as important as our willingness to give. Let's not allow our tiny amount of money, time, or talent to discourage us from contributing to God's work.

## 12. Jesus prays in the Garden of Gethsemane (22:39–44)

**O**n Thursday evening Jesus eats with his disciples a final meal—the Last Supper. He probably knows he'll be arrested within hours, and crucified by morning. He leads his disciples into an olive grove called Gethsemane, just outside Jerusalem. There, on the slopes of the Mount of Olives, he kneels and prays.

"Father," Jesus says, "please don't make me suffer by having me drink from this cup. But do what you want, and not what I want."

His prayer is so fervent that sweat falls to the ground like the giant drops of blood that will fall in a few hours.

Jesus is our model for what to do when the moment we face is more than we can bear. We turn to God and ask for deliverance, but take comfort in knowing that deliverance or not, the God who sustains creation is with us.

## 13. Jesus forgives his executioners (23:26–56)

**T**emple guards arrest Jesus in the garden and take him to the high priest, who convenes an emergency session of the Sanhedrin— the 70-member legislature-court, made up of priests, scholars, and respected elders. After an all-night trial, they convict Jesus of blasphemy for claiming to be God's Son. At daybreak they take him to Pilate, the Roman governor who alone has authority to sentence a local person to death. Pilate initially refuses, but eventually gives in to the persistent demands. He orders an immediate execution.

Soldiers beat Jesus, and then force him to carry his cross to the execution site just outside the Jerusalem walls. They take off his robe, nail him to the cross, and then gamble for the robe, which they treat as a fringe benefit.

"Father, forgive these people!" Jesus says from the cross. "They don't know what they're doing." Six hours later, by about 3 P.M., Jesus is dead.

Years earlier, on a Galilean hillside, Jesus told the crowds to love their enemies and pray for people who mistreat them. At his execution, Jesus practiced what he preached. It's hard to forgive people who hurt us—especially people who don't want forgiveness. But with God nothing is impossible.

## 14. Resurrected Jesus appears to his disciples (24:44–53)

**O**n Friday evening Jesus' body is hastily laid in a tomb for the Jewish day of rest, which begins at sunset. By Sunday morning, he is resurrected. Women discover the empty tomb when they arrive to finish preparing his body for burial.

Jesus appears to his disciples who are gathered in Jerusalem, mourning and probably hiding from the authorities so they don't meet the same fate as their teacher.

Jesus tells them, "The Scriptures say that the Messiah must suffer, then three days later he will rise from death. They also say that all people of every nation must be told in my name to turn to God, in order to be forgiven. So beginning in Jerusalem, you must tell everything that has happened."

Forty days later Jesus ascends to heaven, leaving behind an emboldened band of men who no longer fear death. They will go to the temple, passing the very temple guards who arrested Jesus, and tell the story that has survived the ages. It was their responsibility, as it is ours, to tell the good news that God's salvation lasts forever, and it's for everyone who accepts him as Savior.

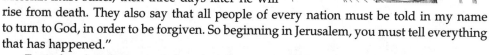

# JOHN

## Why Believe Jesus Is God

Why should we believe Jesus when he says he's God, and that if we believe it we'll live forever?

There are plenty of reasons not to believe it—to call it a lie for feeble souls afraid of dying. After all, one of the earliest creedal statements of faith says, "The Lord is one" (Deuteronomy 6:4, New International Version). Not two or three: Father, Son, and Holy Ghost.

Oddly—especially for a Jewish writer—John never even tried to explain this clash with the Jewish creed. He just said, essentially, one plus one equals one. One God the Son plus one God the Father equals one God. The closest John came to explaining this fuzzy math was to report the words of Jesus: "If you have seen me, you have seen the Father. . . . Don't you believe I am one with the Father and that the Father is one with me?" (John 14:9–10).

Well, no. Many Jews didn't. That's why they condemned him to death: for claiming to be God.

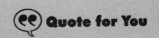

**Quote for You**

"I am the resurrection and the life. Those who believe in me, even though they die like everyone else, will live again" (11:25, New Living Translation).

Decades after the Crucifixion, when John wrote this Gospel, apparently to help Christian Jews explain their faith to traditional Jews, he stopped short of addressing this pivotal issue. Why? Perhaps the explanation is beyond our physics-bound ability to understand it.

What John did, instead, was to show that Jesus was everything we would expect of God. By reporting Jesus' insightful teachings and the most dramatic miracles, John showed that Jesus was master of everything: God's Word, the physical world, the spirit world, life, and death. So how could he not be God?

It's a question whose answer, John says, determines our eternal destiny.

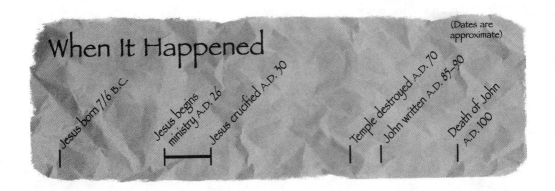

## When It Happened

(Dates are approximate)

Jesus born 7/6 B.C.

Jesus begins ministry A.D. 26

Jesus crucified A.D. 30

Temple destroyed A.D. 70

John written A.D. 85–90

Death of John A.D. 100

# Info You Can Use

 **Background Notes**

**Writer:** The writer never identified himself. But Christians in the second century said the writer was the apostle John, the son of Zebedee.

John, as well as his brothers James and Peter, were Jesus' three closest disciples. John's the only one of these three not mentioned in the book. His conspicuous absence lends support to the idea that he humbly excluded himself from the story he wrote.

Bible experts also say John was the unnamed "favorite disciple" (13:23) to whom the crucified Jesus entrusted the care of his mother, Mary. The Gospel's final verses add that "Jesus' favorite disciple" is the person "who told all of this [Gospel story]. He wrote it" (21:20, 24).

**Time:** The story starts long before the birth of Jesus in Bethlehem. John placed Jesus at the beginning of time. At Creation, Jesus was "with God and was truly God" (1:1). That stated, John jumped ahead to the beginning of Jesus' ministry, which extended for an estimated three to four years, from about A.D. 26 to 30.

John is generally thought to be the last of the four Gospels written. Christians in the second century said John wrote it late in life, while living in the coastal city of Ephesus, in western Turkey. The date of the writing is generally estimated between A.D. 85–90, about 60 years after the death of Jesus. The book's well developed theology adds support to this late date.

If the book was written late, John may have intended it to reinforce the faith of Christian Jews who were locked in a bitter us-them struggle with traditional Jews. Many Christians were Jews, racially. And they still observed Jewish traditions, such as the Sabbath and Jewish holidays. But because they believed Jesus was God's Son, the traditional Jews banned them from worshiping in the synagogues.

**Place:** The story took place mainly in what is now Israel. Most of Jesus' ministry was in northern Israel, in his home region of Galilee. Many of his clashes with Jewish leaders took place in Jerusalem, where he was executed.

**Bottom-Line Summary:** John writes for one reason: "so that you will put your faith in Jesus as the Messiah and the Son of God" (20:31).

He's not interested in telling the life story of Jesus, or reporting lots of miracles—perhaps because the other Gospels had already done that. John wants to convince us that Jesus is deity: God's Son who came down from heaven and temporarily became human. So John reports only the teachings and a few miracles that best prove his point. He skips the parables entirely.

John starts at the beginning of time, saying Jesus was there to create the universe. Then John jumps ahead to the ministry of John the Baptist, who announced the coming of God's promised savior. When Jesus arrives to be baptized and launch his own ministry, John the Baptist declares, "Here is the Lamb of God who takes away the sin of the world!" (1:29).

The first half of the book shows Jesus selecting 12 disciples who will help him, learn from him, and continue his ministry when he's gone. Jesus begins his work by teaching about who he is and why he has come, and by performing miracles that convince many that he is both the promised Messiah and the Son of God. In fact, the seven miracles John reports are what John calls "signs" that prove Jesus is God.

Jewish religious leaders are a hard sell. Some believe Jesus, but many seem convinced his teachings are a threat to the Jewish way of life and that he gets his miracle-working power from the devil.

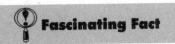
**Fascinating Fact**

For the story of Jesus in one sentence, Bible experts turn to the verse we see on posters at many televised ballgames—John 3:16. "God loved the people of this world so much that he gave his only Son, so that everyone who has faith in him will have eternal life."

The second half of the book tells about Jesus' final week. On what is now celebrated as Palm Sunday, Jesus rides into Jerusalem and is greeted by the cheers of pilgrims who have come to town for the Passover holiday. The words they shout are quotes from the Old Testament about the Messiah, showing they think Jesus is that promised Savior: "Hooray! God bless the one who comes in the name of the Lord! God bless the King of Israel!" (12:13). On Thursday night, Jewish leaders secretly arrest and try Jesus. He is nailed to a Roman cross on Friday morning and dead by afternoon. Sunday morning, however, he is resurrected and talking with his stunned disciples.

The book ends with Jesus challenging Peter, the leader of the disciples, to "take care of my sheep" (21:16). Jesus had described his ministry as the work of a loving shepherd tending the sheep. He tells Peter that this work needs to continue until he returns.

## Influential People

**Jesus,** God's Son, existed since the beginning of time and came to earth in human form to show us what God is like and to teach us how to live as God's people. Because of Jesus' arrival on earth, we have more than abstract teachings to guide us. We have a living example—a model of compassion, humility, and devotion to God and humanity.

**12 apostles,** common, working-class men Jesus invites to help him, learn from him, and carry on his ministry.

**John the Baptist,** a relative of Jesus, prepares the people for Jesus' ministry by calling them to repent of their sins. Fearless in confronting sin, he even criticizes an illegal marriage of Herod the Great's son, who had become a ruler. John is executed for this. But his legacy survives: spiritual truth is worth dying for.

**Key Ideas You Need to Know**

**Word.** John seems intent on confusing us when he starts his Gospel by cryptically referring to Jesus only as "the one who is called the Word" (1:1).

Though this term may confuse us, it helped Romans and Jews in John's day quickly realize he was talking about someone who's more than human. *Word* is from the Greek term *logos*. Romans schooled in Greek teachings used "Word" to describe the cosmic reason behind the universe. One Greek philosopher said the Word "is always existent" and "all things happen through this Word."

For Jews educated in the synagogue, Word was two things: a shortcut reference to Scripture (God's Word), and a description of God's power that could make things happen by merely speaking. So by calling Jesus the Word, John was introducing him to Jews as God's message that has come to life and as God's power that's evidenced in miracles. In fact, it was with just three words that Jesus performed his most dramatic miracle: "Lazarus, come out!" (11:43).

**Trinity.** One of the most perplexing beliefs in Christianity is that there's only one God, but that he exists as three persons: Father, Son, and Holy Spirit.

It's puzzling because the Old Testament says there's only one God and that it's a sin to believe otherwise. Yet Jesus said, "I am one with the Father" (10:30). Jesus also told his followers that after he was gone he would send the Holy Spirit, and that new believers should be baptized "in the name of the Father, the Son, and the Holy Spirit" (Matthew 28:19).

Early Christian theologians debated how to explain the apparent contradiction—three persons, but only one God. Some suggested that Jesus was merely a human and that the Holy Spirit was another name for God. Others suggested Jesus was the one and only God who came in the flesh, which wouldn't explain why Jesus prayed to his Father.

After heated debate, the majority of early church leaders decided to accept what they couldn't explain. A respected theologian named Augustine summed it up this way: "The Father is God, the Son is God, the Holy Spirit is God . . . yet we do not say that there are three gods, but one God, the most exalted Trinity itself."

 **Q&A**

**What does it mean to be born again?** It's a figurative way of describing the change that takes place in us when we become Christians.

Some Bible translations call it being "born again." Others call it being "born from above" or "born of the Spirit."

The apostle Paul puts it this way: "Those who become Christians become new persons. They are not the same anymore, for the old life is gone. A new life has begun!" (2 Corinthians 5:17, New Living Translation).

We're all born, physically. But Jesus and Paul are talking about a spiritual birth that's every bit as real and that produces a life that will never end.

As we mature in our spiritual life, we develop many of the character traits of our Father—such as compassion, patience, and forgiveness.

**Does God make innocent people suffer?** The Bible suggests that sometimes he does.

In Bible times the Jews generally thought all suffering was a punishment from God. That's why when the disciples saw a man who had been born blind they asked Jesus if the blindness was because of his parents' sin or his own.

"He was born blind," Jesus said, "so the power of God could be seen in him" (9:3, New Living Translation). Then Jesus healed the man.

Many of the tragic things that happen to us are because we live in a world affected by sin. Even the natural disasters are presented in the Bible as unnatural because the world God created—before sin entered the scene—was an idyllic paradise.

God, however, can make seemingly tragic things happen to innocent people in an effort to help humanity. In the case of the blind man, this man lived much of his life in darkness. It seems cruel, but we don't know how much God was able to use that healing miracle to change eternity for this man and those who witnessed the miracle.

Christians who have lived long enough to experience God's mercy many times over might say God deserves the benefit of the doubt. Perhaps the blind man, now celebrating with God in heaven, would say, if given the choice, he would gladly have offered his eyesight in exchange for what he's seeing now.

## Red Flag Issues

**Capital punishment.** Christians stand on both sides of this controversial issue. In Old Testament times, God ordered capital punishment for many offenses, including adultery (Leviticus 20:10).

But Jesus seemed to show that the new agreement God made with humanity included changes in capital punishment. When religious leaders brought him a woman caught in adultery, he not only

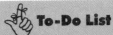

**To-Do List**

- "This is what God wants you to do: Believe in the one he has sent" (6:29, New Living Translation).

- "Unless you are born again, you can never see the Kingdom of God" (3:3, New Living Translation).

- "Everyone who has done good things will rise to life, but everyone who has done evil things will rise and be condemned" (5:29). *Jesus describing Judgment Day.*

- "You shouldn't be so concerned about perishable things like food. Spend your energy seeking the eternal life that I, the Son of Man, can give you. For God the Father has sent me for that very purpose" (6:27, New Living Translation).

- "I tell you for certain that everyone who has faith in me has eternal life" (6:47). *The words of Jesus.*

- "I am giving you a new command. You must love each other, just as I have loved you. If you love each other, everyone will know that you are my disciples" (13:34–35).

- "I am the way, the truth, and the life. No one can come to the Father except through me" (14:6, New Living Translation).

talked them out of killing her, he released her unpunished (8:3). (For more about capital punishment, see Genesis and Matthew, pages 24 and 272.)

**Eternal security.** (See "Once saved, always saved?" Luke, page 293.)

**Drinking alcoholic beverages.** Many Christians consider it wrong to drink alcoholic beverages. Some denominations put it in writing—in their rules of instruction for Christian living. The church leaders order total abstinence and encourage their people to take a stand against licensing places of business that sell intoxicating drinks.

Other Christians see nothing wrong with drinking, as long as it doesn't get out of hand and become addictive or harmful in other ways.

One of the prime arguments for drinking comes from the Gospel of John. In Jesus' first recorded miracle, he turned water into wine during a wedding ceremony (2:1–10).

Also, the apostle Paul told his colleague Timothy to drink wine to help with a stomach problem (1 Timothy 5:23).

Many Christians opposed to drinking alcoholic beverages say this wine was actually unfermented grape juice. But grapes were harvested in the heat of Israel's summer, and without refrigeration began to ferment almost immediately. The wine, however, was often diluted—mixed with water to make it last longer.

Though many Christians see no strong biblical grounds for total abstinence, they stay away from alcohol because of the damage they've seen caused by drinking. The Bible includes some of those kinds of scenes in the escapades of people who got drunk: Noah, Lot, King Belshazzar, and the Prodigal Son. (For more on this topic see Proverbs, page 151.)

##  For the Record: John Abused

**Persecuting Jews.** Nazis liked the Gospel of John. The Nazis and others who persecuted Jews have sometimes done so while quoting this Gospel. Jesus told a group of Jewish religious leaders who were heckling him from a crowd that they weren't children of Abraham. "Your father is the devil" (8:44). The Gospel of John also tends to identify the opponents of Jesus as simply "the Jews," even though Jesus and most of his followers were also Jews.

In the Middle Ages, around the time of the Crusades, Jews were persecuted for being descendants of the race that opposed and killed Jesus, and that refused to convert to Christianity. Jews who didn't convert during the Spanish Inquisition were executed to maintain purity of the "true faith."

Martin Luther, German father of the Protestant movement, had some of history's harshest words for the Jews—which the Nazis later drew from to produce anti-Jewish propaganda. Frustrated in 1543 with their stubborn refusal to convert, Luther called them a "damned, rejected race" and an "unsufferable devilish burden." He offered princes and nobles this seven-point strategy for dealing with the Jews:

- Burn their synagogues
- Destroy their homes
- Take away their prayer books
- Outlaw rabbis from teaching
- Revoke passport and traveling rights
- Confiscate their money
- Force them into jobs of manual labor

In 1994, leaders of the Evangelical Lutheran Church in America condemned Luther's anti-Jewish writings and vowed "to oppose the deadly workings of anti-Semitism in church and society."

# Bible Scenarios You Can Use

## 1. Jesus teaches about eternal life (3:1–21)

Under the cover of night, a Jewish scholar named Nicodemus pays a visit to Jesus. Nicodemus is a member of the Sanhedrin, a 70-member council that makes and enforces Jewish law. Perhaps Nicodemus comes at night to avoid drawing attention to his mission, which is to learn more about Jesus.

Jesus tells him, "You must be born from above before you can see God's kingdom!" When Nicodemus says he doesn't understand how a man can be born a second time, Jesus explains. "Humans give life to their children. Yet only God's Spirit can change you into a child of God."

How do we change? Believe in Jesus. "Everyone who has faith in him will have eternal life." That's the message of the New Testament in a sentence.

## 2. Jesus talks with a woman at a well (4:1–42)

On his way home from Jerusalem, Jesus comes to a village in Samaria. The disciples go to buy food while Jesus waits at the village well. When a woman comes with a bucket to draw water, Jesus asks for a drink.

The woman replies, "How can you ask me for a drink of water when Jews and Samaritans won't have anything to do with each other?"

Jesus said if she knew who she was talking to, she would ask for water that forever quenches thirst. Jesus is talking about his message of salvation, which she accepts.

Just as our body gets hungry and thirsty, our soul needs spiritual food to stay healthy. The spirit's food is God's word. We find it in the Bible, in the advice of others, and in the inner voice of the Holy Spirit.

## 3. Jesus feeds 5,000 who return for more (6:1–40)

A crowd follows Jesus to an isolated hill by the Sea of Galilee. There, Jesus miraculously feeds them all with one boy's lunch of five loaves of bread and two fish.

The next morning the crowd gathers again. Jesus accuses them of coming for food, and says they should be more concerned about food that gives eternal life.

When they ask what God wants, Jesus says it's to have faith in the one he sent. They ask Jesus for a miracle to prove God sent him, just as the miracle of manna bread appearing from the desert sky proved God sent Moses. "The bread that God gives is the one who came down from heaven to give life to the world," Jesus said. "I am the bread that gives life!"

Instead of spending so much energy seeking money that pays for food and shelter, we should seek Jesus.

## 4. Jesus forgives an adulteress (8:1–11)

**A**ngry Jewish leaders bring to Jesus a woman caught in adultery.

"The Law of Moses teaches that a woman like this should be stoned to death! What do you say?" It's a trick question designed to get Jesus in trouble, since only the Roman governor can sentence a person to death.

Jesus stands and says, "If any of you have never sinned, then go ahead and throw the first stone at her!"

One by one the men leave. Jesus tells the woman, "I am not going to accuse you either. You may go now, but don't sin anymore."

When we stand face to face with someone who has sinned, we should follow Christ's example: be slow to judge and punish, but quick with compassion and forgiveness.

## 5. Jesus cries at Lazarus' grave (11:1–44)

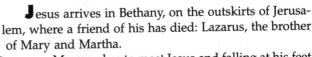

**J**esus arrives in Bethany, on the outskirts of Jerusalem, where a friend of his has died: Lazarus, the brother of Mary and Martha.

Mary rushes to meet Jesus and falling at his feet says, "Lord, if you had been here, my brother would not have died."

Deeply moved, Jesus cries. Then he raises Lazarus from the dead.

Why Jesus cried isn't stated. But those of us who have stood with loved ones heartbroken at a funeral know the painful emotions Jesus must have experienced. Mary hurt, and Jesus hurt with her. Often, the most comforting thing we can do for a grieving friend is to let our genuine feelings do the talking for us—whether the feelings are confusion, anger, or sorrow. Our friend will know we care.

## 6. Jesus washes his disciples' feet (13:1–17)

**H**ours before his arrest, Jesus eats a final meal with his disciples. But first he washes the feet of each man there. In the dusty world of unpaved roads and sandal-clad walkers, this is a common way to show hospitality. Usually, a servant or a child does the washing.

Peter, the most outspoken of the 12, objects. He doesn't think it's right for a rabbi to humble himself in this way, but Jesus insists.

"If your Lord and teacher has washed your feet," Jesus says, "you should do the same for each other. I have set the example."

As Jesus explained before, he came not to be served, but to serve (Matthew 20:28). As followers of Jesus, we do the same. Instead of demanding service, we lend a hand, a towel, or whatever else is needed.

## 7. Peter says he doesn't know Jesus (18:15–27)

**D**uring that Last Supper, Jesus makes a prediction: before the rooster crows in the morning Peter will deny three times that he knows Jesus. Peter vows he'd die first.

When Jesus is arrested a short time later, the disciples run for their lives. The nighttime trial takes place at the home of the high priest. Peter goes there and waits outside with others, including the priest's servants and temple guards. During the wait, Peter is asked three times if he's a disciple of Jesus. Each time he denies it. After the third denial, the rooster crows. Suddenly, Peter remembers Jesus' prediction. He breaks down and cries bitterly as he walks away.

We can all relate to Peter. We've disappointed ourselves—probably more than once. But as Jesus did with Peter, he forgives us and lets us get on with our life—wiser and stronger than before.

## 8. Dying, Jesus asks a friend to help his mother (19:25–27)

**B**y morning, Jesus is nailed to a Roman cross and dying. Standing at the foot of the cross is his mother, Mary. With her is Jesus' "favorite disciple." Though unnamed, he's thought to be John, the writer of this Gospel.

Jesus looks at his widowed mother and says, "This man is now your son." Then Jesus looks at his disciple and says, "She is now your mother." From that day on, the disciple takes Mary into his home.

Even in death, Jesus was still thinking of others. In life, we should do the same. We should help others—especially our family. Often, no one cares more for a troubled family member than we do. So our help may be the best they'll ever get.

## 9. Doubting Thomas sees Jesus (20:24–31)

**A** resurrected Jesus appears to the disciples, but Thomas isn't there. When the others tell Thomas what happened, he says he won't believe it until he touches the execution scars on Jesus.

A week later Jesus returns. This time Thomas is there. Jesus tells him to touch the scars. But there's no need. Thomas replies, "You are my Lord and my God!"

Jesus only gently rebukes Thomas, urging him to have more faith and promising that people who later believe without seeing will be greatly blessed.

It's okay to question religious teachings that don't make sense. Expressing sincere doubts can lead to the discovery of remarkable faith. In time, we can learn to believe that Jesus will do as he says. He came back from the grave, and there's no doubt he's coming back to the earth one day.

# ACTS

## When Talking about Jesus Isn't Cool

Sometimes, talk about Jesus sounds like just another sales pitch. It can remind you of an unwanted phone solicitation in the first calm moment of the evening—a scripted voice that insists, "This isn't a solicitation. It's an invitation."

Yeah, right. An invitation from your wallet to mine. "Click."

For most of us, if we walk across the street and start talking about Jesus to our neighbor, we'll likely get the equivalent of a Click. We might not hear it, but we'll see the disconnection—in slow motion, if our neighbor's polite. Eye contact stops. Fidgeting begins. Brain starts scanning a list of excuses for exiting ASAP.

It wasn't like that in the early days of the church. Peter preached an impromptu sermon, and 3,000 people converted on the spot. But Peter and the other disciples had a unique fire inside them. They saw Jesus come back from the grave, giving them a mission to spread his teachings to everyone. And they had miracle-working power to back up their claim that they represented God.

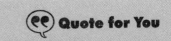 **Quote for You**

"Tell everyone about me . . . everywhere in the world" (1:8). *Christ's last words to his followers, before ascending into heaven.*

Frankly, most of us don't have the passion of the disciples. And most of us can't perform miracles.

But God lives within us. He'll let us know when to speak up, and what to say.

Sometimes we won't have to say anything. Just being there for one another says plenty about the compassionate God we serve. Other times, when they need help that comes only from above, we'll know what to tell them, and they'll know to listen.

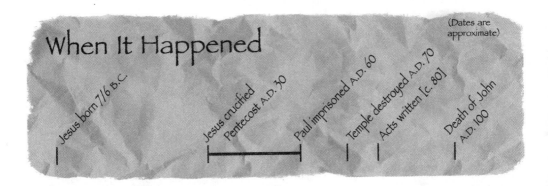

## When It Happened

(Dates are approximate)

Jesus born 7/6 B.C.

Jesus crucified
Pentecost A.D. 30

Paul imprisoned A.D. 60

Temple destroyed A.D. 70
Acts written [c. 80]

Death of John
A.D. 100

# Info You Can Use

## Background Notes

**Writer:** The writer didn't identify himself, but Christian leaders in the second century did. They said the Gospel of Luke and it's sequel, Acts, were written by Luke, a non-Jewish physician who occasionally traveled with Paul (Colossians 4:14; Philemon 1:24).

There's at least a hint of biblical support for Luke as the writer. In some Acts passages—always those starting and ending with a ship voyage—the writer changes from writing about "they" to writing about "we." Whoever wrote this seemed to have been traveling with Paul.

Like the Gospel of Luke, Acts is addressed to a mysterious person named Theophilus. He could be a Roman official who asked for information about the growing Christian movement. He may have been a patron who paid Luke to write a history of Jesus (the Gospel of Luke) and the early church (Acts).

Or he may not have been an individual at all. "Theophilus" means "lover of God." So Luke may have been writing to all who worship God, whether Jew or non-Jew. This would have been an appropriate emphasis in a book written by a non-Jew, and about the beginning of ministry to non-Jews.

**Time:** The story covers the first 30 years of the church. Acts begins shortly after the resurrection of Jesus in about A.D. 30, and ends with Paul under arrest in Rome in about A.D. 60.

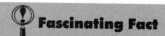

### Fascinating Fact

Believers called themselves followers of "the Way," short for "the way of God" (24:14). "Christian" surfaced about a decade after Christ, in Antioch, Syria (11:26), perhaps as a term coined by name-calling critics. In a similar way, critics of Sun Myung Moon's Unification Church often call the members "Moonies."

It's unclear when Acts was written. Some scholars guess it was in the closing decades of the first century, sometime after A.D. 70. That's because the book's prequel, Luke, emphasizes Jesus' prophecy about the fall of Jerusalem; Romans demolished the city in A.D. 70.

**Place:** Acts begins in Jerusalem, where the disciples witnessed the ascension of Jesus into the clouds and began boldly preaching. Thousands converted, but when Jews started persecuting them, they ran for their lives, scattering to neighboring countries and taking their new faith with them.

By the end of Acts, Christians were worshiping in house churches throughout what is now Israel, Syria, Cyprus, Turkey, Greece, and even Rome, 2,000 miles away.

**Bottom-Line Summary:** As the sequel to the Gospel of Luke, Acts picks up where Luke ends. Jesus ascends into the clouds, giving his final instructions. The disciples are to wait in Jerusalem a few days until God sends the Holy Spirit, who will fill them with spiritual power. Afterward, they are to start telling people near and far about what they learned from Jesus.

Ten days later, the Holy Spirit arrives. The house where the disciples and other believers are waiting fills with the sound of a windstorm. Tongues of fire appear above each person's head, and suddenly the people have the gift of speaking in languages they never learned.

Thousands of Jewish pilgrims from many nations are in town for the harvest festival of Pentecost. They hear the sound and run to the house. They're astonished to hear their native languages. Peter preaches about the prophecies that have been fulfilled in Jesus and in this outpouring of the Holy Spirit. Three thousand people believe him, and the Christian church is born.

Believers start meeting together regularly in the temple courtyard and homes, learning from the apostles, eating together, and financially helping those among them in need. Jewish leaders who had Jesus executed are alarmed that the movement he started is mushrooming. They begin persecuting believers, putting them on trial and imprisoning them. After one believer, Stephen, is killed by a mob, others leave town and take their new faith with them—which helps the church stretch its boundaries.

In response, Jewish leaders order these alleged heretics hunted down. Saul (whose Roman name is Paul) is on a heretic-hunting trip when he has a dramatic encounter with Jesus, which leads to his conversion.

Under the Holy Spirit's direction, Paul and another believer, Barnabas, are sent on a missionary expedition. They manage to start congregations in Cyprus and western Turkey, despite stiff opposition from orthodox Jews. Paul continues his missionary work for about three decades, founding congregations throughout the Roman Empire.

He's eventually arrested in Jerusalem and sent to Rome for a trial that may have ended in his execution. The book closes with Paul under house arrest in Rome, still teaching about Jesus.

## Influential People

**Saul,** an orthodox Jew, persecutes Christians, but later converts to Christianity and becomes a tireless missionary using his Roman name, Paul. During his 30-year ministry he travels some 10,000 miles to start congregations throughout the Roman Empire. One of Christianity's most dangerous enemies, he became one of Christianity's most successful ministers. He's a reminder of how completely God can change us.

**Peter,** leader of the 12 original disciples, boldly preaches the first public sermon after Jesus' resurrection. He, too, is an example of God's power to change people. A few weeks earlier, he denied knowing Jesus because he didn't want to get arrested. Now he begins preaching in front of the very leaders who tried Jesus.

# Key Ideas You Need to Know

**Holy Spirit.** The Holy Spirit is part of the Trinity: God the Father, Son, and Holy Spirit. In Old Testament times, the Spirit's work was apparently limited to certain people involved in special work, such as priests and prophets. When young David was anointed as a future king, "the Spirit of the Lord took control of David and stayed with him from then on" (1 Samuel 16:13).

The prophet Joel, speaking on God's behalf, promised that the time was coming when "I will give my Spirit to everyone" (Joel 2:28). Before Jesus ascended into heaven, he told his disciples to wait in Jerusalem for the Spirit.

"The Holy Spirit will come and help you," Jesus had told them earlier. "The Father will send the Spirit to take my place. The Spirit will teach you everything and will remind you of what I said while I was with you" (John 14:25).

As Jesus promised, the Spirit came and filled each disciple with spiritual vitality that gave them courage to preach about Jesus in the face of life-threatening opposition, and to perform miracles proving their message came from God.

Today, the Spirit lives in every believer (1 Corinthians 3:16). "God's Spirit makes us loving, happy, peaceful, patient, kind, good, faithful, gentle, and self-controlled" (Galatians 5:22).

# Q&A

**Do we have to be baptized to get saved?** Peter, in his first public sermon after Jesus' resurrection, told the people to repent and "be baptized in the name of Jesus Christ, so that your sins may be forgiven" (2:38). But most Bible experts say that baptism isn't portrayed in the New Testament as essential to salvation.

Instead, baptism is a dramatic symbol of the spiritual cleansing we've already experienced. Also, if our baptism method is submersion, when we come up out of the baptismal water we can be reminded of Jesus coming up out of the grave and of the new spiritual life we have because of it (Romans 6:3–4).

Our salvation from a life of sin and for eternal life with God comes through believing in Jesus (John 3:16). As Paul put it, "If you confess with your mouth that Jesus is Lord and believe in your heart that God raised him from the dead, you will be saved" (Romans 10:9).

Should we get baptized? Yes. Jesus did, and so did the early Christians. An Ethiopian official being taught about the faith by Philip insisted on being baptized immediately (8:36). It's a wonderful drama that strengthens our faith and proclaims it in public.

# Red Flag Issues

**Women ministering in the church.** Some churches won't allow women to teach or preach in the church. That's because in some of the apostle Paul's letters to select churches, he bans women from doing so (1 Corinthians 14:34; 1 Timothy 2:11–12).

Other churches permit women to become senior ministers who lead congregations. Christians in these churches say Paul's ban on women in ministry wasn't meant as a general rule, but as guidance for certain troubled churches in a male-dominated era.

For Bible support, these churches turn to Acts. Here, Peter quoted the Old Testament: "I will give my Spirit to my servants, both men and women, and they will prophesy" (2:18). Also, one of Paul's associate ministers was Priscilla (18:18; Romans 16:3). She and her husband even tutored Apollos, a popular Christian preacher (18:26).

Paul also sent his greetings to "Phoebe, who is a leader in the church at Cenchreae" (Romans 16:1). And in one controversial passage, Paul may have identified a woman as one of the apostles. Apostles were an elite group of ministers who had known Jesus. Paul said Junia was "prominent among the apostles" (Romans 16:7, New Revised Standard Version). Other Bible versions say she was "highly respected by the apostles."

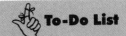

## To-Do List

- "Turn from your sins and turn to God, and be baptized in the name of Jesus Christ for the forgiveness of your sins. Then you will receive the gift of the Holy Spirit" (2:38, New Living Translation).

- "More blessings come from giving than from receiving" (20:35). *Paul, quoting Jesus.*

## For the Record: Acts Abused

**Jehovah's Witnesses and blood transfusions.** Jehovah's Witnesses are reluctant to get life-giving blood transfusions or organ transplants. That's because of Bible passages such as this one: "You must abstain from eating food offered to idols, from consuming blood or eating the meat of strangled animals" (15:29, New Living Translation). Jehovah's Witnesses will, however, use their own blood when stored in preparation for surgery.

The command about blood is from Old Testament Jewish dietary laws. Jehovah's Witnesses extend the law, stretching it out of the context to include a medical procedure that the ancients of Bible times never envisioned (Leviticus 3:17).

The law in Acts was a compromise ruling by the Jerusalem church council. It was an attempt to settle a hot debate among church leaders. Some leaders felt converts should obey all Jewish laws, while others felt non-Jews shouldn't have to do this because the Jewish laws aren't essential to salvation. Only faith in Christ is necessary. The council ruled that non-Jews needed to obey only a few of the more basic rules. But Paul later abandoned even these, insisting that faith in Christ is all we need.

# Bible Scenarios You Can Use

## 1. Jesus ascends to heaven, leaving instructions (1:1-11)

For 40 days after the Resurrection, Jesus appears to his disciples from time to time. In one of these meetings, he tells them to stay in Jerusalem a few days until God sends the Holy Spirit to give them power.

"Then," Jesus says, "tell everyone about me in Jerusalem, in all Judea, in Samaria, and everywhere in the world." Afterward, Jesus ascends into the clouds.

In their lifetime, the disciples could only start the mission Jesus gave them. They began preaching in Jerusalem, then fanned out to the surrounding regions of Judea and Samaria, and finally to some neighboring Middle Eastern nations. As followers of Jesus, this mission is now ours. We can take part by spreading the word where we live and helping fund missions around the world.

## 2. Believers worship together (2:43-47)

As Jesus promised, the Holy Spirit arrives and lives inside each disciple. The Spirit gives them miraculous power to heal and to communicate in foreign languages to the Jewish pilgrims who had come from other nations to celebrate the feast of Pentecost.

Peter preaches a stirring sermon. Three thousand people repent of their sins and are baptized. Afterward, they meet regularly in the temple courtyard to listen to the apostles teach. They also gather in homes to share meals and give thanks to God for all he has done.

Sometimes worship services seem like just one of many weekly chores. But meeting with fellow believers is an important source of spiritual nourishment and joy. If it's not, we can ask God what we should do about it. Status quo won't suffice.

## 3. A husband and wife lie, then die (5:1–10)

**H**elping one another becomes a trademark of the Christian movement. People go so far as to sell some of their property and donate the money to those in need.

One couple sees a chance to make themselves look good. They sell some property and keep part of the money. The remainder they give to the apostles to spread among the needy. But the couple tells the apostles they haven't kept any money for themselves.

Peter says the money was theirs to do with as they wished, yet they lied to the Holy Spirit. Both die instantly, perhaps of shock.

Helping others is a good thing, but not when it's a disguise for helping ourselves. We should give, but not brag about it or exaggerate. As Jesus said, we should try to keep our giving secret (Matthew 6:3).

## 4. Peter converts non-Jews (10:1–23)

**J**ewish law discourages Jews from mixing with non-Jews. But the apostle Peter has a vision that convinces him God is about to fulfill the ancient prophecy that said of the Jews: "I selected and sent you to bring light and my promise of hope to the nations" (Isaiah 42:6).

Immediately after the vision, Peter is summoned to the home of a Roman officer who regularly prays to God.

"You know that we Jews are not allowed to have anything to do with other people," Peter tells the soldier. "But God has shown me that he doesn't think anyone is unclean or unfit." The Roman and his family convert to Christianity.

There's no room for prejudice of any kind in Christianity. God accepts everyone who turns to him, regardless of race, nationality, or net worth. We should accept them, too.

## 5. Paul and Barnabas become the first missionaries (13:1–3)

**B**arnabas and Paul (also known by his Hebrew name, Saul) are part of a ministry team of five men leading a church in what is now southwestern Turkey. One day as these five men are praying, they receive a message from God: "Appoint Barnabas and Saul to do the work for which I have chosen them."

After more prayer, the church sends the two on their way as Christianity's first known missionaries. They board a ship for the Mediterranean island of Cyprus, and continue into northwestern Turkey where they start one congregation after another.

There are no details about what kind of support they got from their home church. But they were certainly sent on their way with money for their ministry, along with prayers that followed them. Those who have devoted themselves to ministry depend on us for both financial support and prayers to guide them on their missions.

## 6. The first church council meeting (15:1–21)

**A**s the Christian church grows, a big controversy develops. Some leaders think non-Jews should observe Jewish laws, such as those requiring circumcision and diets restricted to kosher food. Others disagree.

Peter stands and argues against requiring non-Jewish believers to obey traditional Jewish laws. He tells about his vision and his experience with the Roman soldier. Paul and Barnabas reinforce this by telling about the miracles they've seen abroad among non-Jews. In what is apparently a split decision, the majority agrees to a compromise solution asking non-Jews to avoid meat offered to idols.

We're going to have disagreements with other Christians. But we can work through them, compromising on some issues while standing firm on matters central to the faith. The hard part is figuring out what's central. But God helps us decide what is most important.

# ROMANS

## What Christians Believe

Ask people what they believe about God and you can get quickly confused.

"Which god?" "All religions lead to God." "Jesus is the only way."

Who's right, and who's wrong?

Twenty years into his ministry, after confronting a bunch of distorted religious beliefs—including many among Christians—the apostle Paul wrote a masterpiece of a letter that summed up the most important Christian beliefs. He wrote to Christians in Rome, but what he said has served as a theological guidebook for Christians throughout the ages.

"Theology" is a word that literally means "God talk," or talk about God. As a theology book, Romans isn't like any other book in the New Testament. It doesn't have the riveting stories you'll find in the Gospels or Acts. Instead, it draws from those stories to highlight the underlying beliefs—the ideas on which Christianity is built.

Some of the most important are these:

- Everyone has sinned (3:23).

- God wants to forgive us (3:24).

- We can't earn forgiveness by being good or by following religious rules (3:27).

- We find forgiveness only by having faith in Jesus (3:27).

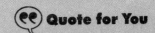 **Quote for You**

"All have sinned; all fall short of God's glorious standard. Yet now God in his gracious kindness declares us not guilty. He has done this through Christ Jesus, who has freed us by taking away our sins" (3:23–24, New Living Translation).

The faith Paul talks about is trusting that Jesus is who he said he is, and did what the apostles testified he did: died and rose again. Perhaps faith is all it takes because God knows that if we believe in the life and teachings of Jesus, we'll live like we believe it.

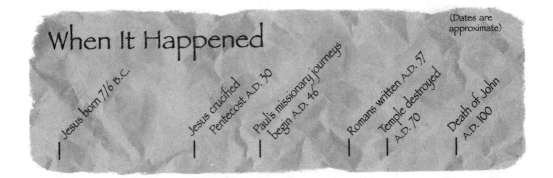

When It Happened

(Dates are approximate)

Jesus born 7/6 B.C.

Jesus crucified Pentecost A.D. 30

Paul's missionary journeys begin A.D. 46

Romans written A.D. 57

Temple destroyed A.D. 70

Death of John A.D. 100

# Info You Can Use

## Background Notes

**Writer:** The writer identifies himself as Paul, once a Jewish scholar known as a Pharisee, and now an apostle of Jesus. Raised in a strict Jewish home and trained by one of the most respected Jewish scholars of his day, Paul became a fierce opponent of anyone who believed that Jesus was the promised Messiah. It was on a mission to search and arrest these alleged heretics in Damascus that Jesus appeared to him. Paul converted to Christianity and became the leader in spreading Christian teachings to non-Jews throughout the Roman Empire.

**Time:** The apostle Paul wrote this letter in about A.D. 57, some 20 years after his conversion, and near the end of his third and final missionary journey.

**Place:** Paul wrote to the Christian congregation in Rome, capital of the Roman Empire. After having started and taught congregations throughout what is now Syria, Turkey, and Greece, Paul said he planned to spend some time in Rome before traveling on to Spain, at the western edge of the empire.

The apostle possibly wrote this letter in Corinth, Greece. It was from there he left for Jerusalem with an offering he had collected for the impoverished Christians suffering from hard times. Unfortunately, when he got to Jerusalem the Jews arrested him because of his alleged heretical teachings.

When he finally did arrive in Rome, in about A.D. 60, it was as a prisoner waiting for trial in the emperor's court. Paul's letters and the history in Acts leave the outcome of this trial unclear. He may have been executed. Or he may have been released, only to be arrested later and executed.

**Bottom-Line Summary:** After two decades of ministry and three church-planting missionary trips throughout the Middle East, Paul feels it's time to move on to new territory. He has never been to Rome, so he writes the Christians there and says, "For years I have wanted to visit you. So I plan to stop off on my way to Spain" (15:23–24).

Romans is a letter of introduction and intent to visit. Paul briefly introduces himself, though most Christians in Rome certainly know him by reputation, and others have met him. More importantly for us, Paul briefly tells the Romans what he believes.

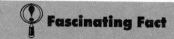

### Fascinating Fact

One of the history's respected church leaders, Augustine (A.D. 354–430), was a party-hearty woman-chaser until he read Romans. A philosopher who dabbled in many religions, he one day felt a strange impression to open the Bible and read the first passage he saw. That passage was Romans 13:13–14. "Behave properly, as people do in the day. Don't go to wild parties or get drunk or be vulgar or indecent. Don't quarrel or be jealous. Let the Lord Jesus Christ be as near to you as the clothes you wear. Then you won't try to satisfy your selfish desires."

In what is considered his finest work—the best and most influential of his many preserved letters—Paul clearly and succinctly explains why and how we should all become followers of Jesus.

Paul says everyone has sinned, and unless our guilt is removed, we can never stand in the presence of a holy God. But God sent his Son, Jesus, to provide a way for forgiveness and to show us how to live at peace with God and ourselves—forever.

All we need to do is trust Jesus. That means believing in him, and trying to follow his advice for living. Though we'll sometimes fall short of God's standard, Paul's good news is that we're not saved through our spiritual success or goodness. We're saved through our faith in Jesus. The first step of faith that we take toward God is the step that determines our eternal destiny. Salvation isn't something we earn. It's something God gives to anyone who wants it. And he wants us all to want it. As Paul's colleague, Peter, so aptly put it: "God is patient, because he wants everyone to turn from sin and no one to be lost" (2 Peter 3:9).

When we're saved, Paul says, the Holy Spirit makes his home inside us (5:5). God's Spirit helps us mature spiritually and develop a godly life. And he gives us the peace that comes from knowing we are indeed God's people.

# Influential People

**Paul,** raised as an ultraconservative Jew, persecuted Christians. He converts and does a complete turnaround—becoming Christianity's most famous minister to the very non-Jewish people that orthodox Jews avoided. As the self-described "worst sinner of all" (1 Timothy 1:15), Paul is a vibrant example of how completely God can change us for the better.

# Key Ideas You Need to Know

**Sin.** It's refusing to do what we know God wants us to do. Everyone has sinned. Even Christians trying to live godly lives occasionally sin when they choose their way over God's way.

**Grace.** It's God's acceptance of us wherever we are in our spiritual journey, coupled with his refusal to leave us there. Paul uses the term to refer to God's willingness to forgive us of our sins even though we've done nothing to deserve it. While we're still in our sin, we cry out for mercy and forgiveness, and God instantly complies. Then he pulls us up out of our sinful habits.

**Salvation.** This is the result of God's grace. We're saved from a painful life controlled by our sins, and saved for life everlasting with God.

# Red Flag Issues

**Predestination.** Some Christians teach that God chooses who will and who won't be saved. This teaching is called predestination, and is common in churches that follow in the theological tradition of French scholar John Calvin (such as Presbyterians and many Southern Baptists).

These Christians find Bible support in passages such as this: "God knew them [the people who love him] before he made the world, and he decided that they would be like his Son. . . . God planned for them to be like his Son; and those he planned to be like his Son, he also called; and those he called, he also made right with him" (8:29–30, New Century Version).

Christians who follow in the theological tradition of English scholar John Wesley and Dutch scholar Jacobus Arminius (such as Methodists and Wesleyans) say God calls everyone to salvation. These Christians teach that although God knows who among us will accept that invitation, he doesn't make the decision for us.

**Homosexuality.** Many Christians today don't know what to think about homosexuality. Even some Christian denominations have started ordaining homosexual ministers.

Is homosexuality a spiritual problem, or is it a physical condition determined by genetics or emotional trauma?

Paul says it's "not normal" and even "shameful." He stops just a hair shy of name-calling when he implies that homosexuals are perverts who will receive "due penalty for their perversion" (1:27, New International Version).

Some argue that Paul wasn't targeting homosexuals, but that he was condemning heterosexuals who practiced homosexuality. But that's not even hinted at in his words. He said men "stopped wanting to have sex with women and had strong desires for sex with other men." Women, likewise, "no longer wanted to have sex in a natural way, and they did things with each other that were not natural" (1:27).

Whether genetics or events in life determine homosexual tendencies, most Christians believe that the Bible urges us not to act on those tendencies. Though it might seem unfair for God to burden us with these powerful desires and not allow us to act on them, single heterosexuals have a similar problem. Many want sexual intimacy, but can't have it because they haven't found a marriage partner.

Some Christians believe homosexuals can be reoriented to heterosexuality. Others believe that everyone—homosexuals included—can benefit from the advice of Jesus: "If you are tired from carrying heavy burdens, come to me and I will give you rest" (Matthew 11:28). Whatever the burden, Jesus promises to help

## To-Do List

- "Don't let sin rule your body. . . . Don't let sin keep ruling your lives" (6:12, 14).

- "You will be saved, if you honestly say, 'Jesus is Lord,' and if you believe with all your heart that God raised him from death" (10:9).

- "Offer your bodies to him [God] as a living sacrifice, pure and pleasing" (12:1).

- "Don't try to get even. Let God take revenge. In the Scriptures the Lord says, 'I am the one to take revenge and pay them back'" (12:19).

- "Pay your taxes" (13:6).

- "Love others as much as you love yourself" (13:9).

us carry it and to learn from it. (For more on this topic, see Genesis, page 24; 2 Samuel, page 90.)

## Romans Well Used

**Protestant movement.** All Protestants—Baptists, Methodists, Lutherans, and more—owe their existence to the Book of Romans. It's here that the father of the Protestant Reformation, Martin Luther, found the courage to challenge the Roman Catholic Church's ancient teaching that people are saved by obeying church rules—and that for a nice donation, people could actually buy their way out of punishment for sin.

Luther read in Romans 1:17—which has become known as the Reformation text—that "God accepts everyone who has faith." We're not saved by doing good works or by obeying church rules crafted by even the best-intentioned ministers.

"The righteous live by a gift of God, namely faith," Luther wrote. When that truth settled in on him he said, "I felt as if I were entirely born again and had entered paradise itself."

In debates that followed, Luther argued that a simple layman armed with the Bible was better off than the pope and bishops without it. He was excommunicated from the Catholic Church, but many Christians rallied around his teachings. And the Protestant movement took hold.

# Bible Scenarios You Can Use

### 1. Jesus dies for humanity's sins (3:21–31)

**B**efore Paul travels to Rome, he writes a letter to Christians there to introduce himself and to give a short overview of his teachings.

"All of us have sinned," Paul writes. "But God treats us much better than we deserve, and because of Christ Jesus, he freely accepts us and sets us free from our sins. God sent Christ to be our sacrifice. Christ offered his life's blood, so that by faith in him we could come to God" (3:23–26, New Living Translation).

In Bible times, people understood better than we do the idea of offering sacrifices for sins. The sacrifice was a symbol of the spiritual death that sin causes. Jesus' death became the ultimate symbol of death, just as his resurrection showed us that God offers a new and everlasting life that is as real as Jesus' appearances to the disciples after the Crucifixion. When we believe that Jesus died for us and was resurrected, God forgives us of our sins and gives us eternal life that starts immediately.

### 2. Jesus' resurrection breaks the death grip sin has on us (6:1–23)

**P**aul anticipates a question: If God is so merciful and forgiving, does that mean we can go on sinning?

"No," Paul answers. Paul says that Jesus has broken us free from the death grip that sin had on us. Paul explains it this way, using metaphors: "When we were baptized, we died and were buried with Christ. We were baptized so that we would live a new life, as Christ was raised to life." We go under the baptismal water, as Christ went into the grave. But we come up again as new creatures.

"The persons we used to be were nailed to the cross with Jesus," Paul continues. "This was done, so that our sinful bodies would no longer be the slaves of sin."

We'll still be tempted by sin occasionally—perhaps more than occasionally. But once we turn our life over to God, sin is no longer our master. Our life will show it, and people will know it.

## 3. Living like God's people (12:1–21)

**O**nce you put God in control of your life, Paul tells the Romans, "Let God change the way you think. Then you will know how to do everything that is good and pleasing to him."

Paul gives the Romans a short preview of what those good and pleasing things will be.

God's people will:

- Use their gifts to help others—whether the gift may be teaching, encouraging, or giving financial help (6–8).

- Love others more than themselves (10).

- Be patient in time of trouble (12).

- Bless everyone who mistreats them (14).

- Be happy with those who are happy and sad with those who are sad (15).

- Be friendly with everyone (16).

- Keep from mistreating people who have mistreated them (17).

- Do their best to live at peace with everyone (18).

- Defeat evil with good (21).

If we are God's people we can expect to start becoming like him: loving and compassionate. We may not perfect the sampling of character traits Paul mentioned, but we'll do the best we can to pursue them out of our desire to please God.

## 4. Obey the laws of the land (13:1–7)

**W**riting to believers in Rome—capital of an empire that sometimes brutally imposed its will on nations throughout the Middle East—Paul offers advice that is probably hard for many to hear without squirming.

"Obey the rulers who have authority over you," Paul says. "Only God can give authority to anyone, and he puts these rulers in their places of power." For that reason, Paul adds, we should respect their right to rule and pay the taxes they demand.

Many of us immediately think of tyrants like Hitler and modern-day dictators, not to mention democratic leaders who abuse their power.

Paul's advice doesn't mean we should ban political activism, let corrupt leaders ignore the law, or remain silent while tyrants exploit the helpless. The apostles made that clear earlier when they took a stand against the Jewish high council's order to stop teaching about Jesus: "Do you think God wants us to obey you or to obey him? We cannot keep quiet about what we have seen and heard" (Acts 4:19–20).

When our leaders intrude into God's business and try to convince us that something morally wrong is right, we're to obey God. Our leaders may pass laws that hurt the poor and abandon the sick, but as Christians we can individually reach out to the needy. And as members of a free society, we can work to change bad laws.

# 1 CORINTHIANS

## Problems with Other Christians

We expect more of our fellow Christians—more kindness, more generosity, and more patience.

But sometimes there's trouble in paradise—more ego, more stubbornness, more conflict.

Often, there's no way to predict where the trouble will erupt. Who would have guessed that the knottiest, naughtiest church in the New Testament would be the one in Corinth, Greece? That's not only a church Paul started himself, it's the church he gave more time and energy to than nearly any other church. In most towns, Paul spent just a few days or weeks teaching the basics of the Christian faith and helping organize a fledgling congregation. But in Corinth, Paul stayed for about two years, carefully guiding the new believers through their spiritual infancy.

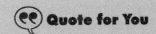 **Quote for You**

"You are tempted in the same way that everyone else is tempted. But God can be trusted not to let you be tempted too much, and he will show you how to escape from your temptations" (10:13).

Yet a few years later, a messenger brought word that the Corinthian congregation was a mess. The people were arguing over who was most important, bickering over how to conduct worship services, and even turning a blind eye to a member who was having sex with his own stepmother.

Unfortunately, many Christians today can relate. We've witnessed—if not participated in—blistering arguments with fellow believers. We've seen ego jousting in God's house. And we've known about blatant sin—such as adultery—committed by members in good standing.

One-by-one, Paul addresses every problem the Corinthian church has—problems Christians still face. He begins with one piece of rock-solid advice, which becomes the cornerstone for everything he has to say. The advice, in a word: unity. The Corinthians are to fight sin, not each other.

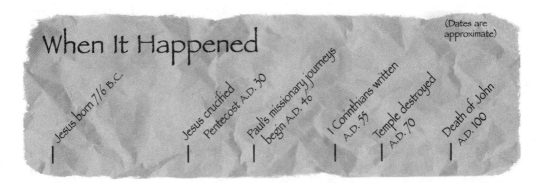

When It Happened

(Dates are approximate)

Jesus born 7/6 B.C.

Jesus crucified
Pentecost A.D. 30

Paul's missionary journeys
begin A.D. 46

1 Corinthians written
A.D. 55

Temple destroyed
A.D. 70

Death of John
A.D. 100

# Info You Can Use

## Background Notes

**Writer:** The apostle Paul wrote this letter. He said so at the beginning: "From Paul" (1:1). And he signed it at the end: "I am signing this letter myself: PAUL" (16:21).

**Time:** Paul wrote the letter in about A.D. 55, some two or three years after leaving Corinth.

Paul first came to Corinth in A.D. 50, during the second of three missionary expeditions. Normally, Paul didn't stay in one place more than a few weeks. But he made an exception for Corinth, staying about two years.

**Place:** Corinth was a busy port town about 50 miles southwest of Athens. Corinth was the busiest and most international city in Greece. That's partly because it was the capital of the Roman province there. But it also controlled two ports linked by a four-mile land bridge between the Aegean Sea in the east and the Adriatic Sea in the west. Merchants sailing between Rome and the Middle East would often stop here and transport their cargo across the land strip. That cut 200 miles off their journey around the tip of Greece, and saved them from the risk of pirates and storms—both of which were common there.

Large ships had to be unloaded and their cargo hauled by wagons to another ship waiting in the other port. But smaller ships could be hauled onto a huge, wheeled barge and slowly pulled across the land strip. A canal was completed there in 1893.

Paul wrote from Ephesus, a large city on the western coast of what is now Turkey. Ephesus, where Paul ministered for three years, was directly across the Aegean Sea from Corinth, about 250 nautical miles east.

**Bottom-Line Summary:** Two or three years after leaving Corinth, where Paul spent a couple of years starting a church, he gets disturbing news. A messenger from Corinth delivers a letter from the church asking Paul to answer some questions and help settle some problems. The issues range from incessant arguing to questions about marriage to confusion about eternal life.

The messenger fills Paul in on additional problems the church leaders neglected to mention—perhaps because they were too embarrassed to bring them up—such as who the Corinthian Christians should consider their leader: Paul, Apollos, or Peter.

Paul responds with a letter that has become known as 1 Corinthians. He starts by reminding them that Christ is head of the church, and that the ministers are Christ's servants who are there to help them, not cause division.

Paul pleads with the Corinthians to stop arguing and work together. He gives advice about marriage, worship services, life after death, and how to keep from damaging the fragile faith of new Christians. And then he closes with the promise that he'll come visit, perhaps staying the winter.

# Influential People

**Paul,** Christian leader and founder of the church at Corinth. His patience with the troubled church, along with his wise advice and his perseverance in helping the people work through their problems, should remind us not to abandon those we care about when they need our help.

# Q&A

**How should the church discipline its wayward members?** For blatant sin—such as adultery, drunkenness, or stealing—Paul recommended having nothing to do with the people until they come to their senses and repent. "Don't even eat with them!" (5:11).

This discipline wasn't intended to punish people, but to correct their behavior and turn them back to God. The Amish people continue to discipline their members through a practice they call "shunning."

In a follow-up letter, Paul advised the Corinthians to stop shunning a man who had done something wrong (Paul didn't say what it was). "Now it is time to forgive him and comfort him. Otherwise he may become so discouraged that he won't be able to recover" (2 Corinthians 2:7, New Living Translation).

> ## Fascinating Fact
>
> Corinth had a bad reputation as a sex city. In some circles, calling a person a Corinthian was like calling them a tramp. A modern comparison from a few years back was to call a young lady a Valley Girl, referring to California's San Fernando Valley. It was generally no compliment to her intellect.

**Should we stop doing something just because another Christian thinks it's wrong?** Yes, if our behavior could damage that person's faith (9:22).

For example, if we don't think it's wrong to drink an occasional glass of wine, but a family member does—and the family member is a new Christian who has struggled with a drinking problem—we should consider giving up the wine for the sake of our loved one. At the very least, we shouldn't drink in front of that person.

But the fact is, we can't please everyone, and we don't need to try. Paul put it well: "Why should my freedom be limited by someone else's conscience?" (10:29).

That doesn't mean we can skip being sensitive to another person's convictions. It just means we don't have to live by them.

# Red Flag Issues

**Speaking in tongues.** Some Christians practice glossolalia (GLAH-sah-LAY-lee-uh), a term that comes from two Greek words meaning "speaking in tongues." Usually, this doesn't refer to people miraculously speaking in languages they never learned—as happened at Pentecost (Acts 2:4–6). Instead, it refers to people making vocal sounds that are incomprehensible without God's help—a kind of heavenly language through which people praise God or deliver messages from God with the help of a translator.

Pentecostal churches stress this practice. Many Pentecostals teach that speaking in tongues proves a Christian is filled with the Holy Spirit.

Paul wrote to the Corinthians about speaking in tongues, apparently to correct some abuses it generated. He described the practice as one of the lesser spiritual gifts, and one that could draw attention to the speaker instead of to God. He insisted that if people spoke in tongues during worship, there should be a translator. Paul said he spoke in tongues, but that in church he would "rather speak five words that make sense than to speak ten thousand words in a language that others don't know" (14:19).

Many denominations frown on the practice, saying it's disruptive and easy to abuse for the purpose of making the worshiper look religious. If it causes divisions in the church, they argue, Paul would have been the first to discard it.

**Women in the church.** Some churches refuse to let women speak in worship services. Women can't preach, teach, or pray.

One main reason is because of advice Paul mailed the Corinthians: "When God's people meet in church, the women must not be allowed to speak. They must keep quiet and listen, as the Law of Moses teaches. If there is something they want to know, they can ask their husbands when they get home. It is disgraceful for women to speak in church" (14:33–35).

Paul gave similar advice to Timothy, ministering in Ephesus (1 Timothy 2:11–12).

Most churches today don't follow Paul's advice, with the notable exception of the Southern Baptists—the largest Protestant denomination in the country—and even

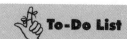

**To-Do List**

- "I beg you to get along with each other" (1:10). *Paul's advice to Christians who keep arguing with each other.*

- "Don't be immoral in matters of sex. . . . Use your body to honor God" (6:18, 20).

- "Love is kind and patient, never jealous, boastful, proud, or rude. Love isn't selfish or quick tempered. It doesn't keep a record of wrongs that others do" (13:4–5).

- "There are faith, hope, and love. But of these three, the greatest is love. Love should be your guide" (13:13—14:1).

- "When you meet to worship, you must do everything for the good of everyone there" (14:26). *Paul's plea for unity in a congregation fractured by disagreements over how to conduct worship.*

- "Be firm in your faith. Stay brave and strong. Show love in everything you do" (16:13–14).

they are not uniform in their practice. Scholars in churches open to women leaders argue that Paul didn't intend his advice to Corinth as a general rule for the rest of the world throughout human history. In fact, it wasn't even a rule he followed consistently, since he had women associates who were teachers and leaders (see Acts, "Women Ministering in the Church," page 314). It was a suggestion he gave to certain churches where some women were apparently showboating and causing divisions in that male-oriented setting. In churches where there was no such problem, the scholars say, there was no such rule.

**Homosexuality.** Paul had harsh words for gay people, declaring that no one who is "a pervert or behaves like a homosexual will share in God's kingdom" (6:9–10). Christians don't all agree with Paul. Some argue that if Paul had known what we do today about the causes of homosexuality, he would have been more compassionate.

Many Christians—perhaps most—consider it a sin to practice homosexuality, though not merely to have the tendency toward it that is never acted on. The sin, these Christians say, is in the act, not the temptation. (For more on this topic, see Genesis, page 24; 2 Samuel, page 90; Romans, page 322.)

# Bible Scenarios You Can Use

## 1. Christians arguing and suing each other (1:10–11; 6:1–11)

**A**bout five years after Paul starts the church of Corinth, he gets word that the Corinthian Christians are bickering. They argue over who their leader is: Paul, Peter, or a popular preacher named Apollos. They argue over worship styles. They even sue each other.

Paul pleads for unity. Regarding leadership, Paul reminds them that it's Jesus who was crucified for them. The three preachers are merely God's servants. And regarding lawsuits among fellow church members, Paul asks, "Aren't any of you wise enough to act as a judge between one follower and another?" Paul knows that Roman courts aren't always sensitive to Christian values such as fairness and honesty, and that the courts tend to favor the rich over the poor.

In churches today, we still bicker over issues, big and small—color of new carpet, worship styles, how to spend the money. Occasionally, we even sue each other because most churches don't have any procedure for settling disputes among their members. It doesn't have to be this way. If Paul could have written just one sentence to the bickering Corinthians—as well as to squabbling Christians today—it might well have been this excerpt from his letter: "I beg you to get along with each other."

If we start there, accepting that unity among believers is critical to the health of the church and to our mission of drawing people to Christ, mountains can get tossed into the sea.

## 2. When half a married couple is Christian (7:10–16)

**S**ome Christians in Corinth who are married to non-Christians are apparently considering divorce. Perhaps they figure they can serve God better remarried to a Christian.

Paul argues against it. He says if the non-Christian spouse is willing to stay married, don't get a divorce.

"The Christian wife brings holiness to her marriage," Paul explains, "and the Christian husband brings holiness to his marriage. Otherwise, your children would not have a godly influence" (New Living Translation).

But if the non-Christian spouse wants a divorce, Paul adds, "then you should agree to it. You are no longer bound to that person."

Marriage is hard enough to nurture when husband and wife share the same values and interests. But when only one follows the teachings of Jesus, marital tensions can mount. Yet the tension is worth it if the love of God breaks through and gives us the joy of ushering our spouse and children into the faith.

Jesus came to help the spiritually sick (Mark 2:17). When we have someone suffering spiritually in our own family, the last thing we need to do is leave them.

## 3. God's greatest gift: the ability to love (12:1—13:13)

**T**he Corinthians quarrel over just about everything. They even debate which spiritual gifts are most important. Prophecy, healing, teaching, and speaking in other languages all vie for top gift—as though God would value a prophet more than a doctor.

"There are different kinds of spiritual gifts," Paul says, "but they all come from the same Spirit." Furthermore, Paul explains, the church needs a wide variety of gifts to function—just as our body needs hands, feet, and eyes to get along.

Though no single gift can make us more important in God's eyes than we already are, Paul says there's one gift that all of us should pursue above every other: compassionate love. It's no coincidence that this gift is the one most likely to end Corinthian squabbles. Paul knows it. He knows, too, that it's the one character trait Jesus praised above all. It's the trait that led Jesus to the cross.

God gives each of us different talents. Some people love to build or repair, some are great speakers, some sing like they're on sabbatical from heaven's choir. But we're wrong to think that the singer on stage is more important than the sound technician hidden in a booth. What's important is that they're both using their gifts in a spirit of love toward those receiving the gift. Our gifts, after all, are from God. We exercise them on his behalf.

## 4. Looking forward to our resurrection (15:35–58)

**S**ome Corinthians are confused about what will happen to them when they die. Greek philosophers have long taught that the soul is immortal, and will live on in some mysterious, impersonal way. But Paul assures the Corinthians that their soul isn't the only thing that will be saved from death. They'll have glorified bodies, just as Jesus did—bodies that have self-awareness, that can be seen and touched, and that can even enjoy a good fish fry.

When we die, our body made from the dust of this earth will instantly give way to a body made from heaven's light. And we will become like "the one who came from heaven."

When we face death—either that of a loved one or our own—it can be heartbreaking and terrifying. But there's comfort in knowing that, compared to the eternity we'll experience with God, death is just a momentary goodbye. And as the prophets Isaiah and Hosea promised, we'll soon praise God by saying, "Death has lost the battle! Where is its victory? Where is its sting?"

# 2 CORINTHIANS

## Picking Your Battles

Some battles aren't worth the adrenaline. We want it one way, and someone else wants it another. Either way doesn't make much difference. In time, most of us learn to pick our battles. We give in on the minor issues and stand firm on the important ones.

We know a big battle when we see it. Our kid wants to drop out of school. Our family is spending more than it earns. Our boss wants us to do something underhanded, to protect the company's profit margin.

Some battles are definitely worth the effort. In fact, they're worth the blood of Christ. They're battles over issues that concern why Jesus came to earth and died—matters that determine a person's eternal destiny.

Paul faced such a battle with the Corinthian church. As a congregation, they were a spiritual mess. They bickered continually, struggled with immorality and idolatry, and were confused about basic Christian beliefs. Paul dealt with this crisis through letters and personal visits. Then came a new crisis. False teachers arrived with a captivating but warped take on Christianity. They repackaged the faith into what Paul called "another Jesus," "another spirit," and "a different message" (11:4). And the Corinthians were buying it.

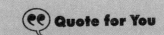 **Quote for You**

"In times of trouble, God is with us, and when we are knocked down, we get up" (4:9).

Paul could have turned his back on this high-maintenance church and considered it a lost cause. After all, he had congregations throughout the Roman Empire looking to him for leadership. But he fought for the hearts and minds of these Corinthians. Why? Because he loved them.

Maybe that's a good criterion for choosing our battles. We fight to defend people we care about.

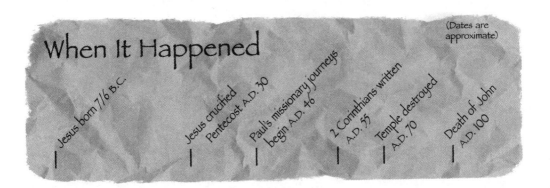

# When It Happened

(Dates are approximate)

Jesus born 7/6 B.C.

Jesus crucified
Pentecost A.D. 30

Paul's missionary journeys
begin A.D. 46

2 Corinthians written
A.D. 55

Temple destroyed
A.D. 70

Death of John
A.D. 100

# Info You Can Use

## Background Notes

**Writer:** The letter is from "Paul, chosen by God to be an apostle of Jesus Christ, and from Timothy" (1:1). Timothy was one of Paul's associates, whom Paul later assigned to the church of Ephesus.

**Time:** Paul probably wrote this letter in about A.D. 55, just a few months after writing 1 Corinthians during his third missionary trip.

Clues from the letter suggest Paul may have written 1 Corinthians in the spring while staying at Ephesus and 2 Corinthians in the winter while in Macedonia. In 1 Corinthians, for example, he said he hoped to winter in Corinth. But in 2 Corinthians, Paul defended his decision not to go to Corinth, but to allow a cooling off period (1:23).

**Place:** Like 1 Corinthians, Paul addressed his letter to the Christians living in Corinth, Greece. He founded this congregation some five years earlier, in about A.D. 50.

Paul may have written from Macedonia, the territory just north of Greece.

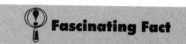

### Fascinating Fact

Paul's efforts in Corinth were apparently successful. A few decades later, a church leader named Clement wrote the Corinthians saying they "bore no malice to one another."

**Bottom-Line Summary:** Paul deals with a second crisis in the Corinthian church. The first crisis, several months earlier, involved squabbling among the members that had produced competing cliques. Paul wrote 1 Corinthians and followed up with what he described as a painful visit. So he left Corinth abruptly and wrote them a stern letter (2:3–4), which convinced the church to seek reconciliation with Paul.

The second crisis erupts within a year of the first. Traveling ministers arrive in Corinth. We don't know who they are or what they're teaching, but given the context clues in Paul's written defense, it seems they're accusing him of:

- being a self-appointed apostle;

- promoting himself over Christ;

- being untrustworthy, since he didn't come to Corinth when he promised;

- barking boldly in his letters but not acting on his threats; and

- pocketing the money he collects for the impoverished Christians in Jerusalem.

Paul calls the intruders "false apostles" (11:13). And he provides ample evidence to counter each of their charges, and reminding the Corinthians of what they already know: he is an honest and sincere minister who cares deeply about them. He has never accepted any salary or offerings from them for himself—even when he was in need (11:9).

# 🗣 Influential People

**Paul,** founding minister of the church at Corinth, pulls no punches in his fight to keep the people from being fooled by false teachers who are peddling a distorted version of Christianity. Paul even reveals deeply personal things about himself—such as failings and sufferings. His openness and frank talk is a model for confronting serious problems. This isn't a time for tiptoeing and trying to avoid hurting anyone's feelings. It's a time for sensitive confrontation. And it may require revealing our own vulnerabilities, to help others acknowledge that they, too, may have made some mistakes.

**Titus,** an associate of Paul's, carries one of the letters intended to mend the relationship between Paul and the Corinthian church. Some relational problems are so emotionally charged that we may need an intermediary.

# ❓ Q&A

**Should Christians avoid marrying or associating with unbelievers?** The question comes from a statement of Paul: "Do not be yoked together with unbelievers" (6:14, New International Version). But the context of the passage isn't marriage or business dealings. It's idolatry. Paul was telling the Corinthians they couldn't remain Christian and continue going to Greek temples to worship idols.

Jesus associated with sinners. And Paul urged Christians married to non-Christians not to seek a divorce, but to be a godly influence in the family (1 Corinthians 7:12–14). That doesn't mean, however, that it's generally a good idea for a Christian to enter into marriage or a business partnership with a non-Christian. The clashing values could make for a rocky relationship. But Paul isn't condemning such a relationship here.

**What was Paul's "thorn in the flesh?"** He didn't say. He said only that it was "to make me suffer terribly, so that I would not feel too proud" (12:7).

We paraphrase Paul today when we talk about someone who's "a thorn in my side." In fact, one theory is that Paul was talking about the Corinthians. Other theories include his never-ending persecution by Jews, or physical problems such as malaria or poor eyesight (he wrote in big letters, Galatians 6:11).

# 🚩 Red Flag Issues

**Praying to saints.** Many Christians ask Mary and other saints of the church to pray for them and help them. This practice is common among people in the Roman Catholic and Eastern Orthodox faiths. Many Protestants, however, consider it idolatry—especially when the prayers are directed at pictures or statues of the saints. As evidence, Protestants cite Bible passages such as this from Paul: "Do idols belong in the temple of God?" (6:16).

Christians who bring their petitions to saints often insist they aren't praying "to" saints but "with" them. They say it's like asking a friend to pray for you. But instead of asking a friend, they ask a saint who they believe led a holy life and is close to God in heaven.

For example, someone having trouble with unanswered prayer might ask Saint Monica to pray for them. Monica apparently prayed 20 years for the conversion of her son, Augustine, who eventually became a church leader.

These Christians also argue that pictures and statues of the saints are no more idolatrous than the family pictures we put on our walls at home or carry in our wallets. Pictures remind us of people and what they represent. So some Christians argue that a statue of Saint Francis of Assisi might remind us how much he loved God's creation, and encourage us to take better care of the environment.

Leaders of the Protestant Reformation, in breaking from the Catholic Church, abolished what has been called "the invocation of the saints," insisting it was equivalent to prayer and tended to elevate humans to the status reserved for God. Protestants also argue there's no reason to believe saints hear our prayers, especially since the Bible says "Christ Jesus is the only one who can bring us to God" (1 Timothy 2:5).

> ### ✍ To-Do List
>
> - "We should stay away from everything that keeps our bodies and spirits from being clean. We should honor God and try to be completely like him" (7:1).
>
> - "Try to get along and live peacefully with each other" (13:11).

**Tithing.** This is the practice of giving 10 percent of our income to the church. The New Testament never instructs Christians to do this, yet it has been a common practice in many Christian churches since the 1800s.

When Paul traveled, he collected an offering for poor believers in Jerusalem. And he occasionally took unsolicited donations to help support his ministry, though he funded his missionary work mainly by making tents. Paul never asked the people to give a tenth of their income or any other set amount. Instead, he said of the Jerusalem offering, "Each of you must make up your own mind about how much to give."

Christians in the early centuries rejected the idea of tithing as too legalistic. Christians do not tithe, they give offerings, wrote Irenaeus, an important Christian leader who lived in the late A.D. 100s. In those days, however, Christianity was an outlawed religion without church buildings to maintain. (For a quick look at how tithing became an accepted practice in the church, see Malachi, page 264.)

# Bible Scenarios You Can Use

### 1. Forgive the sinner who repented (2:5–11)

**P**aul never mentions the man's name, what the man did that was so wrong, or what the church did to discipline him.

Perhaps this is the man who was sleeping with his stepmother, and the Corinthians took Paul's advice to shun him (1 Corinthians 5). Or maybe it was a church member who caused Paul trouble when the apostle visited Corinth a few months earlier, after writing 1 Corinthians. Some Bible experts say it's possible the man was one of Paul's chief opponents, and had argued that there was nothing wrong with honoring their Greek tradition of going to the temples of Greek gods. Marriages and many social functions were held there, but so were sexually explicit rituals.

Whoever the man is, Paul says he has suffered enough. "Now is the time to forgive him and comfort him. Otherwise he may become so discouraged that he won't be able to recover" (2:7–8, New Living Translation).

Heavy-handed discipline isn't a problem in most churches. Typically, we don't take formal disciplinary measures against an errant member—unless it's a pastor. We're so focused on increasing the attendance and the contributions that we're reluctant to confront the wayward person, even though a loving but serious confrontation could lead the person back to Christ. Sometimes, however, we utterly alienate people who sinned. We may not expel them from membership, but we cut them out of the blessed herd socially—forever. Only Satan wins when we go to that extreme.

There's a time to confront, and a time to comfort. May God grant us the wisdom to know the correct timing of both.

## 2. Heaven waits (5:1–10)

The Corinthians are apparently having a hard time believing that their bodies will be resurrected, because Paul writes about this in both letters to them. What they've grown up hearing from famous Greek philosophers is that only the soul (*psyche* in Greek) lives on, and only in some mysterious sense in which all souls are forever reunited with the source of the universe, sometimes called Reality.

Paul assures the Corinthians that they can expect a resurrected body that's as real and wonderful as Jesus had after his resurrection.

"Our bodies are like tents that we live in here on earth," Paul explains. "But when these tents are destroyed, we know that God will give each of us a place to live. These homes will not be buildings that someone has made, but they are in heaven and will last forever." And as Paul said in his first letter, these spiritual bodies will have personalities and recognizable features—but without disease, pain, or death.

We dread death. It's the greatest unknown, and our greatest fear. Perhaps what we fear most is oblivion—the end of our existence. But as Christians, we know better. We know that God will transform us from life to Life. How do we know? "He [God] has given us his Spirit to make us certain that he will do it" (5:5). That sense of immortality deep within us is the whisper of God.

## 3. An offering for the needy (8:1—9:15)

Early in Paul's ministry, Christian leaders headquartered in Jerusalem ask him to collect offerings for impoverished Christians in Jerusalem. It's unclear how the Jerusalem Christians got in a financial bind. There could have been several reasons. Some Christians gave away their possessions to help others (Acts 4:32–37). A famine hit the region (Acts 11:28). And many Jews, some of whom became Christians, came to Jerusalem in their old age to be buried there. The church may have borne the financial brunt of caring for the widows among these pilgrims.

"Don't feel that you are forced to give," Paul tells the Corinthians. "God loves people who love to give."

Throughout the world, there are Christians who need food, clothing, and shelter. Even in our own neighborhoods, there are fellow believers struggling financially. When we see a need and can help, we should. We can't do everything, but we can do something.

# GALATIANS

## Religious Rules We Can Ignore

Some of us grew up obeying a bunch of religious rules we didn't like, couldn't find in the Bible, and felt were being unjustly imposed on us in pulpit-thumping sermons.

You can name some such rules, though they'll vary from one generation to the next. Many of us who've been Christians for a few decades remember the not-so-good old days when the reality of our faith was determined by hemlines, hair lines, and avoiding the movie ticket lines. No mini-skirts for the gals. No long hair for the guys. And no movies for either.

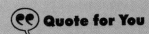 **Quote for You**

"Christ has really set us free. Now make sure that you stay free, and don't get tied up again in slavery to the law" (5:1, New Living Translation).

Not only was it forbidden to drink alcoholic beverages, we couldn't even go to bowling alleys that served liquor—which was nearly every bowling alley.

The spirit of the day was intolerance. And the demands were oppressively out of touch with our constantly changing culture.

In Paul's day, that was much like the condition in Galatia, an ancient region in what is now western Turkey. Paul had taught the people there—mostly non-Jews—that God saves them when they trust in Christ, not when they do religious things. But after Paul left, along came some Jewish-Christian missionaries who disagreed. They convinced many Galatians to obey the hundreds of Jewish laws, most notably eating only kosher foods, observing Jewish holy days, and circumcising the males.

"How were you given God's Spirit?" Paul asked the duped Galatians. "Was it by obeying the Law of Moses or by hearing about Christ and having faith in him?" (3:2).

Today, some Christians say we prove our salvation by studying, or by doing good deeds, or by feeling uplifted emotions. But it's not true. We're saved by God's gift, through faith in his Son. Human-engineered rules to the contrary—such as rules about hemlines, haircuts, and Hollywood—are made to be broken unless the Spirit says otherwise.

When It Happened

(Dates are approximate)

Jesus born 7/6 B.C.

Jesus crucified A.D. 30
Pentecost A.D. 30

Paul's missionary journeys begin A.D. 46

Galatians written c. A.D. 55

Temple destroyed A.D. 70

Death of John A.D. 100

# Info You Can Use

## Background Notes

**Writer:** The letter is "from the apostle Paul" (1:1) to churches scattered throughout the Roman province of Galatia in what is now western Turkey.

**Time:** There's no clear way to tell when Paul wrote this emotionally charged letter, as there are no solid clues in the letter. Bible experts say the theology sounds more like Paul's early letter of 1 Thessalonians (written in A.D. 51) than his letter of Romans (about A.D. 57). Because of that, they suggest a date of about A.D. 55—when Paul was writing the Corinthians. But it's also possible he wrote it a few years earlier.

**Place:** Paul wrote to churches in Galatia, a Roman province in western Turkey between the Mediterranean Sea in the south and the Black Sea in the north. Galatia extends roughly 300 miles north and south, and 100 miles east and west.

Paul started churches in southern Galatia during his first missionary journey. Then he started churches in northern Galatia on his second trip. Paul may have intended his letter to be circulated among all these churches. Or he could have instructed his courier to take it just to the cities where the Jewish-Christian missionaries showed up and caused trouble with their wrong teachings.

**Bottom-Line Summary:** Though Jesus' disciples limit their ministry primarily to Jews, God has commissioned Paul to take the teachings of Jesus especially to non-Jews (Acts 9:15). Paul starts non-Jewish congregations throughout Galatia. There, he assures the people they don't need to follow Jewish laws to find God's forgiveness and salvation. All they need is faith in Jesus, whom God sent. Paul backs up his teachings with miracles.

After Paul moves on, Jewish Christians arrive and offer the Galatians a different spin on the Christian faith. These Jews, who believe Jesus was the Messiah predicted by the prophets, argue that faith in Jesus isn't enough. They say the non-Jews must also obey the laws God gave Moses. There are hundreds of laws covering everything from bathing, to animal sacrifices, to diet, to circumcision for males—the latter of which is the main reason many non-Jews wouldn't convert to Judaism even though they believed in God.

Paul gets word of what's going on, so he quickly writes a letter debunking this teaching. The clash of these two philosophies was, in fact, the first major controversy in the church. Christian leaders supposedly settled the matter in Paul's favor at a Jerusalem summit meeting in about A.D. 49. But some Jewish Christians refused to accept the decision.

In his letter—the most emotionally charged in the Bible—Paul reminds the Galatians of his God-given commission by telling about his conversion and his visit from Jesus. He also reminds them that God accepted Abraham as righteous hundreds of years before the laws of Moses were drawn up.

Jewish law, Paul says, was intended to serve only until the Messiah arrived

(3:19). With the sacrificial death of Jesus, God established a new agreement with humanity, freeing us from these laws. Instead of following rules, Paul says, "you are guided by the Spirit" (5:16).

## Influential People

**Paul,** the apostle famous for his work among non-Jews. Using well-reasoned logic, Bible history, and some occasional bursts of anger, Paul vigorously resists false teachings. The fury of his response serves as a reminder that we need to recognize the seriousness of modern-day false teachings that use a little biblical truth as a springboard into heresy. The best way to combat warped teachings is to clearly and reasonably explain why they're wrong.

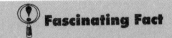
**Fascinating Fact**

Galatians is known as the Emancipation Proclamation of Christianity because it declares that believers are free from the Jewish laws in the Old Testament.

**Peter,** leader of Jesus' 12 original disciples, draws a sharp rebuke from Paul for flip-flopping on the controversial issue about the role of Jewish laws. Peter treats the non-Jewish Christians in Antioch, Syria as equals until some Jewish-Christian leaders from Jerusalem arrive. Then Peter shuns the non-Jews, as Jewish law requires. Peter's mistake shows that even the best of us can be wrongly influenced by others.

## Key Ideas You Need to Know

**Jewish Law.** Many Jewish Christians of the first century believed that since it was God who gave the Jewish laws to Moses, as a means of running the nation and keeping the Jewish people holy and acceptable to God, the laws were still in force. Anyone who wanted to be a follower of the Messiah Jesus, they argued, had to have faith in Jesus *and* obey the Jewish laws preserved in Leviticus, Numbers, and Deuteronomy.

Many of these laws are about crime and punishment. Many are about sacrificial rituals. And many are about moral issues, such as worshiping only God and being honest. Jewish Christians especially emphasized the law about men being circumcised, since it was a reminder of God's contractual agreement (covenant) with Israel.

Paul and many other Christians of his day considered the laws obsolete. That's because God promised to make a new agreement with humanity and write the laws on our minds (Jeremiah 31:31–33). The New Testament teaches that this prophecy was fulfilled through the ministry of Jesus and God's gift of the Holy Spirit, who lives within each believer.

"If you obey the Spirit," Paul wrote, "the Law of Moses has no control over you" (5:18).

Though most laws of Moses are now outdated, the moral laws are timeless. Be kind to others. Don't lie. Don't cheat. Don't seek revenge. Jesus repeated such teachings throughout his ministry.

Had Paul lost the battle over the place of Jewish law, Christianity might have become just another branch of Judaism, alongside the three main branches now: Reform, Conservative, and Orthodox.

**Spiritual Freedom.** Paul teaches that Christians shouldn't feel bound by Jewish rules and traditions. That teaching extends to modern-day religious rules that attempt to impose someone else's convictions on us. As Paul wrote on another occasion, "Why should my freedom be limited by someone else's conscience?" (1 Corinthians 10:29).

But Paul also issued a warning.

"Don't use your freedom as an excuse to do anything you want. Use it as an opportunity to serve each other with love. All that the Law [of Moses] says can be summed up in the command to love others as much as you love yourself" (5:13–14).

As Christians, we follow the teachings of Christ and the leading of God's Spirit within us.

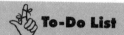
**To-Do List**

- "If you are guided by the Spirit, you won't obey your selfish desires" (5:16).

- "If someone is trapped in sin, you should gently lead that person back to the right path. But watch out, and don't be tempted yourself" (6:1).

- "We should help people whenever we can, especially if they are followers of the Lord" (6:10).

## Q&A

**Should Christian males be circumcised?** This isn't a religious issue for Christians.

God promised to protect and bless Abraham and his descendants (the Jews) in return for their obedience. To help the Jews remember this, God ordered Abraham and his male descendants to be circumcised. "Any man who isn't circumcised hasn't kept his promise to me," God said, "and cannot be one of my people" (Genesis 17:14).

The New Testament is about God's new agreement with humanity. In fact, "testament" means agreement or covenant. And this new agreement is that no one—Jews included—has to follow the ritual laws of the Old Testament. All they need is faith in Jesus. "Everyone who has faith," Paul declared, "is a child of Abraham" (3:7).

Paul had no problem with Christians getting circumcised if it was to open doors of ministry to more tradition-minded Jews. Paul had his non-Jewish associate, Timothy, circumcised for this reason (Acts 16:3). But Paul would never have approved of circumcision as a way to earn God's approval (5:12).

For Christians, the decision about circumcision is made for reasons related to health or customs, not religion.

# Bible Scenarios You Can Use

## 1. Paul publicly accuses Peter (2:11–21)

**P**aul had started churches among non-Jews throughout Galatia, teaching that people didn't need to obey the Jewish laws to find peace with God. All they needed was faith in Christ. But after Paul leaves, Jewish-Christian missionaries arrive and contradict his teaching. They say that anyone who wants to please God must follow the hundreds of Jewish laws in the Old Testament.

In a fiery letter, Paul refutes this many ways. One is to tell a story of how he once corrected the apostle Peter on this very issue. Paul was ministering at a predominately non-Jewish church in Antioch, Syria when Peter arrived for a visit. Peter eats with the non-Jews, though Jewish law forbids it. But when other Jewish Christians arrive from Jerusalem, Peter suddenly stops eating with the non-Jewish Christians.

This is a high-profile snub of the young Christians in Antioch, so Paul confronts Peter in public. "If we can be acceptable to God by obeying the Law," Paul insists, "it was useless for Christ to die."

Though Paul often pled for unity in the church, he didn't shy away from confrontation on important issues. Occasionally, big problems will erupt in the church. Sometimes Christian will have to take a stand against Christian—but in a spirit of compassion for one another and out of a desire to honor God.

## 2. We're all equals in God's eyes (3:26—4:7)

**M**any Jews in Bible times look down on non-Jews. After all, the Jews know they are God's chosen people. In Bible times, men look down on women. It's a man's world, and in many cultures—including the ancient Jewish one—females aren't allowed in schools. Slaves are property—livestock with two legs. The fact is, some Jews greeted each day with the prayer, "Thank you, Lord, that I'm not a Gentile (non-Jew), a slave, or a woman."

Christianity begins changing that. "All of you are God's children," Paul writes. "Faith in Christ Jesus is what makes each of you equal with each other, whether you are a Jew or a Greek, a slave or a free person, a man or a woman."

There's no place for a caste system in Christianity. In the secular world, you can often expect preferred treatment if you're rich, good looking, well connected, or highly educated. But among God's people, a person like that should expect treatment no better than that of a bankrupt, hound dog-faced, socially challenged, high school dropout. Both are beloved children of God and should be treated with honor.

## 3. Following our heavenly nature (5:16–26)

**P**aul tells the Galatians there's a battle going on inside each person. "The Spirit and your desires are enemies of each other. They are always fighting each other."

If we follow the lead of our selfish desires, he explains, we can expect trouble. Paul offers a sample list: jealousy, anger, hate, filthy thoughts, and shameful deeds.

On the other hand, Paul says, "God's Spirit makes us loving, happy, peaceful, patient, kind, good, faithful, gentle, and self-controlled."

These godly traits are sometimes called "fruit of the Spirit." They're not attributes we can develop on our own. They're the work of the Holy Spirit in us—the byproducts of being a Christian and of devoting ourselves to serving God. The Spirit within us gives us the freedom and power to say no to sinful desires that would hurt us.

"Those who belong to Christ Jesus," Paul tells the Galatians and us, "have nailed the passions and desires of their sinful nature to his cross and crucified them there. If we are living now by the Holy Spirit, let us follow the Holy Spirit's leading in every part of our lives" (5:24–25, New Living Translation).

That doesn't mean we won't fail on occasion. But it does mean that sin's mastery over us is broken, and we are free to serve God. Perhaps we should remind ourselves of that whenever we're tempted to do something we know we'll regret later.

# EPHESIANS

## How to Become More Like God

Here's the shocker:

"You were created to be like God" (4:24).

That sounds a lot like a quote from God in the Bible's first book: "Now we will make humans, and they will be like us" (Genesis 1:26). And it sounds like a report of what God, in fact, did: "So God created humans to be like himself" (Genesis 1:27).

But what does it mean "to be like God?" Does it mean we look like him: humanoid? Does it mean we're built to last—for eternity? Or does it mean we're designed for goodness?

It could be all of the above. But in his letter to the Ephesians, Paul zeroes in on the goodness theme. "Be truly holy," Paul explains. "Stop lying and start telling each other the truth. Don't get so angry that you sin" (4:24–26). The list of saintly character traits goes on.

How on earth can God expect that of us? We're not perfect.

Actually, God doesn't expect us to be perfect—at least not in this world corrupted by sin. What he asks is that we let him begin the process: "Let the Spirit change your way of thinking, and make you into a new person" (4:23–24).

In ways we can't fully understand, God starts changing us into the perfect creature he intended humans to be when he first made us. That's the story of the Bible—God working his plan to restore his once perfect creation.

He's not done with us yet. But Paul assures us, "When the time is right, God will do all that he has planned" (1:10).

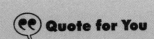 **Quote for You**

"I pray that Christ will be more and more at home in your hearts as you trust in him. May your roots go down deep into the soil of God's marvelous love. And may you have the power to understand, as all God's people should, how wide, how long, how high, and how deep his love really is" (3:17–18).

When It Happened

(Dates are approximate)

Jesus born 7/6 B.C.

Jesus crucified
Pentecost A.D. 30

Paul's missionary journeys
begin A.D. 46

Ephesians written
A.D. 60

Temple destroyed
A.D. 70

Death of John
A.D. 100

# Info You Can Use

 **Background Notes**

**Writer:** The letter says "Paul, chosen by God to be an apostle" (1:1) wrote it while "in jail" (6:20).

Bible experts didn't start seriously questioning this until about 300 years ago. Most experts agree Paul wrote Romans, 1 and 2 Corinthians, Galatians, Philippians, 1 Thessalonians, and Philemon. These books resemble each other in writing style and teaching. Ephesians, however, uses important terms missing from the undisputed books. It also uses familiar words, but with new meaning. In addition, the writing style is more flowery and verbose than Paul's other quick-to-the-point letters.

Some Bible experts say Timothy or another of Paul's associates wrote the letter after Paul died, perhaps to address current issues using their mentor's approach, voice, and name—as a tribute to him.

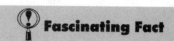 **Fascinating Fact**

Paul was jailed at least three times, given 39 lashes by Jews five times, beaten with rods by Romans three times, and stoned and left for dead once (2 Corinthians 11:24–27). Christian writers in the second century report he was beheaded in Rome.

Others say Paul's writing may have changed over the years, or that Paul adapted his style to match the well-known hymns and prayers he wove into this letter.

**Time:** Paul probably wrote during his two-year imprisonment at Rome, which began in about A.D. 60.

**Place:** The letter is addressed "to God's people who live in Ephesus" (1:1). But that introduction isn't in the earliest copies of this letter. Also missing are Paul's customary greetings to individuals and references to events in the church.

It could be that Paul intended Ephesians to be a general letter circulated to as many churches as possible. But if he intended it for Ephesus, he was addressing a congregation especially dear to his heart. He spent more than three years establishing the Ephesus church—more time than at any other church.

Ephesus was a major port city and capital of the Roman province of Asia, along the Mediterranean coast in what is now western Turkey. Ephesus is thought to have been the world's fourth largest city in Paul's day. Estimated population was 250,000.

**Bottom-Line Summary:** Writing from jail, perhaps in Rome, Paul pens a beautiful, uplifting sermon addressed to the church at Ephesus but suited for any congregation.

Paul isn't trying to settle squabbles in the church, fight off false teachings, or defend his authority—as he did in other letters. He writes only to encourage the believers by explaining that God's plan is to return unity and peace to his creation, beginning with the church and then using the church to help change the world.

Paul starts by assuring believers that God loves them, chose them for greatness, showers them with kindness, freed them from slavery to sin, and welcomed them into his eternal kingdom. As members of God's church, Paul says, believers should be united in their commitment to Jesus and in the use of their diverse gifts, which are intended to serve and strengthen the church.

The apostle calls believers to the highest moral standards and to living in peace with one another. He also warns them to stay close to God, so they'll have all the resources they need to fight off the temptations and evil they'll inevitably face.

# Influential People

**Paul,** a traveling minister, starts churches throughout the Roman Empire. Writing from jail, Paul doesn't focus on his troubles. Instead, he sends an inspiring message to the church, reminding them of their high calling in life and assuring them that he has every confidence in them. By putting others first, Paul is practicing what he preaches (6:21). And he's reminding us to do the same.

# Key Ideas You Need to Know

**Everyday advice for God's people.** In the spirit of Proverbs—a book of sage advice from Jewish elders for young men—Paul closes his letter with practical tips for godly living.

- *Get along with each other.* "Patiently put up with each other and love each other. Try your best to let God's Spirit keep your hearts united" (4:2–3).

- *Treat each other as equals.* "All of you are part of the same body" (4:4).

- *Use your gifts to help others* (4:11–13).

- *Let God help you mature into a better person* (4:23–24).

- *Put others first.* "Submit to one another out of reverence for Christ" (5:21, New Living Translation).

- *Resist evil.* "We are not fighting against people made of flesh and blood, but against the evil rulers and authorities of the unseen world" (6:12, New Living Translation).

# Q&A

**How can we be filled with the Spirit?** By letting God's Spirit within us control our thoughts, feelings, words, and actions.

Paul said that instead of filling ourselves with wine, "let the Spirit fill your life" (5:18). Just as being filled with wine puts us under it's influence, so being filled with the Spirit puts us under God's influence.

Some Christians believe that being filled with the Spirit is an occasional, temporary experience accompanied by speaking in heavenly languages, as happened at times in the Bible (Acts 19:6). But this passage is in the present tense, indicating that believers are to be continually under the Spirit's direction. One such person was the church's first martyr, Stephen, along with his six associates (Acts 6:3).

God's Spirit comes into us when we become believers. And his Spirit guides us as we allow. Paul asked us to give the Spirit full control of our lives, and let ourselves be continually led by the one who can help us understand God's will and make wise choices.

## Red Flag Issues

**Predestination.** Paul said God "predestined us to be adopted as his sons through Jesus Christ, in accordance with his pleasure and will" (1:5, New International Version).

Some Christians say that means God selects (predestines) who will and won't be saved. But others argue that God wants everyone to be saved, and he leaves the decision with us. For support, they refer to passages such as this: "He [God] wants everyone to turn from sin and no one to be lost" (2 Peter 3:9). For more on this, see Romans, page 321.

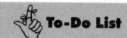

**To-Do List**

- "Live in a way that is worthy of the people God has chosen to be his own. Always be humble and gentle" (4:1–2).

- "We must not let deceitful people trick us by their false teachings, which are like winds that toss us around from place to place" (4:14).

- "Don't go to bed angry" (4:26).

## For the Record: Ephesians Abused

**Husbands as boss of the home.** Christian men have long quoted Paul's command, "Wives, submit to your husbands as to the Lord" (5:22, New International Version). Fortunately for the ladies, Paul's thought begins one verse earlier: "Submit to one another out of reverence for Christ" (5:21, New Living Translation).

In the original Greek language, there's only one verb for the entire section that discusses husband and wife relationships. That verb is "submit" in verse 21. Everything Paul said after that is built on this verb, which presumes that husbands and wives are each putting the other first.

**Slavery.** "Slaves," Paul said, "you must obey your earthly masters" (6:5).

Many Christians today wonder why Paul didn't order Christian slave owners to free their slaves. Perhaps it's because, as far as Paul was concerned, physical freedom took second place to spiritual freedom. Job one was to spread the teachings of Jesus. If that job got done, Paul may have figured, unjust social institutions would crumble.

Paul wasn't interested primarily in starting a slave revolt—or a women's rights movement, for that matter. He wanted to change people's hearts, which is where true revolutions begin. He tells masters to treat their slaves with respect and husbands to put their wives first. If the slave masters and husbands did that, it wouldn't take them long to figure out they should be treating each other as equals.

# Bible Scenarios You Can Use

## 1. Let love be your guide (4:17—5:20)

**W**riting from prison, Paul pens an unusually reflective and thoughtful letter to his dear friends in Ephesus. He sounds much like a father writing to his children, trying to share important spiritual insights he's learned from life.

Bad habits and selfish desires will destroy you, Paul says. "Let the Spirit change your way of thinking and make you into a new person. You were created to be like God, and so you must please him and be truly holy."

Paul doesn't mean they're to be perfect in behavior. "Holy" means dedicated to God. As the Ephesians mature in the faith, Paul says they will gradually get rid of lies, dirty talk, anger, and greed. Instead, they'll become more honest, sensitive, kind, and hardworking.

"Do as God does," Paul says, in timeless advice fit for Christians today. "After all, you are his dear children. Let love be your guide" (5:1–2).

## 2. Family members, put each other first (5:21—6:9)

**P**aul briefly turns to family matters, speaking individually to husbands, wives, children, and servants. But first, he has a message for all of them—a message he repeats when addressing each group: "Put others first."

Husbands and wives are to love and care for each other, doing as much as possible to meet one another's needs. Children are to treat their parents with respect. "Parents," Paul adds, "don't be hard on your children." Household servants, too, are to obey their masters and treat them with respect. But masters, too, are to respect their servants and not threaten them. "They [servants] have the same Master in heaven that you do," Paul says, "and he doesn't have any favorites."

Paul's advice sounds naïve and out of touch with human nature. But he's actually pointing us to heaven's nature that's alive and growing inside believers. We can learn to treat all the people in our lives with respect and compassion because that's what God does, and we're God's people. He rubs off on us.

## 3. How to fight off evil (6:10–18) ▬▬▬▬▬▬▬▬▬▬▬▬▬▬▬▬▬▬▬▬▬▬▬

**P**aul closes his letter with a mysterious warning. He tells the Ephesians that though they live in a physical world they can see and touch, there's also an invisible spirit world teeming with forces of good and evil.

God and his heavenly kingdom are part of that spirit world, helping believers. But there are evil forces waging unseen warfare against Christians. "We are not fighting against humans," Paul says. "We are fighting against forces and authorities and against rulers of darkness and powers in the spiritual world. So put on all the armor that God gives."

Paul compares this heaven-sent armor to the battle gear of a Roman soldier. He tells the Ephesians to strap on truth like a belt, justice like body armor, peace like shoes, faith like a shield, salvation like a helmet, and God's word (from Scripture and the Spirit within us) like a sword.

Live like God's people. That's Paul's message to the Ephesians and to all believers. When we pursue truth, justice, and peace, when we trust in God for our salvation, and when we lean on God's guidance, we've nothing to fear. Evil will attack. But Paul says when it does, "you will be able to defend yourself. And when the battle is over, you will still be standing firm."

We are the church—God's people. Concerning this, there's one sure thing, which Jesus summed up for Peter: "I will build my church, and all the powers of hell will not conquer it" (Matthew 16:18, New Living Translation).

# PHILIPPIANS

## Finding Joy in the Saddest Places

Did you ever try to make a chronic complainer happy?

Take him to a Caribbean beach, where the ocean glows luminous blue from the white sands reflecting the sky—and listen to him gripe about the water plugging his ear. Or invite her to a critic's choice restaurant that specializes in her favorite food, and get a real critic's take.

Imagine what they would say about spending time in jail.

That's where Paul wrote this letter to a small congregation he started in Philippi, in what is now northern Greece. Not only is there no trace of complaint, this letter is the Bible's finest essay on joy. Paul talks about where joy comes from and how we can have it, too.

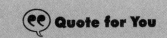 **Quote for You**

"My God will use his wonderful riches in Christ Jesus to give you everything you need" (4:19, New Century Version).

In short, Paul says his joy comes from knowing this: "God accepted me simply because of my faith in Christ" (3:9).

Joy that comes from God's acceptance can overpower and outlast all our tough circumstances in life: water in the ear, indigestion, and false arrest.

And so from jail, Paul is able to write with a straight face and a steady pen: "I am not complaining about having too little. I have learned to be satisfied with whatever I have. I know what it is to be poor or to have plenty, and I have lived under all kinds of conditions. I know what it means to be full or to be hungry, to have too much or too little. Christ gives me the strength to face anything" (4:11–13).

Now that's the kind of person we want as our company. That's the kind of person we want to be. Best of all, that's the kind of person we can be, with God's help.

## When It Happened

(Dates are approximate)

Jesus born 7/6 B.C.

Jesus crucified Pentecost A.D. 30

Paul's missionary journeys begin A.D. 46

Philippians written A.D. 60

Temple destroyed A.D. 70

Death of John A.D. 100

# Info You Can Use

## Background Notes

**Writer:** This short letter is "from Paul and Timothy, servants of Christ Jesus." Paul likely did the writing, but politely mentioned his associate who was with him and who helped start the Philippian church (Acts 16).

**Time:** There's no solid evidence about when Paul wrote this letter. Many Bible experts say he wrote during his two-year house arrest in Rome, which began in about A.D. 60. If this is correct, Paul wrote this letter during the last years of his ministry, which began with his conversion to Christianity about 25 years earlier.

**Place:** Paul wrote to Christians in Philippi, a large city in what is now northern Greece. Then, however, it was in the Roman province of Macedonia. Philippi—named after Alexander the Great's father, King Philip—was on one of the main roads connecting Rome with territories in the east. Paul visited the city twice on his third missionary journey, before his arrest and trial in Rome.

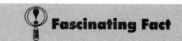

**Fascinating Fact**

Paul's letters are arranged in the Bible, generally, from longest to shortest, starting with the 16-chapter letter of Romans and ending with the 1-chapter letter of Philemon.

It's unclear where Paul was when he wrote Philippians. He said he was in jail, but he didn't say in what city (1:7). Many Bible experts speculate he was in Rome, since it would fit the time frame and because Paul mentioned his "Roman guards" (1:13) and fellow believers in contact with him who were "in the service of the Emperor" (4:22). But there were Roman guards and imperial workers in many cities and in every provincial capital—including Corinth, Ephesus, and Caesarea. Paul said he was jailed many times (2 Corinthians 11:23). Acts identifies three: Philippi, when he started the church (16:23–40); Caesarea, before being transferred to Rome (23:23—26:32); and Rome (28:16–31). He may also have been jailed in Corinth and Ephesus.

**Bottom-Line Summary:** While Paul is in jail he receives a messenger from the church he founded in Philippi. The believers there heard of Paul's arrest, and sent one of their trusted members—Epaphroditus—with gifts for Paul. These gifts may include warm clothing and money to help cover Paul's costs if he is under house arrest in Rome, as many Bible experts suggest.

The Philippian congregation has an unusual bond with Paul, for he has allowed them to help support his ministry with money and gifts. Normally, as with the Corinthians, Paul refuses such support and pays his own way as a tentmaker.

While with Paul, Epaphroditus gets sick and nearly dies. But he recovers. When he does, Paul sends him home with what has become known as the letter to the Philippians. It's an inspiring, joyful letter epitomized in the verse: "Always be glad because of the Lord! I will say it again: Be glad" (4:4).

Paul gives thanks for the longstanding support of the Philippians, for their recent gifts, and for the recovery of Epaphroditus. He also briefly explains to them that his faith in Jesus is what makes it possible to continually rejoice, even in the midst of suffering and imprisonment.

Paul warns the Philippians that one day they, too, may have to suffer because of their faith. If so, he says, they should be brave and remember that God can use suffering to accomplish good. Paul's imprisonment, he says, "has helped to spread the good news. . . . The Lord's followers have become brave and are fearlessly telling the message" (1:12, 14).

## Influential People

**Paul,** a traveling preacher and founder of the Philippian congregation, was a frequent prisoner because his message angers the Jews. From jail, Paul writes the Bible's most powerful treatise about joy—a reminder that our faith can lift us above the bleakest of life's circumstances by reassuring us that we belong to God and to his kingdom that will never end.

## Key Ideas
## You Need to Know

**Joy.** The joy Paul talked about isn't like the happiness adrenaline rush we get from a delightful moment in life, such as the birth of a child, a job promotion, or a relaxing vacation. It's a lasting peace and contentment, no matter what happens. And it comes from knowing that all is well between God and us. When we know that God is with us, we don't have to face problems alone—we can depend on his help and his expertise at turning bad situations into something good.

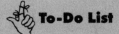

### To-Do List

- "This is my prayer for you . . . that you will do many good things with the help of Christ to bring glory and praise to God" (1:9, 11, New Century Version).

- "Live in harmony by showing love for each other. Be united in what you think, as if you were only one person" (2:2). *Paul's advice to church members.*

- "You live among people who are crooked and evil, but you must not do anything that they can say is wrong. Try to shine as lights among the people of this world" (2:15).

- "Stop arguing with each other" (4:2).

- "Always be glad because of the Lord! I will say it again: Be glad" (4:4).

- "Always be gentle with others" (4:5).

We can be sad, disappointed, and even discouraged by some of the scenes that play out in our life. But far beneath those feelings, at the foundation of our spirit, we can experience the abiding joy of God's presence. It puts a positive spin on the way we approach life.

**Self-sacrifice.** Paul warns the Philippians that because they're Christians they may have to face some of the same kinds of suffering he has endured. Even in our day and culture, which is more accommodating to Christians than the world was in Paul's day, believers still have to make sacrifices. We'll miss job opportunities because of our honesty. We'll lose money because we "give to Caesar what is Caesars," as Jesus put it, by paying all our taxes when others cheat as a way to protect themselves from what they believe is abusive taxation and wasteful spending. And we'll give up some of our time to help others, through ministry in church or simply to lend a hand to a family member or friend.

Paul was a good example of self-sacrifice, having been imprisoned many times, beaten, and even stoned in an execution attempt (2 Corinthians 11:23–25). But Paul pointed to a greater example: Jesus, who came from heaven to minister among us, die for us, and rise to new life to give us a glimpse into eternity. As followers of Jesus, we're called on to be prepared to put aside our own needs to help meet the needs of others.

## Q&A

**Will God really meet all our needs?** Not necessarily in the way we expect. Paul tells the Philippians, "This same God who takes care of me will supply all your needs from his glorious riches, which have been given to us in Christ Jesus" (4:19, New Living Translation).

This, however, comes from a man in jail, who admits to sometimes not having enough to eat or a place to stay, and who is eventually executed.

Clearly, God doesn't always provide food when his people need a meal, or a roof over their head when they need shelter, or a heartbeat when they need to live longer. Jesus himself had no place to call his own (Matthew 8:20). And, like Paul, he was executed. But Jesus, too, had said not to worry about our needs because God will provide (Matthew 6:31–33).

So what need will God meet? The need to live and die and live again. Sometimes that means providing food, shelter, and health. Sometimes it means providing comfort while dying. But always it means providing us with himself—his presence in our life to determine our needs and meet them, whatever they are, and for the rest of eternity.

# Bible Scenarios You Can Use

## 1. Keep yourself humble (2:1–11)

In jail, Paul receives a messenger bringing gifts from the church he founded in Philippi. Paul writes a warm letter of thanks, for the messenger to carry back to the congregation. "Every time I think of you, I thank my God," Paul says. "You have a special place in my heart" (1:3, 7)

Paul doesn't stop with the thanks and praise. A pastor at heart, Paul offers encouragement and advice. One piece of advice seems especially appropriate for helping a praiseworthy church keep from developing a sense of arrogant self-satisfaction.

"Be humble and consider others more important than yourself," Paul writes. "Care about them as much as you care about yourselves, and think the same way that Christ Jesus thought." Then Paul quotes what many Bible experts say is one of the earliest preserved songs about Jesus—about his giving up the glory of heaven to become a servant to help us and even die for us.

Like the Philippians, we're to follow Christ's example and put the needs of others before our own. It won't come natural at first because it's counter-culture. We've been conditioned to make a good impression, look important, and get what we want. There's nothing humble about that. God wants servants willing to help others.

## 2. Running on the highway to heaven (3:12–21)

Using a word picture from the ancient Greek athletic competitions—the Olympian Games in Olympia and the Isthmian Games in Corinth—Paul compares himself to a runner in a race. His goal isn't a crown of withered celery stalks, commonly given to race winners. Instead, the prize he seeks is perfection in heaven—a life completely in stride with God's will and a body as glorious and immortal as the one Jesus had after his resurrection.

"I have not yet reached my goal," Paul says. "I am not perfect. But Christ has taken hold of me. So I keep on running and struggling to take hold of the prize . . . of being called to heaven."

If we could sum up Paul's advice in a sentence, it might be this: run toward Jesus. One way to get there is to follow the example of Paul and other leaders whose behavior shows they are God's people. Many professing Christian leaders aren't worth following. As Paul puts it, "All they think about are the things of this world."

"But we," Paul quickly adds, "are citizens of heaven." And we should run life's race energized by knowing that this is where we're headed.

## 3. Think the good thoughts (4:8–9)

In his closing words, Paul tells the Philippians to take control of their thought life. "Keep your minds on whatever is true, pure, right, holy, friendly, and proper. Don't ever stop thinking about what is truly worthwhile and worthy of praise."

Paul knows that what lingers in our mind comes out in our life, whether it's anger, revenge, lust, greed, or any of the long list of damaging thoughts.

When bad thoughts invade, we can make a conscious decision to give them the boot. For example, many of us are tempted to relive unhappy experiences, such as an argument we lost. We picture the scene in our mind, and argue all over again—this time winning decisively. But as soon as we begin feeling our temper rise and we recognize what's going on, we can evict those thoughts by saying, "You don't belong here. You're not helping me. In fact, you're hurting me. So get out of here."

Many Christians find they can get rid of harmful thoughts by quoting upbeat, encouraging Bible verses, such as these very words of Paul. Others use passages specific to their thought. For lust, there's Job's advice: "I promised myself never to stare with desire at a young woman" (Job 31:1). And for worry: "Don't worry about anything, but pray about everything" (4:6).

Beyond Scripture, we have God's peace-giving Spirit within us to help. "This peace," Paul says, "will control the way you think and feel" (4:7).

# COLOSSIANS

## New and Improved Christianity

For some people, Jesus isn't enough to get us into heaven.

Or so they think.

We need Jesus *and* acts of kindness; or Jesus *and* the right beliefs (such as an emphasis on speaking in tongues, once saved always saved, or regular confessions to a priest); or Jesus *and* obedience to denominational rules; or Jesus *and* the King James Version of the Bible; or Jesus *and* tithing.

It's like Jesus is some kind of detergent that can't get the sin stains out, so we need to add bleach. We package Jesus with something else, creating a "new and improved" Christianity.

But there's nothing new or improved about it.

Christians in the city of Colossae, in what is now western Turkey, were offered much the same brand of reinforced Christianity—Jesus *and* Jewish rules, Jesus *and* visions, Jesus *and* secret knowledge about God, Jesus *and* depriving your body to show you have control over it.

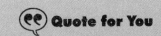 **Quote for You**

"You have accepted Christ Jesus as your Lord. Now keep on following him. Plant your roots in Christ and let him be the foundation for your life" (2:6–7).

The Colossians had heard the authentic Christian teachings from one of Paul's associates, and had believed they were saved through faith in Jesus. But traveling ministers came along later and tossed some additives into the faith. These added teachings seemed to come from Judaism and other Middle Eastern religions.

Paul said these were nothing more than teachings that "come from the powers of this world and not from Christ" (2:8). He would have nothing to do with them. Neither should we.

When It Happened

(Dates are approximate)

Jesus born 7/6 B.C.

Jesus crucified
Pentecost A.D. 30

Paul's missionary journeys
begin A.D. 46

Colossians written
A.D. 60

Temple destroyed
A.D. 70

Death of John
A.D. 100

# Info You Can Use

## Background Notes

**Writer:** At the letter's beginning and end, the writer declared himself to be "Paul, chosen by God" (1:1); "I am signing this letter myself: PAUL" (4:18).

**Time:** Because Paul repeated some of the things he said to the Ephesians, many Bible experts suggest both were written about the same time—perhaps during the two years he was under house arrest in Rome, beginning in A.D. 60.

**Place:** Colossae was a city in what is now western Turkey, about 100 miles east of the bustling coastal city of Ephesus where Paul ministered for about three years. Though Paul never visited Colossae, the church was apparently started by an associate minister Paul sent there: Epaphras.

**Bottom-Line Summary:** While in jail, Paul gets word that religious teachers have arrived in Colossae peddling a distorted Christianity. This new take on the Christian religion has just enough truth to intrigue the church but just enough error to destroy it. Paul apparently gets the news from an associate, Epaphras, who started the church and who came to be with the apostle during his imprisonment.

The intruders are religious philosophers gifted at accessorizing. They take a little from Christianity, a little from Judaism, and some from the mysterious cults in the Roman Empire. And *voila*, they have a new religion that looks deceptively familiar.

To combat the threat, Paul writes a letter to the Colossians. "Don't let anyone fool you," he warns. "These arguments may sound wise, but they are only human teachings. They come from the powers of this world and not from Christ" (2:8).

### Fascinating Fact

A runaway slave was one of two Christians who carried this letter to Colossae. Paul sent the slave, Onesimus, to reconcile with his owner, who was a leader in the Colossae church. Onesimus also carried a separate letter for his owner, which is preserved in the Bible as Philemon.

Paul urges the believers to hold tight to their faith in Jesus "just as you were taught" (2:7). Then he closes with a list of everyday traits that maturing Christians should develop, as well as bad traits and habits they should avoid.

## Influential People

**Paul,** a traveling minister, is widely recognized in his day as the leader among non-Jewish congregations, such as the one in Colossae. Though Paul never met the Colossians, his concern for them moves him to prayer and to action. Imprisoned, he can't go there, but he can write to them. In so doing, he reminds us that when we see problems we can help fix, we should give it our best effort.

# ? Q&A

**What power do evil spirits have over Christians?** None. "Christ defeated all powers and forces," Paul said. "He let the whole world see them being led away as prisoners when he celebrated his victory" (2:15).

Though some Bible experts aren't sure Paul had evil spirits in mind when he spoke about "powers and forces," others say these are likely the same supernatural forces Paul wrote of to the Ephesians, in a letter probably written about the same time. There, Paul wrote, "We are not fighting against humans. We are fighting against forces and authorities and against rulers of darkness and powers in the spiritual world" (Ephesians 6:12).

Jesus didn't wipe out the evil forces. But he showed his power over them by exorcising demons, crushing Satan's efforts to tempt him, and returning from death—a condition caused by evil's entrance into creation.

The Bible teaches that evil spirits are as real as human beings, and able to enter into and control some people. Christian leaders of many denominations report that demon possession still exists, requiring prayers of exorcism. But there's no place for evil spirits in a believer because God's Spirit has taken up residence within us (1 Corinthians 6:19).

## For the Record: Colossians Abused

**Slavery. Men in charge of women.** Paul addresses these two issues, saying much the same thing he did in his letter to the Ephesians. These Bible passages have often been used to portray Paul as condoning slavery and forbidding women's rights. But that's not at all what he had in mind. If people acted on Paul's advice regarding shared submission and mutual respect, the last scene would be equality for all. (See Ephesians Abused, page 350.)

---

### To-Do List

- "Since you have been raised to new life with Christ, set your sights on the realities of heaven. . . . Let heaven fill your thoughts. Do not think only about things down here on earth" (3:1–2, New Living Translation).

- "Stop lying to each other. You have given up your old way of life with its habits" (3:9).

- "Forgive anyone who does you wrong, just as Christ has forgiven you" (3:13).

- "With thankful hearts, sing psalms, hymns, and spiritual songs to God" (3:16).

- "Never give up praying" (4:2).

- "When you are with unbelievers, always make good use of the time. Be pleasant and hold their interest when you speak the message. Choose your words carefully and be ready to give answers to anyone who asks questions" (4:5–6).

# Bible Scenarios You Can Use

## 1. Ask God for direction (1:9–11)

**T**hough Paul has never met the Christians of Colossae, he has heard much about them. Some of the news comes from their founding pastor, an associate of Paul's.

"We have not stopped praying for you since the first day we heard about you," Paul writes in a letter. "We always pray that God will show you everything he wants you to do and that you may have all the wisdom and understanding that his Spirit gives. Then you will live a life that honors the Lord, and you will always please him by doing good deeds. You will come to know God even better. His glorious power will make you patient and strong enough to endure anything, and you will be truly happy."

That's the power of prayer. It's not just a monologue to an invisible person. When we pray to God, it's as though we open up a pipeline to heaven. And through this channel, God supplies us with everything his love has to offer: guidance, wisdom, encouragement, patience, strength, and happiness. All of these are gifts of God, sitting in heaven just waiting for us to ask for them. As Jesus once told his followers, "Ask and you will receive, and your joy will be complete" (John 16:24, New International Version).

## 2. Live like a follower of Jesus (3:1–17)

**I**n words reminiscent of what Jesus once told a Jewish scholar—"You must be born from above" (John 3:3)—Paul assures the Christians of Colossae, "Each of you is now a new person. You are becoming more and more like your Creator."

Paul says this means we begin taking charge of our body and behavior. We become less and less controlled by immorality, greed, anger, and dishonesty. Instead, we become more and more kind, humble, patient, and forgiving.

On those occasions when we don't know what to do or say, Paul offers this advice: "Whatever you say or do should be done in the name of the Lord Jesus." If it will honor Christ, do it. If it won't, don't.

On Planet Earth, we'll never get it perfectly right. We'll occasionally make mistakes, and disappoint ourselves and others. But as we mature in the faith, we'll discover sin won't be the rule. Christ will be the rule. We'll notice it, and so will others.

# 1 THESSALONIANS

## How to Live the Holy Life

"God wants you to be holy."

That's a quote from Paul to the Christians at Thessalonica (4:3). But it applies to all believers everywhere.

To put the quote another way, as Paul did in a letter to the Ephesians: "You are created to be like God" (Ephesians 4:24).

But we aren't God, and we aren't perfect. Yet Paul says "be holy" and "like God." How can we possibly do that?

Paul gives us a clue. His clue suggests that when we read "holy" and "like God" we should substitute a phrase that's perhaps easier to understand: "committed to goodness." It means doing the right thing.

Paul draws us a word picture of what holiness looks like on earth. "Try your best to live quietly, to mind your own business, and to work hard. . . . Then you will be respected by people who are not followers of the Lord" (4:11–12).

Paul's picture continues throughout the closing chapters of his short letter. "Encourage and help each other" (5:11). "Try to get along with each other" (5:13). "Help all who are weak" (5:14). "Be patient with everyone" (5:14). "Whatever happens, keep thanking God because of Jesus Christ" (5:18).

Most of us aren't like this by nature. And we wouldn't hold out much hope of being able to make the necessary changes.

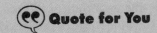 **Quote for You**

"May the God of peace make you holy in every way, and may your whole spirit and soul and body be kept blameless until that day when our Lord Jesus Christ comes again. God, who calls you, is faithful; he will do this" (5:23–24, New Living Translation).

But that's okay. We don't have to make the changes. That's God's job. And Paul assures us, "he will do this" (5:23). We may have been creepy caterpillars, but we're becoming butterflies.

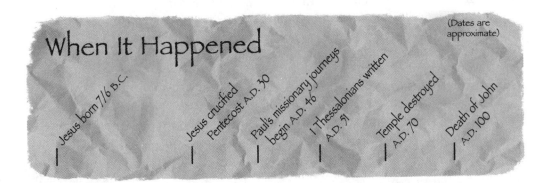

When It Happened

(Dates are approximate)

Jesus born 7/6 B.C.

Jesus crucified Pentecost A.D. 30

Paul's missionary journeys begin A.D. 46

1 Thessalonians written A.D. 51

Temple destroyed A.D. 70

Death of John A.D. 100

# Info You Can Use

## Background Notes

**Writer:** This letter is "from Paul, Silas, and Timothy" (1:1), though it's written in the first person. The writer, Bible experts agree, is Paul, who politely refers to his two ministry associates.

Christian leaders, at least as early as Marcion in A.D. 140, confirmed Paul was the writer.

**Time:** This letter is probably the oldest piece of writing in the New Testament. Paul wrote it in about A.D. 51, just 20 years after the death of Jesus. Paul wrote the letter during his second missionary trip, while starting the church in Corinth. The stories about Jesus were written later, to preserve the testimony of Jesus' original disciples who were dying off.

The timeframe is supported by Bible history and archaeology. Acts 18 says Corinthian Jews brought Paul up on charges before Gallio, the governor of the province. Gallio threw the case out of court. An ancient inscription found at Delphi, a worship center in the region, confirms that Gallio was governor from about A.D. 51–53.

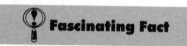

### Fascinating Fact

Paul was a bi-vocational minister. He preached, but he made tents to support himself (2:9, Acts 18:3). Christians generally met in homes and the congregations weren't large enough to fully support ministers.

**Place:** Thessalonica was a busy town for two reasons. It had a seaport and it was on a major road in northern Greece. It drew travelers from it's port in the Thermatic Gulf of the Aegean Sea, and from an east-west Roman road that ran 500 miles across northern Greece and into Turkey.

Charges of disturbing the peace forced Paul to flee Thessalonica after about three weeks. He sailed about 200 miles south to Athens, then traveled another 50 miles southwest to Corinth, which is where he wrote the letter.

**Bottom-Line Summary:** During his second missionary journey throughout the Middle East, Paul has a vision of a man pleading with him to come to Macedonia, a Roman province in northern Greece. Paul does it. He sails across the Aegean Sea and becomes the first Christian missionary to set foot in Europe.

He arrives in Philippi and starts preaching in the synagogue, announcing that the messiah has come: Jesus. Paul is there for about three weeks. That's long enough for him to convince some Jews, along with many non-Jews who have been worshiping God. But many other Jews reject his teaching as lies, and they stir up a riot. This forces Paul to flee for safety (Acts 17).

Paul sails down to Athens, but worries about the new believers he left behind. So he sends Timothy, one of his associates, to check on them. Timothy rejoins Paul in Corinth and delivers a good report. Relieved, Paul writes the letter that becomes known as 1 Thessalonians.

The believers are facing harassment and persecution from their countrymen, so Paul reminds them that Jesus suffered, too. Paul also answers their questions about the Second Coming of Jesus, and gives them practical advice about how to live in a way that pleases God.

## Influential People

**Paul,** a leading minister among non-Jews, is the founder of churches throughout the Roman Empire—including the church in Thessalonica, Greece. Though Paul found a receptive audience in the city, his teachings angered many others and sparked a riot. His departure reminds us that there's a time to talk and a time to walk. We should tell others about Jesus, since many in our "Christian" culture know almost nothing about him. But if they reject the message, we shouldn't try to impose it on them (Matthew 10:14).

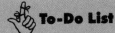

**To-Do List**

- "Encourage and help each other" (5:11).

- "Don't be hateful to people just because they are hateful to you. Rather, be good to each other and to everyone else" (5:15).

- "Never stop praying" (5:17).

**Timothy,** Paul's associate, took the risk of returning to the stirred up city to check on the new believers. Christians look out for one another, even if it sometimes puts us in danger.

## Key Ideas You Need to Know

**Holiness.** Paul prayed for the Thessalonians: "May God himself, the God of peace, sanctify you through and through" (5:23, New International Version). To sanctify something means to make it holy, to set it apart for God's use.

Some Christians teach a doctrine called "entire sanctification," often describing it as a second act of God's grace after we become Christians. They teach that as we mature, we can reach a point where we give ourselves completely to God—holding nothing back. The Holy Spirit then sanctifies us "through and through," destroys the power of sin in our life, and enables us to live in a way that pleases God.

Other Christians teach that sanctification is a gradual process, with peaks and valleys, and won't be complete until we reach heaven.

## For the Record: 1 Thessalonians Abused

**Persecuting Jews.** People throughout the ages—including Crusaders, Nazis, and church leaders—have quoted Paul for biblical support in persecuting Jews. Paul described the Jews as evil people "who killed the Lord Jesus and the prophets and also drove us out. They displease God and are hostile to all men" (2:15, New International Version).

But Paul was a Jew, as was Jesus. Paul wasn't talking about all Jews—just those who attacked Jesus and his followers. And Paul certainly wasn't calling for retaliation. Christianity, as taught and practiced in New Testament times, was a faith of nonviolence, even in the face of attack (Matthew 5:39). (For more about persecution of the Jews, see John, page 306.)

# Bible Scenarios You Can Use

## 1. Living to please God (4:1–12)

**A**fter being run out of town by people who opposed his teaching, Paul writes a letter to those who accepted his message. Paul had been in Thessalonica for only a few weeks, which was long enough to start a small congregation but not long enough to teach the new believers anything more than the bare basics of the Christian faith.

Worried about this, Paul sends Timothy to check on the people. After getting a good report, Paul writes 1 Thessalonians, a letter of encouragement and instruction.

"God wants you to be holy," Paul says. By this, he doesn't mean perfect. He means so completely dedicated to God that others can see it in the way the believers live.

Paul gives the people of Thessalonica—and us—a few examples of what holy living looks like:

- "Don't be immoral."

- "Respect and honor your wife."

- "Don't be a slave of your desires."

- "Love each other."

- "Live quietly."

- "Mind your own business."

- "Work hard."

## 2. Life after death (4:13—5:11)

**T**he people of Thessalonica are anxious for Jesus to return, and seem worried about what will happen to believers who die before Jesus comes.

Paul assures them that Christians who die go to be with Jesus. "When God brings Jesus back again," Paul explains, "he will bring with him all who had faith in Jesus before they died" (4:14).

"All of us who are still alive," Paul says, "will be taken up into the clouds together with them to meet the Lord in the sky. From that time on we will all be with the Lord forever" (4:17).

Though Paul says no one knows when this will happen, he wants Christians to encourage one another with the good news that Jesus is coming again someday. Whether or not we die before that day comes, we'll live to see it.

In the meantime, we live to serve the One who died to serve us.

# 2 THESSALONIANS

## How to Wait for Jesus

Sometimes we've had it up to here, and all we want is out.

Out of the job, with it's abusive workload. Out of a relationship with someone who's favorite pastime is belittling us. Out of a home where kindness is bound and gagged.

Consider this: Imagine yourself in a city you've lived in all your life. Almost overnight, the people turn against you. It's because you did something they think is wrong. Now they hate you. They threaten you. They even commit violent acts against you. You'd want out.

That's what was going on in Thessalonica, Greece. Paul had come to town and converted some to Christianity. But to many Jews there, Christianity posed a threat to all that they believed. A mob of Christian-haters drove Paul out of town, but the Christians of Thessalonica had no place to go. This was their home.

Maybe that's why some Christians started obsessing about the return of Jesus. Paul said Jesus was coming back to set up his kingdom. Persecuted people of Thessalonica wanted Jesus to come right away. To feed their fantasy of quick escape to eternal bliss, some withdrew from the workaday world. But that meant to feed their bodies they needed to rely on the charity of Christians still at work in the world.

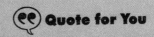 **Quote for You**

"May the Lord bring you into an ever deeper understanding of the love of God and the endurance that comes from Christ" (3:5, New Living Translation).

To the Christians still plugging away, Paul said he bragged about "how patient you are and how you keep on having faith, even though you are going through a lot of trouble and suffering" (1:4). To the others who disconnected themselves from the world and waited around for Jesus to come back, Paul said, "Follow our example. We didn't waste our time loafing" (3:7).

To all of us who've had it up to here, Paul would say don't give up. For between now and the return of Jesus—whenever that will be—there's a world of work to do.

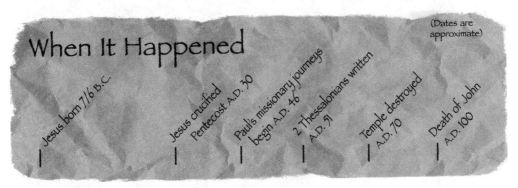

When It Happened

(Dates are approximate)

Jesus born 7/6 B.C.

Jesus crucified Pentecost A.D. 30

Paul's missionary journeys begin A.D. 46

2 Thessalonians written A.D. 51

Temple destroyed A.D. 70

Death of John A.D. 100

# Info You Can Use

## Background Notes

**Writer:** The letter begins and ends with claims that Paul wrote it. It starts by saying it's "from Paul, Silas, and Timothy" (1:1), but the first-person references throughout (such as "I" and "my") suggest Paul wrote it and politely mentions the associates ministering with him. The letter's ending supports this: "I always sign my letters as I am doing now: PAUL" (3:17).

Some Bible experts say clues in the letter suggest someone else wrote it—perhaps Timothy or one of Paul's other associates, writing on Paul's behalf and possibly after his death. The more formal writing style and the appearance of some new teachings about the Second Coming suggest this. Other experts say changes in the letter reflect the changing situation, not a change in writers.

**Time:** Because the two letters address the same topic—the Second Coming of Jesus—many Bible experts say they were probably written about the same time, perhaps a few months apart. Paul likely wrote them shortly after leaving Thessalonica, while staying in Corinth for two years (A.D. 50–52).

**Place:** Paul wrote to Christians in Thessalonica, a busy seaport town on a major road in northern Greece.

**Bottom-Line Summary:** During his second missionary journey, Paul becomes the first Christian missionary to set foot in Europe—taking the message about Jesus to Greece. One of the places he starts a new church is in Thessalonica, in northern Greece. Opposition by the Jews forces Paul to leave after just a few weeks.

The fledgling congregation he leaves behind is persecuted by their fellow townspeople. They're also confused about the Second Coming. Paul encouraged them and answered some of their questions in his first letter, written shortly after leaving them. But new problems crop up, perhaps just a few months later.

Excitement about the Lord's return has nearly consumed the believers. Part of the reason may be because of Paul's teaching while he was in town, his follow-up letter urging them to stay alert and ready for Jesus' return, and the persecution they wanted to end.

### Fascinating Fact

Despite Paul's plea against obsession with end times, many Christians are still captivated by it. As this book goes to press, five of the top ten best-selling Christian paperback fiction books are stories set in end times.

Many are so sure Jesus is coming any day that they see no reason to plant their crops, work in their shops, or take care of their houses.

Paul throws water on their apocalyptic fire. He says Christ's return may not be as near as they seem to think. Certain prophecies have to be fulfilled first. So he tells the Christians to get on with their lives, and to stay away from professing

Christians who hardly do anything more than talk about when Jesus is going to come back.

## Influential People

**Paul,** a traveling minister and founder of the church at Thessalonica. Paul's stern letter to the young church there shows that we shouldn't waste time dreaming about the return of Jesus. We have work to do. For people today preoccupied with the Second Coming, Paul's letter is reminiscent of what the angels told Jesus' disciples after Jesus ascended into heaven: "Why are you men from Galilee standing here and looking up into the sky?" (Acts 1:11). Jesus had just given them a job to do: "Tell everyone about me" (Acts 1:8). It's time to work, not to wait—to focus on helping this world, not enjoying the next.

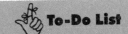

**To-Do List**

- "Never become tired of doing right" (3:13).

## Q&A

**What prophecies need to be fulfilled before Jesus returns?** It's unclear, because the prophecies Paul mentioned were vague and cloaked with mysterious terms.

"That day will not come until there is a great rebellion against God and the man of lawlessness is revealed. . . . He will position himself in the temple of God, claiming that he himself is God. . . . This evil man will come to do the work of Satan with counterfeit power and signs and miracles" (2:3–4, 9, New Living Translation).

What great rebellion? And who is the "man of lawlessness?" The people of Thessalonica apparently knew: "Don't you remember that I told you this while I was still with you?" (2:5).

But we don't know.

Guesses from Bible experts cover a broad range. The "man of lawlessness" might be an evil leader who is anti-Christ; opposed to everything Jesus represents. John refers to many antichrists (1 John 2:18). And history has been filled with them. Some experts guess this wicked man might actually be an evil spiritual entity.

Other experts suggest the phrase might be a code name for the Roman Empire, which tried to wipe out Christianity. Persecution of Christians could certainly qualify as a rebellion against God. So could Roman wars against the Jews. After the Jewish-Roman war that destroyed the temple in A.D. 70, the Romans put insignias of the emperor on the temple site—desecrating the sacred place with idol-like engraved images that are forbidden by Jewish law. Propaganda about that emperor—Vespasian—said he worked miracles.

Paul's intention, however, wasn't to toss out clues about when Jesus was coming back. On the contrary. By briefly quoting information from Jesus (Matthew 24), he was trying to get the people to stop dwelling on the Second Coming so they could get busy fulfilling the commission of Christ's First Coming.

**Red Flag Issues**

**Welfare.** Many people, Christians included, oppose welfare. They think it's abused, and that instead of helping needy people who can't work, it too often encourages lazy people who won't work.

At first pass, it looks like Paul might agree. He said, "If you don't work, you don't eat" (3:10). And he pleads with these people he calls loafers to "settle down and start working for a living" (3:12).

Paul, however, wasn't talking about the kinds of people on public welfare today. He was talking about professing Christians who decided to sit out the rest of their life because they thought Jesus would return any minute.

As for people in financial need and unable to work—widows, orphans, the sick, and refugees—Jewish law featured a welfare system. The needy got donations from the temple and from individuals, and were allowed to pick crops from corners of the fields at harvest time.

One of the Bible's most persistent requests—throughout the Old and New Testaments—is that God's people help those in need. Some people will abuse the system. But a flawed system is better than no system.

# Bible Scenario You Can Use

### 1. Preoccupied with Christ's Second Coming (2:1—3:15)

**P**eople in Thessalonica who become Christians pay a high price. They become targets of ridicule, harassment, and perhaps even the kind of mob violence that drove Paul out of town a few months earlier. Jews in the city consider Christianity a dangerous cult that teaches Jewish traditions are obsolete and that demeans God by claiming Jesus is his son.

Under this constant threat, the people naturally look to God for help. They remember Paul's teaching that Jesus will come again and set up his eternal kingdom, and many become obsessed with the Second Coming. They see it as their rescue—coming at any moment. Some are so certain that Jesus is coming any day that they quit their work.

In time, other Christians feel obligated to pick up the slack and help feed and care for these "people who just loaf around and won't do any work, except the work of a busybody."

Paul urges all the people to get on with their lives and to stop obsessing about the Second Coming. As for the people who bail out of their work responsibilities, Paul offers this rule: "If you don't work, you don't eat."

Many Christians are still obsessed with the Second Coming. Movies, television programs, best-selling books, sermons, and Sunday school series bear witness to the fact that we want to know exactly what's going to happen and when. But only God knows. Jesus told his disciples that even he didn't know when he'd be back (Matthew 24:36). Each day God gives us is a day to live to the fullest—helping others, spreading the good news about Jesus, and enjoying God's creation.

# 1 TIMOTHY

## People Are Watching Us

Have you ever walked into a store at a shopping mall, looked up at the ceiling to the tiny tinted domes that hide the shoplifter-gotcha video cameras, and waved?

You knew you were being watched, so you thought you'd say hello to the watcher.

That's what it's like to be a pastor, or any other church leader for that matter. The only difference is that the camera's always on. People are watching what you do, listening to what you say, and even analyzing what you don't do. Some may have mean motives and are looking for a chance to criticize. But most are watching because they believe you're a godly person—a walking, talking example of the kind of human being they should aspire to be.

Timothy was a pastor. Paul had assigned him to lead the church in Ephesus, a city along the Mediterranean coast in what is now Turkey. Afterward, Paul wrote Timothy. Drawing upon nearly 30 years of experience, Paul offered advice to help the young pastor succeed.

Paul gave practical tips: How to conduct worship services; how to minister to the young and old; and how to help impoverished widows. But perhaps his most notable advice was a description of what a church leader should look like. Paul used words like these:

- Kind
- Friendly to strangers
- Doesn't love money

The list goes on for several verses. The odd thing is that, although Paul said he was describing church leaders, his description applies to the rest of us as well.

People who want to be like Jesus will watch us. Some will follow us. So it's a good idea to be friendly, wave, and live our life as though we are beneath the camera.

## When It Happened

(Dates are approximate)

Jesus born 7/6 B.C.

Jesus crucified Pentecost A.D. 30

Paul's missionary journeys begin A.D. 46

1 Timothy written A.D. 63

Temple destroyed A.D. 70

Death of John A.D. 100

# Info You Can Use

 **Background Notes**

**Writer:** The letter is "From Paul" (1:1). It's in the New Testament because early Christian leaders believed the apostle wrote it.

Many scholars aren't so sure. That's because some of Paul's most important teachings are explained differently in this letter. For example, in Paul's other letters the word "faith" means a person's trusting relationship with Jesus. But here it means Christianity.

Because of this, many scholars speculate that 1 Timothy, as well as 2 Timothy and Titus, were written a generation or two after Paul. The writer wanted to address new problems the church faced by drawing from the spirit and authority of Paul, giving him credit. This was a common and accepted practice in ancient writing—the opposite of plagiarism. Scholars who say Paul wrote the letter explain that the differences in teaching show he wrote it later in his life.

**Time:** It's not clear when Paul wrote the letter. Paul said after he and Timothy visited Ephesus, he assigned Timothy to stay there (1:3). But the travel notes in Acts say both men left Ephesus (Acts 20:4).

This suggests Paul wrote the letter after the events described in Acts—the book that ends with Paul arrested, awaiting trial in Rome, and presumably executed shortly thereafter. But some Bible experts say it might not have happened that way. Instead, Paul may have won his freedom in about A.D. 62 and made another missionary trip, during which he assigned Timothy to Ephesus. In this case, Paul may have written the letter in about A.D. 63, just before he was arrested again and sent to Rome. This second arrest, as the theory goes, led to his execution in about A.D. 64–67, during Nero's persecution of Christians.

**Place:** Ephesus was a major port city and capital of the Roman province of Asia, along the Mediterranean coast in what is now western Turkey. Ephesus is thought to have been the world's fourth largest city in Paul's day. The estimated population was 250,000.

Paul spent more than three years establishing the Ephesus church—more time than at any other church.

**Bottom-Line Summary:** During one of Paul's missionary journeys to start churches, he arrives in Ephesus. When it comes time to move on, he decides to leave behind his associate, Timothy, to pastor the church. Timothy is a logical choice. He's from the same Greek culture as Ephesus, having been raised in Lystra, about 300 miles east of Ephesus. And he understands the Jews because his mother and grandmother are both Jewish.

Sometime later, perhaps while Paul is in Greece, he writes to Timothy. It's a pastor-to-pastor letter, giving guidance on many issues facing these first-generation churches. The topics include how to conduct worship services, how to choose church leaders, how to minister to the poor, and even how to minister to the rich.

## Influential People

**Paul,** a traveling minister, covered about 10,000 miles planting churches throughout the Roman Empire. Though Paul's no longer in Ephesus, the people and their minister are on his mind. So he keeps in touch, writing an encouraging and helpful letter. Many of us are far from those we love. But we can keep involved in their lives by staying in contact through phone calls, e-mail, letters, and visits.

**Timothy,** one of Paul's most devoted associates, worked alongside Paul in Turkey, Greece, and Italy. He handled tough assignments, such as risking danger to deliver letters to persecuted Christians in Thessalonica. He helped Paul start many churches, including those in Corinth and Ephesus. But eventually, it came time for the student to become the teacher. God wants all of us to use our skills and gifts to help the church grow.

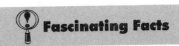

### Fascinating Facts

Timothy was half Jewish, with a Gentile father and a Jewish mother, although uncircumcised. Paul convinced him to get circumcised so the Jews would be more receptive to his ministry. God had ordered all Jewish males circumcised as a reminder of their devotion to him (Genesis 17:10–11). Uncircumcised Jewish males were shunned as pagans.

Paul's two letters to Timothy and one to Titus are called the Pastoral Letters because Paul gives these associates advice on how to pastor churches.

## Q&A

**How can a woman be saved by having children?** It's a mystery what Paul had in mind when he said, "women will be saved by having children" (2:15).

Some Bible experts say this is a reference to Jesus' birth, because the original language refers to salvation "through *the* childbirth." But in the context of what Paul has just said—that women should take a low profile in the church—other Bible experts say he's probably urging women in Ephesus to fulfill their traditional role as homemaker, wife, and mother—and that by doing this, as a ministry, they will be serving God.

Some Bible experts say there was probably a problem among the women believers in Ephesus that prodded Paul to offer this unusual advice. Perhaps some prominent women were becoming so involved in church work that their families were suffering. Though the meaning is unclear to us, Timothy probably knew exactly what Paul meant.

## Red Flag Issues

**Women in the church.** Some denominations refuse to let women take leadership roles in the church.

One of the key Bible passages they quote is 1 Timothy 2:11–12, "Women should listen and learn quietly and submissively. I do not let women teach men or have authority over them" (New Living Translation).

Bible experts, however, point out that in other situations Paul recognized the authority of women church leaders (Romans 16:1–3), some of whom were prophets (Acts 2:17), and one of whom may have been an apostle (Romans 16:7).

It could be that in churches with problems among women—such as in Ephesus and Corinth—Paul restricted women. But where there was no such problem, there were no such restrictions.

As far as Paul was concerned, job one for each local church was that the people be united in fulfilling their mission of spreading the news about Jesus. Anything that became an obstacle to this—such as debates over a woman's role in the male-dominated society—would get temporarily brushed aside. Eventually, as the gospel message of compassion and mutual submission settled in, Paul may have figured that equality would emerge.

As Paul put it in another letter, "Faith in Christ Jesus is what makes each of you equal with each other, whether you are a Jew or a Greek, a slave or a free person, a man or a woman" (Galatians 3:28). (For more on this topic see Acts, page 314, and 1 Corinthians, page 330.)

**Fashion for women.** Some churches frown on women wearing expensive clothing and jewelry. In Puritan New England, the court prohibited women from buying dresses with gold, silver, lace, or embroidery. In the early 1900s, some cities required women's bathing suits to be no higher than six inches above the knee—and officials with tape measures enforced the law. A generation ago, even makeup spurred some fiery sermons.

Today, some Christians—most notably the Amish—take their fashion cue from Paul: "I would like for women to wear modest and sensible clothes. They should not have fancy hairdos, or wear expensive clothes, or put on jewelry made of gold or pearls" (2:9).

Nowadays, that advice could also apply to men, and to dressed-for-success ministers.

Paul probably singled out women because the ladies of his day who were flashy dressers were considered sexually immoral. Today, we can often identify prostitutes on the street by the way they dress.

## 👆 To-Do List

- "Keep on reading the Scriptures in worship, and don't stop preaching and teaching" (4:13).

- "Don't correct an older man. Encourage him, as you would your own father" (5:1).

- "Take care of any widow who is really in need. But if a widow has children or grandchildren, they should learn to serve God by taking care of her, as she once took care of them. This is what God wants them to do" (5:3–4).

- "People who don't take care of their relatives, and especially their own families, have given up their faith. They are worse than someone who doesn't have faith in the Lord" (5:8).

Paul likely wouldn't have trouble with believers today wanting to look nice when they go to church, though there's a point when nice becomes garish. Making fashion statements and collecting show-stopping stares isn't why we go to church. Besides, if we load up on expensive finery and tailored threads, how would the poorer folks feel sitting next to us? It might actually drive them away from the one who deserves to be the center of attention: Jesus.

**Drinking alcoholic beverages.** Though many churches ask its members not to drink alcoholic beverages, Paul told Timothy the opposite. "Take a little wine to help your stomach trouble and the other illnesses you always have" (5:23).

Recent medical studies suggest that light drinking of wine can protect against heart attack, stroke, high cholesterol, and other health problems. Yet many Christians abstain because of their church's teaching or because of problems they know drinking can cause—such as automobile accidents and alcoholism. (For more, see Proverbs, page 151, and John, page 306.)

## For the Record: 1 Timothy Abused

**Persecuting Catholics.** Protestants have sometimes treated Roman Catholics with anger and violence. Protestants have charged, for example, that it's wrong to require priests and nuns to never marry, and it's wrong to order people to eat fish instead of other meat on Fridays.

To back up their charge, Protestants pointed to something Paul said: "Liars will forbid people to marry or to eat certain foods" (4:2–3).

Paul, however, was talking about heretics who came to Ephesus, teaching that anything physical is bad. These false teachers (later known as Gnostics— from a Greek word that means "knowledge") said that the more we deprive ourselves of physical pleasures, such as food and sex, the more spiritual and holy we become. Paul, however, taught that God's creation was good, and to be enjoyed.

Unlike these ancient heretics, priests and nuns voluntarily take a vow of celibacy to devote themselves more fully to ministry, unencumbered by the demands of a family. Though the Bible never requires this of believers, Catholics have required it of their clergy. Catholic clergy are following the practice of Jesus, who remained celibate and who said some people "stay single in order to serve God" (Matthew 19:12). Paul also advocated celibacy as a lifestyle: "Here is my advice for people who have never been married and for widows. You should stay single, just as I am. But if you don't have enough self-control, then go ahead and get married. After all, it is better to marry than to burn with desire" (1 Corinthians 7:8–9). Catholics today are re-addressing this issue in regards to their clergy.

Eating fish on Fridays is no longer required among Catholics, though some Eastern Orthodox churches still practice it. This tradition came from the early Christian practice of fasting on Fridays—the day Jesus was crucified. In time, the fast was limited to meat—considered a luxury in ancient times, as chocolate is today. Fish, however, was easy to catch. So allowing the people to eat fish assured that even the poor could have something to eat.

# Bible Scenarios You Can Use

## 1. How to pray (2:1–18)

**P**aul has assigned his closest friend, Timothy, to stay in Ephesus and pastor the church. Continuing his travels, Paul writes to offer Timothy encouragement and practical advice about running the church.

"I ask you to pray for everyone," Paul writes. "Ask God to help and bless them all, and tell God how thankful you are for each of them." Paul adds that the church should pray for their political leaders, "so that we may live quiet and peaceful lives."

Christians often pray with hands raised. So Paul says he wants the people to "lift innocent hands toward heaven and pray, without being angry or arguing."

Prayer isn't a time to make speeches or scold others. It's a time to talk to God, bringing our requests and thanks. Prayer changes things. It can bring peace in troubled political times. And it can move a mountain of problems out of our way (Mark 11:23).

## 2. Traits of a church leader (3:1–12)

**C**hurch leaders, Paul writes, "must have a good reputation and be faithful in marriage. They must be self-controlled, sensible, well-behaved, friendly to strangers, and able to teach. They must not be heavy drinkers or troublemakers. Instead, they must be kind and gentle and not love money."

Churches sometimes select leaders for the same reasons secular companies do: looks, charisma, and connections. More important than these, says the experienced Paul, is what prospective leaders believe, how they treat others, and how they behave in private.

Church leaders who fit the qualifications and do their job well, Paul adds, "should be paid well" (5:17, New Living Translation).

## 3. Advice for the rich and the would-be rich (6:1–10, 17)

**"P**eople who want to be rich fall into all sorts of temptations and traps," Paul writes. "The love of money causes all kinds of trouble. Some people want money so much that they have given up their faith and caused themselves a lot of pain."

Instead of craving money, Paul says, we should learn to be content with what we have. "We didn't bring anything into this world, and we won't take anything with us when we leave."

Paul tells Timothy, "Warn the rich people of this world not to be proud or to trust in wealth that is easily lost. Tell them to have faith in God, who is rich and blesses us with everything we need to enjoy life."

# 2 TIMOTHY

## How to Know What Matters Most

Watch someone you love die. Listen to what they say. Like no other experience on this planet, it'll reorganize your priorities for the rest of your life.

In a moment—with a single scene or a single sentence—a lifetime of brainwashing by marketers will vanish. These marketers are the folks who've convinced some of us that what matters most are the things that matter least: Our net worth, our career path, the size of our home, the brand of our car, the design of our clothes, the shape of our body.

To discover what really matters most, we can read Paul's last letter to his dear friend Timothy, a young man the apostle said is "like a dear child to me" (1:2). As he writes, Paul's in prison and about to die at the hand of a Roman executioner. It hurts to read this letter. It feels as though we're intruding into a deeply personal moment—as though we've stepped into a room to hear a dying father say goodbye to his son.

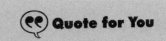

**Quote for You**

"If we die with him [Jesus], we will also live with him" (2:11, New Living Translation).

What we hear is that only two things matter most to Paul:

- His faith in God; "I have been faithful" (4:7).

- His loved ones; "Come to see me as soon as you can" (4:9).

Ring any bells? Does it sound at all like what Jesus said were the two most important laws of life—to love God and to love others?

We may regret plenty of things when we die, but we won't regret either of these.

When It Happened

(Dates are approximate)

Jesus born 7/6 B.C.

Jesus crucified Pentecost A.D. 30

Paul's missionary journeys begin A.D. 46

2 Timothy written A.D. 67

Temple destroyed A.D. 70

Death of John A.D. 100

# Info You Can Use

## Background Notes

**Writer:** The letter is "From Paul, an apostle of Christ Jesus" (1:1).

Some Bible experts say this letter, as well as 1 Timothy and Titus, may have been written by someone else. For reasons why, see the "Writer" section of 1 Timothy, page 374. Other experts argue that the deeply personal nature of this letter confirms what early church leaders said: Paul wrote it.

**Time:** It's unclear when Paul wrote the letter, though many Bible experts say it was probably about A.D. 67, during Nero's persecution of Christians.

The Book of Acts says Paul was imprisoned in Rome about A.D. 60, and was held for two years. But the book ends with Paul awaiting trial—never saying what happened to him.

One popular theory is that the Romans released Paul. Afterward, Paul made another missionary journey—this time to Spain, which is where he told Roman Christians he wanted to go (Romans 15:24). After Spain, Paul returned to Rome during Nero's persecution of Christians. This persecution started in A.D. 64 and continued until Nero died in A.D. 68. In Rome, Paul was arrested again and executed.

**Place:** Paul writes from prison in Rome (1:17; 2:9). He's writing to his dearest friend, Timothy, who's pastoring a church about 1,000 miles away—in Ephesus, a city along the western coast of what is now Turkey.

One of the oldest structures in Rome is Mamertime Prison, a tiny dungeon that was carved out of solid rock 600 years before Christ was born. Early Christian writers said the Romans kept Paul in this dungeon until they beheaded him with a sword.

> ### Fascinating Fact
>
> Paul dreamed of ministering in Spain (Romans 15:24). Though the Bible never reports that he made it to Spain, a first-century church leader from Rome said he did. Clement wrote that before Paul died, he went to the "extreme limit of the west." Spain was the western border of the Roman Empire. Eusebius, a church leader in the A.D. 300s, wrote that after a second visit to Rome, Paul "finished his life with martyrdom."

**Bottom-Line Summary:** Paul is in a Roman prison, expecting to be executed. All his associates have left him, with the exception of a physician named Luke—who is thought to have later written the Gospel of Luke and the Book of Acts. Cold, lonely, and chained like a dangerous criminal, Paul writes what is probably his last surviving letter.

He addresses it to Timothy, an associate he has known for perhaps more than 15 years and whom Paul says is like a son to him. Paul breaks the grim news about what's happening, but says it's okay. He assures Timothy that he has stayed true to God and will soon be rewarded in heaven.

Paul asks Timothy to come as soon as possible, to be with him. He also asks Timothy to bring him a coat (winter is coming) and some scrolls (possibly Bible books to comfort him or blank pages on which to write).

Perhaps because he's afraid Timothy won't be able to make the thousand-mile journey in time, Paul takes this opportunity to encourage and instruct him one last time. Don't be ashamed of Jesus, Paul says—bold words if these are the years Nero is feeding Christians to lions. As a follower of Christ, Paul adds, Timothy can expect to suffer. But if he dies, just as Christ died, Timothy can expect to live, just as Christ lives.

## Influential People

**Paul,** a traveling minister, planted churches throughout the Roman Empire. In jail and facing imminent execution, he stayed loyal to Jesus. Though most of us won't endure death because of our faith, we may endure other hardships because of our commitment to truth and goodness. Paul's letter is a reminder that the temporary price we pay is well worth the everlasting prize we'll receive.

**Timothy,** one of Paul's most devoted traveling companions and dearest friends. Paul called on Timothy to come and be with him in his final days because he loved and trusted Timothy, and was certain he would help. We have a chance to be like Timothy to fellow Christians around the world who suffer because of their faith—whether they are being killed in countries that hate Christianity, or whether they are colleagues passed over for a promotion because they won't cheat others for the benefit of the company.

### To-Do List

- "Never be ashamed to tell others about our Lord" (1:8, New Living Translation).

- "Christ Jesus is kind, and you must let him make you strong" (2:1).

- "Run from temptations that capture young people" (2:22).

- "Be faithful, loving, and easy to get along with" (2:22).

- "Be humble when you correct people who oppose you" (2:25).

## Q&A

**How do we know which religious teachings are correct?** Paul warned Timothy that people would distort Christian teachings. Instead of telling the truth, they'd tell eager listeners "only what they are itching to hear" (4:3).

What people itch to hear is that selfish desire, getting rich, getting even, and getting sexually intimate with another person's spouse are all okay. And throughout the ages, religious teachers have come along who said these are perfectly acceptable. Many have gotten rich by creating distorted religious ideas that people are itching to hear.

"Keep on being faithful to what you were taught and to what you believed," Paul said (3:14). The teachings Paul was talking about were those Timothy learned from what is now the Bible—the Old Testament—along with the stories of Jesus and the letters of Paul and other early church leaders.

We know a wall is straight by holding a plumb line next to it. We know a foundation is level by laying a carpenter's level on it. And we know a religious belief is right by comparing it to the teachings in the Bible.

# Bible Scenarios You Can Use

## 1. How the Bible helps us (3:14–17)

"**T**imothy, you are like a dear child to me," Paul writes shortly before his execution (1:2). Tenderly, the apostle offers the best advice he can: Don't be ashamed of Jesus, be a good soldier of the faith, and study the Bible.

"Since childhood, you have known the Holy Scriptures that are able to make you wise enough to have faith in Christ Jesus and be saved," Paul says. "Everything in the Scriptures is God's Word. All of it is useful for teaching and helping people and for correcting them and showing them how to live. The Scriptures train God's servants to do all kinds of good deeds."

Paul was talking about what Christians now call the Old Testament. But within a few decades of Paul's death, Christians were counting the stories of Jesus and letters of the apostles among Scripture—as part of God's revelation to humanity. Christians read them in worship, lived by the teachings, and passed them on to their children.

Today, we have many versions of the Bible. Some are hard to understand, such as the King James Version, written about the time of Shakespeare. Others are as easy to read as the newspaper, such as the Contemporary English Version. But all of the many popular versions contain exactly what we need to find salvation that lasts forever.

## 2. Dead man talking (4:6–8)

"**N**ow the time has come for me to die," Paul writes.

"My life is like a drink offering being poured out on the altar. I have fought well. I have finished the race, and I have been faithful. So a crown will be given to me for pleasing the Lord. He judges fairly, and on the day of judgment he will give a crown to me and to everyone else who wants him to appear with power."

When we come to the end of our life, if we have time to reflect on it as Paul did, we'll probably have plenty of regrets. Perhaps we'll be sorry we didn't spend more time with our loved ones. We may wish we had been a little more patient and a little more kind. But as we stand on the breath's edge of death, we won't regret knowing Jesus.

We can lose everything—our money, our family, even our life. But even then—with nothing to hold in our hands—we can say with Paul, "I have kept the faith." And that faith is all we need to sustain us in this life and to open the door into the next.

# TITUS

## How to Change a Human

Want to know what much of the world thinks of you as a citizen of this particular country? Hear the word of a Cretan.

He's Epimenides, a poet from five centuries before Christ, describing the people of his own nation: "The people of Crete are all liars; they are cruel animals and lazy gluttons" (1:12, New Living Translation). Paul quotes him in a letter to Titus, who is ministering in Crete. Paul adds that he agrees with Epimenides.

Cross Crete out of that sentence, substitute our nation, and you've got the prevailing international take on us. We make promises we don't keep. With a few exceptions, we do nothing to oppose tyrants who abuse millions, if those tyrants support our economic interests. And here at home we do shoddy work: making tires that spontaneously explode, sports utility vehicles that roll like a ball, and computer software with more bugs than a rotten log.

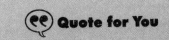

### Quote for You

"God washed us by the power of the Holy Spirit. He gave us new birth and a fresh beginning" (3:5).

Granted, calling all of us liars, cruel animals, and lazy gluttons is an overstatement. Likely, so was the poet's line about Crete. But when we take a slow, hard look at ourselves, we'll see the truth on which the caricature is built. There's more lying than we want to see, more hard-heartedness, and more time wasted—nationally and internationally.

Changing the behavior of our nation and world seems impossible. Paul must have figured the job of changing Crete seemed just as impossible to Titus. Perhaps that's why he reminded him, "We used to be stupid, disobedient, and foolish, as well as slaves of all sorts of desires and pleasures. We were evil and jealous. Everyone hated us, and we hated everyone" (3:3).

God changed Paul and Titus. And he changes the world, one person at a time.

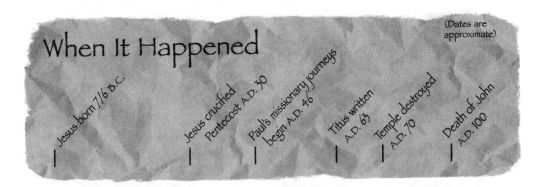

## When It Happened

(Dates are approximate)

Jesus born 7/6 B.C.

Jesus crucified, Pentecost A.D. 30

Paul's missionary journeys begin A.D. 46

Titus written A.D. 63

Temple destroyed A.D. 70

Death of John A.D. 100

# Info You Can Use

## Background Notes

**Writer:** The letter is "From Paul, a servant of God and an apostle of Jesus Christ" (1:1).

Some Bible experts in recent centuries have suggested someone else wrote this letter, as well as the two letters to Timothy. For reasons why, see "Writer," 1 Timothy, page 374. Early church leaders, however, were convinced Paul wrote all three letters.

**Time:** There's no solid clue when Paul wrote the Book of Titus. The only hint comes in the fact that Acts—the book that chronicles Paul's travels—never places Paul in Crete. But this letter says Paul started churches there, and then left Titus behind to finish the job of getting the churches established (1:5).

This suggests Paul wrote the letter after the events reported in Acts, perhaps in about A.D. 63, after being released from imprisonment in Rome. That's about the same time he likely wrote 1 Timothy, a letter that contains much of the same advice to Timothy, who's pastoring in Ephesus.

**Place:** Paul addresses the letter to Titus, who is on a temporary ministry assignment on the island of Crete, about 100 miles south of Greece. The island stretches about 150 miles east to west, and roughly 35 miles north to south, making it about the size of Rhode Island.

Paul plans to send a replacement for Titus within a few months, so Titus can join Paul for the winter in Nicopolis, a city in western Greece.

**Bottom-Line Summary:** During what seems to be a fourth missionary journey that isn't mentioned in Acts, Paul visits the Mediterranean island of Crete and starts churches in several towns. Paul feels compelled to continue his journey, but he leaves behind Titus, one of his closest friends and ministry associates.

Titus' assignment is "to do what has been left undone and to appoint leaders for the churches in each town" (1:5).

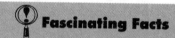

### Fascinating Facts

A thousand years before Paul, Crete was famous for its schools of architecture and engineering. Greeks went there to study. But Crete gradually developed a bad reputation by harboring pirates and mercenaries.

The church was well established in Crete. There are about half a million people living on the island now, and about nine out of ten consider themselves members of the Orthodox Church of Crete, a branch of the Greek Orthodox Church.

Sometime after Paul leaves, he writes Titus a short letter of encouragement and instruction. The letter reads much like Paul's letter to Timothy, whom Paul left in Ephesus to direct the church. Paul tells Titus what qualifications to look for in a church leader. He gives brief directions on how to minister to different age groups, perhaps hitting only the highlights of what he had said in person earlier, before leaving Crete.

Paul closes by telling Titus not to get caught up in arguments with people opposed to Christianity. And he asks Titus to remind the people to be good citizens of Crete by obeying their rulers, and to be good citizens of God's kingdom by performing acts of kindness.

# Influential People

**Paul,** a traveling minister, covered some 10,000 miles in perhaps 30 years of ministry, and started countless churches throughout the Roman Empire. His tireless work is a reminder of the Great Commission that Jesus gave all his followers: "Tell everyone about me in Jerusalem, in Judea, in Samaria, and everywhere in the world" (Acts 1:8).

**Titus,** one of Paul's associates in ministry, is appointed by Paul to organize the churches on Crete. Bringing a religion of goodness to a people well known for their bad reputation must have seemed nearly impossible to Titus. Yet his willingness to accept the challenge is a tribute to his confidence in God's power to change lives. It's also a reminder that God still changes lives today.

# Key Ideas You Need to Know

**Grace.** This isn't a word most people use much, except to ask someone to say "grace," a prayer before the meal. But grace, as it's used in the Bible, means God's expression of love for us. It's unearned love, kindness, or favor. Grace often refers to God's willingness to forgive us and save us when we do nothing to deserve it, other than to ask him.

Paul described grace this way for Titus: "God our Savior showed us how good and kind he is. He saved us because of his mercy, and not because of any good things that we have done" (3:4–5).

# Q&A

**Should we obey corrupt political leaders?** "Remind your people," Paul tells Titus, "to obey the rulers and authorities and not to be rebellious" (3:1).

We immediately think of worst-case scenarios, such as Hitler and some of the

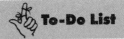
**To-Do List**

- "Always set a good example for others" (2:7).

- "Use clean language that no one can criticize" (2:8).

- "He [Jesus] gave himself to rescue us from everything that is evil and to make our hearts pure. He wanted us to be his own people and to be eager to do right" (2:14).

- "Always be ready to do something helpful and not say cruel things or argue" (3:1–2).

- "Be gentle and kind to everyone" (3:2).

- "Warn troublemakers once or twice. Then don't have anything else to do with them. You know that their minds are twisted, and their own sins show how guilty they are" (3:10–11).

- "Our people should learn to spend their time doing something useful and worthwhile" (3:14).

more recent, butcher-rulers. What would Paul say to Christians living in evil societies run by evil people? And what would he say to those of us in supposedly Christian nations, when our leaders make laws that are unjust?

We can't be sure. But we know this: Paul was writing to believers ruled by Rome—an empire that sometimes brutally imposed its will on nations throughout the Middle East. Paul wasn't interested mainly in social reform. He wanted spiritual reform, perhaps understanding that it would eventually produce social reform.

Paul's advice doesn't mean we should ban political activism, remain silent while corrupt leaders ignore the law, and do nothing but watch while tyrants exploit the helpless. Paul is said to have died opposing Rome's policies against Christians. And Jesus' apostles took a stand against the Jewish high council's order to stop teaching about Jesus: "Do you think God wants us to obey you or to obey him? We cannot keep quiet about what we have seen and heard" (Acts 4:19–20).

When our leaders intrude into God's business and try to convince us that something morally wrong is right, we're to obey God. For example, our leaders may pass laws that hurt the poor and abandon the sick, but as Christians, we can individually reach out to the needy. And as members of a free society, we can work to change bad laws.

**Why didn't Paul order Christian slave owners to free their slaves?** See Philemon, page 391.

# Bible Scenario You Can Use

### 1. Live as a good Christian and citizen (2:1—3)

**T**itus, on the island of Crete, has a daunting challenge. He's to find leaders for the churches he helped Paul start earlier, and get the new believers established in the faith.

The job is daunting because the people of Crete have a horrible reputation that Paul warns Titus is well earned. One of Crete's own writers said they're all lazy, liars, and greedy (1:12).

Paul advises Titus to start by selecting church leaders who have a solid reputation and a friendly disposition. These should be people who agree with Paul's teaching. This teaching emphasizes that salvation comes through faith in Jesus—not through obeying Jewish laws.

Next, Paul describes what kind of people should make up the congregations. Paul gives upbeat traits that may not even closely resemble new believers at the beginning of their spiritual journey, but it's clear Paul sees these traits as attainable goals. The older men should have faith, love, and patience that never fail. The older women "must not gossip or be slaves of wine." The younger women should be "sensible and kind, as well as a good homemaker, who puts her husband first." And the young men should develop "self-control in everything."

People of all ages, Paul says, should be good citizens and respect their rulers. But they should also be good Christians, and follow the teachings of Jesus. They're to be helpful instead of cruel, peacemakers instead of troublemakers, and kind instead of vindictive.

Crete's reputation wasn't much different from ours in this nation. Like ancient Crete, we could quote our own writers to support the charge. But God calls us to change our reputation. Though we can't be responsible for an entire nation, we can be responsible for ourselves. And one person can influence many others for the better.

# PHILEMON

## Getting Along in the Church

It's more important for Christians to get along with each other than it is for slaves to be free.

That's hard to swallow, especially in light of what we know about the horrors of slavery. But it's Paul's message in this letter.

He talked a runaway slave—Onesimus—into returning to his master, Philemon. That's how this book came to be in the Bible. It's a letter Paul had Onesimus personally deliver to the slave owner—a letter asking Philemon to mercifully welcome his slave home as a Christian brother.

The idea seems so incredibly naïve. Runaway slaves were often killed or beaten, but Paul sent Onesimus back to that very real possibility.

Why? The answer starts with this fact: Philemon was a church leader in Colossae. The church met in Philemon's house.

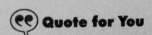 **Quote for You**

"I want your act of kindness to come from your heart, and not be something you feel forced to do" (14).

As an apostle, the highest office in the church, Paul was Philemon's spiritual leader. Paul could have ordered Philemon to free Onesimus and then invited the slave to join him as a ministry associate. Paul told the slave owner as much, but quickly added, "I won't do anything unless you agree to it first" (14).

But if Paul had acted without Philemon's approval, he would have been acting like a slave owner himself—ordering Philemon to do something against his will. Instead, Paul treated Philemon with the same respect he wanted Philemon to show Onesimus. Paul gave Philemon the freedom to make his own choice—something he hoped Philemon would do for Onesimus.

Maybe the reason Paul put such a high priority on Christians getting along is because he knew how much we can accomplish when we're united—and how much damage we can do when we turn on one another.

When It Happened

(Dates are approximate)

Jesus born 7/6 B.C.

Jesus crucified Pentecost A.D. 30

Paul's missionary journeys begin A.D. 46

Philemon written A.D. 60

Temple destroyed A.D. 70

Death of John A.D. 100

# Info You Can Use

## Background Notes

**Writer:** This short letter is "From Paul, who is in jail for serving Christ Jesus, and from Timothy" (1). Paul, however, is doing the writing. That's clear because he speaks in the first person and promises to pay back anything the runaway slave stole to finance his escape: "With my own hand I write: I, PAUL, WILL PAY YOU BACK" (19).

**Time:** It's unknown when Paul wrote the letter. Some ancient manuscripts add a note saying Paul wrote from Rome during his two-year imprisonment, which began in about A.D. 60.

Some scholars doubt this, arguing that it would have been hard for a runaway slave to travel the 1,000 miles from Colossae to Rome. They suggest Paul may have written several years earlier, perhaps from an unrecorded imprisonment in Ephesus, which is about 100 miles west of Colossae.

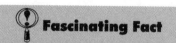

**Fascinating Fact**

Slave Onesimus may have become Bishop Onesimus. There was such a church leader in Ephesus about 50 years after Paul. If Paul wrote the letters of Ephesians, Colossians, and Philemon during his Roman imprisonment—as many scholars believe—Onesimus would have met the people of Ephesus on his way home to Colossae.

**Place:** Paul addressed his letter to Philemon and the congregation that met in his home. Philemon lived in Colossae, a city in what is now western Turkey.

Though the Bible never says Paul visited Colossae, the church was apparently started by an associate minister Paul sent there: Epaphras (Colossians 1:7). When Paul wrote Philemon, pastor Epaphras was in jail with him (23).

**Bottom-Line Summary:** A runaway slave named Onesimus meets Paul. Onesimus converts to Christianity, or perhaps had become a Christian earlier while working in the home of Colossian church leader Philemon. The church of Colossae meets in Philemon's home. (Church buildings weren't constructed until the A.D. 300s, after Rome legalized Christianity.)

Paul convinces Onesimus to go home. In so doing, Paul backs up his teachings elsewhere that say slaves should obey their masters.

But Paul also backs up the rest of his teachings—the part that says masters should treat their slaves with kindness and respect. He does this by sending Onesimus home with a letter for Philemon. The letter urges Philemon to welcome Onesimus home as a brother in Christ. Paul also strongly hints that he would like Onesimus freed to work with him as an associate minister. Then Paul promises to visit Philemon soon—a way of saying he intends to follow up on his letter.

## Influential People

**Paul,** a traveling minister, started churches throughout the Roman Empire and served as leader of the churches. Paul's decision to send a Christian runaway slave back to the slave's Christian master was a hard decision, but one based on a solid principle: Christian unity is essential. When we understand the price Paul asked the slave to pay for this principle, we'll be less inclined to bicker over comparatively unimportant matters, such as the remodeling of the church or the style of music for worship services.

**Philemon,** a Christian, owned the slave, Onesimus. Colossians met for church services in his house. The tone of Paul's letter to him (with compliments, hints, peer pressure tactics, and subtle warnings) suggested Paul thought the church leader might need some gentle pressure to convince him to do the right thing. Sometimes we may need to bring some pressure to bear on fellow Christians to convince them to get with the program—especially when the program involves the well being of others.

**Onesimus,** a Christian runaway slave, takes Paul's advice and returns to his Christian slave master. The faith Onesimus showed in his spiritual mentor is a depth of faith hard for those of us in an independent-minded culture to understand. Onesimus' faith reminds us that there are issues in life more important than our personal agenda.

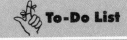

**To-Do List**

- "Show kindness" (10, New Living Translation). *This is Paul's instruction about how slave owner Philemon was to treat his runaway slave, Onesimus. Roman culture understood Philemon was wronged and had every right to punish the slave, but Paul called for kindness instead of revenge.*

 **Q&A**

**Why didn't Paul order Christian slave owners to free their slaves?** "Tell slaves always to please their owners by obeying them in everything," Paul wrote to Titus. "Slaves must not talk back to their owners or steal from them. They must be completely honest and trustworthy. Then everyone will show great respect for what is taught about God our Savior" (Titus 2:9–10).

Paul said much the same to the Christians at Onesimus' hometown church of Colossae and to the Ephesians (Colossians 3:22; Ephesians 6:5–6).

Here, in his letter to Philemon, Paul backs up his words with actions by sending the runaway home. In that ancient culture, so dependant on slavery, how could Paul have done otherwise and still kept the world's focus on Jesus? To imagine what would have happened if Paul had taught abolition, think about the Civil War. The story of Jesus would have gotten lost in the social upheaval.

For Paul, physical freedom took second place to spiritual freedom. Job one was to spread the teachings of Jesus. If Christians got that job done, unjust social institutions would crumble.

Paul wasn't interested in starting a slave revolt. He wanted to change people's hearts, which is where lasting change begins. Though the Bible doesn't say if Philemon freed his slave, given the content of Paul's letter—which was to be read aloud in Philemon's church—it's hard to imagine him doing otherwise.

Imagine yourself as Philemon. The congregation watches you as someone reads aloud from Paul's letter: "Sending Onesimus back to you makes me very sad. I would like to keep him here with me. . . . But I won't do anything unless you agree to it first. I want your act of kindness to come from your heart, and not be something you feel forced to do" (12–14).

# Bible Scenario You Can Use

### 1. Sending a runaway slave home (1–25)

**O**nesimus lives with his master, Philemon, a church leader in the city of Colossae. When Onesimus gets a chance to run for his freedom, he takes it.

On the road he meets Paul, who's recognized as the spiritual leader of churches throughout the Roman Empire. Paul's position on slavery is well established in several of his letters. He teaches that slaves should obey their masters, and that masters should treat their slaves with kindness and respect.

Paul advises Onesimus to go back to his master. Had Paul not been in jail at the time, he likely would have gone with Onesimus. Instead, he sends the slave home with a letter for Philemon and a promise to visit as soon as possible.

In the letter, Paul says that sending Onesimus back makes him sad. Paul knows that Roman law would allow Philemon to execute the runaway slave. But Paul pleads for Philemon to welcome Onesimus back—not as a slave, but as a brother. Paul even hints that he wants Onesimus freed: "I would like to keep him here with me, where he could take your place in helping me."

Paul vows to repay Philemon for anything Onesimus may have taken to finance his escape. "Get a room ready for me," Paul says, in a promise to come and see how things work out.

It's natural to want to run from our problems—to avoid troublesome relatives or to silently look for another job rather than risk a frank talk with our supervisor. But respectful confrontations are usually worth the trouble because they get important words spoken and important emotions released. This can produce healthy changes. And even if we agree to disagree, or to part company, we can do so in a spirit of mutual respect. And even then, the words we speak may plant the seeds for good changes in the future.

In some cases—as with Onesimus—people need the help of a third person to resolve problems. That was Paul's role, and sometimes it may need to be our role.

# HEBREWS

## For Christians About to Quit

There are plenty of reasons Christians leave the church.

Hypocrisy in the church drives many away. But one seasoned believer whom the author knows explained why she stays in spite of hypocrisy: "I'd rather go to church with a few hypocrites than go to hell with them all."

We can gradually wander, like sheep nibbling their way toward danger.

We can dive headlong into a temptation that swallows us whole: money, sex, drugs.

When the writer of Hebrews penned this letter, Jewish Christians were dropping out of the faith for one main reason: to return to their Jewish religion.

Some probably missed the traditions they had grown up with: Jewish holidays, the sounds of the synagogue, and the sense of security from following the laws.

Others couldn't stand the harassment and ridicule they suffered from fellow Jews. Traditional Jews treated Christian Jews as spiritual traitors. Initially, Christian Jews worshiped in synagogues on Saturday and with Christians on Sunday. But before the first century was over, Christian Jews were banned from synagogues.

In the Bible's longest sustained argument, the writer of Hebrews presents compelling evidence to convince these Jewish Christians that the Christian religion fulfills God's promises to Israel. The old agreement between God and Israel has given way to the new and better agreement predicted by

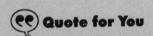 **Quote for You**

"We must be determined to run the race that is ahead of us. We must keep our eyes on Jesus, who leads us" (12:1–2).

Jeremiah. Animal sacrifices are no longer necessary. And the hundreds of Jewish laws written on scrolls have been replaced by the law of love written on the human heart.

This is the next big step in God's plan to save humanity from death and for eternity—the step before Christ's return. The question of Hebrews is this: Why would anyone think they had a better plan than God did? "If we refuse this great way of being saved," the writer asks, "how can we hope to escape?" (2:3).

When It Happened

(Dates are approximate)

Jesus born 7/6 B.C.

Jesus crucified
Pentecost A.D. 30

Hebrews written
A.D. 65

Temple destroyed
A.D. 70

Death of John
A.D. 100

# Info You Can Use

 **Background Notes**

**Writer:** The writer doesn't identify himself. Some early church leaders suggested Paul wrote it. But Bible experts today say that's unlikely. The writer of Hebrews uses a more complex style, and seems to count himself among Christians who never met Jesus (2:3). In fact, Paul met Jesus (Acts 9:5).

Bible experts have suggested many possible writers, including several of Paul's associates: Barnabas, Apollos, Luke, Silas, Epaphras, and Priscilla. But there's no strong case for any of them. As early as A.D. 200, a theologian named Tertullian quoted from Hebrews, identifying the book as "an epistle to the Hebrews under the name of Barnabas."

**Time:** It's unknown exactly when the letter was written. Many Bible experts say it was probably written before A.D. 70. That's when Roman soldiers destroyed the Jerusalem temple. The letter talks a lot about the Jewish temple and the sacrificial system, arguing that Christ's death rendered this system obsolete. If the temple had been destroyed at the time, the writer would likely have mentioned it to bolster his argument.

**Place:** The letter isn't addressed to anyone in particular, and may have been intended as a general letter to be passed among many churches and read in the worship services.

> **Fascinating Facts**
>
> When the New Testament mentions the "Scriptures," it's talking about the Old Testament. Though the New Testament writings were respected and read in church services as early as the first century, Christians didn't agree on which ones to add to the Bible until A.D. 367. And then they declared the Bible a closed book, allowing no further additions.
>
> Hebrews begins the closing section of the Bible, which is called the General Letters. They're "general" because they aren't addressed to anyone, but were probably circulated among many churches.

The writer sends greetings from Italy, suggesting he may have lived in a city there—such as Rome. Clement, a church leader in Rome, quoted from this book in a letter he wrote in A.D. 95.

**Bottom-Line Summary:** Perhaps 20 or 30 years after Jesus was crucified, Jews who converted to Christianity start dropping out of this new religion. They're returning to their ancient Jewish roots.

An unidentified church leader, troubled by this exodus, writes a masterful essay explaining why they should stay. He makes several key points:

- Jesus, as God's son, is better than the Jewish heroes such as Moses.

- Jesus, as sinless, is better than sinful Jewish priests who intercede on behalf of the people.

- Jesus, as the epitome of perfection, is a better sacrifice than the most prized livestock.

- With the arrival of Jesus, the promised messiah, God's former agreement with Israel is obsolete. God has established the new agreement he promised (Jeremiah 31:31–33). This means Christianity is God's plan—the prophesied outgrowth of the Jewish faith.

For Jewish Christians, the writer explains, there's no turning back—for there's nothing to turn back to.

# Influential People

**Jesus,** God's Son, establishes a new agreement between God and humanity. Instead of following hundreds of religious rules, like those in the Old Testament, we're to follow our heart. With the Spirit of God living in us and directing us, we know right from wrong.

# Key Ideas You Need to Know

**Faith.** "Faith is being sure of what we hope for and certain of what we do not see" (11:1, New International Version). It's trusting God and his promises—especially his promise that we can be saved by believing in his Son, Jesus.

**Covenant (agreement, contract).** The Jews and God had a formal agreement—called a covenant. In return for the promised land and God's protection, the Jews were to obey God's laws, which are based on the Ten Commandments. If the Jews failed to live up to their end of the agreement, they would lose God's protection and their homeland. The agreement, which was as binding as a contract, is outlined in Deuteronomy 27—29.

The Jews broke the agreement, and were eventually driven from their homeland. But God made another promise:

"The day will come," God said, "when I will make a new covenant with the people of Israel and Judah. This covenant will not be like the one I made with their ancestors when I took them by the hand and brought them out of the land of Egypt. They broke that covenant" (Jeremiah 31:31–32, New Living Translation).

God describes his new covenant this way: "I will put my laws in their minds, and I will write them on their hearts" (Jeremiah 31:33, New Living Translation).

Hours before his crucifixion, Jesus held up a cup of wine symbolizing the blood he was about to shed. He told his disciples, "This is my blood. It is poured out for you, and with it God makes his new agreement" (Luke 22:20).

The old system of staying in God's good graces by carefully observing hundreds of laws and offering sacrifices is over. It became obsolete (Hebrews 8:13). God put his Spirit in each of us, so we know right from wrong without having to consult a manual. And when we choose wrong, forgiveness sincerely sought is only a prayer away.

# Q&A

**Do we have to obey the Old Testament laws?** Some of them. Moral laws, such as the Ten Commandments, are timeless. Most laws, however, are obsolete—even for Jews. These are laws about such things as what food we can eat, which religious holidays to observe, and how to offer sacrifices.

**Does God punish us in this life?** Sometimes he does, to get our attention and turn us away from sin.

The writer of Hebrews quoted Proverbs by saying, "When the Lord punishes you, don't make light of it, and when he corrects you, don't be discouraged. The Lord corrects the people he loves and disciplines those he calls his own" (12:5–6).

Jesus seemed to confirm that God sometimes punishes us for sin in this life. Jesus did so in a talk with a crippled man he healed. Implying that the crippling came from God, Jesus told the man, "You are now well. But don't sin anymore or something worse might happen to you" (John 5:14).

**Do we have to be holy to go to heaven?** We don't have to be perfect on this planet to make it into heaven. When the Bible uses "holy" to describe people, it means those who have dedicated their lives to God. Instead of doing whatever they please, they try to live in a way that pleases God.

The question comes from a statement the writer of Hebrews made: "Make every effort to live in peace with all men and to be holy; without holiness no one will see the Lord" (12:14, New International Version).

Some "holiness" churches have taught that this means the only people who will go to heaven will be the "entirely sanctified." Entire sanctification is considered by some Christians to be a second religious experience, after conversion. It's said to be an act of God that makes the Christian completely devoted to God. This experience is said to destroy the sin nature and give the person power to overcome sin and to live in a way that pleases God.

### To-Do List

- "Don't let evil thoughts or doubts make any of you turn from the living God. You must encourage one another each day" (3:12–13).

- "We must get rid of everything that slows us down, especially the sin that just won't let go" (12:1).

- "Don't forget to show hospitality to strangers, for some who have done this have entertained angels without realizing it!" (13:2, New Living Translation).

- "We must hold tightly to the hope that we say is ours. After all, we can trust the one who made the agreement with us" (10:23).

- "Some people have gotten out of the habit of meeting for worship, but we must not do that" (10:25).

Most churches, however, (including most holiness churches) teach that a person's eternal destiny is determined when they turn to God in the first place—not after they mature.

## Red Flag Issues

**Backsliding.** Christians don't agree on the topic of Christians abandoning the faith.

Some say it's impossible to backslide. Some Baptists, Presbyterians, and Lutherans teach that once you become a Christian, you can never lose your place in heaven—no matter what sins you commit. This belief is called "eternal security." It's based on several Bible passages, including Jesus' teaching that, to those who follow him, "I give them eternal life, so that they will never be lost. No one can snatch them out of my hand" (John 10:28).

Others teach that it's possible for Christians to abandon their faith. For support, they point to passages such as the parable of the farmer sowing seeds. Jesus said the rocky soil represents "people who gladly hear the message [of salvation] and accept it. But they don't have deep roots, and they believe only for a little while. As soon as life gets hard, they give up" (Luke 8:13).

James adds, in his letter to Jewish Christians, "If any among you wanders away from the truth and is brought back, you can be sure that the one who brings that person back will save that sinner from death and bring about the forgiveness of many sins" (James 5:19–20, New Living Translation).

Some Christians go so far as to say backsliders are doomed. For Bible support, these Christians point to Hebrews, which says, "It is impossible to restore to repentance those who were once enlightened . . . and who then turn away from God" (6:4, 6, New Living Translation). But other Christians see this as a hyperbole—an exaggeration intended to show the danger of leaving the faith. These Christians say the passage means that people who have known the joys of Christianity and yet reject it are very unlikely to return to the faith. But the choice is theirs. For everyone, without exception, Jesus said he'd leave the light on: "Ask, and you will receive. Search, and you will find. Knock, and the door will be opened for you" (Matthew 7:7).

# Bible Scenarios You Can Use

## 1. A new sacrifice for sins (10:1–18)

**W**hen Jews in Bible times commit a sin, they sacrifice an animal to express their sorrow. It's a plan God set up to remind people that sin is deadly serious because it can kill our relationship with God.

Because sin is a killer, the penalty for sin is death. But God allows his people to sacrifice animals to repent of sin. "Life is in the blood," God told Moses, "and I have given you the blood of animals to sacrifice in place of your own" (Leviticus 17:11).

But as God later promised through the prophets, he sets up a new way for people to find forgiveness. He sends his son, Jesus, to die for our sins. "By his one sacrifice," the writer of Hebrews explains, "he [Jesus] has forever set free from sin the people he brings to God."

We Christians sin sometimes. It's not the way we normally walk through our life while following Jesus. But sometimes we trip and fall into sin. When we do, we can hurt ourselves and others, and distance ourselves from God. We sin with our words, actions, and even our thoughts when those thoughts isolate us from others. But the sacrifice has already been made and the forgiveness is available. When we accept God's forgiveness he promises, "I will forget about their sins and no longer remember their evil deeds."

We stand clean before God. The writer of Revelation put it this way, using symbolism to describe a group of God's people dressed in white robes: "They have washed their robes in the blood of the Lamb and have made them white. And so they stand before the throne of God" (Revelation 7:14–15).

## 2. People who have confidence in God (11:1–40)

**T**rusting God is more important than following religious rules—whether they're the Jewish rules in Bible times or church rules today. To make this point, the writer of Hebrews shines the spotlight on a cast of Old Testament people who lived before there were any such rules—before the Ten Commandments, kosher food restrictions, and the Golden Rule of Jesus (treat others the way you want to be treated).

People who predate these rules, but who pleased God, included Abel, Noah, Abraham, Sarah, Isaac, Jacob, and Moses.

What did these people have in common? Faith in God.

"What is faith?" the writer asks. "It is the confident assurance that what we hope for is going to happen. It is the evidence of things we cannot yet see. God gave his approval to people in days of old because of their faith" (New Living Translation).

We can still have confidence in God. We can believe what he says in the Bible. We can assure ourselves that he is working for our best interests. We can know that he will take even the most tragic things that happen to us and use them in good ways.

This kind of faith warms the heart of God. It always has.

# JAMES

## How to Act Like a Christian

Some Christians are more blow than go. They can talk religion, but they have to sit down to do it.

Like armchair quarterbacks, they sound like they know their stuff. But if they really knew what they were talking about, they'd be in the game, not watching from the sidelines.

James was one church leader fed up with listening to do-nothing Christians talk the talk. He wanted to see them exercise some other muscles. So he wrote this letter, as short and jarring as a burst of electricity intended to revive the dead.

"Fool! When will you ever learn that faith that does not result in good deeds is useless?" (2:20, New Living Translation).

James wanted nothing to do with the argument that the Christian religion is a private matter between God and us. It's a public matter. "Prove that you have faith without doing kind deeds," James challenged the reader, "and I will prove that I have faith by doing them" (2:18).

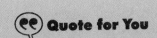 **Quote for You**

"What good is it to say you have faith, when you don't do anything to show that you really do have faith? . . . Anyone who doesn't breathe is dead, and faith that doesn't do anything is just as dead!" (2:14, 26).

What deeds did he have in mind? For starters, Christians stay faithful even when others attack their beliefs. And when Christians see someone who needs food or clothing, they'll help. But James said perhaps the most difficult deed of all—reserved for the maturest Christians—is to have the perfect opportunity to say something nasty, but to keep our mouth shut.

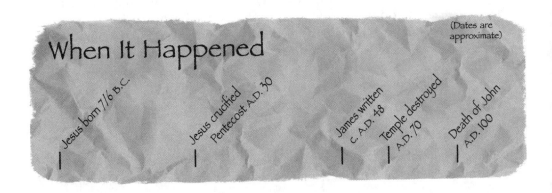

(Dates are approximate)

## When It Happened

Jesus born 7/6 B.C.

Jesus crucified
Pentecost A.D. 30

James written
c. A.D. 48

Temple destroyed
A.D. 70

Death of John
A.D. 100

# Info You Can Use

## Background Notes

**Writer:** The writer identifies himself only as "James, a servant of God and of our Lord Jesus Christ" (1:1).

Four men in the New Testament share this name. But since at least the A.D. 300s, church leaders have said the writer was James, the oldest of Jesus' four younger brothers (Mark 6:3). This is the same person who became leader of the Jerusalem church and who presided over the first church council meeting (Acts 15).

**Time:** It's unclear when James wrote this letter. He could have written it as early as the A.D. 40s, before the church council meeting in A.D. 49. One clue suggesting this is that James spoke highly of Jewish laws—but the council determined these laws were no longer vital. If James wrote the letter this early, it's the oldest piece of literature in the New Testament.

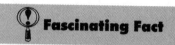

### Fascinating Fact

A monk named St. Francis of Assisi taught that the best preaching had nothing to do with a sermon. Instead, he said it involved helping people—comforting families who've lost a loved one, bringing bread to the poor, visiting the sick. "Preach without ceasing," he said. "If you must, use words."

James could, however, have written the letter anytime over the next 20 years. A Jewish historian of that century said the Jews stoned James to death before Romans destroyed the temple in A.D. 70.

**Place:** James wrote to "the twelve tribes scattered all over the world" (1:1). The 12 tribes generally referred to the 12 tribes of Israel, with each tribe (extended family) descended from one of the sons of Jacob. So James may have been writing to Jewish Christians. Another possibility is that he meant the New Israel—all Christians, both Jewish and non-Jewish.

**Bottom-Line Summary:** James is full of short nuggets of wise advice about how to live the Christian life.

Like the Old Testament book of Proverbs, it covers many topics. For example: thinking before speaking, helping the needy, and resisting the temptation to judge others. "What right do you have to condemn anyone?" James asks (4:12).

But James is most vocal about one particular idea: Christianity is more than a private spiritual experience. If you're truly Christian, you can't keep it to yourself. You'll act on it. People will know you are Christian by the way you behave, by the generosity you show, by the self-control you exhibit, and by the joy of life that you project even when the going gets tough.

## Influential People

**James,** possibly one of Jesus' brothers and leader of the church in Jerusalem, wrote this occasionally forceful letter as a reminder that it can take a lot of energy to propel dead weight into motion. It also urges us to take a hard look at our own life, to make sure we're not part of the dead weight.

## Key Ideas You Need to Know

**Wealth.** Contrary to popular opinion, lots of money is not a good thing.

Jesus said, "It's easier for a camel to go through the eye of a needle than for a rich person to get into God's kingdom," (Matthew 19:24).

His little brother (as many scholars are inclined to identify the writer of this letter), repeats the idea and adds some color. "You rich people should cry and weep! Terrible things are going to happen to you. . . . While here on earth, you have thought only of filling your own stomachs and having a good time. But now you are like fat cattle on their way to be butchered. You have condemned and murdered innocent people, who couldn't even fight back" (5:1, 5–6).

Of course, not all rich people are bad people. But on the basis of what Jesus and James said, they should at least be worried that their money will get the better of them.

How rich is rich remains unclear. Perhaps for clarification of our status, Jesus and James would direct us to someone who has no idea where their next meal is coming from. Wouldn't that be just like Mary's boys?

## Q&A

**Do we have to perform good deeds to get to heaven?** No. That's why Protestant reformer, Martin Luther, said James shouldn't have been put in the Bible.

Luther said the main teaching in James—that faith without works is dead—clashes with one of Paul's main teachings: "You were saved by faith. . . . This is God's gift to you, and not anything you have done on your own" (Ephesians 2:8–9).

But James didn't argue that we're saved by doing good works—that we earn our salvation. Instead, he said genuine faith in Jesus will naturally express itself in kindness. In a way, James was saying that if sin were a disease, and salvation were the cure, compassion would be a side effect we'd have to live with.

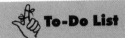 **To-Do List**

- "If any of you need wisdom, you should ask God, and it will be given to you" (1:5).

- "You should be quick to listen and slow to speak or to get angry" (1:19).

- "If you think you are being religious, but can't control your tongue, you are fooling yourself, and everything you do is useless" (1:26).

- "You must not give the best seat to the one in fancy clothes and tell the one who is poor to stand at the side or sit on the floor" (2:3).

- "Resist the devil, and he will run from you. Come near to God, and he will come near to you" (4:7–8).

- "Don't say cruel things about others" (4:11).

- "If any followers have wandered away from the truth, you should try to lead them back" (5:19).

The two men seemed to come at faith from different situations. James apparently ministered among do-nothing believers. And Paul seemed to have ministered among a lot of I-can't-do-enough Gentiles who thought they needed to obey all Jewish laws and customs to earn salvation. Both extremes are wrong.

We're saved by faith. And when we're saved, it shows.

## For the Record: James Abused

**Prayer instead of medical treatment.** Some churches, most notably Christian Science, typically prefer prayer and other spiritual healing techniques over medical science. For Bible support, they quote James: "If you are sick, ask the church leaders to come and pray for you. Ask them to put olive oil on you in the name of the Lord. If you have faith when you pray for sick people, they will get well. The Lord will heal them, and if they have sinned, he will forgive them" (5:14–15).

The Christian Science movement started in 1866, with founder Mary Baker Eddy teaching that sickness and death are only an illusion and that healing is possible through prayer and spiritual enlightenment which transforms a person into the spiritual image of God's ideal.

Christian Scientists sometimes appear in the news when parents refuse to provide medical treatment for their children. Christian Scientists argue that they are providing treatment, though not the conventional type.

The Bible never teaches that sickness and death are an illusion. On the night of his arrest, Jesus was deeply distressed about his imminent suffering and execution (Matthew 26:38).

In addition, when James talks about healing, he doesn't use the medical term. He uses a word that means "whole" and "forgiven." Though prayer may not always heal us in a physical way, we can be assured that God provides the spiritual wholeness that comes through forgiveness.

# Bible Scenarios You Can Use

## 1. Treat the poor with respect (2:1–13)

**S**ince ancient times, rich people have often received preferred treatment. James says it's wrong—the poor deserve as much respect as the rich.

"Suppose a rich person wearing fancy clothes and a gold ring comes to one of your meetings," James says. "And suppose a poor person dressed in worn-out clothes also comes. You must not give the best seat to the one in fancy clothes and tell the one who is poor to stand at the side or sit on the floor. That is the same as saying that some people are better than others, and you would be acting like a crooked judge."

"God has given a lot of faith to the poor people," James continues. "If you treat some people better than others, you have done wrong, and the Scriptures teach that you have sinned."

We Christians today still give special treatment to the rich. We name Christian college buildings and church annexes after them, in recognition of their donations. We vote them into leadership on church committees, since they seem successful in business. And we send our leaders to golf with them, to build bridges of friendship with the influential.

We may court the rich because we want them to give money to the church, and we'd be delighted if they could give us some private tips about how to punch up our net worth. We may avoid the poor because poverty forces us to make a decision about whether or not to help—and we generally want more money for ourselves, not less.

If we do this, we're being more selfish than Christian.

## 2. Real Christians do good deeds (2:14–26)

"**W**hat's the use of saying you have faith if you don't prove it by your actions?" James asks (New Living Translation).

"Suppose you see a brother or sister who needs food or clothing, and you say, 'Well, good-bye and God bless you; stay warm and eat well'—but then you don't give that person any food or clothing. What good does that do? So you see, it isn't enough just to have faith. Faith that doesn't show itself by good deeds is no faith at all—it is dead and useless" (New Living Translation).

The Christian faith changes more about us than the way we think. It changes the way we act. For instance, instead of merely agreeing that it's a good idea to feed the hungry, tend the sick, and clothe the ragged, we're actually doing the feeding, tending, or clothing. If we keep our eyes open, we'll get a chance to put our faith to work one way or another.

## 3. Watch your mouth (3:1–12)

"**T**he tongue is a small thing, but what enormous damage it can do," James says. "A tiny spark can set a great forest on fire. And the tongue is a flame of fire. . . . It can turn the entire course of your life into a blazing flame of destruction" (3:5–6, New Living Translation).

We can tame all kinds of wild animals, James says: birds, reptiles, and sea creatures. But our tongues are nearly impossible to tame, often flailing out of control. "If you can control your tongue," James concludes, "you are mature and able to control your whole body" (3:2, Contemporary English Version).

Most of us know all too well what James is saying. It's as though our tongue has a mind of its own, because it certainly doesn't seem attached to ours. We speak before we think—retaliating, criticizing, gossiping, bragging, lying, and exaggerating.

Often, our tongue is at its most destructive when we're angry. That's why James advises, "Be quick to listen and slow to speak. . . . If you are angry, you cannot do any of the good things that God wants done" (1:19–20). It's tough to comfort the sick when we're telling them off.

Once we make the link between our brain and our tongue—a process that usually takes even more practice than mastering eye-hand coordination—life will become a lot more enjoyable, for us, and for everyone within earshot of us.

# 1 PETER

## Why We Should Suffer in Silence

Suffering in silence when we're in physical pain is a horrible idea. Let's get that straight right away.

If we're in physical pain, we need to tell someone because it means we need help. If we don't get help, the problem will often get worse. A mild infection, left untreated, can enter the bloodstream and kill us.

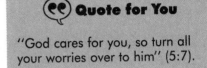

**Quote for You**

"God cares for you, so turn all your worries over to him" (5:7).

Suffering spiritually is altogether different. Here, silence is golden. Consider our model: Jesus standing quietly before his Jewish accusers and Roman executioners.

What good does it do to stand idly by and take the abuse?

Peter gives some examples:

- If you're a Christian woman married to an unbeliever, you have the potential, through kindness, to "win him over by what you do" (3:1).

- If someone in authority over you gives you a hard time because of your Christian values, you have the power "to silence stupid and ignorant people by doing right" (2:15).

- If folks criticize you, the kindness and respect you show them in return will make them "ashamed when they see what a good life you live because you belong to Christ" (3:16, New Living Translation).

In spiritual matters, retaliation prolongs the cycle of suffering. Kindness breaks the cycle.

We can't convince people about the goodness of Jesus and his followers by out-yelling them. But when we offer them humble respect in return for arrogant abuse, we show them what real Christians are made of.

## When It Happened

(Dates are approximate.)

Jesus born 7/6 B.C.

Jesus crucified A.D. 30
Pentecost A.D. 30

1 Peter written c. A.D. 64

Temple destroyed A.D. 70

Death of John A.D. 100

# Info You Can Use

 **Background Notes**

**Writer:** The letter is "from Peter, an apostle of Jesus Christ" (1:1). The writing style is refined Greek—a surprising accomplishment for a Jewish fisherman. But Peter admits "Silvanus helped me write this short letter" (5:12). Silvanus is Latin (Rome's official language). The Hebrew version of this name is Silas. A Christian named Silas traveled with Paul throughout the Greek-speaking world (Acts 15:22).

**Time:** The date of the writing is unknown. Peter could have written it in the early 60s, when Romans became increasingly hostile toward Christians, or shortly after A.D. 64, when Nero blamed Christians for setting fire to Rome.

**Place:** Peter writes "to God's people who are scattered like foreigners" in five Roman provinces in western Turkey (1:1).

He writes from "Babylon," (5:13). That was a Christian code name for Rome as early as A.D. 70 and perhaps earlier. Both empires were rich, powerful, and evil. Both also destroyed Jerusalem.

> **Fascinating Fact**
>
> The Bible says nothing of Peter's death. But early church leaders report that he died during Nero's persecution of Christians. Peter is said to have been crucified upside down on Vatican Hill in Rome, in what is now the courtyard where crowds gather to hear the pope.

**Bottom-Line Summary:** Rome has started targeting Christians as members of a religious movement that may be a threat to the empire. Violent clashes between Christians and Jews have shown it's a religion that can spark trouble. Since it's new, and—unlike Judaism—not approved by Rome, it's considered the source of the troubles.

There have also been nasty rumors about it.

- *Christians are cannibals.* The rumor comes from the Communion ritual, in which believers eat bread and wine that represents the body and blood of Jesus.

- *Christians are incestuous.* They call one another "brothers" and "sisters," and greet each other with a kiss, which was a Middle Eastern custom comparable to a handshake today.

The crackdown on Christianity can involve threats against believers, confiscation of property, physical attacks, and execution.

Peter warns the Christians to expect such suffering. But he urges the believers to hold onto their faith, while treating their attackers with respect. He reminds them of Christ's sufferings, and what it means for eternity: "You were not rescued by such things as silver or gold that don't last forever. You were rescued by the precious blood of Christ" (1:18–19). If they die, they will live again.

When believers are confronted with questions about their faith, Peter says they should be prepared with honest answers, given in a spirit of humility.

# Influential People

**Peter,** a leader among the 12 original disciples of Jesus, is one of the recognized leaders in the emerging church. When people he cares about are suffering because of the message he delivered, Peter has the hard chore of telling them to patiently endure the abuse. Those of us with children who have been bullied know we'd rather offer skills for self-defense. But for the sake of spreading the Christian message, no defense works better than kindness.

# Q&A

**Do we have to be baptized to be saved?** Most Christians say no, though 1 Peter 3:21 might seem to imply otherwise. Peter's original language, however, describes baptism as a "pledge," like one that confirms a business deal. For most Christians, baptism is a public acknowledgement of faith, not a required hurdle we have to jump to get into heaven. (See Acts, page 314.)

**Should we blindly obey our political leaders?** Peter said, "The Lord wants you to obey all human authorities, especially the Emperor, who rules over everyone" (2:13).

But Peter qualified that guideline, long before he wrote this letter.

Shortly after Jesus returned to heaven, Peter refused to comply with the Jewish high council's order to stop teaching about Jesus. Peter said, "Do you think God wants us to obey you or to obey him? We cannot keep quiet about what we have seen and heard" (Acts 4:19–20).

When our leaders intrude into God's business and try to convince us that something morally wrong is right, we're to obey God. (For more, see Titus, page 385.)

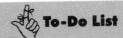 **To-Do List**

- "Behave like obedient children. Don't let your lives be controlled by your desires, as they used to be" (1:14).

- "Quit trying to fool people, and start being sincere" (2:1).

- "Don't be jealous or say cruel things about others" (2:1).

- "Always let others see you behaving properly" (2:12).

- "Most important of all, you must sincerely love each other, because love wipes away many sins" (4:8).

- "Count it a blessing when you suffer for being a Christian. This shows that God's glorious Spirit is with you" (4:14).

- "Church leaders . . . . don't be bossy to those people who are in your care, but set an example for them" (5:1, 3).

# For the Record: 1 Peter Abused

**Slavery and Women's Rights.** Christians in ages past who have supported slavery and opposed women's rights have turned to Peter for ammunition. That's because Peter tells slaves to obey their masters and wives to submit to their husbands (2:18; 3:1).

Peter wasn't condoning slavery or arguing that women should remain second-class citizens. Like Paul in other letters, Peter was pleading with believers to focus on the Christian ideal of putting others first.

Especially at this shaky time in history, when Christianity was under attack, Peter didn't want to portray the faith as a threat to society and a spawning ground for revolution. The social changes would come in time, as the Christian message of equality took root. (For more on slavery, see: Philemon, page 391; Ephesians, page 350. For more on women's rights, see 1 Timothy, page 375; Ephesians, page 350.)

# Bible Scenario You Can Use

### 1. Suffering for being Christian (2:20–25; 4:12–19)

**B**y the A.D. 60s, when many Bible experts think Peter wrote this letter, the harassment and persecution of Christians picks up dramatically. Early on, most of the persecution had come from Jews who treated Jewish Christians as heretics. The Roman Empire, however, considered Christianity as just one of several branches of Judaism—an approved religion.

But now, 30 years after Jesus, the Romans begin seeing Christianity as a new religion. And just as it does with other unapproved religions, Rome starts treating Christianity with suspicion, fearing it may be a secret movement opposed to the emperor. Increasingly, Christians are threatened and mistreated.

Peter urges these Christians to patiently endure the suffering. He says that when they suffer, they are following in the footsteps of Jesus "who set an example by suffering for you."

"Dear friends," Peter adds, "don't be surprised or shocked that you are going through testing that is like walking through fire. Be glad for the chance to suffer as Christ suffered. It will prepare you for even greater happiness when he makes his glorious return."

Unlike Christians in some nations today, most Christians in our country aren't harassed or in danger because of their beliefs. We generally suffer in more subtle ways for our Christian values. We won't cheat our employer, though we may be grossly underpaid. We work hard in a union shop that may want us to slow down. We treat customers fairly, when the company may be more concerned with short-term profits than with customer retention. So we get chided, joked about, insulted, and passed over for a promotion.

As Peter put it, "You are better off to obey God and suffer for doing right than to suffer for doing wrong" (3:17).

# 2 PETER

## Warning: Liars Ahead

Some people will say anything for a buck. We know because they've said it to us—for our buck.

"That outfit looks great on you."

"Your car needed new brakes six months ago."

"A hundred percent of the new tax will go for this need."

We've all lost some hard-earned money to liars, cheats, and swindlers. But it's only money. Sometimes the stakes are higher.

As Peter approached the end of his life he began to see liars sneaking into the church, robbing believers of treasures in heaven. Actually, the robbers weren't targeting anything spiritual; they weren't trying to rob Christians of eternal life. That was only a side effect. The robbers wanted money and sex.

So they passed themselves off as Christian scholars with unique insights into the faith. Sounding smart, they said it's okay for us to sin since we're already forgiven. They practiced what they preached. They apparently collected generous offerings and took pleasure in freeing believers from their sexual inhibitions.

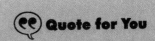

**Quote for You**

"Don't let the errors of evil people lead you down the wrong path. . . . Let the wonderful kindness and the understanding that come from our Lord and Savior Jesus Christ help you to keep on growing" (3:17–18).

"The darkest part of hell is waiting for them," Peter warned (2:17).

We don't follow leaders whose behavior shows they're walking away from God. We follow Jesus.

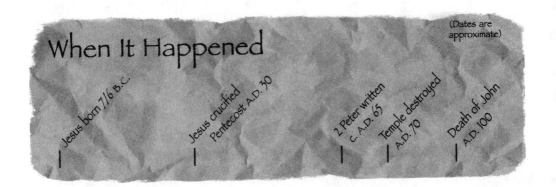

When It Happened

(Dates are approximate)

Jesus born 7/6 B.C.

Jesus crucified Pentecost A.D. 30

2 Peter written c. A.D. 65

Temple destroyed A.D. 70

Death of John A.D. 100

# Info You Can Use

## Background Notes

**Writer:** The letter is "from Simon Peter, a servant and an apostle of Jesus Christ" (1:1).

Some Bible experts doubt it. That's partly because Peter includes Paul's letters among sacred scriptures (3:16). But some of Paul's letters had probably been in circulation for ten years by the time Peter wrote this, and were increasingly regarded as authoritative.

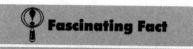

**Fascinating Fact**

Roman Catholics consider Peter the first in a long line of popes—formerly called "bishops of Rome." They base this on Jesus telling Peter, "I will give you the keys to the kingdom of heaven, and God in heaven will allow whatever you allow on earth" (Matthew 16:19).

**Time:** "The Lord Jesus Christ has shown me that my days here on earth are numbered and I am soon to die" (1:14, New Living Translation). The Bible doesn't say when Peter died, but early Christian writers said he was crucified upside down in Rome during Nero's persecution of Christians (A.D. 64–68).

**Place:** The letter doesn't identify where it was written or to whom. It's addressed to all believers (1:1).

Peter said this was his second letter to the people (3:1), so he may have written to the same believers he wrote in 1 Peter: Christians in western Turkey.

**Bottom-Line Summary:** After learning he is about to die, Peter writes an open letter to Christians. He expresses three deep desires. He wants them to:

- continue growing in the faith (chapter 1),

- reject false teachers (chapter 2), and

- live in patient anticipation of the Second Coming (chapter 3).

## Influential People

**Peter,** a leader of the 12 original disciples of Jesus, is one of the leaders of the emerging church. Even as he approaches death, his thoughts are for the spiritual well-being of others. His concern is a reminder that we, too, should be concerned about the spiritual condition of our world. And we should do what we can to point people to Jesus.

## Q&A

**How can we tell dangerous heresy from valid differences of opinion about Bible interpretation?** From the early centuries on, most warped Christian teachings have revolved around Jesus.

- He wasn't really God's Son.

- He only appeared to be human.

- He didn't really die and come back from the dead.

Heresy is any teaching that departs from basic Christian truth—truth such as the divinity of Jesus, the love that God has for us, or the compassion God wants us to show one another.

The Bible and God's Spirit inside us help us know right from wrong. Heresy, on the other hand, tries to convince us that wrong is right.

Christians disagree and debate over secondary issues: the landscaping of heaven and hell, the role of women in church leadership, and the method of baptism (dipping, pouring, sprinkling). But these secondary issues are more like critiquing individual bricks in the church, while heresies undermine the foundation on which the church rests.

**Why is Jesus waiting so long to return?**
For perhaps 30 years, Peter and the other apostles had been saying Jesus was coming back soon. Then false teachers came and started saying he wasn't coming back at all.

Peter said those teachers were wrong. He explained the delay this way: "For the Lord one day is the same as a thousand years, and a thousand years is the same as one day. The Lord isn't slow about keeping his promises, as some people think he is. In fact, God is patient, because he wants everyone to turn from sin and no one to be lost. The day of the Lord's return will surprise us like a thief" (3:8–10).

> ### 👆 To-Do List
>
> - "Keep learning more and more about God and our Lord Jesus" (1:2).
>
> - "Do your best to improve your faith. You can do this by adding goodness, understanding, self-control, patience, devotion to God, concern for others, and love" (1:5–7).
>
> - "Serve and honor God by the way you live" (3:11).

In our physical world, we measure time by clocks and calendars. But in the spirit world, it's as though time is versatile, immeasurable—a bit like a video player that can run anywhere from slow motion to fast-forward. Perhaps the closest we can come to experiencing spirit time is to look over our shoulder at where we've been in our life. In what seems like a moment ago, our children were babies. Now our babies have babies. Decades have passed in an instant. On the other hand, for an elderly man who has lost his wife, each lonely day can seem like forever.

Jesus will come. It doesn't really matter when. In a moment, as our spirit measures time, we'll be with him.

## Red Flag Issues

**Degrees of God's punishment.** Christians debate what exactly will happen to people who reject God. The New Testament uses many vivid terms to describe the punishment: a lake of fire, darkness, dungeons, and destruction, to name a few.

Peter implied there will be degrees of punishment, apparently based on the gravity of sin. He said Christians who abandon the faith and become false teachers will be "in worse shape than they were at first" (2:20). "The darkest part of hell is waiting for them" (2:17).

Some Bible experts speculate that people who hear the Christian message and reject it will be judged more severely than those who never heard it. Others say we shouldn't take Peter so literally—that he was simply trying to say that the false teachers will be held fully accountable for the damage they did. And God determines their punishment.

# Bible Scenario You Can Use

### 1. Fake Christian leaders who hurt the church (2:1–22)

**P**eter expects to die anytime now, because he says Jesus has told him so. A new generation of leaders will have to pick up where leaders of the Jesus Generation left off. Tragically, some of these new leaders are frauds. They pass themselves off as followers of Christ, but they follow only their animal instincts.

"They are immoral," Peter says, "and the meals they eat with you are spoiled by the shameful and selfish way they carry on. All they think about is having sex with someone else's husband or wife. There is no end to their wicked deeds. They trick people who are easily fooled, and their minds are filled with greedy thoughts. But they are headed for trouble!" That trouble, Peter explains, is God's judgment.

"They promise freedom," Peter says, which—based on the way they live—is probably freedom from moral rules. They argue that Christians can live any way they want as long as they believe in Jesus. Peter has two words to describe their teachings: "stupid nonsense."

Our world is full of religions, including many variations on Christianity.

- Mormons revere Jesus and produce kind-hearted followers, but add the *Book of Mormon* as scripture that supersedes the Bible.

- Jehovah's Witnesses revere the Bible, but reject many key Christian teachings: the deity of Jesus, his bodily resurrection, heaven, and hell.

- Unity School of Christianity is an upbeat, positive-thinking kind of faith. But it says there is no literal heaven or hell, no Satan, and that Jesus was no more divine than we can be.

Some of these and other faiths are deceptively similar to Christianity. But once we look closely at them, we discover that some of their fundamental teachings don't line up with the teachings of Jesus. The best way for us to spot distorted teachings is to know the teachings of Jesus and his apostles. Read the Bible. Study it. It'll help you realize when someone is trying to "lead you down the wrong path."

# 1 JOHN

## How to Know We Have Eternal Life

There are so many religions in the world. What are the odds that we Christians have hit on the right one?

Buddhists teach that people can reach a state of impersonal union with Buddha. Mormons say all good people go to heaven, though Mormons will enjoy the highest rewards. Many faiths teach that lots of religions lead to God, like paths up Mt. Fuji lead to the summit.

Christianity is different. It teaches that there's only one way to God. "I am the way, the truth, and the life," Jesus said. "Without me, no one can go to the Father" (John 14:6).

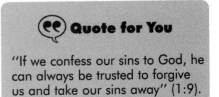

**Quote for You**

"If we confess our sins to God, he can always be trusted to forgive us and take our sins away" (1:9).

First John helps reinforce this message. "All of you have faith in the Son of God," John said of his readers, "and I have written to let you know that you have eternal life" (5:13).

In John's day, there were Christian churches forming that taught the same mistaken messages that some religions teach today, denying the divinity of Jesus. But John wrote to assure Christians that he knew Jesus. He heard the words. He saw the miracles. He witnessed the death, the resurrected life, and the ascension of Jesus. John knew for certain that following Jesus would lead to eternal life. He and the other apostles staked their lives on it, and died preaching it.

How can we know we'll have eternal life, too? We have the writings of John and other eyewitnesses of Jesus' life. We have the Old Testament prophets pointing us to Jesus. And we have the Holy Spirit, who teaches us from the inside out: "The Spirit is truthful and teaches you everything. So stay one in your heart with Christ, just as the Spirit has taught you to do" (2:27).

We can know we have eternal life because we have faith in Jesus.

## When It Happened

(Dates are approximate)

Jesus born 7/6 B.C.

Jesus crucified
Pentecost A.D. 30

Temple destroyed
A.D. 70

1 John written
A.D. 90

Death of John
A.D. 100

# Info You Can Use

## Background Notes

**Writer:** The letter is written anonymously, though the message and the phrasing are clearly in the style of the Gospel of John, which is also written anonymously.

Many church leaders from as early as the second century said John wrote the Gospel and the three letters bearing his name late in his life. (For more, see "Writer," John, page 302.)

**Time:** John is said to have lived to an old age, into the A.D. 90s. That's roughly the time church leaders said he wrote it.

**Place:** The letter doesn't say to whom John wrote or from where. Church leaders in the second century said he wrote an open letter to Christians from Ephesus, a Mediterranean coastal city in western Turkey. The first documented use of this letter was in Ephesus.

Ephesus and the surrounding cities were a virtual stew of varied cultures and religions—an ideal location for mixing new batches of creatively blended religions, like those described in the Gospel and letters bearing John's name.

**Bottom-Line Summary:** John writes to Christian churches warning about a separatist movement of antichrists ("Christ's enemies," 2:18). These unorthodox Christians—apparently forefathers of a heresy that blossoms in the second and third centuries—teach that Jesus was a spiritual being who only appeared physical. These Christians were leaving the traditional church and starting new congregations.

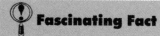

### Fascinating Fact

The heresy John warned about—Gnosticism—is still alive. "The Gnostic says you're saved through knowledge," says Frank Giudici, who teaches ministerial students for Unity School of Christianity. "Well, Unity teaches that. We're Gnostic in that we believe you're saved when you understand that the Christ indwells you." Unity teaches that Christ is in everyone. Unity doesn't teach that there's sin or hell. "Your own false thinking, that's the only thing to be saved from," Giudici says.

The heresy that emerges later teaches that everything physical is sinful, including the human body, and that God is completely spiritual and good. That's why they say Jesus couldn't have been physical. They add that the Crucifixion and Resurrection weren't important in salvation because Jesus didn't really die. We're saved, they explain, through knowledge about Jesus. The heresy—Gnosticism—eventually takes its name from the Greek work for knowledge: *gnosis*. (For an example of Gnosticism today, see Fascinating Fact, above.)

"I am writing to warn you about those people who are misleading you," John says. The apostle warns believers to reject these new slants on the Christian message and to "keep thinking about the message you first heard" (2:26, 24).

# Influential People

**Jesus,** God's Son, came to earth in human form to die for our sins and to show us that there is life after death. John teaches there's just one sure way to God and eternal life, and it's through faith in Jesus.

**John,** one of the 12 original disciples of Jesus, is considered the author of the Gospel of John, the three letters of John, and Revelation. His letter of 1 John, apparently written to all Christians, reminds us that it's important to warn fellow believers about religions that cloak themselves with Christian words but that reject the heart of the gospel message that's summed up in John 3:16. Religions like that have just enough truth to be dangerous.

## Key Ideas You Need to Know

**Antichrists.** John's richly symbolic Book of Revelation spoke of an evil leader called the Antichrist, whom Jesus captures and destroys after an end-time battle. But in 1 John, the apostle used the term to describe all enemies of Jesus.

"As you have heard that the antichrist is coming," John wrote, "even now many antichrists have come" (2:18, New International Version). John said these enemies "came from our own group," indicating they were former members who seceded from the union of believers and started their own congregations based on warped teachings. These antichrists were trying to lure people away from the traditional Christian faith.

## Q&A

**What sin leads to death?** "Everything that is wrong is sin," John says, "but not all sins are deadly" (5:17).

This perplexing verse has left Bible experts struggling to figure out which sins are lethal. Opinions vary widely. Some think John was talking about chronic rebellion against God, which can't be forgiven because the sinner never repents. Others say it's any sin that produces physical death.

### To-Do List

- "Stop loving this evil world and all that it offers you, for when you love the world, you show that you do not have the love of the Father in you" (2:15, New Living Translation).

- "Continue to live in fellowship with Christ" (2:28, New Living Translation).

- "God wants us to have faith in his Son Jesus Christ and to love each other" (3:23).

- "Do not believe everyone who claims to speak by the Spirit. You must test them to see if the spirit they have comes from God. For there are many false prophets in the world" (4:1, New Living Translation).

- "If someone says, 'I love God,' but hates a Christian brother or sister, that person is a liar" (4:20, New Living Translation).

- "Dear children, keep away from anything that might take God's place in your hearts" (5:21, New Living Translation).

Some in the church have identified "seven deadly sins," which include: pride, covetousness, lust, envy, gluttony, anger, and sloth.

## ◈ Red Flag Issues

**Sinless living.** Some Christians teach that we can reach a level of spiritual maturity where we don't sin—or only rarely sin. These Christians generally define sin as doing something we know would displease God—we know it's wrong, and we do it anyhow.

For Bible support, one passage they turn to is this: "Anyone who keeps on sinning belongs to the devil. . . . God's children cannot keep on being sinful. His life-giving power lives in them and makes them his children, so that they cannot keep on sinning" (3:8–9).

Other Christians see in this passage not a plea for perfection but a warning for people who make it a practice to sin, and then try to justify it as a natural part of life.

As John puts it elsewhere in his letter, "Those who have become part of God's family do not make a practice of sinning" (5:18, New Living Translation). "I am writing this so that you won't sin," John adds. "But if you do sin, Jesus Christ always does the right thing, and he will speak to the Father for us. Christ is the sacrifice that takes away our sins and the sins of all the world's people" (2:1–2).

# Bible Scenario You Can Use

### 1. Love each other (2:7—3:24)

**W**ithin a few decades of Jesus' ascension into heaven, most of the original disciples have died. Other leaders emerge who never met Jesus, heard his teachings, or saw his miracles. Some of these leaders start putting their own twist on the story, and splits develop in the church. Many Christians stay with the traditional teachings they've heard all their lives, but some break away and start new congregations with new interpretations on the story of Jesus.

One popular interpretation is that Jesus wasn't actually human, but he only looked human. He was really a heavenly spirit disguised as a human.

John, now an old man, writes to call the people back to the original teachings. This eyewitness of Jesus' ministry says, "We are telling you what we have seen and heard" (1:3). John assures the believers that Jesus came in human form to save us: "Jesus Christ had a truly human body" (4:2). And John reminds them of the central commandment Jesus gave his followers.

"From the beginning you were told that we must love each other," John says. "When we love others, we know that we belong to the truth, and we feel at ease in the presence of God."

John left it to us to figure out what it means to love others. But he implied that love is far more than a feeling: "Even if we don't feel at ease, God is greater than our feelings." Perhaps the love John had in mind is the love Jesus spoke about: "Treat others the way you want them to treat you" (Matthew 7:12).

When people do us wrong—whether or not they're Christians—it can be hard to feel anything but hostility toward them. But we can make a decision to act like a follower of Jesus, even if we don't feel like it. In time, perhaps, our feelings will catch up with our faith.

# 2 JOHN

## Living in an Attitude of Love

We can get mean when we know we're right and someone else insists we're wrong.

We paid the bill and the company cashed the check. But they refuse to believe it until we get from our bank a copy of the cancelled check and mail it—at our expense.

The junior league umpire missed the call, and our son who got his first hit of the season should have been safe on first. But the ump called him out, to the hoots of the crowd and the dismay of the first baseman.

The apostle John wrote what amounts to a memo—only 13 verses—that says we don't have to get nasty about the truth. He was talking about a kind of truth much more important than money or a batting average: the truth about Jesus. Mistakes about Jesus can set people on a lifetime journey away from God.

How should we defend the truth, whether it's about Jesus, a bookkeeping error, or a base runner? In the spirit of love.

The apostle Paul put it this way when advising Christians about false teachers: we should develop the habit of "speaking the truth in love" (Ephesians 4:15, New International Version).

John says when false teachers come to our church, we shouldn't invite them to dinner (10). Though that may seem unfriendly, it can be the most loving response of all. It shows we don't condone their dangerous beliefs. That doesn't mean we should turn all sinners away from our door. Jesus came to help sinners, and he even sought them out. But we hurt them all the more if we do anything that encourages their sin.

Our mission is to point people to the truth—Jesus—but in an attitude of respect and love.

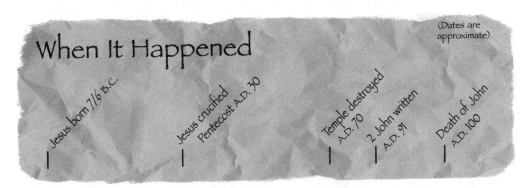

When It Happened

(Dates are approximate)

Jesus born 7/6 B.C.

Jesus crucified / Pentecost A.D. 30

Temple destroyed A.D. 70

2 John written A.D. 91

Death of John A.D. 100

# Info You Can Use

## Background Notes

**Writer:** The writer is identified only as "the church leader" (1:1). Christian leaders in the second century said the writer was John, one of Jesus' closest disciples. The writing style and message of this letter matches that of other writings attributed to John, especially the Gospel of John, along with 1 and 3 John.

**Time:** Church leaders as early as the second century said John wrote this letter near the end of his life, in roughly A.D. 91.

**Place:** It's uncertain from where and to whom John wrote. The letter starts by saying John wrote to "a very special woman and her children" (1:1). This could refer to an individual church with its members. If so, John may have written 1 John as a general letter intended for all churches. And 2 John may have been a special accompanying note to one congregation of which John was especially fond.

Church leaders in the second century said John wrote from Ephesus. It's possible John intended this short note for his home church.

### To-Do List

- "Don't keep changing what you were taught about Christ, or else God will no longer be with you" (9).

- "If someone comes to your meeting and does not teach the truth about Christ, don't invite him into your house or encourage him in any way. Anyone who encourages him becomes a partner in his evil work" (10–11, New Living Translation).

**Bottom-Line Summary:** In 13 verses, John summarizes his five-chapter letter of 1 John. He focuses on three main points:

- Stay loyal to the truth you've been taught about Jesus.

- Love others, because God has commanded it.

- Be wary of people who teach religious ideas that clash with what the eyewitness apostles of Jesus taught.

The false teachers John mentions are traveling ministers spreading lies about Jesus—saying that Jesus wasn't really human, and so he didn't die and wasn't raised from the dead. The ministers live on the donations and hospitality of people in the host cities. But John says people who contribute in any way are helping spread lies about Jesus.

## Influential People

**John,** identified only as "the church leader," is the writer of this short note. He is probably the apostle John, one of Jesus' 12 original disciples. The writer's obvious concern for expressing true religion in a spirit of love can serve as a reminder for us about how to discuss religious matters with people of other faiths—and with our fellow Christians.

# 3 JOHN

## Making People Feel Welcome

Have you ever stepped into a room and felt like an intruder?

Maybe it was a family gathering on a holiday, and you weren't family. Or maybe it was a church you'd never been to before, and everyone else was busy chatting.

Most of us know what a relief it is to find hospitality in an unfamiliar place—the hospitality of a warm handshake, a gentle greeting, and an invitation to make ourselves at home. But most of us also know what it's like when the welcome mat is pulled out from under us.

Third John is a short letter mainly about two people—both leaders in a church. There's Gaius, who welcomes visiting Christian missionaries. And there's Diotrephes, ap-

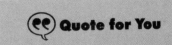 **Quote for You**

"Follow the example of people who do kind deeds" (11).

parently the minister, who won't share the spotlight with anyone. Not only does he not welcome visiting missionaries—even those sent by the apostle John—Diotrephes excommunicates fellow church members who do. That's bad news for Gaius, if Diotrephes finds out.

Writing to Gaius, John commends him for his hospitality and tells him to keep it up no matter what anybody says—Diotrephes included.

"Don't let this bad example influence you," John says. "You are doing a good work for God when you take care of the traveling teachers who are passing through. . . . They are traveling for the Lord and accept nothing from those who are not Christians. So we ourselves should support them so that we may become partners with them for the truth" (11, 5, 7–8, New Living Translation).

We don't have many missionaries pass our way these days. But we do have plenty of opportunities to make folks feel welcome—in our churches, homes, and jobs. We're also able to become partners with missionaries and other ministers by supporting their work.

## When It Happened

(Dates are approximate)

Jesus born 7/6 B.C.

Jesus crucified Pentecost A.D. 30

Temple destroyed A.D. 70

3 John written A.D. 91

Death of John A.D. 100

# Info You Can Use

## Background Notes

**Writer:** As in 2 John, the writer is identified only as "the church leader" (1:1). Christian writers as early as the second century said the apostle John, one of Jesus' original 12 disciples, was that church leader.

**Time:** Early Christian writers said John wrote this letter, along with his other New Testament works, near the end of his life in about A.D. 91.

**Place:** Christian writers in the second century said John wrote from Ephesus, a city in what is now Turkey.

**Bottom-Line Summary:** In the early decades of Christianity, churches are loosely organized. Believers usually meet in homes and are led in worship by one of their own, who's recognized as the minister. The apostles provide guidance, sometimes by coming in person, sometimes by sending associates, and sometimes by sending letters.

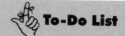

### To-Do List

- "We must support people like them [Christian missionaries and other ministers], so that we can take part in what they are doing to spread the truth" (8).

John has tried sending associates to the unidentified church apparently led by a man named Diotrephes. But Pastor Diotrephes "likes to be the number-one leader" (9). So he turns the visiting ministers away and excommunicates any church members who don't do the same. Perhaps it's his home in which the church meets. Diotrephes also refuses to read to the congregation letters he gets from John.

So John writes to Gaius, a member of this troubled church. John thanks Gaius for routinely welcoming the visiting missionaries. These missionaries say good things about Gaius behind his back. "They say you were good enough to welcome them and to send them on their mission in a way that God's servants deserve" (6).

John tells Gaius to keep up the good work. John adds that he hopes to see Gaius soon. When John arrives, he says he'll tell the church what kind of person Diotrephes really is. If John has any influence among the members—and as perhaps the last living apostle of Jesus, he likely does—the church will soon start taking their cue from Gaius or someone like him. As for selfish Diotrephes, he'll only have what he cherishes most: himself.

## Influential People

**John,** identified only as "the church leader," is the writer of this short note. He is probably the apostle John, one of Jesus' 12 original disciples. John's short letter is a reminder for us to compliment people doing a good job, and to be courageous enough to confront those who are hurting others.

**Gaius,** a church leader, shows kindness and hospitality to traveling Christian ministers even when his local minister orders otherwise. Whenever we need to take a stand, it should be for goodness, because that's the kind of God we serve.

**Diotrephes,** a dictatorial minister, abuses his authority by excommunicating those who disagree with his policy of refusing to welcome Christian missionaries. John's strong rebuke of Diotrephes shows that it's hard for someone with an inflated ego to assume the posture of a servant who works for God. When church leaders think of themselves as chief executive officers issuing commands instead of as workaday people taking their orders from others, they become a speed bump on the highway to heaven; they do little more than slow others down.

# JUDE

## Why Not Sin, Since God Will Forgive?

We sing about God's grace that's greater than all our sin. And we quote the Bible that promises if we confess our sins God will forgive us (1 John 1:9). So the next time we're tempted to indulge our selfish desires, why not?

Why not lie, if it will save us some money? Why not spend all our discretionary income on ourselves, rather than helping others? Why not have sex with someone to whom we're not married?

God will forgive us.

Tell it to Sodom. Or to the snake-bit Israelites on the Exodus. Or to the rebel Israelite family of Korah, swallowed up by an earthquake.

That was Jude's response to Christians of his day whose churches were being infiltrated by false teachers. These teachers said Christians could sin all they wanted without risking their salvation since God has forgiven them—past, present, and future. To prove their point, they sinned.

"They are shameless in the way they care only about themselves," Jude said of these false teachers. "They live by natural instinct because they do not have God's Spirit living in them," (12, 19, New Living Translation).

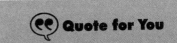

**Quote for You**

"Keep building on the foundation of your most holy faith" (20).

We believers have God's Spirit in us. We know better. We know that in Old Testament times, animals died as a reminder that sin is a matter of life and death. And we know that in New Testament times, God's Son died to save us from sin—not so we could sin all we wanted, but so we'd be free from the power sin has to enslave us.

Contrary to what the heretics said in Jude's day, we're not exercising our freedom when we sin. We're proving our slavery. As Jesus once put it, "Anyone who sins is a slave of sin!" (John 8:34).

(Dates are approximate)

## When It Happened

Jesus born 7/6 B.C.

Jesus crucified Pentecost A.D. 30

Jude written c. A.D. 65

Temple destroyed A.D. 70

Death of John A.D. 100

# Info You Can Use

## Background Notes

**Writer:** The writer is "Jude, a servant of Jesus Christ and the brother of James" (1). Jude is short for the Hebrew name Judah. There's only one Judah in the Bible who has a brother named James. Both men are brothers of Jesus (Matthew 13:55). Jude may have mentioned James because James led the Jerusalem church.

**Time:** It's unknown when Jude wrote this letter. But Paul addressed some of the same issues within about 30 years of the Crucifixion. Paul told Romans not to take advantage of God's grace by continuing to sin (Romans 6:1–2).

**Place:** Jude wrote to all Christians, though we don't know where he was when he wrote.

**Bottom-Line Summary:** Jude writes an open letter to churches. He says he wanted to write a joyful letter about salvation. Instead, he has to warn the church to defend itself.

"Some godless people have wormed their way in among you, saying that God's forgiveness allows us to live immoral lives" (4, New Living Translation).

That's dead wrong, Jude says. And he has the body count to prove it.

He points to famous scenes in history to show that God punishes persistent sin: Sodom and Gomorrah, disobedient Israelites of the Exodus, and an evil prophet named Balaam.

The false teachers are "filthy minded," Jude says. "They are like leafless trees, uprooted and dead . . . doomed to the darkest pits of hell" (12–13). Jude urges true Christians to take a stand for what they know is right, to confront these false teachers with their twisted truth, and if necessary, to show them the nearest exit.

### To-Do List

- "Defend the faith" (3). *Jude's instruction about what Christians should do when people try to prove the Christian faith wrong.*

- "Keep in step with God's love, as you wait for our Lord Jesus Christ to show how kind he is by giving you eternal life" (21).

- "Be helpful to all who may have doubts" (22).

- "Rescue any who need to be saved, as you would rescue someone from a fire" (23).

- "There are still others to whom you need to show mercy, but be careful that you aren't contaminated by their sins" (23, New Living Translation).

## Influential People

**Jude,** the writer of this letter, is probably a brother of Jesus. His stern letter to Christians threatened by false teachings shows that we need to take seriously any attempts to steer the church away from the most basic teachings in the Bible. Today, as in ancient times, common points of attack are to reinvent the identity of Jesus and to downplay the danger of a sinful lifestyle.

# REVELATION

## We Win!

There's one good reason to read this book.

It's to find out that those of us who follow Jesus win in the end. Knowing that changes our life. It gives us power.

Threatened with death if we don't renounce our faith, we humbly refuse. Christians have done so throughout the ages, and are doing so now—as a common occurrence in some countries. They do so because they know heaven's ahead.

Passed over for job promotions because we don't have the killer instinct, we find contentment in serving others. Heaven's ahead.

Discouraged and heart-broken over hatred, disease, and a human race that seems intent on abusing the planet God has entrusted to our care, we learn to love others, help the sick, and give back to God's creation—though we may be in the incredibly shrinking minority. Heaven's ahead.

Christians today tend not to agree much about what they read in Revelation. That's because Revelation was written in code, to protect believers from Romans who were persecuting them. Christians at the time had the key to interpret this message; they knew what the symbols meant. But today, 2,000 years later, most of the key is missing. Even so, we've turned up more than enough of the key to decode the book's main message: Evil loses. God wins.

If we're with God, we win, too.

> ### 🗨 Quote for You
>
> "God's home is now with his people. He will live with them and they will be his own. . . . He will wipe all tears from their eyes, and there will be no more death, suffering, crying, or pain. These things of the past are gone forever" (21:3–4). *A portrait of our future in heaven.*

## When It Happened

(Dates are approximate)

Jesus born 7/6 B.C.

Jesus crucified
Pentecost A.D. 30

Temple destroyed
A.D. 70

Revelation written
A.D. 95

Death of John
A.D. 100

# Info You Can Use

## Background Notes

**Writer:** The writer identified himself only as Christ's "servant John" (1:1). Within a few decades after it was written, church leaders said the writer was the apostle John, one of the closest disciples of Jesus, and author of the Gospel of John and the three letters of John.

About a century later, some church leaders began to question this. They said the writing style wasn't like the apostle John's other works. But the Hebrew-flavored Greek language in which he wrote suggests that if he wasn't the apostle, he was probably a Jew who once lived in Israel.

**Time:** John may have written this book 30 years before his other works, when Nero persecuted the Christians in the mid-60s, executing them to entertain Romans. But most Bible experts say John wrote during the reign of Emperor Domitian (A.D. 90–95), who renewed the Christian persecution. Believers who refused to worship him as "Lord and God" were punished. Many Christians were executed or, like John, exiled to penal colonies.

**Place:** "I was sent to Patmos Island," John said, "because I had preached God's message and had told about Jesus" (1:9). Patmos is a rocky island about 10 miles long and 5 miles wide, almost 40 miles off the western coast of Turkey.

John seemed to target at least the first part of his message, if not all, to seven churches in western Turkey.

John's visions, however, encompass the entire planet, because the visions describe the end of the human race and the beginning of humanity's new life in God's heavenly kingdom.

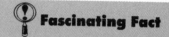

### Fascinating Fact

The number 666, known as the Mark of the Beast, is likely a coded reference to Nero—Rome's most vicious persecutor of Christians. John gave this clue: "You need wisdom to understand the number of the beast! But if you are smart enough, you can figure this out. Its number is six hundred sixty-six, and it stands for a person" (13:18). Hebrew letters have numeric values. Added together, the letters that spell the emperor's title and name—Caesar Nero—total 666.

**Bottom-Line Summary:** Exiled to a small and rocky island between Turkey and Greece, John has a series of fantastic visions about the end of humanity.

Some scenes are horrifying:

- falling stars destroy sections of the earth

- international chaos

- battlefields pooled with blood several feet deep

- God's people martyred.

Eventually, the human race and the world cease to exist.

But in their place, God restores the paradise lost in the Garden of Eden. From the time of Adam and Eve, when sin contaminated a perfect creation, God has been working his plan to remove all traces of sin. John sees the result. "Everything is finished!" God says. God and his people are together, and have settled in for an eternity.

The scenes are beautiful:

- a heavenly city that defies description

- all tears wiped away

- God and his people living together in joy that never ends.

## Influential People

**John,** the author of the book, is possibly one of Jesus' original disciples. His visions frighten many—Christians included. But his final visions assure believers that no matter what happens to us in this life, God is in control and heaven is waiting.

**Jesus,** Son of God, returns to judge all people and take his followers to heaven. This hope is one that offers assurance in even the bleakest circumstances. Whatever our hardships, we press on toward the prize ahead.

## Key Ideas You Need to Know

**Apocalyptic writing.** Like the Old Testament Book of Daniel, Revelation uses a style of writing known for it's vivid poetry and symbolism. The genre is called apocalyptic, from the Greek word *apocalypses*, which means "revelation." That's where the book gets its name.

Writers in politically charged times used apocalyptic symbolism to cloak their messages from rulers who might want to censor or persecute the writers. To talk about the Roman Empire, for example, John refers to it as Babylon (14:8). From at least A.D. 70, and perhaps earlier, Jews used Babylon as a code name for Rome. Both empires were rich and evil. And both destroyed and leveled Jerusalem.

## Q&A

**How can it be heaven if I'm missing some of the people I love most?** If you've ever lost a young child who wandered from home for a while, you know how fixated you were on getting that child back. It dominated your every waking moment. How will heaven be any different?

The Bible doesn't say.

But what it does say God will do for heaven's citizens is this: "He will wipe all tears from their eyes, and there will be no more death, suffering, crying, or pain. These things of the past are gone forever" (21:4).

Some Christians say God may do this by erasing our painful memories. But other Christians say it's hard to imagine God treating us like we're a computer hard drive, and that heaven should be a place for greater awareness and understanding, not less.

So the question remains unanswered, except for the phrase etched onto the quarter in our pocket: In God We Trust.

## Red Flag Issues

**Hell.** Christians have widely differing opinions on what happens to souls who reject God.

There are two main problems:

- Many Christians can't believe a loving God would condemn people to an eternity of torture.

- Most of the Bible's descriptions of hell seem figurative.

The word "hell" comes from a Hebrew word: *gehenna.* This was a constantly smoldering garbage dump in a valley outside ancient Jerusalem. Jesus used various words to describe hell—some of them clashing: fire, darkness (though fire displaces darkness), dungeons.

John says Satan and his followers will be thrown into "a lake of burning sulphur" (19:20), where they will suffer "in pain day and night forever and ever" (20:10).

Christian scholars offer many theories about what hell will be like. Some of the most common:

- It's literally a huge lake of fire, like the sun.

- The only thing we can know for certain about hell is that it's where sinners are kept separated from God.

- Bible imagery of hell's fire and darkness symbolize destruction, implying that sinners will be annihilated. Also, eternal punishment doesn't mean unending torture, but that the result of the punishment—annihilation or separation—will last forever.

- God will forever sustain the souls of sinners, not for punishment but to provide opportunity for reconciliation.

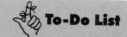 **To-Do List**

- "Don't be afraid of what you are about to suffer. . . . Remain faithful even when facing death, and I will give you the crown of life" (2:10, New Living Translation).

- "Remember the teaching that you were given and that you heard. Hold firmly to it and turn from your sins" (3:3).

- "Worship and honor God. . . . Kneel down before the one who created heaven and earth, the oceans, and every stream" (14:7).

Christians are so divided on this issue that for many, even reading this list will get them hot under the collar.

What happens to sinners isn't up to us. It's in the hands of a God who "never does wrong" and "can always be trusted to bring justice" (Deuteronomy 32:4).

# For the Record: Revelation Abused

**End-time predictions.** Obsession with the "last days" has produced many embarrassing mistakes for the church.

On October 23, 1843, thousands of Americans waited for the return of Jesus—as predicted by end-times specialist, William Miller. Many had sold their possessions. Obviously, Miller's deadline came and went.

More recent end-times specialists have applied Revelation symbols to modern news events. When Iraq invaded Kuwait and provoked the Persian Gulf War, some interpreters turned to Revelation 18 to warn the end was near and that Babylon was about to fall. Iraq's capital, Baghdad, is near the ruins of ancient Babylon.

Other supposed signs of the end-times:

- Chernobyl nuclear disaster. "Chernobyl" means "wormwood," the name of a star that poisons a third of earth's water (8:11).

- Mikhail Gorbachev's birthmark, said to be the mark of the beast (14:9).

Christian books about end-times—prophecies as well as fictional stories based on Revelation—make lots of money for some writers and publishers. That's because many people want to know what lies ahead, and when it's coming. But about all we know for certain is that Jesus is coming to take his followers with him forever, and we don't know when that will happen (2 Thessalonians 2:1; Mark 13:32).

**Flat earth.** At one time, some Christians argued from Revelation that the earth was flat. Now, some critics of the Bible argue from the same passage that Bible writers thought the planet was flat.

The "flat earth" passage: "I saw four angels. Each one was standing on one of the earth's four corners. The angels held back the four winds, so that no wind would blow" (7:1).

As early as the second century, some Christian scholars began arguing that there are no corners on a globe. And a globe is what many ancient scientists said the earth was—at least as early as 150 B.C., when Greeks made the first known globe.

The "four corners" in Revelation refers to the cardinal directions: north, south, east, and west. The wind is a symbol of God's judgment (Jeremiah 4:11–12). In Revelation, angels hold back the destructive winds of God's judgment long enough for God to save the faithful.

In short, the focus isn't on the shape of the planet, but on the mercy of God.

# Bible Scenarios You Can Use

## 1. Turning a blind eye to sinful church members (2:12–29)

**E**xiled on a tiny Mediterranean island for refusing to worship the emperor, John has a long series of dramatic visions, which he records in the Book of Revelation. The first are messages from God about seven prominent churches in what is now Turkey.

One message, directed at Christians in both Pergamum and Thyatira, warns the Christians there to stop turning a blind eye to the heresy and immorality among their church members.

In Pergamum, some of members have jumped into a new stream of thought that says there's nothing wrong with immorality. In Thyatira, a mysterious teacher called Jezebel influences some believers. "You let her teach and mislead my servants to do immoral things," the prophet says, quoting Jesus.

The prophet warns that God will punish these phony Christians and their followers.

There's plenty of room for differences of opinion in the church. We can disagree on which Bible translation is best, whether the death penalty is wrong, or if Christians should be allowed to drink wine with their meal. But there's no room for teachings that clash with the most basic truths of Christian faith, such as the Ten Commandments. We're often hesitant to confront wayward members—even those involved in blatant sins such as adultery or hateful acts. But it hurts them and the church when we condone their actions through our silence.

## 2. Wishy-washy churches with no zest for God (2:1–11; 3:1–22)

John says three of the seven churches have lost their passion for serving God.

Ephesus: "You don't have as much love as you used to. Think about where you have fallen from."

Sardis: "Everyone may think you are alive, but you are dead. Wake up!"

Laodicea: "You are not cold or hot. I wish you were either one or the other. But since you are luke-warm and neither cold nor hot, I will spit you out of my mouth."

After years of serving the Lord, it's easy to slip into routines that wear us down instead of build us up. We have to work at keeping our love for Jesus strong and vibrant, just as married couples have to make decisions to keep the spark of romance alive. If some religious experience seems old hat to us—such as Easter—we can ask God to help us find fresh insights to enliven our celebration. It's hard to imagine him refusing.

## 3. Judgment Day (20:11–15)

After experiencing many visions about events in heaven and earth leading up to the end of human history, John sees Judgment Day.

"I saw a great white throne with someone sitting on it," John says. "I also saw all the dead people standing in front of that throne. Every one of them was there, no matter who they had once been."

The judge is Jesus. "When Christ Jesus comes as king, he will be the judge of everyone" (2 Timothy 4:11).

Godly people, whose names appear in the "book of life," get a life sentence—eternal life. The others are thrown into "the lake of fire." Bible experts disagree about what this lake of fire is. Some take it literally and say it's a place of torment. Others say it's a figurative way of referring to the destruction of everything wicked or to eternal separation from God. In either case, those who want Jesus and those who want nothing to do with Jesus are each given their heart's desire.

We know what it means to be held accountable. That's because we've accidentally written checks for more money than we had. And we've made plenty of other mistakes that cost us time and money. But we live and learn. We become wiser, and it shows in the way we live. The same thing needs to happen in our spiritual life. We can learn from our mistakes. And we can rest assured that if we have faith in Jesus, Judgment Day will be a happy day.

## 4. Heaven ahead (21:1—22:6)

**A**s his visions draw to a close, John sees the most wonderful vision of all. It's the final event in God's plan of salvation: a new creation.

Excitedly, John reports, "I saw a new heaven and a new earth." John knows he's seeing the fulfillment of an ancient prophecy about the coming of an idyllic life. Isaiah, writing hundreds of years earlier, had quoted God saying, "I am creating new heavens and a new earth . . . full of happy people. . . . There will be no more crying or sorrow" (Isaiah 65:17–19).

Gone now are all remnants of sin and the damage it caused. In this new creation, which believers usually call heaven, God lives with his people forever.

John tries to describe this indescribably wonderful place. But how can he adequately describe a spiritual dimension to people who live in a physical dimension? John uses the best images available. Heaven is a perfect cube—like the holiest room in the Jewish temple, where the chest holding the Ten Commandments was kept. Heaven is built of precious treasures: pure gold, pearls, and rare gems. It's a holy place of fantastic beauty.

If we follow Jesus, this is where he'll lead us—to an eternal home more glorious than we could possibly imagine.

# SUBJECT INDEX

# Maps
## OF BIBLE
## TIMES AND
## PLACES

# The Land of Abraham

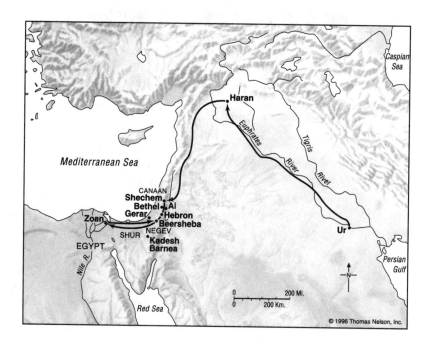

# The Hebrew Exodus
# from Egypt

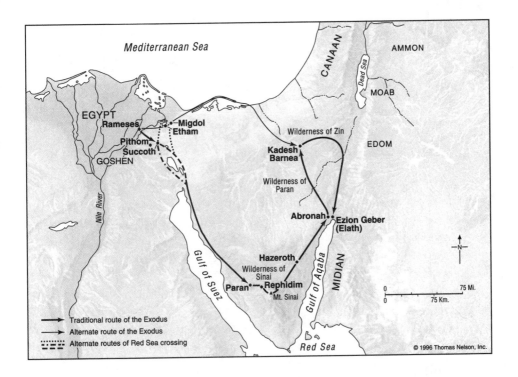

# Israel's Twelve Tribes in Canaan

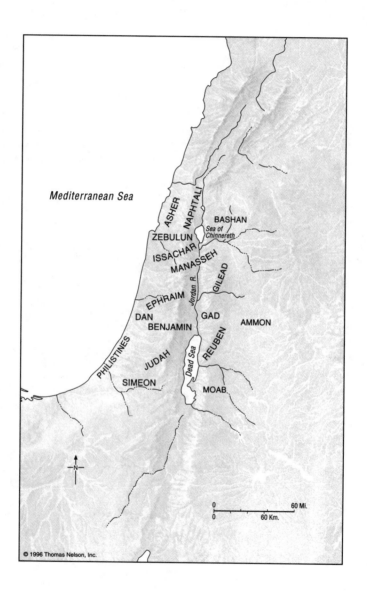

Mediterranean Sea

ASHER

NAPHTALI

BASHAN

Sea of Chinnereth

ZEBULUN

ISSACHAR

MANASSEH

Jordan R.

GILEAD

EPHRAIM

DAN

BENJAMIN

GAD

AMMON

PHILISTINES

JUDAH

Dead Sea

REUBEN

SIMEON

MOAB

—N—

0          60 Mi.

0          60 Km.

# The Kingdom under David

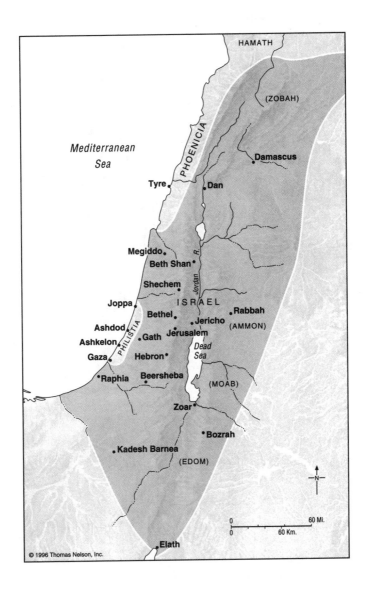

HAMATH

(ZOBAH)

Mediterranean Sea

PHOENICIA

Damascus

Tyre · Dan

Megiddo
Beth Shan

Shechem

Joppa

ISRAEL

Bethel · Rabbah
· Jericho
(AMMON)

Ashdod
Ashkelon · Gath Jerusalem
Dead Sea

Gaza · Hebron

· Raphia Beersheba

(MOAB)

Zoar

· Bozrah

· Kadesh Barnea

(EDOM)

PHILISTIA

Jordan R.

N

| 0 | | 60 Mi. |
| 0 | | 60 Km. |

· Elath

# The Kingdom Divided

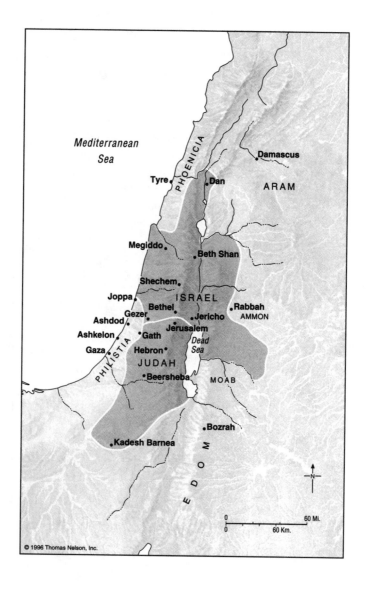

Mediterranean Sea

PHOENICIA

Damascus

Tyre

Dan

ARAM

Megiddo

Beth Shan

Shechem

ISRAEL

Joppa

Bethel

Gezer

Jericho

Rabbah

AMMON

Ashdod

Jerusalem

Ashkelon

Gath

Dead Sea

Gaza

PHILISTIA

Hebron

JUDAH

Beersheba

MOAB

Bozrah

EDOM

Kadesh Barnea

N

0        60 Mi.
0        60 Km.

# The Land Where Jesus Lived

Sidon

Damascus
ITUREA

Tyre

Caesarea
Philippi

Mediterranean
Sea

PHOENICIA

TRACHONITIS
Raphana

GALILEE
Capernaum

Bethsaida?

Hippos

Nazareth
Nain
Scythopolis

Abila
Gadara?

Pella

DECAPOLIS

SAMARIA

Dion

Jordan River

Samaria

Gerasa

Philadelphia

Jericho

Jerusalem

? Exact location
questionable

N

JUDEA

Dead
Sea

0        40 Mi.

0        40 Km.

© 1996 Thomas Nelson, Inc.

# The New Testament World

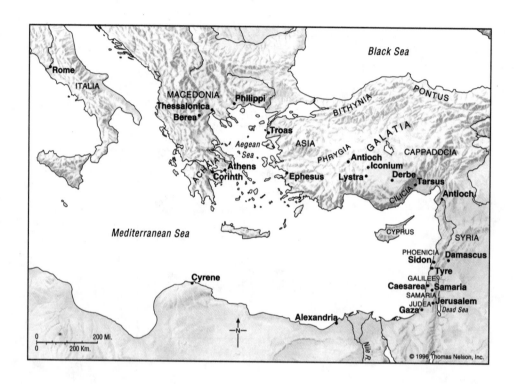

Black Sea

Rome
ITALIA

MACEDONIA    Philippi
Thessalonica
Berea
BITHYNIA          PONTUS

Troas
Aegean      ASIA         GALATIA
Sea                PHRYGIA
ACHAIA    Athens              Antioch    CAPPADOCIA
Corinth          Ephesus   Lystra   Iconium
Derbe
Tarsus
CILICIA          Antioch

Mediterranean Sea

CYPRUS          SYRIA

PHOENICIA   Damascus
Sidon
Tyre
Cyrene          GALILEE
Caesarea   Samaria
SAMARIA
JUDEA   Jerusalem
Gaza    Dead Sea

Alexandria

0          200 Mi.
0     200 Km.
—N—

Nile R.

© 1996 Thomas Nelson, Inc.